Between Ourselves

It is in the tiny struggles of individual peoples
that the great movements of history are most
truly revealed.

Rosa Luxemburg

Between Ourselves

Letters Between
Mothers and Daughters
1750-1982

Edited by

Karen Payne

Houghton Mifflin Company
Boston

Library of Congress Cataloging in Publication Data
Main entry under title:

Between ourselves.

Bibliography: p.
Includes index.
1. Mothers—Correspondence.   2 Daughters—
Correspondence.   3. Mothers and daughters—History.
4. Feminism—History.   I. Payne, Karen.
HQ759.B53   1983   306.8′743   83-10803
ISBN 0-395-33969-3
ISBN 0-395-36571-6 (pbk.)

Printed in the United States of America

D 10 9 8 7 6 5 4 3 2

Houghton Mifflin Company paperback, 1984

*This book is dedicated to my parents,
Jeanette Gallway Payne and Willie Payne,
in loving gratitude for the care
and love they have always given me;
and to Kirk and Amanda
for certain things they have taught me
about love and work and play.*

Contents

CONTENTS

Acknowledgements

First I would like to thank all the daughters and mothers whose letters appear here; in addition to giving permission to use their letters, many of them have generously read and commented on successive drafts of various sections of the book. Thanks in particular to Aurelia Plath, Jessie Bernard, Nan Hunt, Susan Abbott, Ann Scott, Leslie and Morena for loving criticism, support and patience with my *many* drafts of everything.

To my four loving friends who worked closely with me for several weeks at various points, for little or no pay, making even the most awesomely huge or tedious jobs seem fun: Karen Jacobsen, Diana Clarke, Kim Nygaard and Dave Hawkins – thanks for everything, especially for making it possible to complete this book in only one lifetime. Karen and Diana helped immensely with the historical research on the women in Part Two, uncovering sources and writing excellent preliminary drafts of the biographical sketches;* they discussed the content of the book at great length with me and also spent many weeks on more menial tasks such as typing, filing and prodding me to keep up with correspondence. With great efficiency and resilience, Kim accomplished the massive and unamusing task of clearing permission to use all the letters. Dave also worked on permissions and then assisted me in every other task necessary to complete the book, from suggesting new arrangements of the letters within chapters and helping me think about the structure of the book as a whole, to looking after most of the domestic and administrative chores during the last several months of my struggle to finish. Our love for each other has been a constant source of nourishment and hope.

Eileen Fairweather and Jo Chambers gave me many hours of their time while I was working on earlier drafts of the introductions. They are inspiring women and the time we spent working together sustained me for many months thereafter.

For almost three years I met with a group of women to discuss feminist research methodologies; we read and criticised each other's work-in-progress and I benefited greatly from the insights of Wendy Hollway, Jill Rakusen, Lesley Caldwell, Valerie Walkerdine, Maria Roussoun, Leonie Sugarman, Rosie Walden and Lynn Froggett. Loving thanks to Wendy and Jill for also giving me much help outside the group.

At a critical point in time Kate Grant read almost the entire manuscript and made many helpful suggestions. My thanks to her and to numerous other friends who have read portions of this book at all stages, offering encouragement and criticism: Deborah Kingsland, Lennie Goodings, Kaj Holmberg, Kate Grenville, Rosemary Baragwanath, Priscilla Foley, Sue Dimond, Anna Sherbany, Lavender Clarke, Eileen Caedmon, John

---

*Karen Jacobsen worked on Lady Mary Wortley Montagu, Frederika Bremer, Harriet Martineau, Elizabeth Blackwell, Constance Lytton, Winifred Holtby, Amelia Earhart and Edith Summerskill; Diana Clarke wrote drafts for Lucy Stone, Susan B. Anthony, Mary Putnam Jacobi, Queen Victoria, Lella Secor and Hannah Senesh.

Howkins, Frances Pine, Julian Henriques, Claire Chapman, Karen Margolis, Marion Friedmann, John Rowley, Michael Raeburn, Janie Prince, Paul Rusman, Wantje Fritsche, Martha Saxton and Jackie Lapidus.

For assistance in contacting women who had letters to contribute, I am grateful to Zoe Fairbairns, Roz Baxandall, Ani Mander, Blanche Cook, Michael Kidron, Alison Weir, Annette Overby, Gillian Perry and several women at the Women's Buildings in San Francisco and Los Angeles. Harry Katz tracked down some of Elizabeth Blackwell's unpublished correspondence and provided thorough and insightful research about her life. My thanks to Paul Berry and Geoffrey Handley–Taylor for assistance with the Vera Brittain and Winifred Holtby material. Yvette Eastman very kindly gave me access to some of the letters of Annis Ford Eastman and Crystal Eastman; she also wrote an introduction to the letters included here. Special thanks to Ann Hills of the *Guardian* Women's Page and to Steve Parker of *Mother Jones* magazine for arranging to have my request for contributions appear in those publications; also to *Spare Rib, Ms London* and to many newsletters in the women's liberation movement who included notices about my research.

The quality and quantity of material in this book has also been greatly enhanced by the efforts of many women engaged in feminist research. Writers such as Adrienne Rich, Phyllis Chesler, Mary Daly, Dorothy Dinnerstein and Tillie Olsen have sustained me with their courage, eloquence and clear thinking.

Many women's publishing houses, bookshops and libraries have aided my research immeasurably. Thanks to the Schlesinger Library and the Feminist Writers Guild in the USA, the Women's Research and Resources Centre (WRRC) in London – and a very special thanks to David Doughan at the Fawcett Library in London, surely one of the most wonderful places in the world for doing research on women's history.

I would also like to thank Alison Watt, Ian Grant, David Boadella, Frankie Armstrong, Gaynell and Joe Begley, Ellie, Tom Osborn, Tamara Osborn, Luise Eichenbaum, Susie Orbach, the Women's Therapy Centre, the Re-evaluation Co-counselling community, my former teachers at Pitzer College and my therapist, Tamar Selby, for all the ways they have helped me.

My thanks to Lys de Beaumont for typing most of the letters in the book, and to Linda Mason, Jean Beith, Frances Pine and Rachel McCarthy for additional typing. Janet Silver and Sarah Jane Evans were most helpful and astute copy editors. Patricia Walters and Sarah Jackson, who designed this book, were a pleasure to work with as they spent many patient hours changing it until we were all happy.

I am very grateful to all the people who helped make my two-month research trip to the United States in 1980 so rewarding. Loving thanks to Laurie Sparham for coming with me and keeping me going with his support, jokes and sense of proportion; and to Margie and Barrett Coates, Lucy Dubin, Eva Field, Roger Trefousse and Amanda Pope for weeks of hospitality, and for access to cars, telephones and friendship networks – all of which helped immeasurably. Thank you to the friends who loaned me money to help pay for this trip, especially Richard Hinds. Thanks also to Andrea

Heilbron, Holly Coates, Linda and Buddy Gore, Eric Golanty, Mary Ann Zeman, Mandy Mecke, Marsha Gildin and Monica Leff for making that experience – and many others – so worthwhile: these friends have kept me going, wherever I am and wherever they are.

My family has been all that I have needed – or could have wanted – them to be. The courage that my mother has shown in her own life and the loving nurturance that she has given me in mine constantly sustain me. I thank my father for writing me an extraordinary letter of support just when I needed it most; I thank my brother, Kirk, for his stimulating criticism, patient arguing, high standard of writing and, most of all, for giving me so much loving care and help, even though we often disagree; Kerry, Hal and Jeanette have also encouraged me greatly; my sister and brother-in-law, Anne and Audie Jenkins, have touched me very deeply with their continuous outpouring of concern and nurturing.

John Annette has given me steady emotional and practical support for many years; thanks, also, for the use of the cottage and for lending me money. John, along with Kate and Richard Grant, lived with me while I was writing this book; only they, and others who have lived with someone struggling obsessively for four years on a single project, can begin to imagine how much thanks is due them for small and large kindnesses; they have my love, gratitude and more.

My agent, Julian Friedmann, believed in this book from the beginning and helped generously in every way to see it through; his editing skills, business sense and friendship have been invaluable and I am deeply grateful to him.

My editors, Alison Burns (in London) and Nan Talese (in New York), have each made crucial interventions that have improved the shape of the book. I would especially like to thank Alison Burns for knowing when to push and when to shield me from pressure so that I could find my own way. She has been available whenever I needed her and given freely of her time, often late into the night and at weekends. I have loved her humour and relied on her strength; the entire book has been enriched by her talent and insight. She and Dave Hawkins have given me absolutely vital help and encouragement, especially in the final months; this book simply could not have been finished this year or next – and maybe not ever – without their faith in me and in the book, and the sheer hard work we did together.

Editor's Note
All surnames used in this book are the real names of the women writing the letters; the use of a first name only denotes a pseudonym.

Introduction

'Aren't most letters between mothers and daughters mainly gossip?' inquired a taxi driver to whom I had briefly explained the purpose of my journey between libraries one morning. His comment might have shaken me at an earlier stage of my research, but my thoughts turned at once to two of the letters which had come my way recently. The first, from a 25-year-old feminist writer to her mother in the 1970s, had been sent to me by the daughter:

> . . . Now I'm older I can better understand how difficult it must have been for you at times; to let your child kick out and rebel, and make mistakes and get hurt a lot at times, but all the experience I've had has made me the person I am, understanding more and trying to put all that experience to good use with my writing. I think one of the breakpoints was when you realised that my politics and life-style didn't mean I'd one day come crawling home with 3 illegitimate children/VD/heroin marks on my arm/a wooden leg/2 syphilitic parrots and 3 buckets of dung and call it 'Art' – though at times you may have been right to worry!

The second came from a collection of letters from German women and men who had joined the European Resistance in World War II. Rose Schlösinger was arrested and executed by the Nazis. On the day of her execution she wrote to her young daughter, Marianne:

> . . . Now I must say farewell to you, because we shall probably never see each other again. Nevertheless, you must grow up to be a healthy, happy and strong human being. I hope that you will experience the most beautiful things the world has to give, as I have, without having to undergo its hardships, as I have had to do. First of all, you must strive to become capable and industrious, then all other happiness will come of itself.

At the start, I had not known what to expect from these letters either . . .

My initial aim with this book was to discover the ways in which contemporary women endeavour to discuss their intimate relationships, their values, their differences in perspective, their work and their decisions – with their mothers and daughters. Many people had indicated that they thought worthwhile results were improbable – from that taxi driver who voiced the popular notion that talk among women is full of trivialities, to several people who assumed that all letters between mothers and daughters would seethe with guilt and antagonism. There were times when I myself wondered if my researches might confirm these rather bleak expectations.

But women never cease to astonish and inspire me. In the four years that it has taken me to compile these letters, I have talked to hundreds of women in England and the United States and corresponded with many in other countries. At the turning point, when I decided to include women from the nineteenth century, I made the acquaintance of several hundred more through biographies, autobiographies and library archives. These women are writers, doctors, housewives, construction workers, secretaries, political activists, teachers, artists, scientists . . . They are all daughters, many of them are mothers – and their relationships are richly varied. Of course there are common features and I hope that any woman reading these letters will feel a kinship with many of the authors, however different the circumstances of their lives. One particular link is that many of these relationships between mothers and daughters have been significantly affected by issues raised in worldwide movements for women's liberation.

Like other people, I had marvelled at how dreadfully unappealing 'women's lib' appeared in mass-media portrayals; it occurred to me that the ways in which a woman might describe her life and her values to her mother or daughter would offer a richer and more complex portrait of womanhood, as well as of feminism. I chose letters between mothers and daughters rather than between, say, sisters or friends or other family members, because a girl's mother is her most compelling model of womanhood and girls usually imagine that they will grow up to be like their mothers; when they don't, it often comes as an uncomfortable surprise to both sides and seems to call for an explanation.

For much of recorded history, it has not been easy to imagine many different possibilities for women's lives; indeed in most cultures, for innumerable generations, daughters have grown up to lead lives very similar to their mothers'. However, the recurring patterns of women's lives from generation to generation have been interrupted signally at various points in history by major political and technological changes: the industrial revolution, the hard-won advances in educational and professional opportunities for women, improvements in methods of contraception and the numerous periods of struggle for women's rights have had an irrevocable impact. Nearly a dozen generations of women have been involved in those struggles since Mary Wollstonecraft published *Vindication of the Rights of Woman* in 1792; but it is only during the most recent wave of feminism in the 1970s that a woman's relationship with her mother has been seen as such a crucial issue in her journey toward liberation.

Historically, the mother-daughter relationship, like other relation-

ships between women, has been either trivialised or ignored. The days
are not so comfortably distant when the birth of a daughter was a
cause for mourning: an embarrassment to the mother because only
sons have status, and a disgrace to the father's 'manhood'. In more
societies than people generally like to admit, wives could be banished,
divorced and even killed for not producing sons – and it is still the case
today in many cultures that a daughter's birth is bad news to the
family. Under such circumstances, a mother and daughter might have
a hard time perceiving their relationship as anything special, whatever
their bonds of affection; it seems that the 'mother-daughter relationship' has often consisted of mothers pitying daughters the hardships
they would endure and the lack of power they would have over their
lives, and daughters hardly daring to question their mothers' own
hardships or lack of power.

It was not easy to discover the history of this relationship in
standard psychology or history books – which tend to focus on men's
relationships and their struggles for power. The American publisher
M. Lincoln Schuster once said, in the Introduction to *Fifty Famous
Letters of History*, 'Letters remind us that history was once real life':
but even standard collections of letters yielded slim results. I consulted
three anthologies called *Letters to Mother* and found that they were
composed almost entirely of letters from sons to mothers (one had six
letters from daughters out of seventy-three; another had ten letters out
of eighty-four; and the third had fifteen letters from daughters out of
one hundred). It seemed odd not to have letters from mothers, so I
tried *Letters to Children. All* were from fathers, writing mostly to
sons. With a shred of hope I turned to *Women as Letter-Writers*. The
first thing that struck me was that, of the 113 women included, every
biography but one began with the sentence, 'So-and-so was the
daughter of _____' and proceeded to give her father's name only and
make no reference to her mother.* As Virginia Woolf said:

> . . . very little is known about women. The history of England is the
> history of the male line, not of the female. Of our fathers we know
> always some fact, some distinction. They were soldiers or they were
> sailors; they filled that office or they made that law. But of our mothers,
> our grandmothers, our great-grandmothers, what remains? Nothing
> but a tradition. One was beautiful, one was red-haired; one was kissed
> by a Queen. We know nothing of them except their names and the dates
> of their marriages and the number of children they bore.

Women's invisibility in history is regrettable not simply because it
poses problems for people engaged in research. The saddest thing
about it is how women have been deprived of a vital source of inspira-

---

*The single exception was Mary Shelley, author of *Frankenstein* (and wife of the poet, Shelley),
who was the daughter of William Godwin and pioneer feminist, Mary Wollstonecraft.

tion and self-esteem – that sense of pride which comes from appreciat-
ing the experiences and achievements of ordinary people like oneself.
When my mother read an early draft of *Between Ourselves*, her
reaction to the historical material echoed my own feelings of astonish-
ment as I had uncovered letter after letter: 'But I had *no idea* that
women felt these things so strongly all those years ago . . . such love
of freedom . . . such talent and hopefulness . . .'

The media have certainly not ignored the current women's liberation movement, but the women involved are often portrayed as
freaks: it is generally made to seem as if this sort of thing has never
happened before. Attention has been focussed on what women are
fighting against and on the 'unattractiveness' of women getting angry
and wanting to be heard. In contrast, most of the letters in this book
focus on what women find moving, beautiful and worth *living for*. I
have chosen them to show what the history books and popular media
usually conceal: the vitality and the questing spirit of women, both in
the home and in their public activities. For hundreds of years women
have challenged the notion that 'a woman's place is in the home', not
merely out of an ideal of justice and equality, but because they have
had capabilities which demanded action and refused to be quenched.

I began work on this book with the idea that mother-daughter relationships in today's feminist climate would be under particular
strains: that the rapid changes in women's lives would create
traumatic disagreements and differences in this relationship, which
has been concerned primarily with teaching the traditional roles of
wife and mother. I discovered that, when women challenge tradition,
they do often feel that they must justify their actions, above all to their
mothers. There is sometimes strong disapproval, even violent disagreement across the generations. But I also found mothers and
daughters in the past and present who have encouraged each other to
go far beyond the conventional definitions of good mothers and dutiful daughters, and have given each other crucial support in creating
alternatives to values which tend to limit women's lives.

Currents of both fear and hope run through dialogues about
changes in society and in women's aspirations. For these issues affect
the intimate relationships that any woman has with men, with
children, with women friends and – in every way imaginable – with
her mother. Within each mother-daughter relationship there is a
unique conflict between wanting the richest possible fulfillment for
each other, longing to preserve security and needing to break the
mutual dependence. Real liberation for women will perhaps only
come when mothers and daughters can say wholeheartedly to each
other (as Kate does in Chapter Four): I keep on wanting everything,
and I want you to want that too.

Karen Payne, London, 1982

PART ONE

I called her after the heroine of the famous poem, 'The Angel in the House'. . . It was she who bothered me and wasted my time and so tormented me that at last I killed her.

Virginia Woolf (1931)

CHAPTER ONE

Killing the Angel in the House

In 1931, Virginia Woolf was addressing a group of women who were trying to enter professions still barred to them (whether officially or unofficially). She began by explaining that there were no legal impediments whatsoever to being a writer, but that other powerful forces had made it exceedingly difficult for her to practise her chosen profession:

> While I was writing [this] review I discovered that if I were going to review books I should need to do battle with a certain phantom. And the phantom was a woman, and when I came to know her better I called her after the heroine of the famous poem, 'The Angel in the House'. It was she who used to come between me and my paper when I was writing reviews. It was she who bothered me and wasted my time and so tormented me that at last I killed her.
>
> You who come of a younger and happier generation may not have heard of her – you may not know what I mean by the Angel in the House. I will describe her as shortly as I can. She was intensely sympathetic. She was immensely charming . . . She sacrificed herself daily . . . she never had a mind or wish of her own . . .
>
> In those days, the last of Queen Victoria – every house had its Angel. And when I came to write I encountered her with the very first words. The shadow of her wings fell on my page; I heard the rustling of her skirts in the room. Directly, that is to say, I took my pen in my hand to review that novel by a famous man, she slipped behind me and whispered, 'My dear, you are a young woman. You are writing about a book that has been written by a man. Be sympathetic; be tender; flatter; deceive; use all the arts and wiles of our sex. Never let anybody guess that you have a mind of your own. Above all, be pure.' And she made as if to guide my pen.
>
> I now record the one act for which I take some credit to myself, though the credit rightly belongs to some excellent ancestors of mine who left me a certain sum of money – shall we say five hundred pounds a year? – so that it was not necessary for me to depend solely on charm for my living. I turned upon her and caught her by the throat. I did my best to kill her. My excuse, if I were to be had up in a court of law, would be that I acted in self-defence. Had I not killed her she would have killed me. She would have plucked the heart out of my writing . . . Thus, whenever I felt the shadow of her wing or the radiance of her halo

upon my page, I took up the inkpot and flung it at her. She died hard. Her fictitious nature was of great assistance to her. *It is far harder to kill a phantom than a reality.* She was always creeping back when I thought I had despatched her. Though I flatter myself that I killed her in the end, the struggle was severe; it took much time that had better have been spent upon learning Greek grammar or roaming the world in search of adventures.

Even fifty years on, the spectre of the Angel in the House has not completely lost its grip on popular notions of womanhood. Despite the celebrated capability and strength of women in factories during the two World Wars, the 1950s glorified once more the stereotype of submissiveness and self-denial. Most of the people I know grew up thinking there were two kinds of women: good ones and bad ones. Good ones were like the Angel in the House – or at least wanted to be. Bad ones were anything else.

What has changed in the years since Virginia Woolf described the Angel is that several unappealing consequences of such self-effacement have crept in to make a more complex stereotype: the overbearing and engulfing mother who is dependent and obsessive, clings to her children and passes on guilt and fear to them. An important aspect of women's liberation has been to look critically at these sorts of caricatures – to remind ourselves that they contain lies and to ask ourselves what is missing. The truths we most need to hear are not contained here.

In trying to understand the effect of such negative images of womanhood and motherhood, I've recalled many aspects of my own childhood. One of the things I wanted most while I was growing up was to be told that I could accomplish anything, that my strength was greater than I thought, that I should be fearless and try out many things, that I would be loved for trying – and even if I failed.

But this is not what people usually say to girls. Mainly, it seems, girls are taught to be careful. In fairy tales, young women are helpless; they nearly always have good mothers who are dead and wicked stepmothers who force them to stay idle or to do housework. Nice young women do nothing whatsoever to improve their own situations and they wait for men to rescue them. There are few brave and enterprising heroines in fairy tales to make a girl swell with pride and say, 'If she can manage that, then I could too.'

Although notions of 'feminine' weakness and dependence were sharply critiqued in the 1960s and 70s, they seem to have returned in the backlash of the 80s – but this time there is a difference. We have noticed irrevocably the abilities and strength of women all around us, including our sisters, daughters, mothers and grandmothers. Through their unspectacular lives we continually learn about women's courage and our fears. The real lives of the women we love provide evidence and inspiration which we can no longer ignore.

Helen Claes to her daughter Christine, 1974

When Christine Claes Flaxer, a painter living in New York, first wrote to me in 1980 I was at a critical stage of my research. I had not yet uncovered most of the material included in this book, but I had perused many theoretical works on the mother-daughter relationship and I was alternately perplexed and despairing about how the letters I had found related to the theory I was reading. The letters between Helen and Christine completely stopped me in my tracks. Virtually nothing I had read led me to believe that such encouraging letters from a mother to a daughter were even possible in the troubled 1970s: it seemed unlikely that they could be written for at least another generation.

I began corresponding with Helen and Christine, asking them to tell me more about their lives. Meanwhile, I was finding other letters between mothers and daughters which were beginning to show me that what most theories (as well as the caricatures) tend to conceal is how often mothers and daughters inspire each other to take risks and strive for fulfillment.

Helen Claes was born and raised in Detroit, Michigan, the only child of a middle-class family. She studied fashion illustration at college in the 1930s, but her real love was drama; her career as an actress on local radio ended with her marriage in 1941. With her husband, who was a member of the Coast Guard, she spent the war years in California, where they later returned to attend art college. She has worked throughout her life as a volunteer with underprivileged children and senior citizens, drawing on her art and drama skills wherever possible.

At the age of 37, when she had been married fourteen years, Helen issued an ultimatum: 'Let me have a baby or give me a divorce.' Christine, whom Helen calls 'the great adventure of my life', was born in 1956.

Both Helen and Christine say that they consider theirs an 'unusually honest relationship' which they see as the chief factor enabling them to remain very close while Christine was growing up and throughout her adolescence. Life became more complicated when Christine went away to college. Christine explained some of the background to the letters they wrote at that time:

'The most intense struggles between my mother and myself occurred around the time of these letters when I first left home: a time when I so desperately needed to state my independence and when new boundaries had to be set for the relationship.

'In a letter written after I decided to move off-campus during my first year at college, my mother described how she had "floundered in [a] sea of guilt, torn between repressing your individual personality and the ever-nagging fear of creating an unrestrained monster". Giving her blessing and my father's, she went on to say, "We agree that life should be as adventure-filled as you can make it. We have always hoped that you would surge ahead and do some of the really interesting things that most people only dream of." She signed the letter, "Much love and a long, exciting life of adventure, Helen".'

Six months later, when Christine decided to leave college and look for work in New York City, Helen wrote this letter to her:

October 1974

Dear Tina,

I've told several people of your proposed move and among them only Aunt Dorothy gives her unvarnished blessings (I even read her your letter and she thinks you're brave and wonderful). Others took the news with varying degrees of horror with the [next-door neighbours] being the most disturbed. They feel you should be so grateful that you have parents that were willing to send you to college. That you should find some nice 'solid' boy from the 'engineering department' who would be a serious and stabilizing influence on you. Well, that's how it goes – you can't win 'em all!

Dad, of course is worried (so am I) but you are you and no matter where you go I'll never lose you (dead or alive). I'll fear for your welfare at the same time envying your strength of purpose to endeavor to do what you must. Your letter reminded me of my own about Chicago written so many years ago; when my life was new and exciting. I hope with all my heart you have the guts I lacked to keep the fragile flame flickering.

With love and happy hope,
Mom

Helen, who now lives in Detroit with her retired husband, recently wrote me a letter in which she reflected on her ideal of motherhood:

'I like to think of my love for my only daughter as the "slack net" spread beneath a performing aerialist. I hoped that she would not view with alarm or undue apprehension the necessity for its being there, but rather climb as high as she might care to go, secure in the knowledge of its support. It was frightening to know that pulling the corners too tightly could send her bouncing off into oblivion and leaving the knots too loose might plunge her into certain disaster.

'What I wanted most for my daughter was that she be able to soar confidently in her own sky, wherever that might be, and if there was space for me as well I would, indeed, have reaped what I had tried to sow.'

Sylvia Plath to her mother Aurelia, 1956

I shall be one of the few women poets in the world who is fully a rejoicing woman, not a bitter or frustrated or warped man-imitator . . . I am a woman and glad of it, and my songs will be of fertility of the earth and the people in it through waste, sorrow or death. I shall be a woman singer . . .

Sylvia to Aurelia (1956)

Pulitzer Prize-winning poet Sylvia Plath (1932–63) was born in Massachusetts, the eldest child of Aurelia Schober and Otto Plath. Her father was a noted biologist who firmly believed in marriage founded on the concept of the husband's dominance; Aurelia was expected to manage the household and care for the children single-handedly. She was also expected to take notes for Otto's lectures and publications, as well as type and edit them. Aurelia, university-trained and a professional teacher before her marriage, said that she submitted to these demands for the sake of 'peace in the family', but she had sworn that 'no child of mine would ever have to endure tedious jobs' and always encouraged both of her children to study and then find work which would fulfill them.

Otto Plath died of diabetes when Sylvia was 8 and her brother, Warren, 5; Aurelia returned to work to support the family. She did not earn enough to pay for the 'ideal education' she had always dreamed of for her children, but Sylvia was awarded a scholarship to attend prestigious Smith College. Sylvia made excellent marks and began publishing poetry in national magazines, although her letters from Smith reveal that she sometimes felt painfully unworthy of her scholarship and the faith that her teachers and mother had in her. It is hard to imagine that her later grim and compressed poetry could have been written by this same young woman who wrote nearly seven hundred letters to her mother, usually packed with plans, the excitement of learning, a strong belief in her talent and a great capacity to enjoy life.*

After her third year at Smith, Sylvia was awarded a guest editorship at *Mademoiselle* magazine in New York during her summer holiday. When she returned home from the exhausting and exhilarating challenge of New York to find that she had not been accepted into a Harvard Summer School creative writing seminar, she suffered a crisis of confidence in her abilities: she would never be good enough to deserve her scholarship; her performance would not match her promise. She became incapable of reading anything, much less writing anything, and was unable to look for a job. After weeks of deepening depression and fourteen nights without any sleep, she took an overdose of sleeping pills and hid in the space beneath an unused downstairs bedroom, the entrance to which was blocked by a pile of firewood. Police, neighbours and family combed the area for three days without success. Finally, on the third day, Warren heard a thumping noise as Sylvia revived.

In her novel, *The Bell Jar*, Sylvia Plath described her breakdown and recovery: the pressure she felt to perform; the expectation of being popular with boys as well as being a perfectionist in her studies; the fear of letting down her mother who had suffered so much; her experiences with hospitals, psychiatrists and electric-shock therapy; and her gradual return to health.

Sylvia returned to Smith having missed only a semester of study and

---

*Letters from Sylvia Plath to her mother about her work and her relationship with her husband appear in Chapter 3. Most of her letters have been published in *Letters Home*.

graduated the following year Summa Cum Laude with the added triumph of a Fulbright Scholarship to Cambridge University. During her last year at Smith she worked hard and wrote poetry in earnest; she had several poems published (including one in the prestigious *Atlantic* magazine) and won numerous awards and contests. She moved to England in 1955 to continue her studies at Cambridge.

Sylvia continued to write to her mother several times a week, filling her in on the details of her life and constantly reassuring her that she had fully recovered from her breakdown. In an early letter from Cambridge she wrote to Aurelia:

I want to force myself again and again to leave the warmth and security of static situations and move into the world of growth and suffering where the real books are people's minds and souls . . . It is often tempting to hide from the blood and guts of life in a neat special subject on paper where one can become an unchallenged expert . . .

A few months later Sylvia wrote acknowledging her mother's strength and the inspiration she had drawn from her:

3 March 1956

Dearest Mother,
      . . . Already the grounds of Newnham are purple and gold with crocuses and white with snowdrops!

I do want to tell you now how much your letters mean to me. Last Monday those phrases you copied from Max Ehrmann came like milk-and-honey to my weary spirit; I've read them again and again. Isn't it amazing what the power of words can do? I also loved your two letters which came today. I don't know if you've felt how much more mellowed and chastened I've become in the last half year, but I certainly have gotten beyond that stage of 'not listening' to advice and feel that I have been confiding in you through letters more than ever before in my life and welcome all you think wise to tell me. Perhaps you still don't realize (why is it we are so much more articulate about our fault-findings than our praises, which we so often take for granted?) how very much I have admired you: for your work, your teaching, your strength and your creation of our exquisite home in Wellesley, and your seeing that Warren [*her brother*] and I went to the Best colleges in the United States (best for each of us, respectively, I'm sure of it!). All this is your work, your encouragement, your produce, and as a family, we have weathered the blackest of situations, fighting for growth and new life. Perhaps I most especially admire your resilience and flexibility symbolized by your driving,* which seems to open

---

*Aurelia had recently qualified for a driving licence.

new possibilities for a richer, wider life in many other ways, too. I want you to know all this in words, for while I have been most verbal about all the limits in our lives, I don't think I've ever specifically told you all that I love and revere, and it is a great, great deal!

Much, much love,
Sivvy

23 April 1956

Dearest Mother,

Well, finally the blundering American Express sent me your letter from Rome . . . our minds certainly work on the same track!

. . . I have already planned to stay in London three nights and have written to reserve a room for us; we'll just eat and talk the day you come, but for the next two I'll get some theater tickets and we'll plan jaunts to flowering parks, Piccadilly, Trafalgar Square . . . walking, strolling, feeding pigeons and sunning ourselves like happy clams. Then, to Cambridge, where I have already reserved a room for you for two nights . . . I have made a contract with one of my husky men to teach me how to manage a punt before you come, so you shall step one afternoon from your room at the beautiful Garden House Hotel right onto the [River] Cam and be boated up to Granchester through weeping willows for tea in an orchard! Worry about nothing. Just let me know your predilections and it shall be accomplished . . .

You, alone, of all, have had crosses that would cause many a stronger woman to break under the never-ceasing load. You have borne daddy's long, hard death and taken on a man's portion in your work; you have fought your own ulcer attacks, kept us children sheltered, happy, rich with art and music lessons, camp and play; you have seen me through that black night when the only word I knew was No and when I thought I could never write or think again; and, you have been brave through your own operation. Now, just as you begin to breathe, this terrible slow, dragging pain comes upon you,* almost as if it would be too easy to free you so soon from the deepest, most exhausting care and giving of love.

. . . Know with a certain knowing that *you* deserve, too, to be with the loved ones who can give you strength in your trouble: Warren and myself. Think of your trip here as a trip to the heart of strength in your daughter who loves you more dearly than words can say. I am waiting for you, and your trip shall be for your own soul's health and growing. You need . . . a context where all burdens are not on your shoulders, where some loving person comes to heft the hardest, to walk beside you. Know this, and know that it is right you should come. You need

---

*Aurelia's mother was dying.

to imbibe power and health and serenity to return to your job . . .

I feel with all my joy and life that these are qualities I can give you, from the fulness and brimming of my heart. So come, and slowly we will walk through green gardens and marvel at this strange and sweet world.

Your own loving sivvy

Edith Summerskill to her daughter Shirley, 1956

In that same year, another mother was writing to her daughter at a university a hundred miles away. Edith Summerskill (1901–80), Member of Parliament for the British Labour Party from 1938 to 1961, wrote frequently to both her children, Shirley and Michael. The letters to Shirley often provided informative reports on the events of Edith's public life and an analysis of the social and political conditions of the countries she visited, usually with an emphasis on the changing situation of women and how she saw it relating to Shirley as a maturing daughter. Edith also took time away from her busy public schedule to be involved in her children's daily life and, like Aurelia Plath, she encouraged Shirley to choose work that would be challenging and fulfilling.

Edith Summerskill, born in London and educated at King's College and at Charing Cross Hospital, started practising as a physician in 1924. The following year she married Dr E. Jeffrey Samuel, keeping her maiden name. She devoted her life to improving the lot of women and children. Her major campaigns included those for the 'Clean Milk Law' (1949), which significantly reduced children's diseases; the Married Women's Property Act (1964), in which wives were given a right to half-share in joint savings; and the Matrimonial Homes Act (1966), which established that deserted wives could not be turned out of their homes. She fought for the institution of the National Health Service; for the use of analgesics for women in childbirth; against violence and the 'over-emphasis on sex' on television; and against smoking and boxing. As Minister of National Insurance, she paid special attention to industrial injuries compensation and the industrial diseases of miners. In 1961 she was made a life peeress and entered the House of Lords.

Shirley Summerskill (born in 1931) followed in her famous mother's footsteps by becoming a doctor and keeping her maiden name when she married; she has served as MP for Halifax since 1964. She was the UK delegate to the UN Commission on the Status of Women for two years; she then served as Opposition Spokesman on Health and, later, as Under-Secretary of State at the Home Office. She is also honorary vice-president of the Socialist Medical Association and is governor of a group of London primary schools.

In her letters to Shirley, Edith was often the initiator of feminist discussions and she displays an encyclopaedic knowledge of woman's place in world history.* The letter below is one of her shorter, more personal letters, written while Shirley was studying medicine at Oxford University:

December 1956

My Dear Shirley,

As I sat waiting for the result of a division,† Jim Callaghan, MP for Cardiff, came and sat beside me. He said he had just come from a London University debate where you had supported the motion 'That this House has no confidence in the Conservative Government'.

. . . Comparatively few mothers sit in the parliaments of the world, and very few have the pleasure of learning that a student daughter has made such a speech in a debating chamber where the procedure is similar to that of the House of Commons.

I tried to analyse my sudden inexplicable surge of emotion which left me elated and profoundly thankful. It seemed as though I had been psychoanalysed and suddenly from the deep recess of my mind the analyst had unearthed a well-buried fear. The relief was so great that I decided to sit down and write to you before I go to Warrington early in the morning.

My medical and political activities left me very busy during your childhood, and I had at times wondered whether this life of mine outside the home might sow some little seed of jealousy in you which would, with the years, grow into active dislike of these rivals for my affection. This I feared might show itself in a marked distaste for politics and even for the medical profession.

Your interest in Medicine had at least dispelled some of my fears, and then this news tonight finally dissipated all my doubts and forebodings.

Of course I knew that you had interested yourself in politics at Oxford, but this might well have been to please me.

I was simply overjoyed also to realise that you had definitely embraced my political faith in the policy of the Labour Party.

I have observed with some apprehension that the sons and daughters of many politicians take no interest in politics and take no part even during a general election in the political life of a parent. There are others who openly admit that their political views are opposed to those of their parents.

This attitude, which must cause the parents great distress, can only be attributed to the unfavourable reaction of a child to certain pursuits

---

*In one instance (see Chapter 3), Edith documents at great length the achievements of women in the arts and sciences. Their correspondence has been published in *Letters to My Daughter*, ed. Edith Summerskill.
†A vote in the House of Commons.

which absorb a parent's interest to the detriment of home life. Now without the application of any pressure on my part you have found your way to an important debate in which seasoned politicians were taking part.

I felt I was vindicated. The secret fear that it is impossible for a mother who combines a home and professional life not to harbour was completely dispelled. Far from resenting my activities, it seems you are seeking to establish a pattern of life similar to my own.

The shades of the women who blazed the trail that you and I might be free to fulfil ourselves seemed to sit with me on the green benches of Westminster last night. I feel now that you in your turn will go forward to destroy finally those monstrous customs and prejudices which have haunted the lives of generations of women.

Mama

Anne Sexton to her daughters Linda Gray and Joy, 1969–74

By the end of the following decade, some of the customs and prejudices which Edith Summerskill deplored had gradually given way: it was increasingly acceptable to educate daughters, including a college education if the family could afford it, and women's horizons were expanding. Out of the relative prosperity and liberalism of the 1960s the women's liberation movement grew. Women all over the world began to reassess what they wanted to do with their lives, how they wanted to love and be loved, how (and whether) they wanted to raise children – along with demanding a host of legal reforms on a wide range of issues affecting women's lives. Although the feminists were mainly seen as being young and childless, women of all ages, including mothers and grandmothers, were affected by direct challenges to traditional marriage and motherhood.

Anne Sexton (1928–74), another Pulitzer Prize-winning poet, grew up in the same generation as Sylvia Plath and Shirley Summerskill. She was the mother of teenage daughters when women's liberation became a household word, and, although she did not consider herself a feminist, in her life and in her poetry she was continually grappling with many of the conflicts in women's lives which have become the focus of the current women's liberation movement.

Anne was raised in a wealthy Massachusetts family. Her parents had wanted a son and Anne said that she often felt like the unwanted third daughter. She was considered a 'difficult' child, and her adolescent years were even more traumatic for the family. She attended a series of boarding schools where she refused to study, preferring to make as many dates with boys as possible and write letters to her flames all the rest of the time. She eloped with Alfred Muller Sexton (called Kayo) when she was 19 and her first daughter, Linda Gray, was born when Anne was 24. She could not adjust to the pressures of motherhood; she suffered from feelings of inadequacy and severe depression. She attempted suicide on several occasions and was hospitalised by her family.

When Linda was less than a year old, Anne's great-aunt who had been her cherished childhood confidante, died after a long illness. People close to her say that Anne never recovered fully from this loss. The following year, after the birth of her second daughter, Joy, Anne suffered a severe breakdown. After a violent fit of rage, her family again committed her to a mental hospital. Four-year-old Linda and three-month-old Joy were sent to live with their grandparents. Thirteen years later, in an interview given after she had won the 1968 Pulitzer Prize, Anne said:

> Until I was 28 I had a kind of buried self who didn't know she could do anything but make white sauce and diaper babies. I didn't know I had any creative depths. I was a victim of the American Dream, the bourgeois, middle-class dream. All I wanted was a little piece of life, to be married, to have children. I thought the nightmares, the visions, the demons would go away if there was enough love to put them down. I was trying my damndest to lead a conventional life, for that was how I was brought up, and it was what my husband wanted of me. But one can't build little white picket fences to keep nightmares out.

When she was 29, Anne started writing poetry. After her psychiatrist had seen her early writing efforts he said to her, 'Write down your feelings because someday they might mean something to somebody. No matter how despairing you are, there are other people going through this who can't express it, and if they should read it they would feel less alone.' She said that his words gave her a sense of purpose in life, and, throughout the best and worst of times over the next seventeen years until her death, she never stopped writing poems. She took great pleasure in knowing that other people in emotional distress did take comfort from her work, as they attested in the hundreds of fan letters she received from her readers.

Anne Sexton wrote of her experiences of motherhood and marriage, of her yearnings for a belief in God, her attraction to death and her great fear of life. Her parents, daughters, friends and lovers populate her poems. Hers is 'personal' poetry and she intended it to be taken very personally. When she talked about poetry in interviews and letters, she often quoted Kafka's saying, 'A book should act as an axe to the frozen sea within us.' After her death the critic Gerald Burns observed that '[along] with Sylvia Plath, Sexton practically invented the "Poem on a Gruesome Subject".' Certainly both explored the fearful territory of madness, asylums, suicide and shock treatment. Yet they also returned frequently to themes of survival and women's strength; they wrote about creating a self and finding renewal through love and through writing poetry.

Anne wanted her poems to touch and move people, even to goad them into action. From her own experience she had learned that this was possible. She said that an early W. D. Snodgrass poem ('Heart's Needle') had inspired her with the courage to make another attempt at creating a 'normal' family life and to retrieve her youngest daughter, Joy, from her grandparents after a three-year separation.

Shortly after she had embarked on this hopeful new course, Anne's parents died within four months of each other (her mother slowly and painfully of cancer, and her father suddenly of a heart attack). Anne's relationship with them had always been tempestuous, although rarely in the form of direct confrontations since her adolescence. For years after their deaths, her poetry was charged with the unspoken hurt and rage and guilt in her relationship with them. In one poem ('Double Image'), she wrote that her mother blamed Anne's suicide attempts for causing the cancer – and sometimes Anne retaliated by saying that her mother's unlovingness had caused the breakdowns and suicide attempts. However, rather than simply blaming her mother for her despair, she would sometimes acknowledge (as in the above interview) that she was a product of the 1950s and had also suffered from society's limited expectations of women. She yearned for her daughters' greater freedom and she earnestly tried to break conventional patterns of repression and guilt in her relationship with them.

But even with her insight into traditional 'feminine' social pressures and her struggle, through poetry and therapy, to free herself from the bitter resentments of her own childhood unhappiness, Anne never succeeded in achieving the equilibrium and 'normality' she yearned for in her personal life. As Linda Gray Sexton and Lois Ames* have said, 'Always life with Anne was a roller coaster. Her husband and children could never be certain what direction her mood might take. Often she was loving, exuberant, exhilarating to live with but her suicidal depressions and violent expressions of fear and rage were frightening and confusing.' Professional success did not 'keep nightmares out', but combining fulfilling work with being a mother does seem to have enabled Anne Sexton (in common with several other women in this book) to find a deep satisfaction and at times to overcome some of the difficult circumstances of her life.

In August 1973, Joy Sexton (age 18) had Anne committed to a mental hospital and then enrolled herself in boarding school. This letter from Anne was written the following year in response to Joy's apprehensions about coming home from school and living with Anne during the holidays:

21 February 1974

Dearest Joyball with a tiny bit of jellybean cheeks,

I hope my phone call last night was of some help, and I cannot tell you, my dear daisy giver, what it meant to me for you to share your pain and terror and feeling of being cooped up like an animal with me.

---

*Lois Ames is Anne Sexton's biographer, and co-editor (with Linda Gray Sexton) of *Anne Sexton: A Self-Portrait in Letters*.

You must know that I understand only too well. Here I sit at forty-five and have known and often know the very feelings you poured out to me, so what can I say but that MUGGY UNDERS ?ANDS. She knows where you're at, without you telling me I've known where you're at but have felt helpless because you did not want to speak of it to me but to run, run, run – and that too I understand.

The thing is, honey, I'm afraid those feelings go with you no matter what your environment or what cage you look upon at the moment. You do *need* certain limits, rules, despite the fact that you are 18 and in many, many ways a grown woman and want to burst forth upon the world and be free, free as if you were flying your own airplane or skiing the perfect mountain, or galloping on the most beautiful autumn day on the most beautiful horse, etc., etc. I do know how you *want* to be FREE, and can only say like an old philosopher and sufferer that I am[,] that freedom[,] that freedom comes from within and with it comes many responsibilities, and restrictions that YOU must set for yourself. In this life there is no exact thing like freedom, not even in love[,] for it carries with it the necessity to meet the loved one's needs which ideally is simple and natural and joyful. (What I mean is there is not one damn thing wrong with love, but I think one has to get their own animal out of their own cage and not look for either an animal keeper or an unlocker. I am sure that life can have a good enough rhythm for even someone as sensitive as you in time. Loneliness is a terrible thing and to be alone *with* people can be pretty horrible. To keep a closed mouth, as you say, as [if] you are locked in the set of stocks is indeed horrible. If you feel like opening your mouth – then do! And if you want to ever again open it to me, I would be as honored and touched as I was yesterday when I received your heartfelt, suffering letter. It means a great deal to me, more than I can put in words, for I have felt quite alone lately and the fame, the poetry seem to make little difference.

You say I called at just the right moment as though a message, an invisible message had been sent that you were in trouble, and I can only say that your letter came as if YOU had been sent an invisible message that you needed me and that gave me a sense of meaning to my life that had absolutely melted.

If you would like over vacation or over the summer, we can discuss further alternatives to Gould [*the boarding school*] and consult with Daddy, etc. And perhaps your dear Dr Schoen [*Joy's therapist*], although I am pretty broke, I don't think it would hurt you and I could manage to pay for you to see her a little – if you have the courage. I feel she ought to see this letter but will do nothing behind your back.

You do know that 'home' becomes quickly a kind of jail and your resentment against ANY restrictions makes it hard on both of us – I guess you feel guilty about being angry, to no end, of course, in its own way it hurts me although I know it is perfectly normal and natural. And the gas situation is so terrible, and I imagine finding jobs is next to impossible unless the Want Advertiser comes through (which I doubt) and there will have to be a hard look for a job. Even the house cleaning jobs are getting scarce. But we'll put our heads together and think of SOMETHING. I hope you are still looking through the camera's eye. I was indeed amazed by your pictures, extremely original, almost with Xray eyes.

I'm glad you liked *The Death Notebooks*. I am glad you read it. I don't think Linda has. She is too busy. I guess we are all busy, but one does make time for the really important things in life. I treasure your letter more than any I have ever gotten. I love you.

Your daisy lady,
Muggy

This letter was written to Linda on her twenty-first birthday:

3 July 1974

July 3 – looking forward to that WONDEROUOUS [sic] DATE, July 21st when first child, a wonder of a daughter came bursting forth into the world. (In other words happy birthday, in other words, my God! That Linda Gray, that Linda Pie, that stringbean has become that surprising age 21!!!!!!! TWENTY ONE! WOW! ZAP! YIKES! ZOOM! POW!.

What does a mere mother do upon such an occasion? Aside from two pairs of very pretty panties (we Sextons always seem to find ours in rags and tatters it would seem). Well, my darling in her age of ages, what I can I offer up to the gods in thanks for such a woman as you have become, true fighter, true to trust your instinct for right and wrong, a hard worker who can't even afford ketchup in her first apartment/work on her own?

I would tear down a star and put it into a smart jewelry box if I could. I would seal up love in a long thin bottle so that you could sip it when ever it was needed if I could. Instead I, who am lost in stores, and have further lost the Caedmon catalogue, give you bucks. I worked hard for them and I'm sure you realize what kind of work that is –

It would be nice to start them in your OWN saving account to withdraw at will for ketchup by the case or a diamond if it's your present wish, or any damn thing that Linda Gray Sexton who is twenty-one years old might want to do with it, them, dem bucks. I wish they were six million bucks – even more I wish they were stars that would buy you the world. But mothers can't give the world (nor fathers, nor even husbands, lovers or children) – the world sometimes just happens to us, or if we begin with more wisdom than your muggy had, we might help ourselves happen to the world. I feel that wisdom in you and I offer a prayer to it and to its growth.

Dearest pie, today nominated and legally named my literary executor (because I know you know the value, the potential of what I've tried in my small way to write, not only in financial potential for your future income, but maybe, just maybe – the spirit of the poems will go on past both of us, and one or two will be remembered in one hundred years . . . And maybe not).

You and Joy always said, while growing up, 'Well, if I had a normal mother . . .!' meaning the apron and the cookies and none of this type-writing stuff that was shocking the hell out of friends' mothers . . . But I say to myself, better I was mucking around looking for truth, etc . . . and after all we did have many 'night-night time has come for Linda Gray' and 'Goodnight moon' to read and 'Melancholy baby' for your tears.

Forgive. Muggy gets sentimental at the thought of Linda pie, little girl, baby, growing and now grown (in a sense although we never stop growing and learning and most learning comes from the hard knocks). Could you possibly keep the amount of this million bucks titled stars to yourself? It is between you and me although the love with which it's given could be plain to a perceptive observer . . .

KETCHUP DIAMONDS RECORDS BOOKS? Who knows, only Linda.

Four months after this letter was written, Anne Sexton committed suicide. In their 'Epilogue' to *Anne Sexton: A Self Portrait in Letters*, Linda Gray Sexton and Lois Ames wrote:

Anne's death was not unexpected. All those close to her had known that one day she would choose to commit suicide. At home in Weston on Friday, October 4, 1974, she took herself quickly and quietly.*

Only the day before she had returned from a successful reading at Goucher College in Maryland, where the audience had given her an extended standing ovation. The academic year had just begun at Boston University and her students welcomed her home at the airport instead of meeting her in their weekly Thursday class. At Black Oak Road, housekeeping arrangements looked promising: a new young couple had moved into the basement apartment.

The weather that Friday was particularly invigorating – the 'black' oaks and swamp maples were turning color. Anne shared lunch with Maxine Kumin in Newton, and proofread the galley sheets for *The Awful Rowing Toward God* with her as they had done with her previous books. She had planned an evening out with one of the men she was currently seeing.† But despite these signs of renewal and strength, she returned home to her death with no dramatics, no warning, no telephone calls.

Of all those who unconsciously prepared for her death, perhaps

---

*She died of carbon monoxide poisoning in her garage.
†Anne had obtained a divorce from Kayo in November 1973.

Anne herself was the most thorough. By July 1974 she had finished putting her house in order, asking particular friends which of her possessions they would like as remembrances, and offering to write holographs of their favorite poems. She had selected a biographer and prepared the Boston University archive of her manuscripts and letters. After much thought, she had appointed her literary executor, and drawn up a will with specific instructions for her funeral. In the last few years she had repeatedly told family members and friends that she wanted a palindrome from the side of an Irish barn carved on her gravestone. The words RATS LIVE ON NO EVIL STAR gave her a peculiar kind of hope.

She was acutely aware of how her death would affect others. In a letter written in April 1969 to her daughter Linda, she attempted to comfort and to hold, anticipating the day when touch would be impossible.

April 1969

Dear Linda,

I am in the middle of a flight to St. Louis to give a reading. I was reading a *New Yorker* story that made me think of my mother and all alone in the seat I whispered to her 'I know, Mother, I know'. (Found a pen!) And I thought of you – someday flying somewhere all alone and me dead perhaps and you wishing to speak to me.

And I want to speak back. (Linda, maybe it won't be flying, maybe it will be at your *own* kitchen table drinking tea some afternoon when you are 40. *Anytime*.) – I want to say back

1st I love you.
2.   You *never* let me down.
3.   I know. I was there once. I *too*, was 40 and with a dead mother who I needed still. [. . .]

This is my message to the 40-year-old Linda. No matter what happens you were always my bobolink, my special Linda Gray. Life is not easy. It is awfully lonely. *I* know that. Now you too know it – wherever you are, Linda, talking to me. But I've had a good life – I wrote unhappy – but I lived to the hilt. You too, Linda – Live to the HILT! To the top. I love you, 40-year-old Linda, and I love what you do, what you find, what you are! – Be your own woman. Belong to those you love. Talk to my poems, and talk to your heart – I'm in both: if you need me. I lied, Linda. I did love my mother and she loved me. She never held me but I miss her, so that I have to deny I ever loved her – or she me! Silly Anne! So there!

XOXOXO
Mom

CHAPTER TWO

The Men in Our Lives

Traditionally, a mother's primary duty to her daughter has been to ensure that she was marriageable: for centuries the very survival of a woman depended on being attached to a man. Today, for almost the first time in history, mothers and daughters can discuss the role of men in our lives in terms of the quality of our relationships with them, rather than just in terms of security and survival.

The transition to relationships in which women are not always so dependent on husbands and fathers is exciting and liberating, but it is also at times bewildering and painful to both women and men. On the one hand, it opens up possibilities for more fulfilling and mature relationships because of the lessening of women's childlike dependence, but it also causes uncomfortable confusion about what will replace traditional roles and values. Living in these cross-currents of change – which promise fulfillment yet threaten such loss – mothers and daughters have continued to confront and challenge each other about their relationships with men. As it became evident throughout the 1970s that many women were surviving and enjoying their independence, mothers and daughters could have more open-ended discussions about relationships, hopeful that changes in women's aspirations will allow the further development of compassion, courage and nurturing tenderness in both men and women.

Nice Girls Don't (i)

Discussions about relationships with men are often the main battleground on which a daughter struggles for independence from the family in which she has grown up. Fathers, mothers and daughters may express ambivalence about the daughter taking steps away from the 'protection' which the family is supposed to offer. For, although girls are brought up expecting to love men, we are also taught to fear them: to fear being used by men, seduced by them, deluded by them and, perhaps worst of all, to fear not being desirable to The One who could then guarantee our respectability and safeguard us against life's insecurities.

Since the price of not conforming to prevailing codes of respectability has traditionally been so high for women, it is not surprising that many families, and especially mothers, express anxiety when their daughters start exploring relationships with men.* However, among women who have enjoyed a degree of independence and who recognise their capacity for more equal, adult relationships with men (in the family, in their communities and at work), both mothers and daughters find it easier to encourage each other to develop new means of achieving security and self-respect.

Jessie Bernard and her daughter Dorothy Lee, 1961–62

Jessie Bernard, eminent sociologist, scholar and teacher, is best known for her studies of the family and the status of women, particularly in her books, *The Future of Marriage*, *The Future of Motherhood*, *Women and the Public Interest* and *The Female World*. She has also made important contributions to ways of integrating psychological research and social action. Since the 1930s she has been posing challenging feminist questions to social scientists around the world.

Jessie was born in 1903 to a middle-class Jewish family. Her parents wanted her to go to business college but they gave their consent when she decided to attend the University of Minnesota in 1920. There she fell in love with her sociology professor, Luther Lee Bernard (LLB) and married him at the age of 22, when she had just begun work for her doctoral degree. Because he was twice her age and not Jewish her parents refused their consent and Jessie's ties with her family were severed for many years.

After eleven years of marriage Jessie left LLB; their eventual reconciliation was on the basis that they would have children. He agreed, although reluctantly, since he felt it was unfair to bring a child into a war-ridden world. When their first child, Dorothy Lee, was born in 1941, Jessie was 38 and LLB was 61. They later had two sons, Claude (1945) and David (1950). LLB died of cancer when the younger son was less than a year old and Dorothy Lee was 9.

This was the beginning of Jessie's life as a single parent with major professional responsibilities; she continued to pursue her research, write, teach

---

*Nancy Friday's bestselling book, *My Mother/My Self*, explores some of the complex psychological implications of mothers restraining their daughters and inhibiting their sexuality. She underplays the social context of these maternal attitudes – such as the actual risks from which mothers in the past have wanted to protect their daughters and the fact that it is men, not mothers, who have demanded submissiveness and innocence because they find strength and independence 'unattractive' in women. Her book has been heavily criticised for its ethnocentrism and for its mother-blaming stance; although I agree with those criticisms, I think it still offers some important insights. Here, I wish to emphasise the historical/social context without reiterating the psychological explanations, for I think that both types of analysis are necessary to understand the way the mother-daughter relationship affects women's relationships with men. (For several excellent books in recent years on the psychological dynamics, see the Bibliography under Arcana, Chesler, Daly, Dinnerstein, Friday, Mitchell, and Snitow.)

and serve on civic and professional committees and boards. Two years later she took a sabbatical from her teaching post at the Pennsylvania State University and went with the children to Austria for a year's research. Dorothy Lee went to boarding school in Geneva for the year and Jessie, Claude and David lived in Graz with an Austrian family who looked after the children when Jessie's work took her away. It was at this time that Jessie began to write letters to all of her children.*

After a year in Europe, Jessie and the children returned to the USA and Dorothy Lee attended a Quaker boarding school in Philadelphia. In 1959 Dorothy Lee graduated and was accepted at Sarah Lawrence College. After two years there, she moved to England to spend her junior year at the London School of Economics (LSE), where she studied sociology and American history.

While in London, Dorothy Lee wrote many letters to her mother about politics, her courses, and the emerging 'hip' lifestyle; she spent most of the year trying to decide to which cause she should devote her energies, and attempting to fathom what it was men wanted of her. Soon after her arrival she wrote to Jessie:

I am trying to understand . . . this problem which has recently developed for me. I have had several boys (Americans) tell me I was the hardest person they met to get to know. I am very charming when they meet me; I am excellent with people, better than they are: extremely perceptive; what is more I am bright and funny . . . and most of all, good. Oh, yes. I also understand life. Now, after all these compliments they proceed to try to find out what in my past caused me such difficulties. Why aren't I normal?

Dorothy Lee's solution to the dilemma of men's ambivalence to her was to submerge herself in a cause. She wrote to Jessie just before Christmas that year: 'I would love to have someone around me to guide me, to give me direction or a cause . . . I feel guilty a little that with all the training I am receiving I have no ambition to save the world or change people.'

Soon after this, Dorothy Lee became involved with the Campaign for Nuclear Disarmament (CND), working in their office and going on demonstrations. She and Jessie began to correspond about her new relationship with Cecil, a CND organiser.

April 1962

Dear Dorothy Lee,
. . . In your letter you say, 'all is well except for Cecil. I feel a bit of a failure there mostly 'cause there are things I'd like to say and can't find the words and no matter what I still feel alone and oh so sad'. If the

---

*These have been published as *Self-Portrait of a Family*, ed. Jessie Bernard. A selection of Jessie's letters to Dorothy Lee during her teenage years appears in Chapter 6.

reason you can't find the words to say to Cecil what you'd like to say is that you love him, why don't you just say that? Since, as I take it, you aren't demanding anything in return, that is, no commitment, no anything, you needn't feel ashamed or embarrassed to say it. It is my theory that only when you have an exploitative motive in the back of your head is it embarrassing to say you love a person. That is, when you want more than you are willing to give. Or when you want someone for what he can do for you. But if it is a genuine, out-going, generous feeling it seems to me quite all right. I know this is contrary to the *mores* (mainly, I think, because the *mores* were designed to help protect men from designing women). It may make women seem aggressive, something which everyone dislikes. But you surely are not aggressive.

. . . If you want Cecil you should try to get him. I am sure that whatever way is congenial to you will be charming, attractive, and very winning to him. If you succeed, fine; if you don't, well just chalk it up to experience. Some of the most beautiful, talented, and wonderful women in the world have failed to win the men they wanted so you would be in good company. As I said above, I feel as though I am just making stabs in the dark since I know so little about what the situation is but the comments are for your consideration. Use them or not according to how they fit the situation and your feelings. In any event, it is not a world-shaking problem and however it turns out everyone still loves you and thinks you quite a wonderful girl, though causeless. Just be yourself, develop autonomy, don't feel you have to be like the others; take your time about developing and all will turn out well, with only the usual quota of heartbreaks which are the condition of mankind.

In a recent letter to me, Jessie commented on their correspondence while Dorothy Lee was a college student:

'In re-reading the letters to and from Dorothy Lee I am appalled to find how premature Virginia Woolf's report of the death of the Angel in the House was after all. She was alive not only in the House but all around us everywhere even after fifty years. She was very much alive in the early 1960s when Dorothy Lee was a student at the LSE, writing of having to charm, assuage, support the fragile egos of the young men around her. Without a word of tuition on the subject here was my own daughter in effect wrestled to the ground by her male associates in the second half of the twentieth century . . . There she was at twenty writing that it seemed to her "at a certain age boys take over from the girls intellectually, because the really creative thinking seems to come from them." This letter still breaks my heart. How helpless the young women still were only twenty years ago in the grip of that arrogantly male ambience.'

The relationship with Cecil ended amicably a few months later and Dorothy Lee concluded her year abroad with a summer of travelling around Europe and North Africa. In Tangier, she fell deeply in love with Brick, a Harvard drop-out and street musician who refused, on principle, to have a job. From the beginning of the romance with Brick, Jessie walked a tightrope between respecting Dorothy Lee's autonomy and unambiguously asserting her disapproval of the relationship.

This letter was written when Dorothy Lee was in her final year at Sarah Lawrence, while Brick was still in Tangier. Pining for his return, Dorothy Lee was also writing frequently to Jessie about her turmoil over what she could do with her life after she graduated. Jessie wrote in return:

November 1962

Dear Dorothy Lee,

. . . I can't help but keep thinking about your sadness and wishing I could do something about it. I know how hard it is to find one's self and achieve identity (which, I know, is a joke among college girls but which, you must know by now, is a very real problem). It seems to me that there are three things I can do. One is to be a spontaneous mother and try to solve all your problems for you. Definitely not. Another is to give you something to rebel against by, in effect, fighting you. This would definitely hurry the process of finding yourself, but neither you nor I have the temperament for this sort of thing and it would leave scars that might prevent us from being friends and I don't think there is any need to hurry the process. The other alternative is just to let you work out these problems by yourself, however long it takes, and keeping my hands off. I just want you to know that if I do succeed in doing this – which I may not do! – it does not mean that I am rejecting you or abandoning you or deserting you or that I am indifferent or not involved. It's just that I think that will be the best for you. You are having an especially hard time because you have to become independent of a very strong mother but console yourself with the thought that succeeding will mean that you are also very strong. At any rate, darling, know that I am here, loving you very much, yearning like any other mother but abstemiously holding back my impulses to jump in with both feet. Another thing. Would it be proper or not to get a Christmas present for Brick, knowing that he probably can't afford to get us one? If it would be, what do you suggest?

Oceans of love, dearest.

Dorothy Lee's letter in reply expressed her appreciation, saying that the letter had been 'most comforting' and had reconfirmed her belief that Jessie always managed to do and say the right thing at the right time. She asked Jessie not to worry so much about growing-up problems and how to respond to them. The letter ended, 'I love you and do try, in spite of appearances, to be a good daughter.'

The following letter was a reply to Dorothy Lee's request to borrow money in
order to bring Brick home from Tangier:

December 1962

Dear Dorothy Lee,

. . . Do you really want to establish a precedent for protecting him
from his own ineffectualness, for bailing him out of contingencies?
. . . How long can this continue if you have to be a mother to him?
Please really think over these things. I will do what I can to help you,
but this, in my opinion, is not the way to do it.

I know this is a very serious problem for you and my first impulse is,
as always, to rush to give you what you want. But this is one problem I
cannot solve for you or even help you solve. You will have to deal
with it yourself. This is one of the responsibilities of independence and
adulthood. I know you will feel resentful because you are unaccus-
tomed to having me turn you down on anything. You may hate me for
a while. I can take it, darling. Be as angry as you like. But ask yourself,
too, if it's me or circumstances that make you mad. Believe me,
dearest, I do love you.

Despite Jessie's objections to the relationship with Brick, they were married
soon after Dorothy Lee's graduation. Seventeen years later, Jessie says:

'I finally capitulated; I did not want to lose her; I gave the marriage my
blessing. Then watched its slow disintegration. I watched her gallant,
unflagging, finally desperate struggle to save it. But, inevitably, it came to an
end. She could win every battle but one, the battle against his alcoholism.'

After nine years of marriage they separated and divorced. Dorothy Lee now
lives in Washington D.C. and works for a company which monitors the U S
Congress, keeping track of committees, caucuses and other congressional
units.

Nice Girls Don't (ii)

Most of us were not taught to view our bodies as our own, for our own
pleasure and purposes – but as something which a man will one day possess
and enjoy. Teachings about sex have traditionally focussed on how and why
to stay away from it and what men will think of us if we don't; we are
expected to be heterosexual – but not sexual. For a woman, sex is mainly
referred to in terms of loss: the loss of her virginity, of her innocence and, if
she is unmarried, of her 'reputation'.

These sorts of teachings have long been an important consideration in the
survival of women, and mothers have often been forced to ignore their
daughters' health, pleasure or sense of well-being in the interest of making
sure that men would find them 'attractive'. Sometimes they have had to be

physically brutal and inflict lifelong pain to help their daughters meet men's standards: even such damaging practices as footbinding and clitoridectomy* are often carried out by the girl's mother or under her mother's supervision. In our society, teaching daughters to be appealing to men has meant a wide variety of things, from telling them that they shouldn't appear too intelligent or independent, to the contradictory instruction to be constantly aware of looking attractive while remembering that 'boys only want one thing' (and nice girls don't give it to them).

None of these repressive practices occur because mothers *want* to cripple their daughters; they arise out of religious and social codes and are passed on out of genuine fears that women can never find love, security or respectability if they do not play by the rules. The mother's own life may even be a case in point: she may feel that to disagree with her husband would undermine her own security.

Jessica and her mother Nancy, 1970

Nancy was brought up in a wealthy English family, the eldest of two children. Her higher education was brought to an abrupt end by World War II and she never returned to it. At the age of 22 she married a newly-chartered accountant with whom she had fallen in love just after the war. Their son was born the following year, Jessica four years later. Nancy saw her job as creating and running a 'good' home. As the children grew older she spent increasing energy pursuing her other interests, such as painting.

Jessica was sent to boarding school when she was 10. At 21, after earning a History degree at Edinburgh University, she moved to London and began working as a secretary. Two years later she met Alex, a civil servant with a promising career ahead of him. In her parents' eyes he was unacceptable. Jessica sent me this description when she offered her letters for publication:

'My whole life up to the age of twenty-three had involved trying to please my parents. I found my mother incredibly overpowering and dismissive of anything I did or even *felt* that she didn't agree with or approve of. I ended up not allowing myself to think or feel things that were unacceptable – a recipe for disaster!

'This first letter represents one of the peaks in our confrontation. They had decided (after meeting Alex once) that the relationship should not continue and they informed me over dinner one night that I must stop seeing him.

---

*For over 1000 years in China, girls from the age of five were deliberately crippled; their pus-filled bloody feet were concealed in ornately embroidered slippers. All this, because men found small feet sexually arousing. Footbinding became illegal only at the beginning of this century.

Female genital mutilation (clitoridectomy and infibulation) also inflicts excruciating lifelong pain on girls and women. It is done for the purpose of 'purifying' women and enhancing men's sexual pleasure (while literally cutting out the woman's pleasure). It is still practised in parts of Africa and the Middle East. (See Bibliography, Daly and Dworkin.)

'They were staggered to discover that it wasn't as simple as they thought. I said I had no intention of ending the relationship. The battling went on through that evening and culminated the next day in an argument which ended up with my father hitting me hysterically. I crouched by my bed, stupefied and appalled, and also laughing in that very contorted way that one sometimes does in horrifying situations.'

Alex arrived shortly thereafter and a 'cross-examination' began; Jessica's parents objected mainly to the fact that he had been married (though he had been separated from his wife for two years and they were filing amicably for divorce), and that he lacked the right middle-class pedigree:

'My parents have a very definite idea of how to survive and they couldn't understand that there are other ways of surviving which don't require rigid adherence to a set of rules. My mother couldn't imagine her life without her house, her status, her husband; those are the only things which gave her security. Sadly she doesn't have a sense of security within herself and in the letters it is obvious that she couldn't imagine me being secure if I didn't pay close attention to questions of status.

'One of the most confusing things was that I knew my parents did not agree on many things, certainly about sexual morality. I vividly remember my mother once asking me outright if I slept with Alex and I said yes. We were both smiling and she said, "I thought so." She said she'd found some birth control pills of mine about two years before when I'd been seeing a different man. She didn't seem – and she wasn't – at all bothered. The memory I have of that conversation is of two girls together, giggling. Thus, her attitude in the letters about my sexuality was very disconcerting. It has to be seen in the context of a decision she made (which she repeatedly told me she had to make) to stand by my father no matter what. Hence, my feeling of betrayal.'

11 June 1970

Dear Jessica,
    We were unable to get hold of your 'friend' on the telephone this morning and I feel that several things remain to be said to you, which you are at liberty to show to him.
    Your conduct and way of life has created havoc with your father and with me – but for the last time. I fully support your father's attitude, and am not prepared to hide your distasteful way of life for your convenience anymore.
    As you know, there is nothing about this young man that particularly appeals to us; but had he been presented from the beginning as the man you wished to marry, we might have been able to accept a distasteful situation. However, in view of your obvious lack of desire for marriage, you must realise that we are not prepared to entertain or meet a series of your lovers.
    You have spoken a lot about honesty; you seem to know as little of

the effect of this so-called honesty as you do of real love; and your life so far is the worst possible foundation for happiness. You are 23, and may well live to be 83; in my opinion you are well on the slippery slope to lack of self-respect and a future of misery and uncertainty. I can assure you real love rests upon consideration for one's partner and upon trust and I cannot see that people who have slept around and hurt other people deeply (including parents) have much choice of becoming anything but increasingly selfish and self-interested.

Your father and I can assure you that we have no intention of our deep bond of affection being upset further by your headstrong and selfish attitude of all take and no give. We can advise and warn and the only steps we can take are financial; and as we have already said, we are not prepared to give you any more financial help. If you dissipate what you already have, you must be prepared to expect no more; we see no reason why either of us should will money to you that any Tom, Dick or Harry will relieve you of. My great regret is that your father has worked so desperately hard all his life, and has forgone things he always wanted, in order to provide not only the best possible education for his daughter, but also some protection for her future. We are both deeply disappointed in your lack of fastidiousness and plain common sense.

If you wish to come home you will always be welcome as our daughter, but you must be aware that you have strained not only your relationship with us but have also caused a tremendous strain upon our own. That, however, is more firmly cemented than ever, and I sincerely wish that I could think that you also could find the happiness and content that your father and I have achieved.

later in the evening
. . . Your father and I are human beings of some sensitivity and standards that are not unknown to you; we are not just here to provide every wherewithal and to submit to discourtesy, kicks and insults and then come up smiling, waiting for the next blow. We have a relationship with each other which is the most important thing in our lives now. Please don't add any more burdens to your father who has spent his whole life in helping other people . . . If you are pleased to accept his material gifts, then you must respect his moral standards and principles and try to make him happy in return.

Well, Jessica – you've been like the Sorcerer's Apprentice this time – forces have been unleashed that you cannot control; do not think for a moment that we condone or accept your living with this man or that we are prepared to meet him again. Nor do we think that a series of lovers is preparation for happiness in the future; you will always find a home and welcome with us, but we are not prepared to give hospitality to these people, or to meet them anywhere else. Your father's attitude is entirely consistent with what he has said to you over the years, and you must accept a large responsibility for damaging your own 'image'. In fact, you are a very selfish and spoiled child, and you had better begin to grow up, before you hurt many more people.

Mummy

[*Note from her father, attached:*]

Dear Jessica,

Your mother has collapsed again after writing her letter and I have just recovered after reading it myself . . .

P.S.   Jessica, I have just read what your father has written and cannot add any more except to beg you to think of our feelings. It seems to me that the most sensible step to take would be to come back home and take a job up here; it would help you to forget this unhappy affair.

My love to you,
Mummy

In her correspondence with me, Jessica explained something of her feelings at that time and what she feels she has learned after several years of bitter estrangement:

'The events that precipitated these letters were more fantastical than most fantasies. During this period I experienced terrifying desolation and betrayal. My parents seemed to me to be deliberately out to destroy me. They were trying every possible means to make me do – and be – what they wanted. I had been brought up dependent on their assessment of me, and I found myself having to break from that dependence at a time when I was being completely undermined by them. The alternative seemed to be madness and for very short periods of time I would get close to what I suppose madness is. Subsequently, for a period of years, I was in a semi-permanent depression.

'After nearly a dozen hostile and, increasingly, threatening letters from my parents [*only the first is included here*], communication between us ceased for nine years. I felt as if I had lost their love. I even worried that they might try to have me committed to a mental hospital – but I always thought I could produce their letters as proof of their mental instability and my sanity. On the other hand, I was worried that if anyone ever saw these letters, they might believe that I was as bad as they had tried to persuade me. Alex had even resorted to tearing up some of them before I saw them, because they were making me so upset.

'I'm really pleased at how much I am able to distance myself from the letters now (although I have always been able to laugh at them – through the tears). Now I feel a kind of liberation: at last I am able to shake myself free from the shocking spirit of these letters and what they stood for. I feel proud of the way

I stood up for myself under terrible pressure, yet continued to communicate my love for my parents. And I feel proud of what I have learned and discovered – and continue to discover – as a result of all the horrors of that period: the strength and self-respect that I might never have developed without the very confrontation that threatened to destroy me.'

14 June 1970

Dear Mum and Dad,

I hope you realise that if you decide to 'dismiss' my relationship with Alex, that dismissal also dismisses me . . . and even if the relationship were to cease, I could find no cause to 'return to your fold'. You see, there would be no mutual feeling, no point of contact, no reason for me to have anything to do with you, or you with me, except to receive 'handouts of financial assistance', which you KNOW I dislike and continually refuse.

I find your statement 'don't expect any more from us', not unnaturally, amazing. You have still not realised that I do not expect anything from you. I have never – as long as I have thought about it – considered it a right to be handed money etc., and you have both witnessed countless occasions of my refusal to accept. I have also expressed once or twice that I feel you should spend your money on yourselves and that your children should take second place now. After all, you've done a hell of a lot for us.

You have both been utterly shocked. I do not deny shocking you, nor condone shocking you. But, *you* have asked the questions; I really don't know why you asked them if you didn't want them to be answered. You would have preferred me to tell lies, but that policy would lead to our being even more distant from each other. Telling lies leads to more lies, and then more lies, which by that time are unconvincing and lead to lack of trust . . .

So, having asked the questions, now armed with information which has shocked and upset you, you wish to cut me off from you. (Surely, you must see a lot in me that you do not understand? Does that mean that it is necessarily wrong or harmful?) The path that you have chosen was not the only course of action . . . For what is undoubtedly the last time, I will try and make you understand.

. . . Alex loves and respects me; it is this very love and respect which you choose to dismiss that leads him to wish to strive after marriage with me. He does not feel ready for it yet. I feel exactly the same as he: marriage, but not yet. I wish to prove myself to him first, to be capable of standing on my own feet, and to be capable of supporting him emotionally. At the moment, he is giving me more than I am giving him. We want both our lives to be stable before embarking on a joint one. Do not imagine that I think marriage is easy. I think it would help us all if you accepted that I observe other

people and their marriages, that I think about them extremely
seriously. You are pointing out traps to me that I already know. You
must accept that and thus accept that I am an intelligent form of
human life!

I have nearly finished. I hope you are still reading.

I am aware that your relationship has suffered many blows. (Do not
imagine that I was trying to play you against each other; you are both
different people and have different ideas; I have often heard
arguments about the fundamental differences you have. I do not
expect you both to hold the same views on everything; nor do you.)
When I told Mummy things, she ASKED questions. I only hope that
your relationship has been cemented by all this disruption: my
relationship has. People must resolve their differences if they are to
continue to have any rapport: you have both clearly been able to do
that in the past. It is now time WE resolve our differences: you and I.
That is, if there is a mutual wish for any rapport. You, Mummy, often
said that children and parents do not choose each other. Is it not
reasonable to expect there to be differences between us? . . .

I am your child and am not rejecting you, even if you reject me. By
my words, 'not rejecting you', I DO NOT mean that I am leaving the
way open for advice and help (material or otherwise). I mean that I
accept you as parents who do what they think is best, I love you and
respect you. I do not ASK you to change in any way, but I do believe
that the ideal attitude a parent can adopt is pretty similar: to accept,
love and respect its offspring. I do not ask you to condone what is
totally alien to you, but I do not think it is beyond you to recognise my
powers of judgment, and to ignore what you do not wish to see (many
other parents do).

To accept, I know, is very difficult, but judgment IS, after all,
relative. There are many girls whom you and I know whose relationships with men you would consider unacceptable and immoral, and I
WOULD TOO . . . If you consider I am being a whore, that is your
affair. What is important is MY attitude to the relationship: because if I
did not love, then I would be a whore. I do love, and feel a tremendous
responsibility to the person I love. If I were to feel a responsibility to
you first, there would be no love. I feel it is irresponsible to deceive
and betray love and would never do it. I also feel that one must
(mutually) work hard at it, and I will work bloody hard. Try also to
remember that I am aware that most marriages are pretty poor
examples. If there is no deceit or betrayal, there is often no support
either between the two people and rarely do they work hard at love
and marriage.

It is within the control of both of us to resolve our differences, and I
do most sincerely want to resolve them.

I am sure you must have had an awful weekend. I hope one day you realise your fears about me are unfounded, not only your fears that I shall end up in the gutter, but your fears that I do not love you and that I do not care about you. Some of your accusations are impossible to answer and this is one of them.

I cannot think any more, I am afraid, except to say that if you succeed in destroying any relationship of mine, be it this one or any friendship, you would at the same time destroy yours and mine. I told you last week how strong my relationship was with Alex. You said on Saturday that this relationship must end. It simply CANNOT, WILL NOT end. The vague doubts I have had are completely dispelled now, and I hope will never come back. If our love were not so strong (Alex's and mine) he would have left long ago, and I may have given in to you and bowed to your orders.

Please remember, if I were to do what you wanted, I would have no self-respect, and I would expect none from you.

I hope that one day we can be truly friends. Meanwhile, the world will carry on. I must end, and wonder when I will see you again.

Love,
Jessica

Nice Girls Don't (iii)

Despite the prevailing disapproval and worry about the 'new morality' of the 1960s, throughout the 1970s numerous women and men were deciding to live together without getting married – either as a 'trial period' to see if they wanted to make a deep long-term commitment or, in other cases, without intending ever to get married even if they decided to stay together. Some parents felt that their sons and daughters were wise to take time to discover more about themselves, to explore their relationships and find out whether they wanted the same things from life as the people they happened to fall in love with. But there were still many parents, from every type of background, who were shocked and upset that their children (especially their daughters) would consider having a sexual relationship without the proprieties and safe-guards of marriage.

Pat and her mother Janet, 1972

Pat grew up in a small town in Ohio. Her mother and father were employees of the American government all their working lives. They met and married while they were at business college; Pat's mother went on to become a secretary and her father a management consultant.

Pat always felt that her parents were miserable in their full-time work and she has chosen instead to work in fulfilling part-time jobs. She has a master's degree in electronic music and recording media; she is an electronics technician and works freelance on commercial container ships. She is also part-owner of a collectively owned and operated restaurant in Berkeley, California.

On the subject of the men in her life, Pat says:

'Occasionally I'm still hit by the old "if I'm not married I'm nobody" and "here I am at thirty years old and still not married". But then there are times when I know I'm not married out of personal choice. From living with my first boyfriend [*Tony, who is the subject of these letters*] I know how easy it would be for me if I was married to defer to the other person and not take care of my own needs in many ways. It's difficult enough to get my personal work done in life without the distraction and time commitment of a full-time relationship. I don't feel strong enough to maintain my own sense of individuality if I make a "commitment" to someone else. My partner would have to be someone who is an intense worker – who would not have time to demand too much from me . . . My parents, of course, could not conceive of the possibility that I would not marry. My mother had always *strongly* stressed the security factor of marriage. She truly believed I could not possibly find true security outside of marriage. Thus at the end of my first year of University when I wrote to tell them I was planning to live with Tony, the thing I most needed to stress was my ability to survive.'

1 August 1972

Dear Mom and Dad,

. . . I'm not moving back home after I graduate. There is really nothing for me there (aside from being with the family). I am contented, happy, and settled down in a place where I don't mind living. What would you rather have: me as a mature adult, handling my own affairs and making my own decisions . . . or me as a 'child' depending on you for everything? I want to be able to handle my own financial matters after I graduate. It is time for me to stop accepting money from you and start supporting myself. I don't want to limit my world to one thing or one place or one set of ideals.

My roommate is moving out at the end of this term. There is a possibility that Tony will move in. We have talked about it and it seems like the logical thing to do since we might as well be living together anyway. I hope you have realized by now that I am not a little girl any more. I firmly believe we have made the right decision and so does Tony. We are happy together and we have much to learn and gain, and much to experience by doing this. Also, if I am living with a man I will feel safer living in an area where rapes and robberies are a common occurrence.

I assume you think that living together is morally wrong as opposed to marriage which is morally 'right'. I feel that two people can be just as close and happy living together, and they do not need a marriage contract to make theirs a 'legal' partnership. If marriage is a form of 'security', then I don't want that form of security. Security alone is not a valid reason for two people to be together. This is what I believe and I want you to be able to accept it and be aware that this is what I really am.

Much love,
your daughter, Pat

8 August 1972

Dear Pat,

I don't know what reaction you expected from us after reading your Air Mail letter to us this week. Naturally we are disappointed at your apparent lack of appreciation and respect for us, as well as respect for yourself. We did the best we could for both our girls, and expected to see you graduate, as did Sharon [*Pat's sister*], knowing where you were going and with both feet on the ground. As it is, you seem to be in a confused state, changing your major for the third time and not knowing exactly what you want or where you are going.

When you gave us the snow job several months ago, convincing us that you wanted to move from the dorm into an apartment, even though we had a few misgivings as to the advisability of it, our trust and confidence in you overruled our doubts and we gave our consent. At that time you seemed to be acting with mature judgement with goals firmly set. We are now convinced that you weren't as prepared as we thought you were to handle the outside world.

You always prided yourself on dating fellows who respected you. What happened along the way that you can no longer demand such respect? Aren't you able to look ahead and visualize what may be in store for you in two, five, or ten years? When this fellow has finished with you and moves on to someone else, and when you meet THE ONE you will want to spend the rest of your life with, will he want to settle for secondhand, used merchandise?

No Pat, we didn't expect you to move here after graduation. You had wanted to go to grad school, and we had made plans to see you thru after your graduation. We wanted to give you every opportunity to fit yourself for self-support. If you are willing to throw all this away, there is nothing we can do about it since you are now an adult and must make your own decisions. If you believe Tony is THE ONE in your life, then he will be willing to wait for you to attain your goals. You have your whole life ahead of you and one more year or less shouldn't make any difference.

Naturally we are disappointed that you do not want to spend your quarter break with us, but you know what is best so far as your studies are concerned. We do want you to be able to retain your good grades and graduate when you planned, and hope that you will reconsider what you proposed in your letter so that we will want to put you

through this last quarter. Of course you realize that would be impossible if you should go through with it.

How about Tony's sweet mother, the one who mailed the violin to
you? Are you a girl whom he would like to take home to meet his
mother? Would she condone such an arrangement? Is he considering
her feelings? I'm leaving the remainder to be said by your daddy.

Your loving
Mom

P.S.   Whatever will I do with the pretty blue print corduroy bed-
spread I have just made for you?

Honey, anytime you want to come home for a visit, your room will
be waiting for you. Your husband, if and when you get one, will also
be welcome. Here is a picture of the happy family that once was
[family snapshot enclosed].

[Note from her father, attached:]

Pat, as you can well understand from what your mother has written,
you know we do not condone your proposal to shack up with Tony.
You stated in your letter that you wanted to be independent and make
your own decisions. We have let you do just that. However, if you
decide to go through with your proposal, God pity you. Here are some
of my proposals:

1. Be sure and get some insurance.
2. Get acquainted with income tax rules and regulations.
3. Don't expect any more financial assistance from us.
4. Straighten up and fly right. You will be all the better off if you
    do.

If you are going to live with a man I will expect him to support you. I
pray that you will give this matter some serious thought. Let us know
your decision so we can know where we stand financially.

Daddy

Pat writes:

'It's really difficult for me to say what my parents deepest reasons were for
opposing my living arrangements with Tony.* I think for my mother it was
loss of control and religious. With my father, it was economic. Deep down
inside my parents probably realised how much they had over-protected me
and they must have been fearful that I was incapable of making an intelligent
decision, having had no experience in making decisions with them.

---

*Approximately six months after Tony moved in, he met Pat's parents. Pat says, 'They fell in
love with him and wouldn't let him out of their sight, especially my dad. Dad would drag out his
old navy scrapbooks to show Tony and even asked if he had ever smoked marijuana (in a
curious, non-hostile way).'

'I felt that my mother derived her morals entirely from what other people believed and she was too insecure to do any thinking on her own. I used to really resent this side of her personality. – Now I see that, given the circumstances, and the authoritarian nature of my father, she really had no choice. She had no encouragement to think on her own; in fact, she was encouraged not to. My father made all the decisions in the house when I was growing up. I had a painful first few years away from home when I went to college because I was also terribly dependent on my father's judgement.

'When I received my parents' letter, I felt a mixture of fear and ridicule. I wanted them to accept who I was (unlike my sister who was content to tell them what they wanted to hear, true or not). I didn't feel that I could live with myself if I didn't tell them the truth, even at the risk of losing their approval. I have never lost the need for it, and sometimes I'm amazed at how it still "runs" me and motivates my behavior and perception of myself, especially in relation to men.'

Anne Sexton to her daughter Linda Gray, 1969

The first three mothers in this chapter were all writing to daughters who were over 21, had been through university and, to all intents and purposes, were adults who could and should be responsible for their own lives. But Anne Sexton, poet and mother of two daughters,* found herself dealing with similar issues of sexuality and parental authority while her eldest daughter, Linda, was still a teenager. Anne wrote this letter when Linda, then aged 16, was away at camp as a Counselor-in-Training (CIT) (Judy, who is mentioned in the letter, is the daughter of Anne's best friend, the poet Maxine Kumin; Kenny was Linda's boyfriend):

3 July 1969

Dear Linda Pie,
. . . I'm sorry you're so sort of homesick, sweetheart, god damn it. I used to get so homesick at camp and god damn it I remember how it feels. I'm sorry too that I didn't write sooner. I have been so lonely . . . too lonely to write I guess. I like calling better because then you're right there. I know a letter from me isn't as good as one from Kenny, but I can't do a thing about that. Believe it or not, you're going to love me a lot longer than you'll love him. Even if I say my mother was mean, I still love her and anyhow she wasn't *that* mean. I exaggerate everything I fear.
. . . Earlier this week I had a heart-to-heart talk with Judy. She advising me on what it's like to be a young girl and me telling her about

---

*Further letters and biographical information on Anne Sexton and her daughters can be found in Chapter 1.

possibly you wanting to go on the pill for birth-control reasons . . . Naturally I didn't go into the specifics of you and Kenny, but I did value her advice. Seeing she is on the pill and is a *little* older and wiser than you are (and yet younger and more hip than I am), I thought she might have some wise words . . . And she did. Today she brought in a poem she wrote to you. It doesn't say it's to you but I guessed from the poem. It's a good poem and I told her to send or give it to you. I think you'll like it although you may resent the message. The main message is that it's a trap. Nevermind me telling you what it says. I just called Judy and she said I could send it to you . . . She said she's worried that you'll say its none of her business. I said to her, 'Do you think she'll be angry with me for talking about it with you?' She said, 'Well, we're too good friends for her to mind too much.' I hope you don't, bobolink. It's just that I have no one to go to for advice. Hardly Daddy, who thinks you should never go on the pill, even for cramps: 'You suffered with cramps, Anne, so let her. Letting her go on the pill is giving her a license to steal.' 'But Kayo,' I answered, 'a relationship between a boy and a girl who are in love, no matter what they do, is not stealing.' 'But a nice girl wouldn't do that!' 'Kayo, a nice girl is one who is kind to people and loves people.' 'You're too god damned liberal'
and so forth . . .
Linda, I think Kenny is right. The right thing, the nice thing, the kind-toyourself thing is to wait until it will be something special, not just fumbling on the grass or on a couch or in a car. Wait for a bed. That won't happen for years and I do really think it is something worth waiting for. I really think it's better to wait until you're older and readier to handle it. But no matter what you do I'll stick by you, Linda. As Dr. Deitz points out, girls in other cultures have married and had babies by the time they're sixteen. But still, pie, you don't live in another culture do you!

Now I won't give you another lecture about drugs but will save that for later. They worry me too.

As you can see you've been very much in my mind!!!!!! I keep having internal dialogues with you about all this. They are never arguments . . . We get along too well when we have serious talks. Usually we agree but I don't want to be too 'liberal' and hurt you in any way.

I hope you like Judy's poem . . . You can send it back to me after you've read it.

. . . Continue to be a good CIT dearest. I know you will gain a lot of experience and growth from this summer. Is it fun to be in a cabin with all the older girls? You might try talking over some of these things with them. Just to get their approach. Judy says if you ever want to talk

things over with her she'll be glad to . . . Your friends this summer
might be [some help]. I know I'm your good friend (if not your best)
but I'd like you to have many and varied friends.

I ADORE YOU

XXXXXXXXXXXXXXXXXXXXXXXXXXXXXXXXXXXXXXXXXX
XXXXXXXXXXXXXXXXXXXXXXXXXXXXX
))))OOOOOOOOOOOXXXXXXXXXXXOOOOOOOOOXXX
XXXXXXOOOOOOOOOXXXXXXOOOOOOOXXXXX
OOOOOXXXXXOOOO

Jackie Page to her mother Lynn, 1980

Jackie Page was raised in a farming family in rural Colorado. She attended
Colorado University and was married at the age of 23. Her son, Chris, was
born when she was 25, and her daughter, Ashley, six years later. When
Ashley was a year old, Jackie and her husband divorced. At the time when
this letter was written, Jackie was living in Oregon and teaching in a private
alternative high school for students with problems. She wrote to me about
the effect that this letter has had on her relationship with her mother and with
her children:

'I left home at 17 but at 35 I'm still in the process of cutting those everlasting
apron strings. The following is a letter I wrote to my mother to explain how I
felt about [Matt] a man I had chosen to live with rather than to marry. The
idea of living with a man, especially since I have two children and live in a
traditional kind of neighborhood was, in her eyes, *unforgivable* – at least
where her daughter was concerned.

'In the three years since the letter, there have been brief periods when the
tensions between us have eased slightly, but then become worse again.
Overall, I've come to understand through this confrontation that being a
mother is no piece of cake – and probably never was – especially if there's a
father to deal with as well as the kids. My mother has had her hands full with
my brother and me and my dad, and she probably feels she still does. We've
had some hurt feelings over things, though none so painful as this big
mangling of feelings – but my Mom will always be my Mom. I have to be my
own person; it must be by instinct, because I wasn't raised to be, but I love her
and I admit that it would be nice to have her approval. So *my* lesson is that I
need to be very accepting of Chris and Ashley as people in their own right.
That, I'm learning, is not as easy as it sounds.'

Jackie had said to her mother that she never seemed interested in how Jackie
felt. Her mother had replied, 'Sit down and tell me in a letter':

30 July 1980

Dear Mother,

How I feel? Well, it's complicated but I'll try to give you some idea. I feel like I'm approaching a time in my life that's more comfortable than anything I've felt right up to writing this letter to you. Now for sure I'm not talking economics when I say comfortable. I'm addressing my equivalent to your financial security/insecurity. The thing I'm talking about is self-confidence. I feel confident that I made the right decision about divorcing Ron; I am confident in the riches I possess for giving my children the confidence and desire to grow and live; I am confident in my own decisions, in my ability to meet responsibilities financial and otherwise; and last, but I assure you not least, I am confident in the love, affection and friendship I feel for Matt Blender from Jersey.

I know you have written Matt off as some kind of ne'er-do-well and I know the reasons why: 1. his appearance; 2. because I neglected to mention his last name when I introduced you; 3. you figure he's sponging off me because he's unemployed or something; and 4. the 'shack-up' in your own words. Now just as this letter is by no means to be confused with a statement of defense for any of my actions, neither am I in any way asserting a defense for Matt, he needs no defending. Maybe what I can do, though, is just tell you some of the things I like most about him. To start off with, I've never felt more comfortable around any other adult in my life. Matt has an intense love of life and ability to live that, well face it, I can't resist. I love the way he has of communicating with Chris and Ashley (it's on a level with the rapport Chris has with Dad) I liked the way Matt was supportive of me when I was troubled (understatement) by Ashley's behavior (the stuff you saw her doing at the airport at Christmas) and I admire the intelligence I see in his responding to Chris and Ashley.

The fact of the matter is, I like, love, whatever, the guy so much that I want to spend the rest of my life with him and the commitment we have made to each other is that kind. The subject of marriage comes up a lot. I feel very married to Matt now, only better. Marriage offers perhaps one thing that is worthwhile, maybe two, but if you asked me to define them I'm sure they aren't the same things you would think I should think, and they aren't really worth going into here. Actually, Matt and I may well one day get married for those reasons of mine.

As far as Chris and Ashley are concerned, now don't think me cold, but it's part of my lesson to them that there is more than one way to perceive the world and that's important now – more than ever I guessed. It's hard being a kid and having realities be obstacles, but Chris and Ashley are bright, they want to be happy and they know about loving, so in the longrun what else is there really?

Now I know you and Dad are feeling like I've acted horribly, like a bad child who really knows better. I've hurt your feelings, probably embarrassed you and disappointed you miserably and I feel sorry that it had to happen. I guess by your standards, all that is true about misbehaving, but not by mine. I feel badly for you both, though, that you don't have the confidence in me that I have. It would be so great for me if you could listen and understand when I say that I don't have all the answers, just like you don't. All we really do anyway is live through a series of accidents and mistakes, insights and successes. I'm not saying my way is better than yours, I'm only saying that it is my way and we can either part ways here or get to know each other somehow and see if we can practice some lesson in perceiving the world in our different ways.

love,
Jackie

Mothers as Wives: A Lesson We Don't Forget

As girls grow up there seems to be continual tension between wanting to be like their mothers and wanting to be different. Many mothers also seem to have mixed feelings about similarities: wanting their daughters to be like them and have similar values – yet wanting them to have a 'better' life, not to get hurt and make the same mistakes.

'Do as I say, not as I do', goes the popular saying. But however greatly we are influenced by teachers, churches, television, girls' magazines and fairy tales, it is from the behaviour of our parents that we learn our most enduring lessons about what it means to be a woman and what to expect from relationships between women and men. Only too often, the significance of this teaching is acknowledged by how strongly it is denied. I have been involved on two occasions in women's groups where there was an assignment to 'close your eyes and think of all the ways you are like your mother': after a few minutes, every woman in turn opened her eyes and said all the ways she was *different* from her mother! I had to laugh when I started describing this exercise to my mother and she said immediately, 'the only thing I can think of is all the ways that I'm different from my Mom.' (She was able later to think of some similarities between them.) I have heard of this happening in several other women's groups: after each woman has convinced the group that she is not in the least like her mother, she can then begin to remember some of the characteristics they have in common.

Sometimes daughters don't want to think about the ways they are like their mothers because they are hurt and angry about the negative patterns they have 'inherited' from them. In order to be free they have had to question the assumptions they learned while growing up and make a conscious effort to lead lives different from their mothers'. Several of the mothers whose letters appear in this chapter have also endeavoured to change harmful patterns in their own lives, giving their daughters new models of womanhood and loving relationships.

Charlene Baldridge to her daughter Lou, 1981

Charlene Baldridge was born in 1934, the youngest of three daughters of a middle-class suburban Chicago family who believed that home, family and marriage were the ultimate goals for a woman. Her mother was an alcoholic, but she vowed to remain sober when Charlene was 6. She never touched another drink and Charlene only found out about the alcoholism when she was 19.

Charlene had a strikingly mature singing voice and her family decided that she should receive private training for a career in opera. But she was afraid to go out alone, even to a restaurant; she became frightened at the prospect of fame and convinced herself that marriage, rather than a career as a singer, would fulfill her. At 20 she married a charismatic and unreliable suitor (Bob O.); she left him three years later when their second son was only 5 months old. She began taking opera workshop classes at the University of New Mexico and worked full-time in a bank to support her two children. In 1958 she married Sam, a man with whom she had sung in local theatre musicals. He died of a heart attack two years after Lou was born.

Charlene moved to San Diego to be near her parents; she found a job as a bank clerk and took singing jobs when she could find them. In 1963 she married Jay (he is referred to as 'Dad' in the following letter and he is the only father Lou has known). Jay had four sons and it was necessary for Charlene to continue working in the bank to support their large family. She had to give up her job in 1972 when she underwent surgery twice in the same year; the surgery left her with no singing voice.

With the children grown and married she decided to pursue her dream of a college education. She began writing poetry and held a job as music and theatre critic for the local newspaper. Her poetry has been published by a number of women's presses and she currently contributes articles about the fine arts and women's issues to magazines and newspapers around the country.

Lou married Dave at the age of 20. Both are students at the University of California, San Diego, and active Christians. Dave is a bank-loan officer and Lou works during college holidays as an aide in a group home for severely retarded young people.

When Charlene sent me a copy of one letter she wrote to Lou, she explained her perspective on her differences from her daughter:

'Lou's letters from college are filled with her God. He was the God of my youth, as well, but I've become separated from Him as a result of the Women's Movement. I'm not a radical feminist, as you can tell from my letter to Lou; however, I strongly wish for her the opportunity to be all she can be.

'Because I was so sheltered, because I made such shatteringly naive choices in life, I wanted Lou to be different. Wanted her to have more information with which to make choices . . . informed choices. I don't know whether I've done right or not. I know she loves me. And I think she's stronger than I was at 20. But, I did manage to muddle through somehow, and I don't feel anything was wasted, nor do I regret anything, for it is all part of me. As for her future, I wonder. The feminist in me has got to be lurking somewhere in her consciousness, but due to her fundamentalist beliefs, her love commitment with Dave includes *subjugation*. Fine, perhaps. Hope I'm around to see how that is negotiated between them, as I know it must be.'

The following is Charlene's 'Letter to a Daughter When She Didn't Know Which of Two Suitors to Marry':

6 January 1981

Dear Lou:

You either know by now or are more confused than ever.

You are my daughter, and it's hard to say, 'Objectively, I see this happening: . . .' because there can be no objectivity where we're concerned. However, I think we are enough alike that I can get some insight into what's going on, because I feel the same way. Thank God you don't have to choose right now. Maybe time and getting to know both Larry and Dave better will give you more criteria on which to base a decision. Of course, the romantic in me says, 'Let your heart be your guide.' And yet, each time I followed my heart, and impulsively did what I was led to do, sorrow followed. You are different than I in that you are not as head-strong and romantic. You must remember, I was very naive and totally Pollyanna about life at the time I met and married Bob O. He was Prince Charming – a man of the world – all grown up, so handsome, so intelligent. I saw none of his bad side, and even denied it for years, when deep in my brain I knew what he was.

You have better judgement than that. You've told me you see both Larry and Dave *with* their faults.

Dad was the only choice of mate I made in which my reason was stronger than my heart, and it was a wise choice.

The romantic in me says, 'Dave is going to be a very boring middle-aged man. Larry will always be a kid.' But only you know if that is true. And if you're not 100% sure, don't marry either of them. That's not to say you won't always long for the other in many ways. You wouldn't want to be so consumed. Unless you believe that 'forsaking all others' means keeping other men out of your mind and remembrance as well.

Naturally, I want what seems best for you, and I keep thinking Dave is 'best' for you because of his stability and seriousness and his seeming ability to be successful at whatever he does. These same qualities may seem boring or make Dave seem stodgy, but you have to be alone with him, I don't. I think I understand his reticence to be physical with you and I admire him for it, but I feared for awhile that perhaps he had a weak libido, and I'd hate to see you married to someone less passionate, less affectionate than you are.

I love Larry for his enthusiasm and openness and his wonderful sense of humor. And his strawberry blonde hair, his tallness and thinness, and his artistry. And I love him because so easily he calls me 'Mommy.'

I am, always have been, a terrible judge of character! You know I always bring home the homeless, give money to the charlatan, and open my heart to any who needs me. Who am I to give you advice?

I hate to see either of them hurt, and I hate to see you so grieved over the necessity (real or imagined) to choose. I understand your feelings that you must choose, but urge you to keep on being open with both young men. Perhaps your God will make it abundantly clear to you and to them what His will is for the three of you.

I understand Dave's reticence and Larry's impatience. This is a basic characteristic of each. You musn't allow your 'ripeness' for marriage and motherhood to get in the way of your choice. I think you've reached that dangerous place in the physical development of women like us where every cell is crying out for a mate, for motherhood, to suckle, to do all those things God in his wisdom gave us to do through the eons since creation; however, He didn't give you the gift of reason and intelligence and the opportunity to use them to see them wasted.

Your doctor sees that biological ripeness for child-bearing. The time *is*. Larry is ready to marry you, to carry you off on a white charger, to show you where the unicorns live, to give you a beautiful child, to be your Lochinvar. But is he ready for all that goes with it? And are you, really?

Dave too sees your ripeness and responds to it with his heart, soul and intellect. He knows he cannot do what his every cell tells him. He would marry you now, ask you to quit school now, bear his child, and would love you, love you, and be ready for all that goes with it – and would help you grow, but his time is *not*. He loves you so much that he realizes what is best for you both, and in so doing, also that he risks losing you because of your very readiness.

You must un-ready yourself. You're right, you have to put from your mind marriage as a goal unto itself, apply all your energy to your dorm duties and your studies, finish school, and pray for wisdom.

Maternity and marriage will come, but later. Stall off those cells which cry out. They'll still be there in 3–5 years, and so will all your wonderful qualities.

I realize that I have unwittingly pressured you. I long for your happiness, and I long for your baby. But, I'll still be here, darling. I promise.

I see myself as a participant in a fertility rite as old as the world, and I can't help myself. The circle must be completed. You are my eternity, womanchild of mine. And I am sorry for this. And this is the sorrow of every woman. And in this knowledge, I forgive my mother, my grandmother, my great-grandmother, my great-great-grandmother . . . it is all I can do.

Isobel to her daughter Catherine, 1980

Isobel, who is Australian, married in her mid-twenties and ran her own pharmacy business during the years when she was bringing up her two sons and one daughter, Catherine. After returning to university in her fifties to study for a degree in French, she spent a year in France qualifying as a teacher of English as a Foreign Language; since then, she has been teaching in Sydney.

Catherine grew up in Australia and worked in the film industry for five years, before moving to London. She has completed an MA course at an American university and plans to teach Creative Writing on her return to Australia.

She wrote to me about the background to her mother's letter:

'My mother claimed that she brought me up to be "selfish" and urged me to stay ignorant of domestic skills so that no man would expect me to be a traditional housewife-and-mother support system; she took it for granted that I would have a satisfying career of my own. She also sees that women's physical desire can be at least as powerful as a man's, and that because women's desire involves more than the body, we're very vulnerable.

'Her encouragement of my independence was all the stronger because she felt that she had been too ready to put her own needs below that of her husband. She had done this with my father, but refused to do it for Edward, her second husband. That marriage ended after only eighteen months, when she was in her early sixties. The basic problem was that it became clear that Edward had always depended on a mother, a wife or a secretary and was expecting Isobel to provide the same kind of total support. After the initial anguish of her divorce from my father, my mother had begun to enjoy her life and didn't want to give this up to "mother" Edward.'

When this letter was written, Catherine was working on her first novel. Isobel is responding to news of Catherine's first sales of short stories for publication, and to the news that she had begun her feminist education by reading *Damned Whores and God's Police: A History of Women in Australia*:

17 June 1980

Dearest Catherine,

It was lovely as always to get your last letter and to hear the good news about selling your stories; the sales side of it all, in itself, is interesting as well as being essential to keeping the whole affair viable (as Father would say) – there's something nice about getting a business proposition off the ground and has creative merit on its own; far from being a flash in the pan as you say, you will probably find you won't be able to cope with the business side and still go on with the novel. However, that kind of problem will be a pleasure to deal with . . .

This will surprise you. I too have been reading and thinking about our position as women and ask myself how it is that I was so successfully conned? It must have gone very deep with me since I'm only now really able to see what happens to women. I think I told you I was reading *The Three Marias* about the same time you were reading *Damned Whores and God's Police*, and it hit me as never before how cunningly the whole trap is set. You've been smart enough never to be snared because for most of us, once we have children they (the men) know we are side-tracked for a long time.

Modern girls have found and are finding ways around it and men have to go along with it if they want the comforts of sex and so on in a nice environment – but it doesn't work unless the man is very nice.

Bill of course is too conceited and pleased with himself ever to change or see what he's missing and he is selfish with everyone, not just with women.* I think the blatant way he used everyone showed that he thought himself a god who was above ordinary laws of decency, and there again, although you suffered you weren't caught and that's where your own good sound common sense and intelligence have been able to save you. If we were not very sexy or didn't need men in that way it would be simple, but nature has made it infinitely more difficult for women than men. I've reserved *Damned Whores* at the library where there is a long waiting list, so that's a good sign, don't you think?

No wonder I couldn't stand Edward for long once we were living together and this time, like you, I've never even considered that it might be my fault as I did with your father; all I ever think is how lucky I was to get out of it so easily. I love my life now and love being free and hope it goes on for a long time.

Sam and rising damp have moved out and he assures me there will never be any more trouble. It was much worse than I had guessed and I

---

*'Bill was a man I had been in love with for the past year. The relationship ended very violently because I wanted more independence, time for my writing, etc. It was that relationship as well as the books I was reading that made me a feminist.'

was lucky to strike such a clever little man to sort it out . . . Now that the damp problem is out of the way I can get the repainting done and that is about all in the big job line. I'm always finding little things to do and the house is looking nice and well cared for, which is nice. I really enjoy these odd jobs especially those that are tedious and if you *could* get a man in to do them he would grizzle all the time. I repainted the arbour at the back and after I had put the first coat on (which didn't take a long time) suddenly I remembered when your father did it I had to come out and say, 'Oh how quickly you did it and isn't it lovely.' No one said it to me but I did to myself and had all the satisfaction as well . . .

lots of love,
Mum

Sharon to her mother, 1978

Shortly before Christmas 1978, a short article about *Between Ourselves* appeared in *Ms London*, a magazine handed out to young women during Monday morning rush hour. As a result of reading the article, Sharon sent me the following letter which she had recently written. She gave no details about her life beyond what is in the letter.

September 1978

Dearest Mum,

I know you think I sleep around and drift from day to day but I don't. I've got a steady relationship, just because I'm not married doesn't mean I'm immoral or anything. I do want to get married but not just yet. I want you to know your daughter is going to have a happy marriage. Bob and I will get married if it works out. And if it doesn't, if we can't stand each other's guts then we'll just end it and thank God it wasn't marriage. It's acceptable today, living with somebody, because people have realized that before tying yourself physically and mentally to somebody for your whole life, you ought to be sure.

Perhaps you could come and spend a weekend with us and see for yourself? We could go to the theatre and out to dinner. It'll do you the world of good.

It's terrible having to explain like this to you because I know it must hurt so much. You did it for my sake sticking with dad all those years. Maybe you were right not to leave him, I don't know. But I'm telling you mum, no man is going to come home drunk – whether it's once a year or once a week – and treat me like dirt. And no man is going to beat me – I don't give a damn how many 'worries' he has. What did you get out of it? A bloody nothing. He left you and didn't even bother to ask about his own kids.

I hate putting salt into your wounds but they're mine as well. I appreciate it was harder in your days. You had no choice as a woman. You were practically dependent on a man.

I want to make up to you those years you suffered bringing me and Andrew up – when people still looked down on one-parent families.

Please write soon and tell me when you can come. Bob is looking forward to seeing you.

Sharon

Nan Hunt and her daughter Diana, 1975–78

Nan Hunt, a poet and playwright, was born in Wisconsin and raised in Indiana, the eldest of two children. She attended the University of Texas where she was active in the civil rights movement and became a feminist while earning her BA in English/Humanities. She later earned an MA from the University of Florida. She married at 21 and divorced her husband when their daughter Diana was 5. She married Jim six years later and their daughter Erica was born in 1960. When Erica was 12, Jim died of a cerebral haemorrhage and Nan became a single parent for the second time. She had become involved with a man twenty-two years younger than herself, shortly before Jim died; she and Ray are now married and live in Los Angeles.

Nan has had careers as a social worker, a director of a mental health association, and a college English instructor; she has also taught in the writing program at the Los Angeles Women's Building. She is now a Poet-in-the-Schools and teaches adult writing workshops. She is a co-author of *Dark and Bright Fires: Women's Collective Autobiographies* (in which she also performed when it was produced as a play at the Women's Building and at various California colleges and art centres). She is a contributor to *Ariadne's Thread: Women's Journal Writing.*

Diana is a manufacturer's representative in Tennessee. She described her view of the relationship with her mother in a letter to her:

> We both understand that even though we might have different talents and different methods of expressing ourselves, we are still basically alike. We both want very badly to push ourselves to the fullest, derive as much pleasure as we can from this life, and at the same time try to make our loved ones happy too. That's the only concern we should have about one another . . . as mother and adult daughter.

At the time when these letters were written, Diana was completing her BA in psychology at the University of Georgia and was in love with Harry, a man she had known for about a year. She and Nan wrote frequently during this period about many important aspects of their lives: Erica (who still lived with Nan); work; friends; plans for the future; and the ups and downs of their relationships with men.

After a telephone conversation in which Nan had voiced her concern over Diana's feelings of insecurity in her relationship with Harry, they exchanged letters:

27 October 1975

Diana dear,

. . . I want you to know that what I want for you is whatever will help you keep developing to your fullest potential. You should *want much* for yourself: much love, stimulating experience, knowledge, giving to others, and *much* outlet for your abilities. Don't settle for a little bit of any of these things. It was mainly when you wanted to settle for less, that I wanted to persuade you otherwise when you were growing up. Now, though I have no prerogative to do so, I'm still tempted at times to persuade you a certain way, but it is a friendly, loving and not demanding persuasion – just motherly inclination. I do more than tolerate, I *accept* your differences, and I love you very much.

Lots of Love and Kisses,
Mom

16 November 1975

Dear Mom,

Received your check and sweet note; thank you for the support – I often don't feel like I get much around here. I'm so determined to accomplish what I know I'm capable of . . . This check will get me over a big hump and prevent me from flunking out with an attack of nerves. I'm trying to work as much and anywhere I can until I get out of school. Then I will have full-time work, if I can find it.

I can understand your fears about my men associations, I would feel the same if the tables were turned.

I don't cook for either Harry or myself more than about 2 times a week – we eat out together anytime he is not out of town. When we eat in, he usually does the shopping and always pays for it. I do not think I'm being abused and especially compared to other girlfriends of mine.

I wonder how I would be if my life up to now had been different – but the fact is I've been intimately involved with only one man at a time. I've been very lonely at times when tradition says I would have no cause to be; it still hasn't stopped hurting to discard my romantic notion that somebody other than me will take care of me and keep me protected from all the sins of the world. It is very hard for me to balance my dependent and independent feelings. What I want from a man right now, Harry provides – emotional support, no criticism, good sex, a decent social partner, no tantrums or using me to beat out his frustrations about himself – and his physical presence. He makes no decisions for me; he gives me no money.

From a purely financial standpoint we both would be better off sharing rent. But there are problems to consider that could be harder to resolve than just making money. I'm hard-headed, opinionated, selfish about a lot of things and so is he. Sometimes it is a lot easier to be gracious to one another when we each are somewhat guests in each other's home than it is when we are both using the same place – anyway that's my rationale.

I love you.
Di

Six months later, Diana felt confident enough in her relationship with Harry to propose a solution to her dissatisfaction at not living with him. She wrote to Nan that he was willing to 'gypsy it' for a while and spend most of his time at her apartment, and that they had agreed to look for suitable apartments next door to each other.

Over the next year, Diana's relationship with Harry continued to improve in some respects, and Diana wrote to Nan about her mounting conflicts between feelings of dependence and desire for independence. Nan's reponse (below) initiated a lengthy dialogue:

10 July 1977

Diana darling,

I was worried about you when you were fearful of your relationship with Harry. I just hate for you to have any more stress. Life should have some happy times for you, so I'm glad to hear from your letter that Harry has been loving and attentive.

Yesterday I had a discussion with the man who rents Erica's room. He is an engineer near retirement age – divorced and recently broken up with a woman he was living with. He was adamant in his belief that it is the *man* who suffers the most by living alone. He says women should realize how indispensable they are. Single men are really isolated without a loving person in their lives – they end up failing emotionally or physically.

I was impressed to hear him say this because I have observed this also.

He pointed out that men are not very honest with each other, so they can't form deep relationships with each other, whereas women friends are more open. I *know* this is true . . .

Ray is in a similar position to yours: he wants me to make a long-term commitment. He is a wonderfully good friend and lover. He does much for me and I for him. The only thing that keeps me from him is my own restless need for variety of experience (not sexual experience) and time to spend on learning and writing, which requires aloneness. I don't want the responsibility of having to look after another person's life and yet I'm reluctant to 'wing it' all by myself – to do without love . . .

I love you so very much, my beautiful, capable daughter.

Mom

16 July 1977

Dearest Mama,

Got your letter today and felt so much support and loving things coming from you in it – thank you for being both my mother and a good, wise friend.

It is wonderful to have a mother – mothers always want a Utopia for their children and probably forget how much growth they themselves gained from stressful times. I hear the love and concern for me in your remarks about how you don't want me to have any more stress but only happy times, but I feel like I've never come out with a negative from the times I have endured stress – I gain insights about myself and other people and though it may be painful at the time, I don't know any better way for someone with a personality as hard-headed and opinionated as myself to really learn.

I agree with your male friend and your insights about why men probably suffer more than women when a relationship ends. My problem with it is: why don't men change or learn from that kind of insight instead of bemoaning it? Why can't men learn to be more open with each other and even if it is hard to find other men to be close with, why can't they keep trying? Surely the great feeling they could gain from even having a few close open relationships with other men (non-sexual) would be reward enough for the hard work involved. Maybe they really aren't in touch that it takes two people and each has as much responsibility as the other person to make it work. When it is good with a woman maybe they attach too much importance to the 'magic' the woman has instead of giving themselves credit too that it is so neat . . . And that it can happen again if they're willing to start fresh with another person/woman . . .

You said that Ray wanted you to make a long-term commitment but you didn't want to do that because of your need for a variety of experi-ence (not sexual) and time to spend on learning and writing which requires aloneness. Somehow all that does not sound too shallow to me, and if it is a reality for you, it conceivably could be a reality for Harry . . . I was interested in your statement about how you didn't want the responsibility of having to look after another person's life and yet were reluctant to 'wing it' all by yourself. Why do you feel a long-term commitment carries with it an agreement of responsibility to look after another person's life? If I could understand that sentiment from you, maybe I could understand Harry better – that sounds like a tape from him. I don't *want* anybody to look after my life – I can do that quite satisfactorily, thank you. And for someone else to use that as a reason for us not having a long-term commitment implies that I am somehow requiring it when it is really the other person's neurosis. My feeling is that the other person ought to try to deal with his own

problem so that it is not a stumbling block to our relationship getting
bigger and better . . .

Got to stop and create (yuk)! I love you so much too. And I've been
meaning to tell you how your letters have had an added dimension to
them since you've been going to the Jung Institute and even more so
when you started meeting with your support-system women friends.
Your choice of words to express yourself about potentially emotion-
laden topics that we might have a difference of opinion about has been
more factual and precise than in the past . . . I appreciate this unseen
side of you because it helps me keep from getting sidetracked from
what I want to communicate back to you – sidetracked into defending
my own emotions that might not be as developed or the same as yours.
For my own reasons of wanting to be close to you and communicate
honestly with you, this helps me so much. Thank you.

Di

20 July 1977

Dearest Diana,

I love getting such a newsy and discursive letter from you. Good
question, Why don't men change or learn from pain? The answer may
be because of their social conditioning to be rigid, thrusting, pushing,
insisting on their way – on hiding their pain even from themselves, as
opposed to feminine conditioning to be pliable, adaptable, to go at
goals more indirectly or patiently – to be able to express pain, even
despair and ask for comforting.

When this term is over, try to get a hold of the book *Amor & Psyche*
by Erich Neumann. The myth of Psyche is a searching study into the
feminine psyche – but also it seems to describe the process of what is
happening on a universal basis between men and women – as women
become conscious of their powers and struggle toward individuation,
it causes a painful separation between the sexes. But eventually the
imagination of many men will be fired by the struggles and changes
they see happening in women. They will begin to learn and change
into adults. Most men have been arrested in the 'little boy playing big
man' role all their lives. Women can't save men; they can only work
toward solving themselves while they continue to love men – but
insisting that the love be between two real individuals . . .

I do believe that that *old kind* of self-denying-immersion in passion
must be replaced by tender friendship and companionship between
men and women . . .

Back to your letter . . . It is true that Harry's reservations may be
very similar to my own. You know, consistency was never my big
virtue. I'm always seeing the other side of things. At least Ray and I are

living together and sharing expenses. My other defense is that there seems to be a much greater gulf between Ray and me: our ages, and our interests. We make some fine compromises but someday those compromises may grow too irksome.

Also, there are some days when I think I just want to be alone for a long period of time – but with the option of returning to love and companionship. If Harry is in that same state of mind as I am, he just isn't a likely candidate for a full-time permanent or near permanent relationship. I would like to selfishly breeze in and out – whereas Ray is steady, a home-bound nest-loving man. I think you are fairly nest-loving.

Perhaps Harry would like for you to be able to breeze in and out of your relationship happily and casually. But I'm not at all sure you could stand that kind of relationship or *should*.

Remember that I'm a *veteran* now – I've been through all the love and marriage, passion, lovers, babies, commitment, responsibility and more responsibility. I'd like to be loose. But Harry hasn't really had all that much responsibility to anyone but himself (or maybe he feels his mother is a big drag on his emotions), nor has he raised children, etc., so I don't quite understand why he should be so world-weary at his age . . .

Your friend at the office sounds delightful. I agree that you can just be spontaneous and not analyze everything. That analyzing behavior of yours came as a surprise to me after I hadn't seen you for a couple of years. You had been in the work world and most probably thought you needed to be cool and rational in order to survive. But I still have the image of that blonde, pig-tailed girl who jumped up at the sound of music to twirl and dance around the room. Or the enthusiastic five-year-old who dragged her playmate Marta over to hear the pretty music on Saturday mornings when I played ballet or symphony records. I remember you as absolutely guileless and full of intense enthusiasm . . . Don't kill off that passionate child at the core of you. I get teary-eyed writing this . . .

Thank you for telling me that my communication has added dimensions lately. I certainly feel that my life has wide and interesting dimensions. As for my choice of emotion-laden words, that was/is my tendency toward hyperbole absorbed from Mary P. I'm sure it has often made you feel like I was slapping all that heavy emotion on you – and you didn't see it as intensely as I seemed to. Remember, it was always my perspective and I wasn't insisting that it be yours.

And darling, I don't really expect your emotions to be the same as mine about a given person or situation . . .

When we talk eye-to-eye, you probably feel the need to *preserve* your integrity as an individual – your separateness, your equalness, your perception of the world – from the encroachment of my motherly concern, power or experience. There is so much between us, sad and good. I find you a fascinating person. So there is more than mother-daughter love. You-really do enrich my life and *teach me*.

Love and hugs,
Mom

Later, Diana comments that a few men give her hope but that 'men as a group are a mess,' and Nan replies:

. . . Passion in love is not enough – there must be equality of *respect* and comradeship. Men as a group *are* a mess, but our liberation is going to force them to look inward to find the missing feelings – that is if their imaginations are not too stunted already. Do you see why I would prefer a young man not yet warped and propagandized by the dumb world?

After nearly four years, Diana's and Harry's relationship broke down under the strain of their differences about commitment and Diana's growing sense that Harry did not want to deal with tension or dissatisfaction in his life, except by heavy drinking. She wrote about rejecting the traditional female pattern of putting up with men who 'take it' in the cruel, hard world and then expect to come home to the warm safety of home and 'let it all out'. She did not want a life of nagging Harry and then going to other women for comfort about 'what big babies men are', and she wrote bluntly to Nan: 'If he can't find other resources for dealing with his frustrations and finding solutions for his problems other than emotionally beating up on me, then I don't want him.'

While she was still living at home with Nan, Erica (Nan's younger daughter), aged 16, began a relationship with Bryan, a teacher at a nearby university, who was several years older than her. She has since put herself through university and is now completing an MA in psychology. She and Bryan are still together, living near Nan and seeing her frequently.

Diana had written to Nan about her concern for Erica's well-being and Nan responded:

6 January 1977

Diana dear,
. . . In your *so-thoughtful* letter about Erica, I think you sized up the situation quite accurately. Erica has not yet stayed over night at Bryan's apartment but went on a trip with him to Carmel and Tahoe to be with his brother and his girlfriend. I worried a good deal over whether to let her go – but mostly in fear of auto accidents or her own rash risk-taking on ski slopes. I felt that all I could do was check on Bryan. I had a Department of Motor Vehicles check on him, and he

has a clean driving record except for one traffic ticket. I asked for references from the University where he teaches and studies. I got phone numbers and addresses of places they would visit in Northern California, and she telephoned me at intervals.

Remember that Erica is the child whose first sentence was 'I do me my' (I'll do it myself) and whose nursery teacher noted her resistance to adult authority at age 4. At the same time she was always dressing up to 'be the Daddy' in play with other children. To say that I've had difficulty being a role image for her is an understatement!

With Jim [*her first husband, Erica's father*] dead, I've received the role of the *heavy*, the depriver, the one who thwarts her urges. At least with you, Jim and I were a fairly solid front and that was important I think, that you couldn't play us off against each other – although very frustrating to you.

I have managed fairly well to train Erica to take many responsibilities – for earning her spending money, for making her own clothes, for making and keeping appointments, for the consequences of her own actions. She has absorbed *some* of my value system about fairness, tolerance of others, kindness, honesty, etc.

I do not want to be the tyrant in her life *and* I *will not* let her make my life miserable with hatefulness. She did that for nearly three years after Jim died – everything from verbal abuse in front of other people to hitting and kicking me. I resisted all this and struggled to keep the margin of control, but my God it has taken a toll on me! However, I would resist her latest demand if I thought it would be a positive move. I talked this over with Bunny* before I got your letter . . . She felt it was inevitable that Erica would take her life into her own control very soon, and the best I can do is point out the problems she will face, express my considered opinions on the reasons not to leave home, but not try to force her to stay. However, I've already made it clear that if she goes to live with Bryan, I'm not continuing to pay her expenses – either she or Bryan will have to take those on . . .

I'll also let her know that if she changes her mind and wants to come back home, she can of course. I'll probably not be able to hold onto this house much longer, and she may have to be willing to live in small quarters with me and perhaps Ray. So, with love but not approval, I'm letting her go ahead and make her plans. I'm trying to make friends with Bryan and assess what kind of person he is. He seems to be unusually intelligent, sensitive, and very tender toward Erica. I can't help but feel happy for her to experience love and tenderness from a man – even if it becomes short-lived. I have felt her deprivation of manly love very keenly. If he continues to be decent and considerate

---

*Bunny Flarsheim, whose relationship with Nan is described in Chapter 3.

of her I'll be more than pleased. If *she* will seek positive experience, learning, and loving, intimate relationships, I'll feel like a successful Mother.

Erica is just *beginning* to learn that *she* is the cause of the results (in school, on the job, etc.) in her own life. I think it best for me *not* to be the catalyst for her rebellion – let her rebel against other things – then perhaps she won't have that deafness and blindness about what I'm trying to teach her, that rebellion causes.

So, since I talked to you on the phone, I've come to decisions about the attitude I'll take. I felt that I was *the enemy* to you for too long, and I refuse to take that role again. With me consenting but advising against – remaining a friend and well-wisher – Erica should begin to find out who the real enemies in life are and perhaps soon enough to make good decisions for herself . . .

Love, Mom

Vickie to her mother Lucy, 1978

Vickie grew up in a middle-class American family. She has a PhD in Sociology. She had just turned 30 when the following letter was written: her mother had stopped speaking to her six months earlier because she had discovered that Vickie was having a sexual relationship with a man who lived with her. For ten years Vickie had been renting out rooms in her house to friends, some of whom had been lovers with whom she had very close relationships. Though she had never felt inclined to get married, the relationships (which generally lasted about two years) were important to her and continued as strong friendships even after the men moved out of her house.

The silence between Vickie and her mother was broken when Vickie's younger sister, Adelle, came to visit and their mother phoned to find out what flight she would take home. It was an unpleasant phone conversation followed by an even more unpleasant letter from her mother which was an attack on Vickie's 'morals' because she refused to get married. When Vickie sent me the letter below, she included a covering note:

'My reply to her letter was incredibly nasty and vicious. I believe that the relationship between a mother and her daughter can be the most destructive of all conceivable relationships, even more so than between a husband and a wife in a bad marriage. I've certainly found that it was in my case and I believe it is not at all uncommon . . .'

July 1978

Mom –

If anyone seems bitter, it is you – so I write you nasty letters and sit around and dwell upon some remark you made till I've completely blown it up out of proportion and am so enraged I have to write a nasty letter to let it out. Was I nasty on the phone – NO! – for reasons of your own, you took a pretty simple statement and made it into something you could use to be upset about and vent your anger. I do get awfully upset by the occasions you seem to fabricate in order to express your dislike of me. After months of not speaking, it was even more upsetting. I guess I'm still vulnerable to your attacks. I try to tell myself that you're just a person who happens to be my mother, but that I should just consider you a person as any other I happen to know and that way it wouldn't be so upsetting. But no matter how hard I've tried, I can't achieve that kind of emotional distance. But I certainly will continue to try – there is no way I'd want to be emotionally vulnerable to you – I don't trust you not to hurt me and put me down.

And please stop the pretence of being the victim – I never said I blame you for anything, not that I think you didn't make mistakes but I really think you and Dad suffered more than any of us did. I don't have particularly fond memories of family life but I have some good ones and I wasn't unhappy. If I really thought it was just you and Dad who had such problems, I wouldn't be so opposed to marriage and family life but it's obvious that it's nearly the norm. So why would I want to risk it in my own life? I'm not unhappy in my existence now. It is you who condemn my life, not me. I think it is a better alternative to marrying anyone I've yet known and I feel certain I'm better off than had I married anyone. So what would I be blaming you for? I like myself and have no real bitterness towards anyone. I do dislike things in you, just as you dislike things in me.

And the thing I especially dislike is using me to work out your internal hysteria and drama. If you cannot be friendly towards me – I much prefer the strategy of ignoring me and avoiding contact. You probably don't realize that your letter was uncalled for; I'm sure you feel righteous in writing it – well, I think it's *sick* . . .

I really don't even see the connection between my remark on the phone and your bizarre letter, calling me cheap and unappreciative of anything you've ever done for me. I think I'll just throw your letters away before reading them – actually I couldn't read this one, I threw it away after a few paragraphs but I took it out of the garbage today to read it. It takes about 24 hours to be able to deal with the nastiness – it's too much of a shock to my system when I get such a gust of it in the mail. Thank heavens – I'd hate to be so used to it again. What happens if you suppress your nastiness – does it make you tired and listless? I guess you're still not a happy person – I hope moving to a new town helps – it might I think. You need a more exciting place to live.

In the meantime, try not to vent your discontent on me – I don't think you should make one of your kids take the brunt of your unhappiness anymore. I refuse to have to put up with this sort of thing any longer. Drive me away if you wish, but believe me it's working.

Vickie's mother replied by returning this letter to her, with the following comments in red ink next to Vickie's signature: 'Never "love Vickie". (How can I love someone who so obviously doesn't love me?)'

Don't Tell Your Mother

Why does the incest victim find so little attention or compassion in the literature?. . . So many authorities assert either that incest did not happen, did not harm her, or that she was to blame for it.

Judith Herman and Lisa Hirschman (1977)

Young people are supposed to do what they are told by people in authority; children are not allowed to say no to their fathers. Yet, in cases of incest, daughters are often blamed for being sexually abused by their fathers. The question is asked, 'Why didn't she stop him?', as if it was a contest between equals.

People do not blame a child for being battered or suggest that the child 'asked for it'; the criticism falls on the parent, because no child behaves so badly as to deserve brutality and lifelong emotional scars. But many women who survive incest have grown up accepting blame for the way they have been abused. In the beginning of an incestuous relationship, a daughter may love (and/or fear) her father and want to please him. Later, realising that there is something wrong in what has happened, she must cope with feelings of betrayal (because he knew all along it was wrong) and her own terrible guilt (because sexual violations are often not seen as being the fault of the man involved – we hear how the woman 'asked for it'). In other cases, the daughter may think from the beginning that there is something wrong with her father's sexual advances, but feel unable to stop it because she is too frightened, guilty or confused.

Self-blame is the reason daughters often give for remaining silent about incest despite the fear and pain they suffer; they feel too 'wrong' to deserve comfort or help. And they especially feel the loss of their mother's approval (even if she does not know). Many daughters also see their mothers as being too weak to stand up against the father. In a family where the father is sexually exploiting the daughter, the mother's weak position in the family is a major obstacle to the daughter asking for the protection she needs. It is not the mother's fault that the father is behaving irresponsibly and harmfully, but the daughter, who is relatively powerless, needs someone to stand up for her. *Only when girls can see themselves and other women as strong, can they view their mothers as powerful allies who could help them.* In a family where the father is not seen as being all-powerful with some magical key to right and wrong ('Don't ask questions, just do XYZ because I say so!'), a daughter who was sexually molested by her father would be much more able to speak out about what was happening to her. She could challenge his authority and feel unashamedly deserving of her mother's help and protection.

Terry Wolverton to her mother, 1980

Terry Wolverton grew up in Detroit, the only child of a working-class family. Her parents were divorced when she was a year old; her mother, then 24, went to work as a secretary. A few years later she married a man who had worked in an automobile factory until he joined the Air Force during World War II, and since then had worked in a gas station. Both of them worked while Terry was growing up. They wanted a more comfortable life and aimed for middle-class status; their dream was to raise Terry's social standing through education. Her mother told her: 'I would scrub floors to help you get to college.'

The following letter is taken from the script of a performance entitled 'In Silence Secrets Turn to Lies/Secrets Shared Become Sacred Truth'. Terry wrote and performed this piece for an exhibition called 'Bedtime Stories: Women Speak Out About Incest' which took place at the Women's Building in Los Angeles in October 1979. She has subsequently performed it on local television. 'Bedtime Stories' is an exhibition of artwork, writing, performance and videotapes by women who, as children, experienced sexual abuse by members of their families. The exhibition was a part of the year-long Incest Awareness Project.* This project brought together artists, feminist activists, social service organisations and members of the community, to raise public consciousness about the problems of incest from a feminist perspective.

Terry, who is now an artist living in Los Angeles writes:

'The sexual abuse of children in the family is shockingly widespread; it is estimated that over twenty-five million women in the United States have experienced incest. Yet, its occurrence is shrouded in secrecy, a conspiracy of silence (in the name of family privacy) which isolates the victim and protects the perpetrator. Popular culture and psychoanalysis have fed us myths about the seductive teenage daughter (Lolita), the cold and sexually frigid mother, blaming always women for their own victimization. These myths keep women from bonding together in self-defense, keep us blaming one another and ourselves. Only by speaking out about our own experiences can we challenge these myths; as feminists we can apply our own analyses about the causes and effects of incest, we can make our voices heard. This belief is the basis of the Incest Awareness Project: that by speaking out we transform ourselves from "incest victims" into "incest survivors".

'Through the support of other women in the project, I determined to speak to my mother about my experiences of being molested by my stepfather from the ages of 5–11. In doing so, I was breaking twenty years of silence that had echoed across our relationship.

---

*Co-sponsored by 'Ariadne: A Social Art Network' and the Gay and Lesbian Community Services Center in Los Angeles.

'My mother and I have always had a close relationship; in fact, she had shared with me many of the abuses she had suffered in her relationship with my stepfather. However, I never felt safe to tell her about my incest experiences while she was married to him. I feared the consequences: that I might have to confront him with my accusations, that I would be the cause of breaking up their marriage and be blamed for it, or that my mother would fall apart emotionally and I would have to take care of her. I have learned, in working on the project, that many children take on the burden of total responsibility in an incest environment.

'In August of 1979, I went to visit my mother (by then divorced from my stepfather), and after two days of blushing, stammering, and choking on the information, I was able to tell her my experience. Her initial reaction is described in the letter which follows.

'This experience was the catalyst for creating my performance, which deals with my twenty years of silence about incest, and the effect of that silence on my self-image and my life. I begin by speaking about my role in the family, how "being a good girl" was equated with silence, not upsetting anybody. I reveal all the things I kept silent about: sexual abuse, physical and emotional violence, alcoholism. I then talk about how I internalized that silence, by editing all those parts of my personality and experience that were unacceptable or too upsetting, and how this became a form of lying, to others and to myself. After tearing away the veil of lies that has masked my experience, I call upon the nine women who have been influential and supportive of me in speaking out, my lesbian feminist community which has helped to restore me to myself. I conclude the performance by reading this letter to my mother:

[1980]

Dear Mother,
On the eve of my twenty-fifth birthday, I decide to stop being a liar. I confront you with the truth that I was sexually molested by your husband when I was a child.
'Did he have . . . *intercourse* with you?' you ask.
'No,' I answer, and you are relieved.
I notice that you are not surprised by this truth, but rather, surprised that I have spoken it.
I have broken a taboo   the words are spoken   irretrievably
I cannot take them back, and I can never again pretend to be your good girl.
Nothing will be the same for us now, though we may pretend it is. I don't want to pretend it is.
'Why didn't you tell me before?' you demand suspiciously.
I am guilty. I have been a liar/why am I now telling the truth?
'Why do you tell me now? Just when things are going well for me. Are you trying to punish me?' And you look so dangerous, Mama, in your

guilt and grief, that I almost wish I could restore the calm between us,
silence this secret I have spoken.
'No,' I reply. 'I do it for myself. To value my own truth. It is for my
own life that I tell you.'

I have to remind myself that it is not I
Who brings this pain into our lives.
I have to remind myself that ending this silence
is a gift that I give to my life.
and to other women's lives, and that ultimately
this is the most sacred gift that I can ever give you,
Mama,
my own truth.
With love, your daughter, Terry

Ella to her mother, 1980

Ella is the eldest of four children of a middle-class family from the North of
England. When she was 13 her father started having a sexual relationship
with her; it continued until she felt powerful enough to say 'No', when she
was 17. The relationship did not include sexual intercourse and it was a long
time before Ella called it 'incest'. She did not tell anyone about this relationship until nearly ten years later when she decided to speak out about it in a
feminist women's group.

She explains how she now sees the experience and the difficulties she faced
in breaking the silence:

'It was in the context of a loving, trusting relationship. My father was somebody who represented right and wrong to me, which is why it was so difficult
to understand what was happening to me at that age.

'One grows up with the idea that male sexuality, male passion, is somehow
a woman's fault, something you're responsible for. As a little girl, I can
remember being taught not to sit in a certain way, not to stand in certain ways
– and it's very complicated to learn all those things, because you're supposed
to be sexy and attractive to men; at the same time, you're not supposed to
lead them on, you're supposed to know what the balance is. Of course, I now
realise that men must take responsibility for their own sexual feelings . . .

'I felt very miserable about relationships within my family. I was terribly
worried about my mother, and very guilty. I didn't know whether she knew
or not. One of the things I resent most is how it damaged my relationship with
my mother. It put such a barrier between us. It was all kept a secret and I felt
very paranoid in my relationship with her.

'I thought, and still do think in many ways, that my parents had a very
good marriage. They were close and I thought that they had the perfect relationship and that I was the one responsible for spoiling the relationship, for
breaking up the family. It never came to that, but I always thought that if

anybody found out, there would be a terrible split in what I saw as a very secure family. And I'd be responsible for that.

'It is good that the women's movement has begun to look at incest and that support groups are starting up. I am worried, however, that by calling it rape they will lose a lot of women and girls who won't see what is happening to them as 'rape'. I also disagree with the substitution of the words 'sexual abuse of girls' instead of incest (because it says nothing about the family!). I feel it is too soon to make another taboo out of the word incest, before we've had time to explain what we mean by it.'

Ella wrote the following poem when she was 30, shortly after she first spoke out about her incest experience in her women's group:

INCEST

Mummy
What happened to your anger?
Did you hold it all in
And squeeze out stale tears
At night?

Was your guilt that of being a woman
Large and fertile
Whose massive menstrual flow
Clotted on number two towels
Burned with newspaper and shame
At the bottom of the garden
Or smouldered in secret in the kitchen boiler?

Your body swollen again with childbirth
You struggled tired from the shops
While we clung to the pram and your love
Demanding attention

Your delicate hands held his head in your lap
And comforted even the oppressor
As you built with him a kingdom
Where his ego reigned supreme.
It was him we worshipped
Not you, his modest mistress
Tired and worthy
Whose hands went out to us when we fell.

You did not warn me of the ways of men
So that when he came to me
I felt it was the greatest privilege

I did not see his lust
Only this mythical giant choosing me to caress
What an honour.
And I felt very special
(Young and lovely)
Compared to you.

Though I feared you
I thought it was alright
To submit to your hero
Since his love was real –
He was so tender and so magical.
You recommended him.

Later I realised my crime, appalled.
The giant shrank
As I recoiled from him in horror
Disgusted in my body and our shame.
I inherited thus your life long guilt
And worse –
Much worse
For years I feared to love you.
For him I kept a scared pity
From you, in pain I turned away.
And only now with new awareness
Can I know you are my sister and my friend
In joy that you're alive
I hope my love now manifests.

Bringing the Truth Home

Even in very difficult families, people often draw great strength and comfort from each other; bonds of nurturance can be formed which prove unbreakable over a lifetime. This is what people often long for in times of change or great distress. 'Home is where, when you have to go there, they have to take you in', I remember my father saying – a definition that always made more sense to me than the proverbial 'blood is thicker than water'.

But honesty about the most complicated or hurtful aspects of life is not easy within many families: sexuality, divorce, rape or abortion would be spoken about in hushed tones, if at all. It is hard to predict the reaction which close family members will have to hurtful events or major changes in one's life. The following letters show both the difficulty that mothers and daughters have in sharing some of their most critical life experiences and the sense of relief and greater understanding which such revelations can precipitate.

Linda and her daughter Jenny, 1982

Linda was born and raised in a small midwestern American town, the second of six children of a strict Presbyterian working-class family. Her parents were divorced when she was 16 and her mother then worked full-time to support the family. Linda was married at 19 to Mike, a bus driver. They had five children by the time they were 30. Although they both believed in the importance of a strong family life and shared similar moral values, they often disagreed on how to raise the children. Linda was gentle and fairly permissive; Mike, who had been severely beaten as a child himself, became increasingly violent towards their sons and extremely protective and possessive of both Linda and their daughters. After twenty-five years of marriage they obtained a divorce on the grounds of incompatibility.

Jenny, the eldest daughter, left home at 18 and worked her way through college. She was active in the anti-Vietnam War movement and, through her involvement in that protest as well as the reading she did in her first year at college, became a committed feminist and socialist.

The following letter was written eight years after Linda's divorce from Jenny's father:

July 1982

Dear Jenny,

. . . I would have liked to have told you about this in person, but I don't want to wait with it. For about a year now I've been really looking at myself and realizing the changes that have occurred in my personality and total outlook. Our letters to each other have helped me so much to open up even more . . . and Mary and Pamela [*her two youngest daughters*] have also pushed me. They've asked many times since the divorce, 'How will you and Daddy feel when one or the other of you dies?' Wow, how do we know? Anyway, upon examining this, especially the last year, I realize that Mike's and my marriage being dissolved was not all his fault. Not that I ever felt that exactly but I always felt like the 'injured party'. Now I can see, through some of my experiences and looking back on our marriage, that I was not always easy to live with and deal with. I was too agreeable and too dependent and that is absolutely annoying to anyone – but particularly to someone with Mike's personality. He was totally in love with me and I with him, and he really put much into the marriage that I took for granted. I allowed him to do all the thinking, planning, etc. It's not easy to have to make all the decisions, in fact, it's downright irritating.

So one Saturday morning about three weeks ago I called him to tell him that I realized this, that it wasn't his fault and I wanted him to know before anything happened to either of us. He was really appreciative and thanked me profusely. Then he called me back on Sunday and said some very meaningful things. I have felt relief since then and no longer have any animosity toward that situation.

There are two reasons why I'm telling you this. One is that you may feel like it's easier for you to talk to Mike or me about things without holding back anything that you may have felt in the past would be hurtful or annoying to us. Maybe it has cleared the air a little. The other reason is that this was mentioned in a Christian seminar I attended last year; the man leading the seminar said that when this is done you have such a feeling of relief – as I have. I didn't do it with that in mind and only realized what he had said after I ceased to have this feeling of animosity. He also suggested that we pray for God to open the heart of the recipient to accept our acknowledgement. I did that and Mike was very receptive which made it much easier. His response was also gratefully accepted.

I also hope that this is accepted by each of our five children. I want you to realize that it was done for Mike and for me but also for each of you to know that we don't hate one another, but each take our share of the responsibility for the divorce.

I love you very much and am very anxious to see you and meet Jim [*Jenny's lover*] whenever that time arrives. I feel so blessed that you are so happy now and only want that to remain in your life from now on. I hope you know that when each of you (my children) are happy, that's when I am most content.

My love to Jim and to your household too,
Mom

Jenny writes:

'My mother and I spoke on the telephone soon after I received her letter and I told her how moved I was by her generous gesture of reconciliation and what a difference it would make in all of our lives that she does not see herself as a victim anymore. Besides effecting a great healing, it was a strong statement that she does not see herself as powerless and passive, but as someone who can take action based on what she believes. I told her she was one of my models of courage and integrity – and a heartening example to us all that long-term relationships of caring and commitment are still possible in this world of easy divorce. I think she might have been a bit surprised by that: she knows I don't believe in marriage and I know she worries about it – especially since I had recently written to her that Jim and I have decided that we want to have children together.* She asked what I felt about our long-term commitment.'

---

*See Chapter 5.

July 1982

Dear Mom,

. . . You asked about commitment. Yes, we do have a strong commitment to each other and we would make doubly sure we know how we both felt about that before having a child. We won't get married because neither of us believes that it is a good social institution. But as you know, 50% of marriages end in divorce so I don't think that you or I or anyone else could rationally believe that marriage is any sort of guarantee of security. I wish there was some alternative way to make a public, social declaration and celebration of our love and commitment. But there isn't. I think (as I mentioned at Christmas) that the laws regulating the institution of marriage are evil, unjust, and keep women down. I want no part of it, even if I'm one of the fortunate women who could be an exception. It is part of my commitment to all women to refuse the social privileges which marriage bestows (e.g. it's easier to get credit and mortgages, people believe you're a real person not just a weirdo, etc.). But as long as women are safer and more legitimate being married, then it will be unsafe for women to leave their bad marriages. I suppose it may bring me some discomforts in my life – but feeling insecure in my relationship with Jim *isn't* one of them.

We both seem to feel very secure, to trust and admire one another, and we have discovered that we are good at enduring and triumphing over conflict and differences. We have an extremely joyful sexual relationship which, in addition to the pleasure it gives, also seems to create a very primitive, almost infantile bond. That level of trust permeates many aspects of our togetherness. I know that it is only because the rest of the relationship is so loving and trusting that the sexual relationship can be so blissful. The safety of feeling bonded on many levels means that it feels OK to take risks, to say our true feelings, even when they may cause hurt or difficulties. *That* is what gives me my feeling of security with Jim – and him with me. That in addition to knowing we love and respect each other, it is safe to say anything, so that feelings don't get buried and out of control. Our commitment is to continue to cherish each other and to protect the relationship from lies or buried feelings which might threaten it.

I think we both realize that there are very few people in the world who are willing or *able* to live out this particular kind of commitment. I especially know that most men are still uncomfortable with emotional honesty (though I see that beginning to change). But Jim is very good at it . . .

It is lovely to talk about these things with you – I look forward to hearing your response to it all. Everyone here sends their love.

with much love and hugs and kisses,
Jenny

Sarah Grace to her children, 1980

Sarah Grace left her husband and family after their children were grown, to live and work elsewhere more happily. Before this letter was written, she had told all her children that she was a lesbian and their reactions had ranged from loving and complete acceptance to revulsion.

Sarah explains:

'All of my children were in great conflict over the clash of values that came to the surface when I left home: my ex-husband, Alan, was telling them that I was selfish, and uncommitted to anything, and that the pain all of them were feeling was due to my selfish wish to "find myself". He told them that the result of searching for who you are and following a dream is to cause great pain to people who love you and care for you, and that it is thoughtless and inhuman. He said that the only real joy in life comes with continued commitment to something "solid" – meaning socially acceptable. The letter was my answer.'

27 December 1980

Dearest Karen, Larry, Jay, Sandy and Andy,

I am writing all of you a joint letter, and mailing copies to each, because I have something important to say to all of you.

I know that my leaving has set loose a lot of dynamics that all of us have to deal with (and I am including myself), but there is one that I am particularly concerned with. It has to deal with the 'selfish' aspect of all this, the motivation that led me to leave this family unit and go off in pursuit of things that have been needing to be done within me for a lot of years.

I think it important for me to tell you that I have never changed my basic philosophy that I taught all of you . . . I believe that it is important to follow a star and to do with your life what will make you at peace and fulfilled . . . You are all doing that in your lives, each in your own way . . .

I believe in commitment. And I am still committed. I am committed to all of you children, to mother and to love and to cherish our relationship. I am committed to live out my philosophy that one has to find peace within oneself or life is meaningless. I am committed to trying to help all of you understand that what I am doing is the outgrowth of needs to create and fulfil what has been put inside me as a person. Lesbianism is part of that, but surely all of you must be aware that it is only one small part of the overall who-I-am.

I know that Alan believes, and is imparting to all of you, that the belief in following your star is unrealistic, foolish, and leads to destruction. I need all of you to know that I do not believe that. I believe that it is ultimately the only way to find peace and to exist as a full human being. And I do understand, and hold no anger, over the fact that that is how he sees reality. It is not how I see reality.

So that leaves all of you with what ultimately is left to each of us alone anyway: you need to make your own decisions on what is the reality for you. Maybe, even after reading this letter, you will believe, as Alan does, that commitment to work and to family must come before everything and that that is the only path to joy and fulfilment. Maybe you won't. Either way, it really doesn't matter. What you decide is best for you, is best for you . . .

I love all of you, passionately and deeply, and I hope this letter will help all of you put things, for yourself, into perspective.

Love,
Mom

Sarah's daughters did not respond in writing, but her eldest son, Larry, wrote back immediately. She offered me his reply as an example of the positive response that men are having to women's liberation – which has, sadly, been hidden from history in the same way that many other encouraging aspects of the liberation struggle have been hidden:

> Madre,
> Mom, Mother, Sally, Hey you! . . . Really enjoyed your letter and I'm glad to hear you are doing well . . .
> You asked me what I thought of the last piece you've written.* Well, that's kinda hard for me to answer. First of all, it shows a freedom within yourself from old chains. That, of course, is good. It shows that you have passed this freedom on to Sandy. Also admirable. The thing is, I guess I felt intimidated a little by it. I think that is because you are so strongly defining your womanhood that it infringes on my sense of malehood. More power to you! I really believe that what you are doing in the article is good. Because it made me feel a little uncomfortable, it made me examine the things inside of me that caused the feeling. Often growth only comes through self-examination and a little bit of pain. When wimmin† such as you set forth these ideas, they are certainly the essence of social change. The society we live in, and especially the one down here in the south, is strongly male-oriented. People such as you who set forth these ideas that challenge men too – that hit us guys in the face when we read them – can only do us all good. More power to all humans who can see the need for social equality. More power to you.
> You know, I know a lot of folks there in Springfield are kinda freaked by the direction you have taken. They were brought up according to the rules of society, spend their lives trying to live out the ways that they were taught. The trouble is, a lot of people have been mass hypnotized or brainwashed by TV, schools, church or temple, and other social organizations. All men are created equal said the slave masters. Any way you can help liberate people of their chains, they should welcome . . .

---

*This was an article on teaching her daughter, Sandy, to take pride in her womanhood when she begins menstruation.
†This is the spelling of 'women' that Sarah uses in her writing.

Julie and her mother Elizabeth, 1980

Julie left home when she was 17 because she wanted to break away from the conservative Middle America community where she had been raised. At 19 she was living in Norway, studying and working as an *au pair*. While she was on a weekend trip to the countryside, a 40-year-old man broke into her hotel room at 3.00 a.m.; he brutally raped and beat her, smothered her with pillows and tried to strangle her. She struggled against him for nearly two hours, crying out and hoping that any minute someone in the hotel would hear her and come to save her. No one heard and Julie finally was released by the rapist.

There was a trial and the rapist was allowed to go free; he was acquitted on the grounds that there was only circumstantial evidence – Julie's word against his. Her lawyer, an extremely kind and sensitive man who had supported her in pressing charges, had warned her that they would probably not win the case but that the trial would set a beneficial precedent that would help other women who are raped.

Five years later, Julie said:

'The first thing I wanted to do when I was released by the rapist was to kill myself – I did not want to go on living with this horrifying experience. The police questioning was another nightmare; I was being tortured all over again. I had fought with all my strength during the rape and now I fought again. I said I would not go through with it, that I did not have to suffer any more. In order to sustain what strength I had left I had to make the decision not to endure the brutality of the police procedures – which they constantly reminded me were for my own good. There was no consideration for me as a woman; their procedures were determinedly humiliating and dehumanizing. I had to stand up for myself and refuse their form of 'protection'. My lawyer understood this and aligned himself with me. He shielded me from any further interrogation and made sure that I was out of the country when the trial took place.

'I didn't tell my mother because I couldn't bear to think how much it would hurt her to know that one of her children had suffered something so horrible. My father died when I was seven and I had seen my mother suffer so much raising five kids on her own. She had not had any support in her own painful life; she had never protected herself in any way or sought comfort for her own pain; she just bore it, heroically. I wanted to protect her from any more suffering. Looking back on it, I probably could have told her and she would have been strong. I desperately wanted to tell her and have her comfort me. But I had always taken responsibility for her suffering; I had never made any distinction between her pain and my own and it seemed very dangerous to ask her to take care of me. My fear was that she would be so distressed by this terrifying news that I would have to be strong and comfort her. And I just couldn't bear any more suffering, especially not my mother's.

'I was also terrified that my mother would identify with my pain rather than with my strength. I needed to have my strength affirmed and to feel the strength of other women.

'My mother had always supported my independence; it was something we were both struggling for. I couldn't allow anything to threaten that; I couldn't allow either of us to give up the fight. As long as she didn't know about the rape, she would continue to relate to me as a strong woman. The strength I had to survive came from her. Yet, ironically, I was not allowing myself to ask from her the care and protection that I had always felt she deserved during the painful times of her life.

'I now realize why I needed to achieve separation from my mother's pain. In denying myself her protection, I ended up supporting one of the very principles I wanted to oppose: I was seeing my mother as one of life's 'victims', rather than acknowledging her resilience and strength.

'My mother was not the only one it was difficult to tell. Because of the way rape is viewed socially, I was afraid of being treated like a victim by anyone who might find out. At that time I didn't have the strength to deal with other people's ignorance or pity. Another problem with telling anyone about being raped is that our society blames the woman who is raped for what happened to her. We've all grown up with the sickening cliche, 'if you had stayed at home, this never would have happened.' Of course I know that women in my home town (and everyone's home town) are raped as often as anywhere else. But until people stop hating and fearing women's sexuality, and stop blaming women for men's violence, I think it will remain very hard for women to speak out truthfully about the pain and horror of being raped. We need to feel secure that we will receive compassion rather than blame.

'I chose to tell my sisters about the rape. I felt that they could be strong for me because they wouldn't identify with my pain or feel responsible for it in the way my mother might have done. Two years later, when my mother wrote to say that my sister, Kathy, had told her that I had been attacked, I was both furious and sad. There was a desperate fear of lifting the shield of protection; however, her letter was the beginning of my realizing that I deserved to allow her *to be my mother*.

'The letter was also the beginning of my healing, because I realized that I had the right to tell people about what I had been through: I didn't have to protect everyone else from knowing the horror of rape. It has taken me a long time to recover from my constant fear. An important part of the process has been my commitment to rejecting the social concept that women are weak. It was the refusal to see myself or any woman as a victim that enabled me to overcome my fear that I would never again be as strong and unafraid as I had been before I was raped. I have only just begun to know any real liberation from this pain.

'When my mother wrote this letter she had no idea of the severity of the attack, nor any knowledge of the legal procedures I had been through. In many ways our letters served to perpetuate my pattern of protecting her at any cost':

8 September 1980

My dearest Julie,

. . . Last night I asked Kathy if something terrible had happened to you in Norway because when you were home one summer I overheard you telling Debbie about something bad that had happened. I felt that you would tell me sometime when you wanted to, but you never have and I felt I wanted to know because I love you very much and I don't want you to feel that you can't tell me anything. I want to give you all the love and support I can, especially when you really need it. Please feel you can tell me anything, honey. I'm not going to condemn you. We all need to support each other in our family and that's what I want to do. I know it must have been a terrible experience and I'm only thankful that you were able to get away and had friends there to go to . . . I'm sure it must have been a terrible experience. Were you able to see a doctor or therapist and have some help from anyone like that? Who was the biggest help to you?

Oh, Julie, I feel so bad that I couldn't have comforted you or been there to love you and be with you . . . I really worry about you being alone some places . . .

[Later that night]

We just finished talking on the phone. It is so good to hear your voice. I would have sent this before, but I was worried about how you would react to it . . .

All my love always,
Mom

24 October 1980

My dearest Mother,

My absence of written communiqué is no sign of how often I am thinking of you. Daily my thoughts are with you. My studies and work at the gallery are extremely demanding of my time. At the moment, the only time I have for myself is when I am driving in my car and often even that is robbed from me if I have a passenger . . . This is when, if I haven't had a chance earlier, I speak to you – can you hear me momma, can you feel my love, my support, can you feel my struggle and my calling for you . . . my dear sweet momma . . . I want to come home for a while to be with you – I need you now more than ever.

Mom, about your last letter that you wrote me, about Kate's wedding and your experience with Kathy and your concern for me – I wept for days, we shouldn't have been apart at this moment in our lives. I wrote and wrote for pages and hours to you, to Kathy, of my pain, of my anger, of my intense sadness, of my confusion. I feel paralyzed at the moment as I write now, as I cannot find my freedom through words on paper, as I cannot engage in conversation with you through this means, I can only be alone in my expression yet again. I need to be with you, I need to weep and weep and feel your protective embrace around me, your committed love – I am shaking and crying at the moment as I desperately need to be with you – to share our lives together, to trust each other – to expose ourselves to each other so that we might once and for always liberate these painful burdens we carry with us through our lives – which if not dealt with can dangerously stunt our growth – I feel angry with Kathy that she was not sensitive to my need to be the one to tell you – but my dear mother, know that you were always with me – that you were my strength, my symbol of life – and that is what I needed most if I was to continue my life – you gave me life – and continue to do so – I will be with you soon and we will talk – don't be afraid – I need you to be strong – when we are together we can be weak in each other's arms – until then be strong.

> Never leave me momma,
> I love you deeply,
> Julie

Jan and her mother Dorothy, 1974

Jan and Dorothy wish to remain anonymous. Jan was 18 when the following letters were exchanged.

October 1974

Dear Mom,

Health-wise I'm OK but I've been through some unfortunate experiences as of late. Day before I left for my New York visit I went to the doctor for a check-up. He examined me and told me I was 6 weeks pregnant. I was shocked. He offered to give me an abortion that day but I knew I had to prepare myself emotionally and I also wanted to continue with my New York trip.

My first thoughts were that I could never have an abortion, but the more I thought it over and the more Al and I discussed it I realized it was the only thing I could do.

The day of the abortion Al and I went to the clinic at 10 a.m. I saw a counselor; we discussed my feelings and she felt my decision was carefully thought over and one I believed in. She also explained the actual procedure: dilation, suction and then a scraping of the womb.

I can only feel fortunate that I live in a time when abortion is legal and I did not have to suffer through an unwanted pregnancy or find means of an illegal, unsafe abortion. The other women there – one 35, one 50, one 15; all making an important decision about their lives.

I was pretty calm about it. The counselor was there with me as well as a doctor and a nurse. I was given a local anesthetic but I swear I never knew such physical pain existed. I thought I would die or leap off the table (they said my cramping was much worse than usual). But when it was over so was the pain.

Immediately after, they led me into a small room where Al was allowed to come sit with me. It was then I cried and I haven't cried since. The feeling was mostly of relief – the pain was gone but most of all the pregnancy.

I knew from the start that I would tell you, but I waited till now to give you the reassurance that I'm alright. I'm too close to you not to tell you. I guess I still fear that I'm the little girl that will be punished. I just want to be understood. I know you will feel sad but don't feel disappointed. Just understand.

The night after the abortion I had a dream. I dreamt that I was walking down a street in New York. A young boy, 16 or so, offered me a ride. We drove and drove all the way to Mississippi and gradually he became younger until he was about 8 years old. He lived in a big house by a lake. Then Al was in the dream – we were telling the boy we wanted to make love with him to show him how much we loved him. Then his mother came home and we left. To me, that symbolized our love for the child even though we had to leave it behind and realizing that it had found another place.

Please write me of your feelings. I'm glad that I felt I could write you of this. I will see you and talk to you soon.

Much Love,
Jan

November 1974

Dearest Daughter,

Your adolescent years have provided us with the usual tense moments that all parents must associate with 'growing-up'. Your wailing despair with hair and figure. Your ups and downs with 'first-lover' and the gradual moving away from the once close companionship that you shared with your father.

As you know the 'new sexuality' was not hard for me to accept. I think I was relieved to know that we were now living in an era that allowed a young woman to explore her sexual curiosity without the shame of feeling *ruined* or the necessity of having to 'marry the boy'. You are not a promiscuous girl and when you did lose your virginity we discussed it thoroughly along with the responsibilities it entailed.

I think my only real days of despair came when you entered into this 'live-in' relationship with Al. It was neither the 'live-in' that bothered me nor the fact that he is almost twice your age but the knowledge that he is a deeply *disturbed* person. I was afraid for you.

During the week-end that dad and I spent with the two of you, we were so shaken by his violent mood-swings. On our long drive home the silence was broken only by my tears and dad's laments of disbelief.

Now I have before me the letter telling of your recent abortion. It's difficult to explain how very saddened I am – not by the loss of a grandchild but by the necessity to deny some spark of human potential, its existence. I, who would not knowingly step on an ant, do understand how you have done what you *had* to do. At eighteen, with your life before you, you are not ready for a child nor are you ready for marriage to its father. This unfortunate 'flying Dutchman' who drifts from coast to coast, crashing with friends until they can no longer abide his temper could provide neither emotional nor financial support for a 'family'.

I think my real sorrow stems from the fact that you had to undergo this traumatic experience. That you had to make this decision, endure the physical pain and mental anguish; the knowing loss. And finally that I should, somehow, have 'been there' to comfort, to hold you in my arms and tell you (although we would both know, deep inside that it wasn't) that everything was all right –

With my love,
Dorothy

PART TWO

There was a bird's egg once, picked up by chance upon the ground, and those who found it bore it home and placed it under a barn-door fowl. And in time the chick bred out, and those who had found it chained it by the leg to a log, lest it should stray and be lost. And by and by they gathered round it, and speculated as to what the bird might be. One said, 'It is surely a waterfowl, a duck or it may be a goose; if we took it to the water it would swim and gabble.' But another said, 'It has no webs to its feet; it is a barn-door fowl; should you let it loose it will scratch and cackle with the others on the dung-heap.' But a third speculated, 'Look now at its curved beak; no doubt it is a parrot, and can crack nuts!' But a fourth said, 'No, but look at its wings: perhaps it is a bird of some great flight.' But several cried, 'Nonsense! Can you suppose that a thing can do a thing which no one has ever seen it do?' And the bird – the bird – with its leg chained close to the log, preened its wing. So they sat about it, speculating, and discussing it; and one said this, and another that. And all the while as they talked the bird sat motionless, with its gaze fixed on the clear, blue sky above it. And one said, 'Suppose we let the creature loose to see what it will do?' – and the bird shivered. But the others cried, 'It is too valuable; it might get lost. If it were to try to fly it might fall down and break its neck.' And the bird, with its foot chained to the log, sat looking upward into the clear blue sky; the sky, in which it had never been – for the bird – the bird, knew what it would do – because it was an eaglet!

There is one woman known to many of us, as each human creature knows but one on earth; and it is upon our knowledge of that woman that we base our certitude.

For those who do not know her, and have not this ground, it is probably profitable and necessary that they painfully collect isolated facts and then speculate upon them, and base whatever views they should form upon these collections. It might even be profitable that they should form no definite opinions at all, but wait till the ages of practical experience have put doubt to rest. For those of us who have a ground of knowledge which we cannot transmit to outsiders, it is perhaps more profitable to act fearlessly than to argue.

Olive Schreiner, Woman and Labour *(1911)*

CHAPTER THREE

Dangerous Dreams

Stepping Out of Place: The Nineteenth Century and Before

. . . We should place our aspirations and our dreams very high – and I also think it is a source of disappointment to make all the interest of one's life depend on sentiments as stormy as love.

Marie Curie to her daughter Eve (1932)

Women must convert their 'love' for and reliance on strength and skill in others to a love for all manner of strength and skill in themselves. Women must be able to go as directly to the 'heart' of physical, technological and intellectual reality as they presumably do to the 'heart' of emotional reality. This requires discipline, courage, confidence, anger, the ability to act, and an overwhelming sense of joy and urgency.

Phyllis Chesler, *Women and Madness* (1972)

'Raising tempests' was a common charge brought against women who were accused of witchcraft in the Middle Ages – a charge we might find ridiculous if the results had not been so cruel and depraved. Millions of women throughout Europe were tortured, stoned, beaten and burned to death throughout the fourteenth, fifteenth and sixteenth centuries.* Other charges, ranging from healing the sick to engaging in love outside marriage or holding individual opinions on theological or social matters, could also condemn a woman to torture and death. One of the most substantial pieces of evidence that could be brought against an alleged witch was that she was an unmarried woman.

By the nineteenth century, society no longer saw fit to torture and burn spinsters, healers or radical thinkers. But latter-day tempest-raisers, women who stepped out of place, were viewed with considerable alarm and they often paid a high price in social ostracism and family censure. Although women's desires to take on challenges outside the home were hindered by such models as the Angel in the House, the obstacles which bedevilled their dreams were not always so ethereal: women were prevented by law from

---

*The American 'witchcraze' was considerably more modest, both in brutality and in the number of women who were attacked.

entering into well-paid, interesting work. Until 1875 in England it was *illegal* as well as socially unacceptable for women even to attend most colleges or universities.

In her classic study of sexist attitudes in Western culture, Kate Millett has remarked on the irony of certain of these popular prejudices about 'ladylike' behaviour:

> The issue of women's entrance into the professions is a spectacular case of the contradictions in the chivalrous mentality . . . Women have always worked. They have generally worked longer hours for smaller rewards and at less agreeable tasks than have men. The issue of employment was simply their demand that they be paid for their efforts, have an opportunity to enter the most prestigious fields of work, and when paid, be allowed to retain and control their earnings. Even before the industrial revolution brought them to the factory, women had always done menial labour, most of it physically exhausting and tedious, much of it agricultural. Yet . . . 'decorum' found it outrageous for a lady to use her mind rather than her hands and back . . . Pioneers in each field met with ruthless and nearly overwhelming opposition in law, medicine, science, scholarship and architecture.*

The 'Woman Question', as the nineteenth century referred to it, was a grave preoccupation of families, churches and politicians, in much the same way as economic recession and nuclear weapons are today. Popular sensibility was dominated by angry perplexity about why women might want to have spheres of influence outside the home – with growing numbers of women pointing out that, the joys and cares of domesticity notwithstanding, there was no reason to suppose that housekeeping and intimate relationships could possibly satisfy every talent, ability and inclination which half the human race might harbour.

The 'Woman Question' made new and often painful demands on the relationships between mothers and daughters. Because of the risks and sacrifices involved in defying tradition, it was very difficult for a mother to step out of place – or to encourage her daughter to do so. All too often it meant sacrificing half a life – the comfort of home and family – in order to fulfil one's dreams; the expectations of Victorian marriage allowed little chance of combining family life with dedication to other projects. Nonetheless, women did frequently manage to give loving support to their mothers and daughters – even with the uneasy knowledge that, throughout history, women have been called every name from 'insane' to 'demonic' for acting according to their dreams.

---

*Six decades before Millett's *Sexual Politics*, Olive Schreiner had spoken pointedly about the sexual division of labour in primitive societies, at that time necessitated by women's constant childbearing and childcare: 'Women naturally took the heavy agricultural and domestic labours, which were yet more consistent with the continual dependence of infant life on her own, than those of men and the chase. There was nothing artificial in such a division; it threw the heaviest burden of the most wearying and unexciting forms of social labour on woman, but under it both sexes laboured in a manner essential to the existence of society . . .'

Lady Mary Wortley Montagu to her daughter Mary Bute, 1751–53

I would be content to endure some inconvenience, to gratify a passion that is become so powerful with me, as curiosity.

Mary Wortley Montagu (1717)

If there is one woman who represents independence and adventure – insofar as these were possible for women during the eighteenth century – it must be Lady Mary Wortley Montagu (1689–1762). Her mother died when Mary was only 3, leaving four children to be brought up by the family nurse; Mary's father, as a member of England's ruling aristocracy, had little time for his children. Mary was not given a classical education like her brothers, but was largely self-taught through her haphazard investigation of her father's library. When she was 23, she eloped in order to escape an arranged marriage.

At a time when it was considered unwise and improper for women to travel, Lady Mary crossed war-torn Europe with her diplomat husband and lived for a year in Constantinople. She was the first European woman to visit the Islamic world and she became famous for the informative and perceptive letters she wrote from abroad to her sisters and friends. She also achieved notoriety when she had her children 'engrafted' against smallpox according to the local Turkish custom; vaccination was not practised in England at that time and upon her return people flocked to her home in London to inspect her children's scars. She propagandised for a time about the beneficial effects of the practice but medical prejudice was too strong and she gained few converts.

A notable society woman wrote that when Lady Mary returned from her travels in the East she appeared 'a very singular person, who neither thinks, speaks, acts or dresses like anyone else'. Nonetheless, she frequented the court of King George I and maintained friendships with important literary figures – notably the poets Alexander Pope and William Congreve.

But Mary had an independent and nonconformist spirit; she became disenchanted with court life, with its petty scandals and social superficiality. She and Pope quarrelled and he attacked her publicly, his acid wit making social life difficult for her. At 50, she decided to leave England and travel as her fancy dictated. Her 'wifely duties' do not seem to have concerned her overmuch; she and her husband maintained a respectful correspondence but they never met again. Once she had seen her daughter prosperously married to Lord Bute, assistant to the Prince of Wales, she set off on her own and travelled throughout France and Italy for eight years. In 1747 she settled in a village near Venice where she lived for nearly fifteen years, content with gardening, reading, occasional travel and writing lengthy letters to her daughter. She returned to England the year before her death at the age of 73.

1 November 1751
[My Dear Child]

. . . I am so far persuaded of the goodness of your heart, I have often had a mind to write you a consolatory epistle on my own death, which I believe will be some affliction, though my life is wholly useless to you. That part of it which we passed together you have reason to remember with gratitude, though I think you misplace it; you are no more obliged to me for bringing you into the world, than I am to you for coming into it, and I never made use of that commonplace (and like most commonplaces, false) argument, as exacting any return of affection . . . In the case of your infancy, there was so great a mixture of instinct, I can scarce even put that in the number of the proofs I have given you [of] my love; but I confess I think it a great one, if you compare my after-conduct towards you with that of other mothers, who generally look on their children as devoted to their pleasures, and bound by duty to have no sentiments but what they please to give them . . . I have always thought of you in a different manner. Your happiness was my first wish, and the pursuit of all my actions, divested of all self-interest. So far I think you ought, and believe you do, remember me as your real friend.

28 January 1753
[My Dear Child]

. . . I will therefore speak to you as supposing [your daughter] not only capable, but desirous of learning: in that case by all means let her be indulged in it. You will tell me I did not make it a part of your education: your prospect was very different from hers. As you had no defect either in mind or person to hinder, and much in your circumstances to attract, the highest offers, it seemed your business to learn how to live in the world, as it is hers to know how to be easy out of it. It is the common error of builders and parents to follow some plan they think beautiful (and perhaps is so), without considering that nothing is beautiful that is displaced . . . thus every woman endeavours to breed her daughter a fine lady, qualifying her for a station in which she will never appear, and at the same time incapacitating her for that retirement to which she is destined. Learning, if she has a real taste for it, will not only make her contented, but happy in it. No entertainment is so cheap as reading, nor any pleasure so lasting. She will not want new fashions, nor regret the loss of expensive diversions, or variety of company, if she can be amused with an author in her closet. To render this amusement extensive, she should be permitted to learn the languages. I have heard it lamented that boys lose so many years in mere learning of words: this is no objection to a girl, whose time is not so precious: she cannot advance herself in any profession, and has therefore more hours to spare – and as you say her memory is good, she will be very agreeably employed this way. There are two cautions to be given on this subject: first, not to think herself learned when she can read Latin, or even Greek . . . True knowledge consists in knowing things, not words . . .

The second caution to be given her (and which is most absolutely necessary) is to conceal whatever learning she attains, with as much solicitude as she would hide crookedness or lameness – the parade of it can only serve to draw on her the envy, and consequently the most inveterate hatred, of all he and she fools, which will certainly be at least three parts in four of all her acquaintance. The use of knowledge in our sex, besides the amusement of solitude, is to moderate the passions, and learn to be contented with a small expense, which are the certain effects of a studious life – and it may be preferable even to that fame which men have engrossed to themselves and will not suffer us to share. You will tell me I have not observed this rule myself – but you are mistaken: it is only inevitable accident that has given me any reputation that way. I have always carefully avoided it, and ever thought it a misfortune. If she has the same inclination (I should say passion) for learning that I was born with, history, geography, and philosophy will furnish her with materials to pass away cheerfully a longer life than is allotted to mortals. I believe there are few heads capable of making Sir I. Newton's calculations, but the result of them is not difficult to be understood by a moderate capacity . . .

The ultimate end of your education was to make you a good wife (and I have the comfort to hear that you are one): hers ought to be to make her happy in a virgin state. I will not say it is happier – but it is undoubtedly safer than any marriage. In a lottery, where there are (at the lowest computation) ten thousand blanks to a prize, it is the most prudent choice not to venture. I have always been so thoroughly persuaded of this truth, that, notwithstanding the flattering views I had for you (as I never intended you a sacrifice to my vanity), I thought I owed you the justice to lay before you all the hazards attending matrimony: you may recollect I did so in the strongest manner.

6 March 1753

I cannot help writing a sort of apology for my last letter, foreseeing that you will think it wrong, or at least Lord Bute will be extremely shocked at the proposal of a learned education for daughters, which the generality of men believe as great a profanation as the clergy would do if the laity should presume to exercise the functions of the priesthood. I desire you would take notice, I would not have learning enjoined them as a task, but permitted as a pleasure, if their genius leads them naturally to it. I look upon my grand-daughters as a sort of

lay nuns: destiny may have laid up other things for them, but they
have no reason to expect to pass their time otherwise than their aunts
do at present; and I know, by experience, it is in the power of study not
only to make solitude tolerable, but agreeable.

Frederika Bremer to her mother Brigitta, 1831

Frederika Bremer (1801–65), one of Sweden's foremost women writers, was
raised in a wealthy conservative family who believed in strict discipline in
order to shield young girls from evil. She and her sister were confined to their
darkened rooms during most of their unhappy childhood, and were given
very little to eat because their parents wished them to remain delicate.
Frederika detested her life of idleness and, against all expectations of proper
behaviour for an upper-class young woman, was determined to have a career
as a writer (intending thereby to raise money for charity). Her first book,
Tales of Swedish Life, was written in secret and published in 1828 under a
pseudonym. Two years later her identity was made public when she was
awarded a Gold Medal by the Swedish Academy, for her second volume of
Tales. After that, she felt on surer ground in demanding time away from
cloistered family life for her writing.

Throughout her life, Frederika Bremer continued to work as a novelist and
journalist. Her books were widely read in England and America and in 1843
she was awarded the Large Gold Medal of the Swedish Academy. That same
year she founded a network of Women's Associations to organize social-
work projects for the benefit of children living in conditions of poverty and
disease.

After a visit to America in 1851 she decided to devote her life to the complete emancipation of Swedish women who, at that time, had virtually no
civil rights: any unmarried woman was legally a minor and could not marry
or inherit property without her parents' consent. Frederika successfully
campaigned for women to attain adult status at the age of 25. Swedish
women were also barred from the teaching profession, and only married
women with sufficient knowledge of the Scriptures were allowed to engage in
such trades as haberdashery and dressmaking. Frederika established a
'seminarium' to train women as teachers and succeeded in obtaining legal
reforms which enabled unmarried women to work in trades previously
closed to them.

Inspired by her American visit, her play *The Bondsmaid* compared the lot
of women to that of slaves – a theme frequently echoed in the nineteenth-
century struggle for women's rights. Frederika Bremer was also one of the
first people to proclaim that women had a special role in procuring world
peace. In 1854, *The Times* in London published her appeal calling for women
to form an international Peace Alliance to stop the Crimean War; she invited
women everywhere to join hands as sisters, disregard national boundaries
and strive to end all wars. *The Times* in its editorial the following day replied:

'. . . women are at their best in the quiet corner of their homes . . . We have never heard that women's ambitious attempts to improve mankind have resulted in any real progress.'

Undaunted by such diatribes, at the age of 55 Frederika set off on her own to travel for five years; she visited Switzerland, Belgium, France and Italy, and then continued on to the Middle East. When she returned, she wrote one of her most popular books, *Life in the Old World*, a narrative of her journey through Palestine and Greece. Four years after her return, she died of pleurisy.

This letter was written shortly after she had been awarded her first Gold Medal by the Swedish Academy:

25 October 1831

My Dearest Mother,

Ah! what a joy it is to be able to turn in full confidence to the one whom we have to thank for our existence. I say, thank; for life seems now to be of value to me. Formerly it was not so. My youth has not been happy: on the contrary, it has been a time of suffering, and its days, to a great extent (this is indeed truth), have passed away in a continual wish to die. But now it is otherwise. As a compensation for that long time of suffering and compulsory inactivity, another has succeeded, which gives me the means of usefulness, and therefore also of new life and gladness. We hope, we desire, my sisters and I, nothing else than to be able to do some little good, whilst we are wandering here on earth, and according to the power that is given to us, to work for the good of others, and live ourselves in peace and harmony; and perhaps our joyless youth, if it has deprived us of some of the enjoyments of life, may in some measure have led our minds to higher aspirations, and to a stronger desire for real usefulness.

At this moment my plan for the future is the following: to spend as little as possible of my own fortune upon myself, so that I may be able as much as possible to devote my life to acquiring all the means that may be of service to me in the development of my mission as an authoress. Never have I felt so much that I have been created for this aim as now; never have I felt my intellectual being, as it were, grow, strengthen, gain stability and clearness, as now; knowing what it is to desire to live and learn, and never to have had the joyful hope (to speak in the language of St Paul) 'to be a vessel formed to honour'. The desire and the hope that I become to you and to my sisters a subject of rejoicing, is to me – how shall I express it? – a spur of roses.

Yes, dearest mother! what I have often felt, what I have often wanted to say to my beloved ones at home is, I am happy. Never has any one enjoyed their life more fully than I do at this moment. The brightening thoughts within me, which promise such sweet harmony for my soul in future, contribute much to this: and then my own little quiet room. Oh! dear mother, if I should be at home next winter, do you think I could get a little garret in Mr Bruhn's house? It is more important for me than any one can believe, to have a little quiet nest of my own, where I can be quite undisturbed. In the suite of apartments in our house this would be impossible; but in the garret it would be delightful, if it only can be managed.

George Sand to her mother Sophie Dupin, 1821–31, and to her daughter Solange, 1852

The French novelist Amantine Lucile Aurore Dupin (1804–76), who called herself George Sand, is probably most often remembered for dressing like a man and having love affairs with famous artists such as the composer Frédéric Chopin and the poet Alfred de Musset. Yet she wrote some eighty novels and plays; she was also an ardent socialist, and was greatly respected in the early days of the Movement of 1848 as the unofficial Minister of Propaganda. She was earning her living by her pen a good hundred years before women in France received the vote; and she was one of the first women to combine motherhood with writing and full involvement in the public world.

Aurore (as she was called by her family) was the firstborn child of Sophie Delaborde, daughter of a humble tavern-keeper, and Maurice Dupin, an officer in Napoleon's army. Sophie's humble origins earned her the lasting contempt of her mother-in-law who believed Maurice had married beneath himself. Maurice died when Aurore was 4; from then on, she was raised by her mother and grandmother who bore each other unreserved hatred and battled for possession of the girl. When Sophie moved to Paris after a few years, leaving her in the care of her severe and repressive grandmother, Aurore suffered bitterly under numerous new restrictions designed to make her a little lady and to eradicate any trace of her mother's passionate tempera-ment or her own vitality and imagination; she was later to be driven to dis-traction by her grandmother's tales depicting the beautiful and passionate Sophie as a scarlet woman. Her misery was compounded by beatings administered by the maid, and by cruel rationing of visits to her mother. It was with relief that, at 12, she was sent to Paris to be educated in an English convent where she gained a reputation for staging irreverent theatrics and audacious pranks. In her last year she made a complete about-face and decided to become a nun.

Her grandmother, wanting to put a stop to this notion, withdrew her from the convent and decided it was high time Aurore was married. Aurore, only 15, was horrified but kept quiet about her vocation which, in any case, rapidly receded as she submerged herself in ancient philosophy, Enlighten-ment essays and classical poetry, in an effort to improve her education. Nobody objected to Aurore's loss of faith: what alarmed them was her independent spirit. She shocked almost everyone with her daily romps on horseback and the unconventional medical education she was receiving through touring neighbourhood villages with her tutor, who set broken bones and amputated infected limbs.

That Aurore should study anatomy by drawing human bones, brought to her by a young medical student, was the final straw for village gossips. When word got back to Sophie in Paris, she immediately fired off a letter designed to intimidate her daughter back into the bounds of propriety. Seventeen-year-old Aurore replied politely but firmly that horse-riding was good for her health and that she felt her virtue insulted by insinuations that she might allow her teacher to make amorous advances.

In answer to the additional accusation that she was a fool to be so bookish, Aurore continued:

18 November 1821

My Dear Mother,
. . . Why must a woman be ignorant? . . . Supposing I should one day have sons and that I should have derived enough benefit from my studies to teach them, don't you think the lessons of a mother are worth as much as those of a tutor? But to reach this point one must be married, and, for that say you, I shall only find a giant or a coward. In that case I might never get married, for I no longer believe in giants and care not for cowards . . . I won't look for a man capable of becoming the slave of his wife, because he would be an imbecile; but I don't believe that a man of intelligence and wit would want his wife to seem timid and fearful when she was neither one nor the other . . .

Within six months, Aurore met Baron Casimir Dudevant; after a brief court-ship, they decided to marry. She was delighted by the birth of their son, Maurice, scarcely a year later. Dudevant, who proved to be a man of neither intelligence nor wit, became increasingly drunk and abusive and the marriage deteriorated over the next few years. A daughter, Solange, was born in 1828, to the consternation of her parents who had virtually given up on the marriage and were rarely civil to one another. Aurore asked her husband for a separation when Solange was 2; he refused.* Then began years of legal battles over separation and custody of the children, which finally resulted in Dudevant gaining custody of Maurice and Aurore winning Solange. Aurore went with Solange to Paris, where she began writing books and articles under the name George Sandeau (after she and her collaborator–lover Jules Sandeau parted company, Aurore kept the name George Sand).

Even as an adult, Aurore was frequently distressed to the point of illness by her relationship with her mother. Since the death of her father, she had

---

*Divorce was abolished in 1816 and remained illegal in France until 1884.

endured agonies from her mother's wild swings of mood: one minute Sophie would rage against her daughter, hurling abuse and unfounded accusations; the next she would overwhelm her with maternal tenderness and understanding. When Sand became famous (and infamous) overnight, Sophie was predictably unpredictable, veering between praise and attack. Nonetheless, it was Sophie who recommended that Aurore wear men's clothing: it was cheaper and more practical and would free her from the restrictions which both laws and custom imposed on her movements in Paris. Since Aurore's greatest desire at this point was to attend the theatre as often as possible (and to stand in the pit, which was cheaper than buying a seat but reserved only for men), she was delighted by her mother's ingenuity – and by the freedom she gained.

In her autobiography, George Sand wrote of her mother: 'The first letter I wrote, on resolving to oppose my husband in court, was to her. The affection she returned to me was spontaneous, total, unwavering. Almost two years went by during which she became for me what she was in my childhood.'

The following letter must have been written just before that loving interlude. Aurore does not give any hint of the imminent break-up of her nine-year marriage:

31 May 1831

My Dear Maman,
    You are not feeling very cheerful, are you, because you are still going to be alone. Congenial companionship is very difficult to combine with liberty. You like to have people with you, but you hate any kind of constraint, and that is just like me. How is one to reconcile one's own desires with other people's? I really don't know. Perhaps one really ought to shut one's eyes to a great many little things, to tolerate a great many imperfections in human nature and to resign oneself to certain annoyances which are inevitable whatever one's circumstances may be. Are you not rather severe towards transient wrong-doing? It is true that you forgive easily and forget quickly; but are you not a little hasty in condemnation? For me, my dear, liberty of thought and action is the first of blessings. If one could combine with that the little cares of bringing up a family it would be much sweeter, but is that at all possible? The one is always a nuisance to the other, liberty to one's home-circle, and one's home-circle to liberty! You are the only judge in the question of which you would prefer to sacrifice! I know that my own greatest fault lies in the fact that I *cannot* submit to the least shadow of constraint. Everything that is imposed on me as a duty becomes odious at once; whatever I do of my own free will is done with all my heart. It is often a great misfortune to be made like that and all my failings towards other people when they do occur, originate there.

But can one change one's own nature? If people are very indulgent to this fault of mine I find that it corrects itself in the most wonderful way. But when I am perpetually reproached about it, it gets much worse, and really that is not out of a spirit of contradiction; it is just involuntary, irresistible! I really must venture to tell you, dear Maman, that you have very little idea what I am really like. It is a long time now since we lived together and you often forget that I am now twenty-seven years old and that my character was bound to undergo many changes since I was quite a girl.

You seem to impute a love of pleasure and a need of frivolous amusement to me that I am far from possessing. It is not society, and noise, and theatres and new dresses that I want; you are the only person to make that mistake, it is liberty that I long for. I want to be able to walk out quite alone and say to myself: 'I will dine at four, or at seven, just as I like. I will go to the Tuileries through the Luxembourg instead of the Champs Elysées if the whim seizes me.' That would please me far better than the ordinariness of ordinary people and the stiffness of drawing-rooms.

If I meet people who are dense enough to take my innocent fantasies for hypocritical vices I cannot persuade myself to take the trouble to undeceive them. I only know that such people bore me, misunderstand me . . . yes . . . and outrage me! I make no answer. As far as I am concerned they are wiped out. Is there anything to blame in that? I seek neither vengeance nor reparation for I am not vindictive: I simply forget. I know people say I am not a serious person because there is no hatred in me and I have not the pride to justify myself.

Oh, God! What is this frantic desire to torment each other, which possesses human beings? This frantic desire to reprove each other's faults bitterly, to condemn pitilessly, everyone who is not cut upon our own pattern.

You, dear Maman, have suffered much from the intolerance and false virtues of high-principled people. How terribly at one time they blackened your beauty, your youth, your independence, your happy facile character? What bitterness poisoned your brilliant destiny! If you had had a tender indulgent mother who opened her arms to you at each fresh sorrow and said to you, 'Men may condemn you, but I absolve you! Let them curse . . . for I bless you!', what a comfort it would have been to you in all the disgustingness and littleness of life!

So someone has been telling you *that it is I who wear the breeches*. It is not a bit true, if you were to be here for twenty-four hours, you would see that it was not. On the other hand I have not the slightest desire to see my husband in petticoats. Let us each wear our own clothes and be equally free. I have my faults, but my husband has his, and if I were to tell you that ours is a model household and that there is never a cloud between us you would not believe me. There is good and bad in my circumstances, just as there is for everyone else. The fact is that my husband does just as he likes. He has mistresses or does not have them, as his appetite dictates to him; he drinks muscat grape juice or plain water according to his desire at the moment; he saves or spends just as he feels inclined; he builds, plants, makes changes, and rules the property and the house just as he intends. I have not a word to say in any of it.

I don't mind because I know he is a good organiser, that he is more inclined to be economical than to waste money and that he loves his children, and looks at everything from the point of view of their welfare. As you may see, I have no feelings for him but esteem and confidence and since I have given the property entirely into his control, I suppose no one will continue to suspect me of wishing to dominate him.

I need so little, nothing but the same income and the same standard of comfort that you have. I should be satisfied with an allowance of three thousand francs a year, considering that I can already add to it with my pen. For the rest, it is only fair that my husband's absolute liberty should be reciprocal; if that were not the case he would become hateful and contemptible to me, and that he does not wish! I therefore live quite independently. I go to bed when he thinks it is time to get up. I can start off to La Châtre if I like, or just as easily to Rome; I come in at midnight, or at six in the morning. It is entirely my own business. Please judge anyone who criticises me for it with the head and the heart of a mother, for both ought to be on my side.

I shall go to Paris this summer. The more you show me that I am dear to you and that you are pleased to have me with you, the happier and the more grateful you will find me. But if I find bitter criticism and offensive suspicion in your orbit (it is not from you that I fear them) I will make room for the more powerful, and without vengeance, without anger, I will enjoy the peace of my own conscience and my liberty. You really have too much mind and heart not to realise soon that I do not deserve all this hard treatment.

Good-bye dear little Maman. My children are well. Solange is lovely and naughty. Maurice is too thin really, but such a good boy. I am so pleased with his character and his mental development. I rather spoil my fat little girl. But the fact that Maurice has become so sweet now reassures me for their future.

Write soon, dear Maman.
Kisses with all my soul.

By contrast, Aurore's relationship with her daughter, Solange, did not keep up even the appearance of such warm openness. Solange suspected (quite rightly) that her mother had always preferred Maurice, and over the years her relationship with her steadily increased in bitterness. Solange did not have her mother's love of hard work, but wanted the fine things that money could buy. She married a sculptor, Auguste Clesinger, mistakenly believing that he had a fortune (he had vainly hoped the same about her). Aurore was eager for the match and provided Solange with a handsome dowry which Clesinger soon dissipated. Aurore was furious; she and Solange never achieved a reconciliation.

Solange separated from her spendthrift and violent husband in 1852. To escape from his threats she went to live in a convent, where she immediately found the dull routine intolerable. Worst of all, she was dependent on her mother for an increase in her allowance in order to leave the convent and begin a new life in Paris, in the style to which she hoped to become accustomed. She wrote to her mother from the convent:

Having to live in this isolation, with the sound and movement of life all around me – people laughing together, horses galloping, children playing in the sunshine, lovers being happy – it is not so much a matter of being bored as of being made to despair.

People wonder how it is that girls without minds of their own or any sort of education allow themselves to drift into a life of pleasure and vice! Can even women with judgement and warm affections be sure of being able to steer clear of all that . . .?

Aurore, eager not to be manipulated by this emotional blackmail, responded immediately and without sympathy to her daughter's threat to become a prostitute:

I spent many of the best years of my own youth living in what you call 'isolation' working hard between four dirty walls, and let me tell you that, though I regret a great deal, I don't regret that . . . It may be that your husband does not wholly deserve to be so bitterly disliked or so impulsively put aside . . . In my view it is not very pretty of you to complain of the immediate consequences of a resolution which you took entirely of your own accord. The only thing which will console you is money . . . and a great deal of it . . . I could only give you what you need by working twice as hard as I do now, and if I did that I'd be dead in six months, since even my present programme is beyond my strength – besides, even if I could work twice as hard and keep at it for a few more years, what is there to say that it is my duty to turn myself into a galley slave or a complete hack merely to supply you with money to burn? What I can give you, you shall have. You can treat this house as your home, on the sole condition that you don't upset everybody with your idiotic behaviour, or drive them to distraction with your ill-natured ways . . . What I will not do is to pretend to sympathise with the difficulties and privations that you will have to endure in Paris . . .

So you find it difficult, do you, being lonely and poor, not to step into a life of vice? . . . It is all you can do to endure being cooped up within four walls while women are laughing and horses are galloping outside? 'What a horrible fate!' as Maurice would say . . . All right then, just try a little vice . . . just try being a whore. I don't think you would make much of a success of it . . . a woman has got to be a great deal more beautiful and more intelligent than you are before she can hope to be pursued, or even sought out by men who are eager and anxious to pay for her favours . . . men with money to spend want women who know how to earn it.

I have known young women who have fought down the impulses of heart and body, scared to death that domestic unhappiness might trick them into giving in to the mad impulse of a moment, but I have never known a single one of them, brought up as you have been in an atmosphere of personal dignity and moral freedom, who has dreaded unhappiness and isolation because of such dangers as you talk of.

Aurore and Solange managed to patch things up during the fight for custody of Solange's daughter, Jeanne, who in fact died during the proceedings. Solange then moved to Paris to pursue her career as a prostitute. She enjoyed success in her chosen profession and shared the details in vivid letters to her mother. But Aurore would not take the bait offered:

I'd like to be able to laugh at the fantastic travel adventures that you tell me of with such relish. But I can't help feeling that there may be a great deal of sadness and difficulty lying in wait behind all your gaiety . . . do at least keep me informed of your whereabouts, and when you're tired of your never-ending search for amusement – come here and be bored. At least it will give you a chance to catch your breath.

Harriet Martineau to her mother Elizabeth, 1833

My business in life has been to think and learn, and to speak out with absolute freedom what I have thought and learned.

Harriet Martineau

Harriet Martineau (1802–76), popular English writer on political economy and leading journalist of her time, was born and raised in Norwich, the sixth of eight children in a liberal middle-class family. A sickly and unhappy child, born without the sense of taste or smell, she became deaf at the age of 12. Her Unitarian parents believed in good education for girls as well as boys, so Harriet attended excellent schools, although, unlike her brothers, she was not sent to university. Elizabeth Martineau seems to have been a moralistic and undemonstrative woman; well into adulthood, Harriet expressed resentment that her mother did not give her either affection or approval while she was growing up. Even after Harriet became a bestselling author, she was intimidated by her mother and became unusually quiet and unhappy in her presence.

Harriet did not want the limitations and constraints of a Victorian marriage and there was only one alternative for a respectably unmarried woman: to remain a daughter. After finishing school, she kept up appearances and sat dutifully in the parlour, sewing and receiving callers. However, she now began to write articles on the current political scene, published anonymously. She would work early in the morning and late at night in order to seem suitably ladylike and idle when people were around.

When she was 24, her father died and his business immediately went bankrupt, leaving the family almost penniless. Harriet took in sewing to help support the family, but her articles were becoming increasingly popular and soon provided an indispensable source of income for the family. It then became acceptable for her to write during the daytime. In 1830 she began writing *Illustrations of Political Economy*, a series of tales which simplified and explained the new ideas of Adam Smith, David Ricardo and T. R. Malthus. For a young woman in the 1820s to worry her head over such 'masculine' matters was considered quite a scandal – but her monthly instalments sold over 10,000 copies each for two years as people clamoured for enlightenment about the social and economic upheaval which England was facing.

Harriet Martineau was an outspoken advocate of women's rights. She wrote extensively in her journalism about the need for girls to be educated, the situation of working women, problems of domestic violence and inequalities in the marriage laws. She was a longstanding friend of Florence Nightingale* and helped to publicise Florence's reforms in the nursing profession and her advanced ideas on public-health issues. After travelling in America in 1834, Harriet wrote *Society in America*, in which she made her major theoretical statement about the position of women, comparing it with the position of slaves. Her book was heavily criticised by the press on both sides of the Atlantic, but it sold well and she received numerous grateful letters from women readers.

Although a committed feminist in her writings, Harriet had contradictory attitudes about women in general, and about woman's-rights activists in particular. She rebelled against the prevailing stereotypes of 'masculine' and 'feminine' but she never succeeded in rejecting them entirely. Thus she often found herself identifying with men because she was 'successful', and despising most women because they were not. Ultimately, this contradiction brought her to grief: when she was offered a prestigious position as editor of a new economics journal, she turned it down. Her doubts about her ability to overcome what she saw as her feminine weakness were reinforced by her

*See pp. 99–111.

brother's disapproval of her accepting such an unladylike post; she turned instead to the more acceptable task of writing a novel. She also became bedridden for five years.* She was eventually cured by hypnosis and continued writing and publishing until her death at the age of 74. In addition to *Illustrations of Political Economy* and *Society in America*, her best-known works include her *Autobiography* and her novel, *Deerbrook*. She also wrote children's books and several articles and books on history and travel.

This letter was written soon after the initial success of the *Political Economy* series had brought Harriet a measure of independence. She was enjoying living on her own when her mother and aunt decided to move in with her:

8 July 1833

Dearest Mother,

I have rather put off writing, feeling that I have much to say, and now I must write after all more briefly than usual. Mrs K. has told you that I am well, and so I go on to what you most want to know next. About our future. I know of no risks that you are not at present aware of, and I have no fresh doubts. You are aware that I must travel, after 1834, for a year or little short of it; and we all know that my resources depend on health, and in some degree on popularity. I say 'in some degree', because I am pretty sure that I can now never be without employment unless I choose . . .

My advice is that we begin modestly, – with a house which we may keep *after a time*, when our income may be reduced. With prudence I think we may hope to live comfortably on our means, while I may be laying by something against a time of rest, if it should please God to preserve my health. I see no other plan which promises equal comfort for the three parties concerned, and if you are willing to trust to our industry and care, so am I; and I have no doubt we shall make one another happy, if we at once begin with the change of habits which our change of position renders necessary. I fully expect that both you and I shall occasionally feel as if I did not discharge a daughter's duty, but we shall both remind ourselves that I am now as much a citizen of the world as any professional *son* of yours could be. You shall be most welcome to my confidence, as ever, and to any comfort that may be derived from living in the same house, and meeting at the same table, and taking frequent walks, and having many mutual friends. My hours of solitary work and of visiting will leave you much to yourself; this you know and do not fear; so now the whole case is before you, and you know exactly under what feelings I say 'Come'. I may just

---

*Although there was undeniably a psychosomatic component to her invalidism, Harriet did suffer from polypous tumours and prolapse of the uterus.

mention that I see no sign of disapprobation on any hand, though there are naturally doubts here and there as to how a removal from a place where you have lived so many years may affect you. *We*, however, know that removal to be necessary, whether you come to London or fix your abode elsewhere; there is another chance, dear mother, and that is, of my marrying. I have no thoughts of it. I see a thousand reasons against it. But I could not positively answer for always continuing in the same mind. It would be presumptuous to do so; and I especially feel this when I find myself touched by the devoted interest with which some few of my friends regard my labours. I did not know till lately any thing of the enthusiasm with which such services as I attempt can be regarded, nor with what tender respect it could be testified. I mean no more than I say, I assure you; but, strong as my convictions are against marrying, I will not positively promise. As for my money prospects, the sale [of the *Illustrations*] *cannot* now fall below the point of profit, and large profit; and there is the cheaper edition to look to, which everybody says will yield an income for years to come . . .

Yours most affectionately,
H. Martineau

Elizabeth Blackwell to her mother Hannah, 1844, and to her stepdaughter Kitty, 1887

Elizabeth Blackwell (1821–1910), the first woman to obtain a degree in modern medicine, was accepted as a medical student as the result of a misunderstanding. The administration at New York's Geneva College had referred her application to the students – who, thinking it a spoof by a rival school, accepted it. From then on she needed an iron will to carry her through the long years of isolation and hostility from townspeople and colleagues as she fought, first to study medicine and then, once she had earned her degree, to work as a physician.

From her family, however, Elizabeth had full encouragement. She grew up in Cincinnatti, Ohio, the third of nine children; from the time of her father's death when she was 17, Elizabeth and her two sisters worked as schoolteachers to support their large and destitute family. There was no question of a family prejudice against women working. Her parents, both devoutly religious, had been in the vanguard of English and American social reform, including campaigns for the abolition of slavery and for women's rights. Two of Elizabeth's sisters were writers; another sister (Edith) also became a doctor; and her two brothers married two of the foremost women activists in nineteenth-century America, Antoinette Brown and Lucy Stone.* From an

---

*See pp. 97–9.

early age Elizabeth felt outrage at thoughts or actions which violated her moral, religious or social values. She was an intense woman, and she viewed her commitment to medicine almost as a spiritual quest, entirely compatible with her family's crusade against evil and injustice.

Elizabeth's struggle to become the first woman doctor served another, very important function in her life: it provided an outlet for her passions which, she felt, would never be wholly fulfilled in intimate relationships with men. At 24 she wrote in her journal, 'I felt more determined than ever to become a physician, and thus place a strong barrier between me and all ordinary marriages. I must have something to engross my thoughts, some object in life to fill this vacuum and prevent this sad wearing away of the heart.' Recognising that there was slight chance of finding a mate who would tolerate, much less encourage her goals, she determined to subordinate her emotions to work. Suppressing her desire for social contact and frivolity in *any* form in order to pursue her aims, she formed few close friendships and paid a high price for the satisfaction of achievement.

Elizabeth Blackwell won many victories for herself and for other women in the face of fierce resistance. After completing her training in Paris and London, she decided to establish her practice in New York: she was not allowed to work in hospitals; no one would rent consulting rooms; and when she lectured on childbirth, sex and women's health, she was jeered at in the streets. Finally, with the help of her sister, Dr Emily Blackwell, and Dr Marie Zakrzewska, she founded the New York Infirmary for Women and Children. In the UK, she was the first woman to have her name entered on the Medical Register and she helped to found the National Health Society. She organised the first medical college for women, the Women's Medical College of the New York Infirmary, where she created opportunities for women to gain clinical experience. This college was also the first medical training facility to have a Chair of Hygiene, a post which Elizabeth Blackwell held until she was appointed to the Chair of Gynaecology at the New Hospital of the London School of Medicine for women in 1875.

In 1854, at 33, realising that she would never marry and feeling keenly the loneliness and isolation of her position, Elizabeth adopted a homeless 7-year-old waif, Katherine (Kitty) Barry, who became both step-daughter and helper. As she grew older, Kitty was her secretary, assistant and occasional travelling companion. Elizabeth's letters to Kitty suggest dutiful concern rather than emotional intimacy, whereas Kitty seemed to regard her step-mother as a paragon, deserving of devotion, admiration and respect. During Elizabeth's travels Kitty was looked after by the Blackwell clan, and Elizabeth wrote frequent newsy letters filled with practical and moral injunctions. However, she seems to have mellowed considerably as she grew older and in the excerpt below (from a thirty-page letter written when Elizabeth was 66 and Kitty was 40), it appears that their affection grew stronger over the years.

Elizabeth's relationship with her own mother, on the other hand, was always warm and loving, although she rarely took her mother into her confidence or told her about the real problems she faced. Her mother's letters were full of religious advice and Elizabeth was constantly reassuring her about the state of her soul. She often used humour as a way to avoid worrying her mother and the letters are in that sense evasive. They do, nonetheless, offer an unusual perspective on Elizabeth, who otherwise gives the impression of living an admirable but somewhat cheerless life.

These first two letters were written shortly after Elizabeth left home; she was teaching school at Henderson in Kentucky, a slave-owning state:

5 March 1844

Dear Mother,

. . . I dislike slavery more and more every day; I suppose I see it here in its mildest form, and since my residence here I have heard of no use being made of the whipping-post, nor any instance of downright cruelty . . . But to live in the midst of beings degraded to the utmost in body and mind, drudging on from earliest morning to latest night, cuffed about by everyone, scolded at all day long, blamed unjustly, and without spirit enough to reply, with no consideration in any way for their feelings, with no hope for the future . . . To live in their midst, utterly unable to help them, is to me dreadful . . . The mistresses pique themselves on the advantageous situation of their blacks; they positively think them very well off, and triumphantly compare their position with that of the poor in England and other countries. I endeavor, in reply, to slide in a little truth through the small apertures of their minds, for were I to come out broadly with my simple, honest opinion I should shut them up tight, arm all their prejudices, and do ten times more harm than good.

I do long to get hold of someone to whom I can talk frankly; this constant smiling and bowing and wearing a mask provokes me intolerably; it sends me internally to the other extreme, and I shall soon, I think, rush into the woods, vilify Henderson, curse the Whigs, and rail at the Orthodox, whose bells have been going in a fruitless effort at revivals ever since I have been here. Not mind, mother, that I really have such diabolical feelings against the poor Orthodox in general and particular, but I have an intense longing to scream, and everyone here speaks in a whisper . . .

[Your daughter,
Elizabeth]

[c. 1845]

My Dear Mother,

I'm afraid from the sad tone of your letter that you think you're going to die very shortly, but such I assure you is not the case, as I can prove to you if necessary from scripture and common sense; on the contrary I can prophesy many a long and much brighter year in which one of your greatest delights will be to visit me in my beautiful residence near Boston, where I shall present to you my adorable husband, and my three daughters, Faith, Hope and Charity, and four sons, Sounding Brass, Tinkling Cymbal, Gabriel and Beelzebub. (Do not imagine however that I'm going to make myself whole just at present, the fact is I cannot find my other half here, but only about a sixth which would not do.) There are two rather eligible young males here whose mothers have been some time electioneering for wives; one tall the other short, with very pretty names, of good family and with tolerable fortunes, but unfortunately one seems to me a dolt and the other a fool so I keep them at a respectful distance, which you know I'm quite capable of doing . . .

. . . I'm very much obliged to you for your interest in my soul which is quite natural as you had some hand in giving it to me, but you need not be uneasy for I think a great deal on interesting serious subjects, read the bible and pray in a very good fashion so all will come right presently.

Now my dear mother believe me full of natural affection and with a great desire for your growing fat.

Your daughter
Elizabeth

After she had retired from medical work Elizabeth wrote the following letter to Kitty (Kitty was 40):

20 January 1887

My Dear Child,

I will now really try to comply with your earnest and repeated request that I will note down for you some of the facts of my past life. I should hardly care to do so if I were not prompted by my affection for you. For as I draw nearer the borderland, the individual life seems to grow so small, in comparison with the grand whole, that I should be well content to let my useful work speak for itself, whilst the very imperfect worker were forgotten. And indeed the wonderful light of the other life seems often to shine so joyfully into this one, that I almost forget the past and present in an eager anticipation of the approaching awakening.

But affection, dear child, shall hold me to my task of recording what I know will be of interest to you. The little unknown child, whom I took to myself 33 years ago, at a very dreary time of my life, and whom I carried up to bed in my arms, has proved a real daughter to me, and this record shall be a legacy of my affection to her.

[Elizabeth first describes her life as a teacher after her father's death, the hardship of supporting the family, her horror at slavery, her growing attachment to spiritual matters, her campaigning for women's rights. She then moves on

to the period of her decision to become a doctor: 'an idea which was destined to mould so completely my whole future life.']

The idea was first forced upon my attention by a valued lady friend of the family [Miss Donaldson] who was a sufferer from a most painful disease requiring surgical intervention . . . She asked me whether, as I had health, leisure and cultivated intelligence, it was not a positive duty to devote them to the service of suffering women.

The thought of studying medicine was to me so utterly repugnant that I instantly put it aside and tried to forget it. I had always despised the body, as the greatest hindrance to all that I most valued. I disliked everything that related to our physical organisation, even studies in natural history were antipathetic to me. I cannot at all trace the source whence I derived this contempt for the body, but I well remember trying as a child to subdue my body. When going to school in New York I had tried to go without food for days, and had tried to sleep on the bare floor . . . This spirit of asceticism and deep-rooted opposition to the conditions of human existence was rudely shocked by Miss Donaldson's prayers that I should become a physician. And doubtless had the proposition continued to present itself in relation to the special studies requisite for such a course, I should never have taken the matter up. But as the idea would occur to me again and again, other quite different aspects of the question presented themselves.

Much was said in the public press of that date, respecting a notorious abortionist living in New York, a certain Madame Restell, who had a luxurious establishment, a fine carriage, a pew in a fashionable church, and was really a very clever woman. She was always spoken of as a 'female physician': and the term, then, meant an abortionist. This seemed to me a really wicked perversion of what should be a very honourable position and title. I keenly felt the degradation involved in the unnatural and wicked career of this fashionable woman whom the one-sided law vainly tried to stop. Swedenborg's phrase, 'redeem the halls', often occurred to me; and the question whether it would not be a glorious moral battle to redeem the title 'female physician' to a true and noble signification continually forced itself upon me.

I therefore wrote to six well-known physicians in different parts of the U.S. for counsel as to whether it would be a good thing for a lady to become a physician and, if so, what course she should pursue. The replies received were identical in substance. All agreed that a thoroughly qualified woman physician would be a great boon to society; but all equally agreed that it was impossible for a woman to become an equally educated physician, and that it would be foolish and even improper to attempt such a course. These answers made a great impression upon me. I accepted the first part and rejected the second part of the counsel. I reasoned that if a thing was a great good in itself, there must be some way of doing it – and I would do it! I was young, strong, accustomed to study, and I needed an absorbing occupation.

This felt need of engrossing occupation and effort requires a statement of one of the chief reasons which finally decided my work. It has often been thought by superficial observers that only a hard and unwomanly nature could have taken up and fought through the difficult task of opening to women the strongly barred entrance to the medical profession. As a matter of fact, from the age of seven, when I first fell in love with a golden-haired rosy-cheeked little fellow in my aunt's school, who seemed to me like a little angel, I have always been keenly susceptible to the influences of sex both in attraction and repulsion. Indeed so different has been my experience in this respect from the stereotyped (but I think utterly misleading) notions respecting men and women, that I should not hesitate to record facts from time to time, which may help to form truer data for future judgements on this important subject.

Up to this date I had scarcely ever been free from some strong attraction which my sober judgement condemned but which nevertheless made me uncomfortable, often very unhappy, and yet which I seemed powerless to eliminate from my daily life. I hold my own personal or other attractions in very low esteem, or rather it never occurred to me to consider them; and I was extremely shy. At that very time when the medical career was suggested to me I was experiencing an unusually strong struggle between attraction towards a highly educated man with whom I had been very intimately thrown and the distinct perception that his views were too narrow and rigid, to allow of any close and ennobling companionship.

I grew indignant with myself at a struggle that weakened me, and resolved to take a step that I hoped might cut the knot I could not untie and so recover full mental freedom: I finally made up my mind to devote myself to medical study, with the belief that I should thus place an insuperable barrier between myself and those disturbing influences, which I could not wisely yield to, but could not otherwise stifle. I long retained a bunch of flowers which had passed between us, done up in a packet which I sentimentally but in all sincerity labelled 'young love's last dream'.

I look back now with real pity at the inexperience of that enthusiastic young girl who thus hoped to stifle the master passion of human existence. But it was then a very truthful effort, and after some weeks of fierce mental contest, I drew a deep breath of relief and prepared for the fresh departure in life.

I have always enjoyed one great blessing in life, *viz*: the fullest sympathy of my own family. The mother and nine brothers and sisters who were left to struggle through life on my father's death were a very united family. So when I determined to study medicine, although none of us realised what the study might involve, it was with the entire approbation of all the dear brothers and sisters that I prepared for my studies. We were all very poor in worldly goods. My first step therefore was to accept a position as music teacher offered to me at Asheville amongst the mountains of North Carolina, in a school kept by a clergyman who was also a physician and where I hoped to commence a course of medical reading as well as gain money . . .

The excellent head of the Asheville school, the Rev. John Dickson, proved an intelligent and sympathetic counsellor; he gave me the use of his library, and under his direction a course of medical reading was commenced. Considerable time was needed before the natural distaste to medical subjects could be overcome. It was an irrational prejudice and I resolved to conquer it; and in the end I became thoroughly ashamed of my repugnance to the physical side of human nature and entered at last with thorough interest into my new studies: but the struggle was not an easy one.

One day a fellow teacher laughingly brought me a 'subject for dissection'. It was a cockchafer that had been smothered in a pile of pocket handkerchiefs and it was jokingly offered me to try my skill upon. I accepted the task and absurd as the fact may seem, it proved a difficult one. I seized the insect with a hairpin, placed it in a shell, and then opened my pearl-handled pen-knife to make an incision – but I could not make it. I stood over that shell for an hour before I summoned up resolution enough to cut into the insect and discover only a little dry yellowish dust! Clearly however a greater victory was then gained than I was aware of at the time: for in the serious and necessary studies of a later date, I never experienced again a similar repugnance . . .

Lucy Stone to her mother Hannah, 1846

Lucy Stone (1818–93) was one of the earliest women's rights activists in America. Elizabeth Cady Stanton, a revered leader of the suffrage cause, said of·her: '[she] was the first person by whom the heart of the American public was stirred on the woman question.' She was born the eighth of nine children to Francis and Hannah Stone. Hannah had objected to raising children around the 'bad influences' in her husband's tannery yard and, although he believed in a husband's right to rule, he had yielded; the family was living on a farm by the time Lucy was born. At 16, Lucy began teaching in local schools. Faced with her father's lack of support for her further education, she continued teaching in order to put herself through college. She gained a reputation as a talented and conscientious school teacher and by the age of 24 was earning an impressive salary for a young woman of her day. She succeeded in becoming one of the first women students admitted to the liberal

Oberlin College in Ohio – although when she graduated at the top of her class in 1847, she was forced to sit in the audience while a male student read her valedictorian speech.

Like many American suffragists, Lucy Stone began her career working for the abolition of slavery; after slavery was abolished she continued to work for the rights of women until her death at 75. She travelled and lectured throughout the east coast of America and helped found and edit the *Women's Journal*, an influential suffrage newspaper which was published for almost forty years.

Lucy's carefully considered decision to marry Henry Blackwell, brother of Elizabeth Blackwell, America's first woman doctor,* was based on his agreement to devote himself to her work for women's rights (which he faithfully did). Their marriage also set another precedent: she decided to keep her own name after she married. They had one daughter, Alice Stone Blackwell (1857–1950), who worked with her parents on the *Journal* and became a poet and political activist in her own right.†

In 1869 the American suffrage movement was divided when Lucy Stone and Susan B. Anthony** had a major policy disagreement over whether or not to support the Thirteenth Amendment to the Constitution, which would give black men the vote but still exclude women. Lucy Stone favoured supporting the Amendment, while Susan B. Anthony's faction argued that this would drastically delay the progress of the women's struggle. They also disagreed about the liberalisation of the divorce laws, which Lucy did not want included in the suffrage campaign. Three years before Lucy Stone died, Alice Stone Blackwell was instrumental in re-uniting the factions.

In this letter, written in her last year at Oberlin College, Lucy defends her intention to become a public speaker for the Anti-Slavery Society:

1846

. . . I know, Mother, you feel badly about the plans I have proposed to myself, and that you would prefer to have me take some other course, if I could in conscience. Yet, Mother, I know you too well to suppose that you would wish me to turn away from what I think is my

---

*See pp. 91–7.

†Alice Stone Blackwell edited the *Women's Journal* for thirty-five years. In 1887 she also began editing the 'Woman's Column', a collection of items about suffrage which was syndicated to newspapers around the country. After her mother's death she became more radical and involved herself in numerous causes which went far beyond the sphere of suffrage. An avowed socialist radical, she deplored the suppression of free speech, repressive measures under the Espionage Act and the deportation of radicals, and she worked tirelessly in political campaigns. She helped found the League of Women Voters in Massachussetts on the premise that women should remain an autonomous political force and not rely on the two-party system to accomplish their aims. In 1930 she published a biography of her mother. During the next decade she went blind and she died in 1950 at the age of 93.

**See pp. 116–18.

duty, and go all my days in opposition to my convictions of right, lashed by a reproaching conscience.

I surely would not be a public speaker if I sought a life of ease, for it will be a most laborious one; nor would I do it for the sake of honor, for I know that I will be disesteemed, nay, even hated, by some who are now my friends, or who profess to be. Nor would I do it if I sought wealth, because I could secure it with far more ease and worldly honor by being a teacher. But, Mother, the gold that perishes in the using, the honor that comes from men, the ease or indolence which eats out the energy of the soul, are not the objects at which I aim. If I would be true to myself, true to my Heavenly Father, I must be actuated by high and holy principles, and pursue that course of conduct which, to me, appears best calculated to promote the highest good of the world. Because I know that I shall suffer, shall I for this, like Lot's wife, turn back? No, Mother, if in this hour of the world's need I should refuse to lend my aid, however small it may be, I should have no right to think myself a Christian, and I should forever despise Lucy Stone. If, while I hear the wild shriek of the slave mother robbed of her little ones, or the muffled groan of the daughter spoiled of her virtue, I do not open my mouth for the dumb, am I not guilty? Or should I go, as you said, from house to house to do it, when I could tell so many more in less time, if they should be gathered in one place? You would not object, or think it wrong, for a man to plead the cause of the suffering and the outcast; and surely the moral character of the act is not changed because it is done by a woman.

. . . But, Mother, there are no trials so great as they suffer who neglect or refuse to do what they believe is their duty. I expect to plead not for the slave only, but for suffering humanity everywhere. ESPECIALLY DO I MEAN TO LABOR FOR THE ELEVATION OF MY SEX . . . But I will not speak further upon this subject at this time, only to ask that you will not withold your consent from my doing anything that I think is my duty to do. You will not, will you, Mother? . . .

Florence Nightingale and her mother Fanny, 1851–62

My present life is suicide; in my thirty-first year I see nothing desirable but death. What am I that their life is not good enough for me? O God, what am I? . . . Why, Oh my God, cannot I be satisfied with the life that satisfies so many people?
                                                                Florence Nightingale (1850)

Florence Nightingale (1820–1910), the founder of modern nursing, spent the bulk of her life not as a practising nurse but writing thousands of bureaucratic letters and numerous reports on medical reform. At the age of 34 she worked as a nurse for eighteen months during the Crimean War. Her chief contribution to the suffering soldiers who kissed her shadow was as a hospital administrator, arguing about open windows, toothbrushes, endless red tape

– and paying out of her own pocket to have the laundry washed in hot water. Her efforts resulted in a dramatic lowering of the death rate from infection in Army hospitals and barracks.

She lived to be 90, but spent a good deal of her life as an invalid; she was frequently told by her doctors that she was on the brink of death and must rest, yet she worked day and night, driven by ambition and by the nightmare she had faced in the Crimea. Upon her return in 1855 she convinced Queen Victoria of the necessity of setting up a Royal Commission to investigate the health of the Army and, illness and exhaustion notwithstanding, produced her own massive report which was highly respected as a resource on military medical administration. *Notes on Hospitals* revolutionised the theory of hospital administration and construction and throughout the second half of the nineteenth century she acted as consultant on the building and management of many European hospitals.

Florence Nightingale's life is obscured by legend. Occasionally, the familiar Lady-with-the-Lamp all-sweetness-and-light myth gives way to a caricature of neurosis and manipulative ambition; both, however, contrive to diminish her as a person and her significant contribution to medical care.

She was born into a wealthy and well-connected family and bred for idle gentility. Together with her elder sister, Parthenope, she was educated at home by her father, William (always called W E N). The Nightingale sisters studied Greek, Latin, German, Italian, history and philosophy. Florence's desire to study nursing arose in adolescence and persisted despite all the distractions or threats her family could muster. She was an outrageous disappointment to her mother, Fanny, who only wanted her to accept the proposal of one of her numerous eligible suitors. Florence was beautiful, witty, and accomplished in the womanly arts of piano and reading aloud. She was in great demand in the 'best' society and eminently suited to realising her mother's social dreams. But she was captivated by the contemporary spirit of social reform. Furthermore, she believed that she had been 'called' by God to hospital nursing. By the age of 30 her sense of calling had not diminished in the slightest, although her mother's continued frustration of her goal had led Florence to suffer from hallucinations, insomnia, complete disinterest in social life, and an acute desire to die.

Of course, Fanny had not set out deliberately to make her daughter suicidal. She merely wanted what every good Victorian mother wanted: a dutiful daughter who would become a dutiful wife. She was understandably mystified by Florence's passion for the nursing profession; it was a highly disreputable form of work which in those days often meant that a woman would spend her life in drunkenness, filth and possibly prostitution. Even after fourteen years (Florence had been 'called' at 16), Fanny had not made the slightest concession to her daughter's alarming inclinations, nor shown any interest in discussing the suggestions Florence put forth of places where she might receive 'respectable' medical training. And if Fanny was adamant, her elder daughter, Parthe, was hysterical: hospitals could not be mentioned without bringing out the smelling salts to revive Parthe, whose delicate sensibilities recoiled from this immoral and degrading topic.

Eventually, a few friends of the family became so alarmed by Florence's mental and physical health that they began hatching plots to extract her from the clutches of her family. Trips to Italy, Switzerland and Egypt, and lengthy sojourns in Paris, did nothing to distract her from her calling; she would not be reconciled to her station in life as a much-sought-after, beautiful, rich woman. While on holiday in Egypt with family friends (the Bracebridges), Florence began to show every sign of losing her mind and her will to live. Selma Bracebridge cut the holiday short and they returned home via an infirmary in Germany, where Florence worked for two weeks while her companions holidayed in Munich. Florence had known about the Institution of Deaconesses in Kaisersworth for five years. It was the one place where she thought that Fanny might conceivably permit her to study nursing, because the Deaconesses were a holy order of nuns whose conduct was above reproach. Unlike the Sisters of Mercy in Paris (with whom Florence had also corresponded), they were neither Roman Catholic nor exposed to the filth and moral danger of city life.

On most of her trips abroad Florence had managed to sneak away from her family and investigate foreign hospitals and slums. From this informal research she almost certainly had a greater grasp of conditions in hospitals throughout Europe than any other woman in England; and she was also ahead of most doctors in this broad experience. But her detour to Kaisersworth at the age of 30 was her first opportunity to spend a significant length of time within any type of medical environment. She was jubilant at the end of her visit, during which she had been allowed to help look after children and observe administrative procedures – medical procedures being considered too sordid for a woman, particularly one of Florence's breeding.

This proved too much for Fanny, however, and, upon her return, Florence was sentenced to be at Parthe's beck and call for six months; as Parthe's 'slave' she could not mention nursing, or, indeed, hardly have a private thought. She again became depressed. But this time, Florence finally decided that she must follow her own will, irrespective of her family's views. Fanny gave way only under pressure from respected family friends and the evident decline in Florence's health. Parthe was so overwrought that she was ordered by doctors to take a cure at Carlsbad, a well-known spa located near Kaisersworth. Everything was held in strictest secrecy in order that the family name should not be disgraced, and preparations were made as if for a holiday-cum-rest-cure. Fanny and Parthe went to Carlsbad, and Florence returned to Kaisersworth.

Once at Kaisersworth, she tried to communicate the harmlessness of her occupation:

July 1851

Dear Mother,

. . . On Sunday I took the sick boys a long walk along the Rhine; two Sisters were with me to help me to keep order. They were all in ecstasies with the beauty of the scenery, and really I thought it very fine too in its way – the broad mass of waters flowing ever on slowly and calmly to their destination, and all that unvarying horizon – so like the slow, calm, earnest, meditative German character.

The world here fills my life with interest, and strengthens me in body and mind. I succeeded directly to an office, and am now in another, so that until yesterday I never had time even to send my things to the wash. We have ten minutes for each of our meals, of which we have four. We get up at 5 . . . Several evenings in the week we collect in the Great Hall for a Bible lesson. The Pastor sent for me once to give me some of his unexampled instructions; the man's wisdom and knowledge of human nature is wonderful; he has an instinctive acquaintance with every character in his place. Except that once, I have only seen him in his rounds.

The operation to which Mrs Bracebridge alludes was an amputation at which I was present, but which I did not mention to —— knowing that she would see no more in my interest in it than the pleasure dirty boys have in playing in the puddles about a butcher's shop. I find the deepest interest in everything here, and am so well in body and mind. This is Life. Now I know what it is to live and to love life, and really I should be sorry now to leave life. I know you will be glad to hear this, dearest Mum. God has indeed made life rich in interests and blessings, and I wish for no other earth, no other world but this.

Florence received no encouraging reply. She continued her training at Kaisersworth, which she did not consider prepared her for anything except further training at a large urban hospital. With increasing urgency she wrote again to her mother at the end of August when she had almost completed her internship: 'Give me time, give me faith. Trust me, help me. Say to me, "Follow the dictates of that spirit within thee" . . . My beloved people, I cannot bear to grieve you. Give me your blessing.' Neither Fanny nor Parthe responded to her appeal.

When she rejoined them she was in high spirits and good health, bursting with plans to continue her studies. Years later, Florence gave an account of the reunion: 'They were furiously resentful. They would hardly speak to me. I was treated as if I had come from committing a crime.' Parthe even alleged that her cure had failed because she had been so anxious while Florence was working. In the months that followed, Fanny used this as a reason for forbidding any discussion whatsoever of nursing: Florence's wicked ambitions were destroying her sister's health.

It was at this point that Florence – in a world of high-society parties and London shopping, feeling a suppressed ambition which was again making her life seem grotesque and unbearable – spewed out 'Cassandra', a vitriolic protest against the enforced leisure of upper-class women (this formed Part Two of a longer philosophic work entitled, 'Suggestions for Thought to Searchers after Religious Truth'):

Why have women passion, intellect, moral activity – these three – and a place in society where no one of the three can be exercised? Men say that God punishes for complaining. No, but men are angry with misery. They are irritated with women for not being happy. They take it as a personal offence . . .

And women . . . go about teaching their daughters that 'women have no passions.' In the conventional society, which men have made for women, and women have accepted, they *must* have none, they must act the farce of hypocrisy, the lie that they are without passion – and therefore what else can they say to their daughters, without giving the lie to themselves? . . .

Women often strive to live by intellect. The clear, brilliant, sharp radiance of intellect's moonlight rising upon such an expanse of snow is dreary, it is true, but some love its solemn desolation, its silence, its solitude – if they are but *allowed* to live in it; if they are not perpetually baulked or disappointed. But a woman cannot live in the light of intellect. Society forbids it. Those conventional frivolities, which are called her 'duties', forbid it. Her 'domestic duties', high-sounding words, which, for the most part, are bad habits (which she has not the courage to enfranchise herself from, the strength to break through), forbid it . . .

What wonder, if, wearied out, sick at heart with hope deferred, the springs of will broken, not seeing clearly where her duty lies, she abandons intellect as a vocation and takes it only, as we use the moon, by glimpses through her tight-closed window shutters?

The family? It is too narrow a field for the development of an immortal spirit, be that spirit male or female. The chances are a thousand to one that, in that small sphere, the task for which that immortal spirit is destined by the qualities and the gifts which its Creator has placed within it, will not be found.

The family uses people, *not* for what they are, nor for what they are intended to be, but for what it wants them for – its own uses. It thinks of them not as what God has made them but as the something which it has arranged that they shall be. If it wants someone to sit in the drawing-room, *that* someone is supplied by the family, though that member may be destined for science, or for education, or for active superintendence by God, i.e. by the gifts within.

This system dooms some minds to incurable infancy, others to silent misery.

Disgorging her venom in prose did not quieten Florence's spirits. She felt as trapped as ever by the conditions she decried in 'Cassandra' and surreptitiously continued to seek nursing positions. When she was finally offered a job, she was 32, and she decided she must move away from home. Parthe raged herself into a state of frenzy and collapse; Fanny had to be revived with smelling salts. When the hiring committee heard of her family's disapproval, Florence's appointment was withdrawn and only after lengthy negotiations was she reinstated. At this point, her father could bear the family turmoil no longer. In a timely gesture of support he gave her an allowance of £500 a year – a generous sum meant to enable her to maintain her standard of living. Fanny refused to give her blessing, saying: 'It would be useless upon what I consider as being an impossible undertaking.' The 'impossible undertaking' was the post of 'Superintendent of the Institution for the Care of Sick Gentle-women in Distressed Circumstances' in London's Harley Street.

A year later, when Florence was offered a position as Superintendent of Nurses at King's College Hospital in South London, familiar lamentations broke out. By this time, however, the opposition was weakening, and Fanny implored her to nurse babies or seek a private post: anything, but anything, was preferable to working in a hospital.

Perhaps only something so romantic as the Crimean War could have prevented a final schism in this desperate family. With her relatively wide experience, her detailed reports on hospital conditions, and her perseverance in bending the ears of her powerful contacts (not least, the Secretary of the War Office, Sidney Herbert), Florence had convinced herself and everybody else that the scorned profession of nursing would be redeemed on the battlefield under her scrupulous supervision, and that the miserable lot of British soldiers could be improved by the angelic ministrations of nurses.

Her biographer, Cecil Woodham-Smith, spared no mercy for Florence's family: 'Her appointment caused a sensation . . . No woman had ever been so distinguished before, and Fanny and Parthe were ecstatic. Forgetting they had brought her to the verge of insanity by their opposition, they congrat-ulated themselves on the scope of the experience which qualified her for her mission. They immediately came to London to share the excitement.' Parthe shared fully the spirit of family pride, writing to a friend:

> The Government has asked, I should say entreated, Flo to go out and help in the hospital in Scutari. I am sure you will feel that it is a great and noble work, and this is a real duty; for there is no one, as they tell her, and I believe truly, who has the knowledge and the zeal necessary to make such a step succeed . . . The way in which all things have tended to and fitted her for this is so very remarkable that one cannot but believe she was intended for it.'

Florence was unimpressed by their conversion. Although the following letter of blessing from Fanny was among the few personal possessions which she took with her to the Crimea, there is evidence in her future writings that it was too little, too late:

[1851]

Dear Florence,

God speed you on your errand of mercy, my own dearest child. I know he will, for He has given you such loving friends* and they will always be at your side to help in all your difficulties. They came just when I felt that you must fail for want of strength, and more mercies will come in your hour of need. They are so wise and good, they will be to you what no one else could. They will write to us and help you in that and all ways. They are an earnest of blessings to come. I do not ask you to spare yourself for your own sake, but for the sake of the cause. Ever thine.

From then on, glory crowded in upon glory. Florence was revered and Fanny (from whatever motives) could not get enough of it. The glory was all in London, with Fanny; the exhausting labour, excruciating suffering and infuriating incompetence was with Florence in the Crimea. The inept and negligent Army Medical Corps was not grateful for Florence's interventions – nor, certainly, for her public acclaim. She was now obstructed in her nursing duties, not by two distraught women, but by an enormous and time-honoured bureacracy; now there were intractable male egos rather than delicate feminine sensibilities to be threatened by her intelligence, her efficiency, and her tireless dedication to a wholesale reorganisation of the hospital at Scutari on both medical and administrative levels.

After a year of toil and frustration for Florence in Scutari, a public meeting was called in London 'to give expression to a general feeling that the services of Miss Nightingale in the Hospitals of the East demand the grateful recognition of the British people'. The meeting was overcrowded and wildly enthusiastic. A brooch was presented, inscribed by Queen Victoria, 'To Miss Florence Nightingale, as a mark of esteem and gratitude for her devotion towards the Queen's brave soldiers from Victoria R 1855'. A fund was started, to 'establish an institute for the training, sustenance and protection of nurses, paid and unpaid'.

Fanny was overjoyed and wrote to Florence:

29 November 1855

. . . The 29th of November. The most interesting day of thy mother's life. It is very late, my child, but I cannot go to bed without telling you that your meeting has been a glorious one . . . the like has never happened before, but will, I trust, from your example gladden the heart of many future mothers.

---

*Selma and Henry Bracebridge accompanied Florence to the Crimea, as chaperones.

For her part, Florence was desperately tired and overworked. However much Queen Victoria and her mother might esteem her and despite the affection she earned from the soldiers, the Army Medical Corps loathed her popularity; they continued to undermine her and tried to prevent her from working. Despite their best efforts, however, they never entirely succeeded. In the year since her arrival and her hard-won reforms, the rate of death from infection at Scutari had dropped from 42 percent to 2 percent. Florence replied wearily to her mother's exuberance: 'My reputation has not been a boon in my work – but if you have been pleased, that is enough.'

Florence returned from the Crimea in 1855, ill and exhausted after eighteen months of struggle. Over the next several years her letters to her mother were factual and infrequent, steering clear of disagreeable topics. Although Fanny sent frequent gifts of fresh flowers and fruits to Florence's home in London, Florence consistently favoured her friends and her father with her confidences and her long letters. (Throughout her life she maintained an active correspondence with her father, pouring out her thoughts and activities in great detail and reminding him on a few occasions that 'my letters are for you alone'.) There were long periods when there were no letters or visits because Florence was ill and working too hard; even at the best of times, she found any contact with her family too upsetting. Aunt Mai (her father's sister), who lived with Florence and managed many of her affairs, was charged with strictly guarding her from her family for long periods of time. She wrote letters reporting on Florence's activities and state of health, intercepted any letters which came in reply, and insured that no visits were contemplated. Florence's generally poor state of health allowed her to appropriate months and even years to herself and her work; she deemed life as an invalid more constructive than an active existence in which anyone might intrude, offer invitations or expect her to socialise.

Florence enjoyed a great deal of prestige – although no real power – after her return from the Crimea. She visited Queen Victoria and Prince Albert several times in Scotland at Balmoral and succeeded in impressing them so much that, after their first meeting, the Queen wrote to the Commander-in-Chief: 'I wish we had her in the War Office.' In one of her few letters to Fanny during this period (25 September 1856), she made an offhand remark about meeting the Secretary of State for War while visiting the Queen and Prince: '. . . The Queen has wished me to remain to see Lord Panmure here rather than in London because she thinks it more likely something might be done with him here with her back to me. I don't but I'm obliged to succumb . . .'

What needed to be done, in Florence's view, was to reorganise the War Office. Lord Panmure did not want all the bother of wholesale reform and, Queen or no, the scheme was opposed, delayed and ignored for nearly a year. Finally, a Royal Commission was appointed with Florence's loyal ally Sidney Herbert as chairman. Florence was overjoyed. Over the next few years she was engrossed in preparing reports and statistics for the Commission and she drove everyone she could enlist into a frenzy of work. Her 'cabinet' of helpers

included her Aunt Mai, her nephew Arthur Clough, as well as eminent
medical men, statisticians and politicians. The Commission succeeded in
establishing new procedures which reduced the rate of death from infection in
barracks, improved the training of army medical personnel, and provided
soldiers with more comfortable living quarters and a better diet.

Catastrophe struck when Sidney Herbert died in August 1861, after a
three-year illness during which Florence had worked him remorselessly,
because 'without him I can do nothing'. When he died she was grief-stricken;
she collapsed entirely for several months. Without him, there could be no
more grand campaign in the War Office; she was, after all, an outsider and a
woman. However, she was still asked to fight smaller battles: arguing over
the construction of a new military hospital; organising medical services
during the American Civil War; planning strategies for medical provision in a
near-miss war between England and America (the Canadian Expedition)
which was averted by the intervention of Prince Albert; and so on. Florence
wrote to Fanny six months after Sidney Herbert's death:

7 March 1862

Dear Mother,
     . . . I have lost all. All the others have children or some high and
inspiring interest to live for – while I have lost husband and children
and all. And am left to the dreary hopeless struggle . . . It is this desperate guerrilla warfare ending in so little which makes me impatient
of life. I, who could once do so much . . . I think what I have felt most
during my last three months of extreme weakness is the not having one
single person to give one inspiring word, or even one correct fact. I am
glad to end a day which can never come back, gladder to end a night,
gladder still to end a month.

Florence had made a conscious decision not to marry before she went to the
Crimea. Having struggled against her family for most of her life, she could
not – given the choice – willingly undertake yet another set of obligations,
and spend the rest of her life arguing with a husband about where her 'duty'
lay. But, though she firmly renounced intimacy, she did not relish solitude; at
various points in her life, she expressed deep bitterness that her 'calling' left so
little time and energy even for friendships. Under the conditions described in
'Cassandra', marriage would have meant the absolute death of her vocation;
and she was probably accurate in her assessment that it was unlikely that she
would be lucky enough to marry under any other conditions. When she was
considering the proposal of Richard Monckton Milnes, a man she loved and
admired, she had written:

I have an intellectual nature which requires satisfaction and that would
find it in him. I have a passionate nature which requires satisfaction and
that would find it in him. I have a moral, and an active, nature which
requires satisfaction, and that would not find it in his life . . . I could

satisfied to spend a life with him in combining our different powers in some great object. I could not satisfy this nature by spending a life with him in making society and arranging domestic things.

The letter to Fanny after Sidney Herbert died is one of her few admissions of vulnerability, in which she dared admit the drawbacks of her decision not to marry – a 'choice' which, to this day, provides critics with ammunition for attacks on her character.*

With Sidney Herbert, at least, she had had a 'marriage of true minds'. Both Sidney and his wife, Liz, had been utterly devoted to Florence and they had championed her work to the point of sacrificing their own domestic routines, cancelling family holidays and working to exhaustion to satisfy Florence's impatience. Within a short period, however, Florence also lost the three other people who were closest to her. Dr Alexander, her colleague and ally since they worked together in Scutari, died in February 1860; Arthur Clough, her nephew who had lived and worked with her since her return from the Crimea, died only a few months before Sidney. But the blow which Florence probably most resented in her adult life was the 'abandonment' of Aunt Mai who had been with her in the Crimea and had stayed with her ever since their return to London. After years of pressure from family and friends, in early 1860 Aunt Mai returned to her own family.

In 1857, Florence had written about Aunt Mai and Fanny:

The REAL fathers and mothers of the human race are NOT the fathers and mothers of the flesh . . . For every one of my 18,000 children, for every one of these poor tiresome Harley Street creatures, I have expended more motherly feeling and action in a week than my mother has expended on me in 37 years . . . I have had a spiritual mother without whom I could have done nothing, who has been all along a 'Holy Ghost' to me and lately has lived the life of a porter's wife for me.

When Aunt Mai left she began to lash out against all womanhood. She had never had great faith in women and had always suspected that men were better friends and allies. Writing to her friend 'Clarkey',† in December 1861, about the support she had received from Sidney Herbert, Dr Alexander and Arthur Clough, she was more convinced than ever:

---

*In a review of *Florence Nightingale: Reputation and Power* by F.B. Smith, Richard Shannon says that the purpose of the book is to expose her 'as a consummate confidence-trickster: an hysteric, a bully, a liar, a manipulator, an ingrate, an intriguer, a bluffer, a well-born meddler with a lust for authority, sexually infantile, a betrayer, dogmatically ignorant, avid for fame . . .' (*TLS*, 28 May 1982). There is no doubt that she was ambitious, that she made errors in judgement and that she was often not a very pleasant person. Although she could be charming at times, she was also known for being unsympathetic, and for demanding to get a job done at almost any human cost. However, one cannot help but wonder what 'sexually infantile' (read: unmarried) is doing in the same list as 'bully, liar, betrayer . . .'. Precisely what magnitude of character-flaw is it (and still, in 1982) to be a spinster?

†This was her affectionate name for Madame Mohl, an old family friend.

. . . you say women are more sympathetic than men. Now if I were to write a book out of my experience, I should begin, *Women have no sympathy*. Yours is the tradition – mine is the conviction of experience. I have never found one woman who has altered her life by one iota for me or my opinions. Now look at my experience of men . . .

No woman has excited 'passions' among women more than I have. Yet I leave no school behind me. My doctrines have taken no hold among women. Not one of my Crimean followers learnt anything from me – or gave herself for one moment, after she came home, to carry out the lesson of that war, or of those hospitals. I have lived with a sister 30 years, with an aunt four or five, with a cousin two or three. Not one has altered one hour of her existence for me. Not one has read one of my books so as to be able to save me the trouble of writing or telling it all over again . . .

This letter was written within a few months of Sidney Herbert's and Arthur Clough's deaths. Florence was nearly demented with grief and loss and her allegations about the women she had known are manifestly unjust. Aunt Mai had not been the only woman to stand by Florence. Alongside her, Selma Bracebridge and 'Clarkey' had pitted their good social standings against Fanny's early recalcitrance; all three had written lengthy letters to Fanny, implored Florence to stand up for herself, and acted as 'chaperone' on the rare occasions when Florence was allowed out of the house. Selma and her husband had also tasted the horrors of Scutari for thirteen months, acting *in loco parentis* to lend respectability to Florence's presence there, meanwhile working day and night as she did. Liz Herbert, too, had often pleaded Florence's case before Sidney when he thought a cause was lost and Florence wanted to carry on. And in 1860, one of Florence's cousins, Hilary Bonham Carter, had come to serve as her private secretary and maid for an indefinite period. (This was cut short only by Florence's insistence that she must return to her own work as a sculptor and not play the traditional feminine self-sacrificing role when she had talents of her own to develop.) Not least, Harriet Martineau* wrote many articles in support of Florence's work and often steered interesting projects her way. Nonetheless, the highest accolades were always reserved for Aunt Mai – so hers was the deepest betrayal. Florence refused to speak to her for twenty years.

But her anger did not stop there. Anyone might be forgiven for supposing that the author of 'Cassandra' was a staunch feminist. But Florence had never been a great sympathiser with the suffrage cause† – for reasons which may

---

*See pp. 88–91.
†Throughout the 1860s Florence Nightingale carried on a debate with John Stuart Mill about women's rights, their entry into medical schools, and the suffrage campaign. Her argument against the suffrage campaign was, in many ways, a very radical position. She wrote to Mill in 1867, '. . . that women should have the suffrage, I think no one can be more deeply convinced than I . . . (but) there are evils which press much more hardly on women than the want of the suffrage . . . Till a married woman can be in possession of her own property there can be no love or justice . . .'

She was asked in 1867 to join the National Society for Woman's Suffrage and refused; but in

also explain her harsh accusations against the very women who had been most devoted to her. It appears that she never recovered from her early experiences in which the full weight of society's limiting restrictions on women were forced upon her by her mother and sister. Despite the numerous daring, intelligent and supportive women whom she met and worked with, Florence never seemed able to overcome her feelings of distrust, based on her relationship with Fanny and Parthe. She felt that she could not rely on women and never really believed most women capable of anything other than petty domestic tyranny. Her journal entry in 1857 about 'the real fathers and mothers' indicates that she did not think that Fanny had mothered her – certainly not in any positive sense. Her resentments about Fanny are also evident in 'Cassandra', where she twice notes that in order for heroines in novels to have lives of any interest, their mothers (and often their entire families) must be killed off by the novelist before the story can begin. Thus, in her view, all interesting women are orphans; all women who are not doomed to be orphans are doomed to be uninteresting.

As a woman struggling in a man's world, Florence had learned to latch on to powerful men in order to achieve her aims. She had internalised the negative view that society had of women's abilities; all the parts of herself that she felt were admirable, she labelled 'man-like'. Thus, she could neither respect women in general enough to wish them more status in the world, nor transcend her early experiences enough to credit the support of women when it came.

Florence's father died in 1873 and she was forced to stop working for the next seven years in order to nurse her mother. Fanny died when Florence was 60; they had eventually made their peace and, in the final years, it was frustration rather than anger that Florence expressed at having her work interrupted. She wrote to 'Clarkey' after Fanny's death (June 1881):

> I cannot remember a time when I have not longed for death. After Sidney Herbert's death and Clough in 1861, twenty years ago, for years and years I used to watch for death as no sick man ever watched for morning. It is strange that now I am bereft of all, I crave for it less. I want to do a little work, a little better, before I die.

Florence Nightingale lived to be 90 and managed to do more than 'a little work' in her remaining years. Before Fanny's illness had demanded her attention, Florence had been active in the reform of the Poor Law, the establishment of district nursing, and the reorganisation of the Nightingale Nursing School. She had also worked for nearly two decades as an adviser on health

---

1868 she became a member and in 1871 she allowed her name to be added to the general committee. Six years later, she revised her views on women doctors and signed a petition urging the admission of women to medical degrees at the University of London.

in India, writing reports, collecting statistics, and meeting with officials on their way to and from service in the distant colony. As soon as Florence returned from her enforced absence at home, she began crusading for liberal reforms in Indian local government and advising the new Indian Viceroy. She finally retired from the Indian campaign in 1894, at 74, after thirty years of lobbying and research on wide-ranging issues connected with sanitation, including housing, irrigation, taxation and land distribution. In 1882 she was called on one last time by the War Office to provide a party of nurses for the Egyptian campaign; upon receiving reports on medical conditions she helped set up a committee of inquiry to investigate inefficiencies in the Army Hospital Corps and to suggest guidelines for reorganisation.

By 1896 she was partially blind and she quietly withdrew from active life. Three years before her death, when she had become completely blind and senile, King Edward VII bestowed upon her the Order of Merit, the first time it had been awarded to a woman.

Louisa May Alcott and her mother Abigail, 1843–75

Work is and always has been my salvation, and I thank the Lord for inventing it.
Louisa May Alcott

Louisa May Alcott (1832–88), author of *Little Women*, was born in Germantown, Pennsylvania, the second daughter of Amos Bronson Alcott and Abigail May Alcott (known in the family as 'Abba' or 'Marmee'). Louisa grew up around Concord, Massachussetts, in an atmosphere of transcendental philosophy and New England liberalism, exemplified by Emerson, Hawthorne and Thoreau – all of whom were friends of the Alcott family.* Daily life was governed by the uncompromising moralism which accompanied this wave of philosophic and political idealism and, even when she was very young, Louisa's parents frequently discussed her moral failings with each other and with her. She was constantly made aware of her imperfections, the gravest being her strong-willed and passionate nature.

Louisa's feelings towards her parents were nonetheless tender and affectionate; as an adult, she often lived with them and seems to have enjoyed their company. Abba, the model for 'Marmee' in *Little Women*, was as warm and loving as her namesake (although a good deal less conventional in her views). Bronson, his incessant moralising notwithstanding, was a very affectionate father. However, he was often carried away by his idealism and rarely earned an income which would support his family. He preferred to hold philosophy seminars, which meant that the family existed in penury and

---

*Her parents were also staunch supporters of the Abolitionist movement and the campaign for women's rights. Abba kept up a friendship with the extraordinary anti-slavery activist Lydia Marie Child; Bronson was friendly with some of the most radical feminists of the day, including Lucy Stone (p. 97) and Elizabeth Cady Stanton.

humiliating debt until Louisa managed to produce what she called 'rubbishy tales for they pay the best'.

From an early age, Louisa had been made aware that she would be expected to assume responsibilities that her father was above taking seriously. When she was 11, Abba presented her with an engraving of a sick mother and a hard-working daughter, with the accompanying note:

12 March 1843

Dear Louisa,

I enclose a picture for you which I always admired very much – for in my imagination I have thought you might be just such an industrious good daughter – and that I might be a sick but loving mother, looking to my daughter's labors for my daily bread.*

Mother

Not surprisingly, several of Louisa's letters to Abba include a list of her recent earnings. She tried various ways of earning a living, including teaching, sewing and domestic service to families in the Boston area. Inspired by Florence Nightingale,† she worked as a nurse during the Civil War; however, after only three weeks she came down with typhoid pneumonia and had to return home. Her first financially successful book was *Hospital Sketches*, which was based on her nursing experience. Before writing *Little Women*, she had several stories published in national magazines: one, called 'Happy Women', she had produced upon being paid a large cash advance to write 'one column of advice to Young Women'. She recorded this 'enthusiastic moment' in her journal: ' "Happy Women" was the title, and I put in my list all the busy, useful independent spinsters I know, for liberty is a better husband than love to many of us. This was a nice little episode in my trials of an authoress, so I record it.'

She wrote *Little Women* in 1868 to please her publisher and because her father thought it was a good idea. With its publication she became famous and achieved financial security for her entire family. She began the second part of *Little Women* immediately after publication of Part One, amidst a deluge of entreaties from her fans around the country. Her journal entry for 1 November reports: 'Girls write to ask who the little women marry, as if that was the only end and aim of a woman's life. I *won't* marry Jo to Laurie to please anyone.'

Like her parents, Louisa May Alcott was an ardent feminist. She and her sister were the first women to vote in Concord, the birthplace of American

---

*This sentiment was echoed repeatedly over the next thirty-three years until Abba's death. In 1875 she wrote to Louisa: 'my daughters will give me their care for the short future now left me to work in.'
†See pp. 99–111.

independence, and Louisa was a regular contributor of forthright articles to the *Women's Journal* (the newspaper founded by Lucy Stone and Henry Blackwell). She financed a clinic for women doctors in Boston from the proceeds of her books; she used her influence to get her publishers to bring out books on the suffrage movement; and she corresponded with Lucy Stone and Susan B. Anthony* on the subject which she believed to be 'the most vital question of the age: the emancipation of the white slaves of America'. In many ways, Louisa's feminist credentials are impeccable. Echoing her own activism, many of her female characters in the stories written after *Little Women* also desired an independent life. (The heroine of 'Rose in Bloom', for example, says to a man who has just proposed marriage, 'A woman has a right and duty to a profession. Would *you* be content to be told to enjoy yourself, then marry and do nothing more til you die?')

In her personal life, the issue was not so easy to resolve. Louisa was virtually addicted to self-sacrifice and had no idea how to live for herself. After her mother died, she wrote in her journal: 'I think I shall soon follow her, and am quite ready to go now that she no longer needs me.' Her letters and journals reveal that she was never very happy, and it is arguable that her deeply-held conviction of her own evil nature might have made her miserable in any circumstances. It seems as if self-sacrifice was her 'neurotic' adaptation to her family and femininity, much as illness was for Florence Nightingale and Olive Schreiner.† Self-sacrifice did not make her happy, but it made it possible for her to cope with her guilt about never being content to be just a 'little woman'. Even when the family was well out of financial difficulty, Louisa continued to ruin her health through overwork, tormenting herself with a sense of obligation to earn more money.

The closest she could come to a resolution of these conflicts was to work: by writing best-sellers she could reconcile service to her family with her own fiery spirit, which longed for an outlet. She used the term 'vortex' to describe her frenzied state of energy and concentration when she worked – sometimes for weeks at a time, with scarcely any food or sleep. Scattered throughout her journal are notes reminding herself to 'work slowly for fear of a breakdown'. When she re-read her 1868 journal eight years later, she noted in the margin: 'Too much work for one young woman; no wonder she broke down.' Yet she loathed being interrupted and she continued writing until the year she died (*Jo's Boys* was written in 1886 and stories were still appearing in 1887 and 1888).

Louisa May Alcott's first book was *Flower Fables*. It consisted of stories written for Emerson's daughter and was published shortly before she wrote this letter presenting a copy to Abba:

---

*See pp. 116–18.
†See pp. 99–111 and 134–39.

25 December 1854

Dear Mother,

Into your Christmas stocking I have put my 'first-born', knowing that you will accept it with all its faults (for grandmothers are always kind), and look upon it merely as an earnest of what I may yet do; for, with so much to cheer me on, I hope to pass in time from fairies and fables to men and realities.

Whatever beauty or poetry is to be found in my little book is owing to your interest in and encouragement of all my efforts from the first to the last; and if ever I do anything to be proud of, my greatest happiness will be that I can thank you for that, as I may do for all the good there is in me; and I shall be content to write if it gives you pleasure . . .

I am ever your loving daughter,
Louy

The following letter was written at the start of a crucial year for Louisa – she wrote *Little Women* between May and July and it was published in October:

January 1868

[Dear Marmee]

Things look promising for the new year. F. [has paid] $20 for the little tales, and wrote two every month; G. $25 for the 'Bells'; L. $100 for the two 'Proverb' stories. L. takes all I'll send; and F. seems satisfied.

So my plan will work well, and I shall make my $1,000 this year in spite of sickness and worry. Praise the Lord and keep busy, say I.

I am pretty well, and keep so busy I haven't time to be sick. Every one is very clever to me; and I often think as I go larking round, independent, with more work than I can do, and half-a-dozen publishers asking for tales, of the old times when I went meekly from door to door peddling my first poor little stories, and feeling so rich with $10.

It's clear that Minerva Moody is getting on, in spite of many downfalls, and by the time she is a used up old lady of seventy or so she may finish her job, and see her family well off. A little late to enjoy much may be; but I guess I shall turn in for my last long sleep with more content, in spite of the mortal weariness, than if I had folded my hands and been supported in elegant idleness, or gone to the devil in fits of despair because things moved so slowly.

Keep all the money I send; pay up every bill; get comforts and enjoy yourselves. Let's be merry while we may, and lay up a bit for a rainy day.

With which gem from Aristotle, I am, honored Madam, your dutiful and affectionate,

L.M. Alcott

Regards to Plato.* Don't he want new socks? Are his clothes getting shiny?

Most of Abba's letters were systematically destroyed by either Abba or Louisa to eliminate comments which in retrospect displeased them. This one somehow seemed acceptable and escaped the purge:

30 December 1875

My Dear Louy,

. . . We interchanged little gifts at Christmas . . . a book called 'Thrift' by [Samuel] Smiles – capital for this leaky craft you are working so hard to tow into safe waters – it is full of fine instruction. I ought to have had it 40 years ago. May is charmed with it – Father does not think he needs it. Thrift is more of a positive virtue than I was aware of – it gives dignity to life, to economize the means of living – and what we save from our luxuries often enables us to furnish the necessities of life to others. May and I have chosen this word as our talisman for the year 1876 – so she buys a book for $1 and draws a prize of a diamond ring worth $45 – ha ha . . .

The Darwin theory of evolution is done up well by E. P. Whiffle. The illustration is coarse but effective. C— is going thru Darwin scientifically – there's where he gets his devil. Long life to him. I wish he would gobble all the men up, with their 'tails and vertebrates' – the women could then rule the world and bring some order out of chaos – some right out of this complicated mess of wrong. You see a little of it in N.Y. – and Boston is waking up to the knowledge of evil, [which] is devouring it's best substance in that doomed city – corruption is in their counsels and crime stalks in their streets unheeded – let me hope that as our roughest get educated in young days, virtue will finally prevail. I will not whine but hope on.

. . . I wish you a happy New Year. Health, Prosperity and all the happiness you are capable of – one chain of bliss – no links of woe.

Marmee

By the age of 40 Louisa had fulfilled the vow she made when she was 20: the family was completely out of debt. She had also been able to send her sister to Paris to study art and had even invested money in railway bonds for her parents' security in old age. She wrote twenty books in all. Her major publications include *Moods* (1865); *Little Men* (1870); *Eight Cousins* (1873);

---

*Her name for her father.

Work (1873); 'A Modern Mephistopheles' (1877); and *Jo's Boys* (1886). She died at the age of 55.

Susan B. Anthony to her mother Lucy, 1870

Susan B. Anthony (1820–1906) was one of the early members of the women's rights movement in America and became its most central and committed figure. She was brought up in a Quaker family in rural Pennsylvania, the second of eight children of Lucy and Daniel Anthony. With the customary Quaker dismissal of 'female inferiority', her parents strove to enlarge their children's horizons, first by building a school for them at their mill and, later, enabling Susan and her elder sister to attend a seminary near Philadelphia. Susan and her sisters all worked as teachers from the age of 15. Their father was criticised because the family did not need the daughters' wages to survive, but he was active in political reform movements – including suffrage – and he wanted his daughters to be independent. With his piety and radical politics, Daniel was a major influence in Susan's political development; both her parents attended the founding conference of the Women's Rights Movement in Seneca Falls in 1848 and it was from Daniel's enthusiastic reports of Elizabeth Cady Stanton's resolution demanding woman suffrage that Susan became interested in the movement. By all accounts, Lucy Anthony rarely spoke to her children and they always felt her to be remote. From an early age, however, Susan viewed her mother's domestic labours as a terrible ordeal and she never forgot how determinedly she ran the family farm alone after Daniel's death in 1862.

Susan B. Anthony never married and devoted virtually her entire life to the struggle for women's rights. At 84, after more than fifty years of unremitting struggle, she was given an outstanding welcome in Berlin by the International Council of Women (an organisation she had helped to found) – and was moved to tears by their unexpected tribute. She did not discount her own efforts, but she often undervalued them and underestimated how much she was loved and respected. Feeling that her own speeches were wooden and stilted, she had always esteemed, and given most credit to, such gifted orators as Elizabeth Cady Stanton – her closest and most loyal friend. Yet her own contribution as organiser had supplied the backbone for the suffrage movement. She raised money and organised numerous conventions and petitions; she often provided the essential arguments for other people's speeches; she exercised wide influence as editor of *The Revolution*, a women's rights newspaper; and she sustained the much-needed motivation for renewed assaults upon the legislature. Her own perseverance, sincerity and integrity attracted many sympathisers to the cause – and she continues to inspire people today.

In the long years of struggle, there were many times when the setbacks seemed greater than the advances: when vicious caricatures in the press hit hard and harmed the entire suffrage movement; when hostile audiences booed her from the platform; when senators laughed outright at the thousands of signatures on petitions (the fruit of two whole years' hard work); when even her old and dear friends from her abolitionist and temperance days had turned against her, fearing the taint of her radical and visionary demands for women's rights in both personal and political life. Nonetheless, although often discouraged, Susan never lost faith in the ultimate success of the movement, believing that, if women dedicate their lives, then 'failure is impossible'. She battled on when many other suffragists fell from view, burdened by family demands or discouraged after the Thirteenth Amendment (which extended the vote to black men) had failed yet again to include women. She kept the cause of woman suffrage abreast of the times, integrating it with other economic, political and social issues in a radical manner. She favoured liberalisation of the divorce laws and supported measures which would give women greater economic independence. She also recognised the needs and importance of working women and fought for trade-union representation for them. In many ways she was more radical than many of her contemporaries in either Britain or America, having more in common with the radical suffragists in the north of England than with the more fashionable suffragettes.*

Sadly, Susan B. Anthony did not live to see the completion of her great life-work. It was not until 1920, with the Nineteenth Amendment, that women's right to vote was written into the Constitution – a full fourteen years after her death. The struggle, dated from the first Women's Rights Convention in Seneca Falls, had lasted seventy-two years.

This letter to her mother, Lucy, was written on Susan's fiftieth birthday. The year had started with an impressive display of strength at a Washington convention, where confidence ran high after the suffrage victory in the territory of Wyoming the previous year and Britain's recent decision to give women taxpayers the vote in municipal elections. This elation was boosted by a further victory in the territory of Utah, giving ample cause for celebration on Susan's birthday.† Even the press had been friendly, and this seemed to mark the turning of the tide. She little knew that a further fifty years of struggle lay ahead.

15 February 1870

My Dear Mother,
    It really seems tonight as if I were parting with something dear – saying good-bye to somebody I loved. In the last few hours I have lived over nearly all of life's struggles, and the most painful is the

---

*The Cause by Ray Strachey and One Hand Tied Behind Us by Jill Liddington and Jill Norris (Virago, 1978) give the history of these two movements.
†These territories refused to reverse their decision for the sake of statehood; eventually, when Wyoming was admitted to the Union in 1890, it became the one state where women could vote.

memory of my mother's long and weary efforts to get her six children up into womanhood and manhood. My thought centers on your struggle especially because of the proof-reading of Alice Cary's story this week.* I can see the old home – the brick-makers – the dinner-pails – the sick mother – the few years of more fear than hope in the new house, and the hard years since. And yet with it all, I know there was an undercurrent of joy and love which makes the summing-up vastly in their favor. How I wish you and Mary and Hannah and Guelma [*her sisters*] could have been here – and yet it is nothing – and yet it is much.

My constantly recurring thought and prayer now are that the coming fraction of the century, whether it be small or large, may witness nothing less worthy in my life than has the half just closed – that no word or act of mine may lessen its weight in the scale of truth and right.

Mary Putnam Jacobi to her mother Victorine, 1870

Mary Putnam Jacobi (1842–1906) became one of America's foremost physicians in the late nineteenth century despite the many obstacles preventing women from achieving adequate medical qualifications at that time. Although Elizabeth Blackwell had passed through medical college in 1849,† over ten years later the doors of the major medical schools were more tightly shut than ever.

Mary's background had not predisposed her to tolerate any such frustration of her ambition. She was the eldest of eleven children (four of whom died when very young). Her parents, Victorine and George Palmer Putnam, were liberal and had always encouraged her plans and projects (George in particular), valuing her precocity as a child and her determination as a young adult. Even though George, a publisher, found medicine a 'repulsive' profession for a woman and would have preferred Mary to become a teacher or pursue her considerable literary talents, he struggled to remain in accord with her, ultimately accepting her decisions and supporting her financially when the family's means would allow.

This is not to suggest that there were no disagreements. In keeping with George's English Victorian upbringing and Victorine's New England background, pride of place was given to The Family. For the most part, as daughter and eldest sister, Mary accepted these responsibilities. When asked

---

*Alice Cary was a popular writer of the day. Alice and her sister Phoebe were regular contributors to *The Revolution*, and their home in New York was a well-known rendezvous for writers, artists, musicians and reformers. Susan had once referred to this Cary 'salon' in a lecture on 'The Homes of Single Women', in order to dispel the widespread fallacy that single women were unwanted and helpless creatures, dependent on some male relative for their livelihood.
†See pp. 91–7.

to delay her studies at the New York College of Pharmacy for two years in order to help her mother with her younger brothers and sisters, she conceded to the request without much argument or resentment. On another occasion, however, it was her 'femininity' that was at issue. Her father wrote to her when she had just left for the Women's Medical School in Philadelphia:

> Now, Minnie, you know very well that I am proud of your abilities and am willing that you should apply them even to the repulsive pursuit (for so it is in spite of oneself) of medical science. But *don't* let yourself be absorbed and gobbled up into that branch of the animal kingdom ordinarily called strong-minded women! . . . All I want to say here is that I do hope and trust you will preserve your feminine character and, with all your other studies, study a little of the proprieties and elegancies of life. Be a lady from the dotting of your i's to the color of your ribbons – and if you must be a doctor and a philosopher, be an attractive and agreeable one and don't abandon yourself so entirely to the snares of metaphysics that you find yourself beyond all influences of faith and trust in the only chart we have to guide us to a happy immortality.

Mary's reply has been lost, but it would appear from her father's later letters that she responded in a lively fashion and somewhat more critically than would have been considered appropriate for a 'lady' of that period.

Mary had always been most attracted by the scientific and academic side of medicine. In view of the increasingly obstructive policies of American colleges, she resolved, after receiving an MD for the various courses completed in New York and Philadelphia, to enter and qualify at the École de Médecine in Paris.

She wrote to her mother when she arrived:

16 April 1867

My Dear Mother,
  . . . You speak of English prejudices. You must know that French prejudices rest upon an entirely different ground from those that obtain in England or America. An Englishman would say that it was indelicate to admit women to study medicine, a Frenchman, that it was dangerous. The French disbelief in women is so rooted, and their social system is constructed so entirely on the principle of keeping young men and women as far apart as flame and gunpowder, that they would consider as a perfect absurdity any attempt on the part of their own countrywomen to study medicine . . . It was upon my appreciation of this kind of prejudice that I based my calculation in coming to Paris instead of to London. I knew well enough that I was not 'dangerous', and that Frenchmen would instantly perceive that I was not, and when once that first difficulty was overcome, that I could be much more at my ease here . . .

Entry to this prestigious establishment was not gained as smoothly as she had hoped, though it would appear that her persistence (coupled with a deliberate absence of the ribbons and giggles so disapprovingly predicted for women medical students) did eventually convince the French professors of her serious intent. Once she had gained admission, the quality of her work and the depth and breadth of her understanding not only surpassed their expectations of her as a woman but also put her in a league above almost all her male counterparts. She earned her PhD after five long years, spent battling first for admission, then for financial security (she wrote articles on French politics for newspapers back home) and, finally, enduring a long wait for the medical schools to re-open after the Franco-Prussian War and ensuing civil turmoil. Throughout her doctorate she received the highest possible commendations in her examinations; her thesis was much praised, and she later received a bronze medal for her overall achievement.

It was during this period in Paris that most of her letters to her mother were written. She wrote regularly to both parents, but, feeling that her mother was weighted down by family responsibilities and cares at an age when she still needed gaiety and excitement in her life, Mary made herself particularly responsible for enlivening Victorine's domestic duties with cheerful, newsy letters:

5 February 1870

My Dear Mother,

I have just received your letter speaking about my examination, and I was delighted to get it, for your last was no less depressing than depressed. I realize keenly how much you need some change of scene, and some little excitement and positive pleasure, such as you could not fail to derive if you saw some of your children succeeding in what they undertake, especially your boys. Be assured that it is one of the great objects of my life, to bring this stir and excitement and success into yours; not pecuniarily – I feel I shall never be rich – I am not cut out to make money – it must rain down upon me before I shall get much of it. But I hope to gain enough to fulfil one legitimate desire; as for the illegitimate ones, there will be no harm in having them starved out . . .

Even though she could not always sustain this tone, it is clear that she wanted constantly to reassure her mother, to alleviate any fears that Victorine may have had about her chosen direction, and to demonstrate that she could survive in a man's profession:

25 March 1867

My Dear Little Mother,

You are too good to bother yourself with so many speculations as to my possible causes for 'blueness'. As you do not specify the letter which gave you so much alarm, I am unable to explain it. I can only say in a general way, that in the first place I am hardly ever blue, in the second I should take good care not to write home while in such a mood, so I do not understand what could have been said in my letter to sound so dreadful . . .

22 April 1867

My Dearest Mother,

. . . I am so sorry you should get anxious about me, or be so 'homesick' for me. I cannot bear to think of your 'wearying' after me – your boy-girl. I believe, with feminine perversity, you care more about me, precisely because I am of so little account to you as a daughter, but am more like a son. Since I have actually brought that situation upon myself, I must at least endeavor to do credit to it. I have a fair prospect here of becoming a thoroughly educated physician, and unless I am, I certainly will never undertake to practice medicine. But such being the prospect and opportunities, I am obliged to make the most of them, and put all homesickness aside until the end is accomplished. But when I once get home – you may be sure I will never leave you again. You are so young, so near my own age (you know there is less difference between your age and mine than between mine and Herbert's [*her second youngest brother*]), we shall have good times together yet . . .

Shortly after her third examination, when it seemed that the end of her doctorate was in sight, Mary wrote to her mother about her long-term plans. Her father wanted her to teach in a women's college, but she was determined to enter the New York Academy of Medicine (as it happened, political events were to delay her fifth and final examination by just over a year*):

13 January 1870

My Dearest Mother,

I received yesterday your letter written just after Christmas . . . It was the day after each of us had passed an examination, – and I at least was quite tired with the preparation for it.

. . . I am somewhat amused at your supposing for an instant that I would go to [the women's college] and very much amused that that blessed father considers it 'more respectable than etc.'. It would be worth while to spend four years at one of the first medical schools in the world – to move heaven and earth and run into debt and what not, for that end! I have already sufficient terror of the demoralization

---

*These events – the Franco-Prussian War, the surrender of the Emperor, the growth of the Paris Commune, the second siege of Paris and the ultimate suppression of the Republicans by the government – stimulated Mary's political development. It was an exciting as well as a depressing time, and she returned home dedicated to radical ideals.

imminent from the atmosphere of New York, with its very slack interest in medical science or progress, its deficient libraries, badly organized schools and hospitals, etc. I am doing my best to accumulate a sufficient fund of original force to make headway against these adverse influences, and to subordinate them to my purposes, instead of allowing them to subordinate me. But to isolate myself completely from medicine and the medical world would be suicidal, and a pure waste of force and time. I am prepared to live in a garret in New York as I have done in Paris – to double my thumb into the palm of my hand when it pushed through my glove – to wear rubbers, with a hole in the heel over shoes that had a hole in the toes, to keep clear of parties for lack of new clothes, etc., etc. All this I have done, and thrived on it, but I should stifle in clover at a girls' college.

Immersion in technical studies is like arsenic eating, – once begun, you must go on, and at a continually increasing dose. I am really astonished to find how this absorption grows upon me. I take a lively interest in politics, when I can hear the papers without reading them, but I hardly open a book that has not some reference to the physical sciences or medicine; and all society that is not of this world, although delightful at short doses and long intervals, bores me if prolonged – or a least would if I ever prolonged it.

Do not suppose that I labor under any illusions in regard to success. I have a fair prospect, and I certainly shall exert every energy to serve the patients who may honor me with their confidence – and thus justify the confidence of others. But it is scarcely possible for a physician to become rich by purely medical means – that is, only visiting his patients when it is necessary, never cajoling or flattering them – devoting his time to the advancement of science rather than to the extension of his clientele. I look upon a rich physician with as much suspicion as a rich priest – and I know perfectly well that since the public are entirely incapable of judging in the higher ranges of intellectual activity or acquirement, the public suffrage will never be in proportion to the amount of trouble taken to acquire knowledge and train intellect. But when one has reached a certain point, one becomes entirely indifferent to this public suffrage, one's entire attention is concentrated, first upon the opinion of the very limited public whose competency one really respects.

The objects that I have in view are the following:

1st. To honestly earn my living 'in that state of life to which it has pleased God to call me'.

2nd. To pay my debts.

3rd. To educate the younger children, those three dear little boys.

4th. To buy you silk dresses, and to succeed sometime and somewhere in sending Edith to Europe.

5th. To accumulate a medical library equal to the library that

Theodore Parker left to the Athenæum, and to secure its enjoyment for all medical students, especially women, for all future generations in New York.

6th. To have a fund by which I can pay the services of a reader during the last ten years of my life, when I shall most probably be blind.

So much for the ends – not too extravagant as you perceive – which depend upon 'filthy lucre'. The others, moral and intellectual, depend almost exclusively upon the amount of knowledge and ability I may succeed in acquiring, and the amount of influence I may be able to exercise, by dint of ideas, obstinacy, force of character, or tact.

These objects are:

1st. The creation of a scientific spirit (which at present does not exist), among women medical students.

2nd. This by rigid training, according to training I may have myself received, and ideas that may be more or less original.

3rd. *Entrée* into the New York Academy of Medicine, in virtue of special medical work that I have already laid out.

4th. Pursuit of numerous important problems in Experimental Theraputics.

As a mild social effort by the side of the technical business which should and must absorb me, I intend having social receptions, when it shall be *de règle* for the guests to come in afternoon dresses instead of silk. This to be intended, not as a crusade against silk, but a demonstration *à la Quaker*, that social enjoyment is not necessarily connected with fine clothes, and that people excluded from other houses by lack of means, may find at mine, comfort and refreshment . . .

When Mary finally returned to America, she was 29. Although she failed to fulfil the first of her aims outlined in the letter above (the library), she did, in 1880, become the first woman member of the New York Academy of Medicine, and in this capacity made available to female colleagues the resources of the Academy's superb library. For sixteen years she lectured at the Women's Medical School, exacting a very high standard of work from her students. Her lectures were unusual for their breadth as well as depth, and when this ultimately became a source of conflict with other staff (who felt that she was intruding on their specialist domains), she resigned rather than compromise her approach. All the while she had maintained her own medical practice and managed to publish over a hundred articles in medical journals, dealing mostly with pathology, neurology, paediatrics, physiology and medical education. She also became involved in the suffrage campaign and wrote a pamphlet called ' "Common Sense" Applied to Woman Suffrage', which was published in 1894. She was instrumental in founding the Working Women's Society and, later, the League for Political Education to carry on suffrage work.

Marriage presented the all-too-familiar conflict for a woman with Mary's goals: two engagements had been made and broken off before she settled for Dr Abraham Jacobi in 1876. What she feared in marriage were the restrictions it might place on her as a professional woman. She had written to her father in 1865 after she decided to break off her first engagement: 'Do I not above all things need freedom of action, and power to carry out the intellectual schemes that are so dear to me as anything else, and might not this other kind of person greatly interfere with that?'

Although she felt under no great social or familial pressure to marry, she did, in time, develop a clear idea of what kind of person 'this other' would have to be. Two years later she wrote to her mother:

29 May 1867

My Dear Mother,

. . . I have no particular desire to marry at any time; nevertheless, if at home, I should ever come across a physician, intelligent, refined, more enthusiastic for his science than me, but who would like me, and for whom I should entertain about the same feeling that I have for Haven [*her eldest brother*], I think I would marry such a person if he asked me, and would leave me full liberty to exercise my profession. Otherwise – no.

Abraham Jacobi seemed to fit the bill, as well as sharing Mary's political sympathies. They had three children: the first boy died very young, the second at the age of 8. Mary never really recovered from this last blow, dear to her though their surviving daughter was.

Around the age of 51, Mary developed a brain tumour which increasingly affected her speech and she eventually became a mute invalid. Right up to her death some thirteen years later, she struggled to maintain communication with her family and friends, and even managed to keep a detailed scientific account of the tumour's progress. She died at the age of 64.

Queen Victoria and her daughter the Crown Princess Victoria Louise, 1867-71

Queen Victoria (1819-1901), was the only child of the German Princess Victoria Mary Louisa of Saxe Coburg and Edward, Duke of Kent, the fourth son of King George III. Although the King had seven sons and five daughters, Victoria was the only direct heir to the English throne.* She grew up ignorant

---

*Princess Charlotte, the only legitimate grandchild of the King, died in childbirth after more than fifty hours of labour; her son, heir to the throne, died at birth. The Duchess of Clarence, married to the King's third son, had two children who died in infancy. The King's two married daughters were childless and his sons mainly preferred mistresses to wives: hence the scarcity of legitimate heirs. Edward, Victoria's father, lived with a mistress for twenty-seven years; in the hope of producing an heir to the throne, he finally began looking for a suitable wife only after Princess Charlotte's death.

of her destiny until the age of 12, when she discovered by 'accident' (while reading a royal genealogical chart which someone had left among her books) that she would become Queen of England. She said that she 'cried much on learning it'.

Victoria's father had died when she was less than a year old and she was brought up by her mother and a German governess. The dominating memory of Victoria's childhood was of her mother's perpetual vigilance: she felt that she 'was extremely crushed and kept under and hardly dared say a word'. Until the day she became Queen, at the age of 18, she always slept in her mother's bedroom and she was never allowed to walk downstairs without someone holding her hand.

Despite her earlier reservations, Victoria relished her sudden independence and the responsibilities of monarchy. She fell deeply in love with her cousin, Albert, Prince of Saxe Coburg, and they were married when they were both 20 years old. Their famous reign gave her much satisfaction and happiness, but when Albert died at only 42 she retired from public life for many years, inconsolable.

Of their nine children, the eldest, Victoria Louise (1840–1901), married the Crown Prince of Prussia, Frederick William ('Fritz'). It was a political match but they loved each other and were united in their idealism: they resolved to dedicate their lives to the creation of a unified, constitutional and democratic Germany. For thirty years, however, they waited for Frederick's father, King William I, to die or abdicate so that Frederick could ascend the throne and put through their reforms. But the King lived on, falling steadily under the sway of Bismarck, and Prussia veered in the opposite direction, toward autocracy and militarism.

As the daughter of Queen Victoria (whom Bismarck saw as being Prussia's arch-enemy – long before she was), Victoria Louise found herself in an impotent and unpopular position. At Bismarck's urging, the Prussian people distrusted her. Despite her adopted loyalties to Prussia, she always remained very English in her manners, dress and liberal ideas; her vivacity and habit of speaking her mind jarred in the formal Prussian court and made her many enemies. She had five children (the eldest of whom would become Kaiser Wilhelm) and, while waiting for real power, she busied herself with prison reform and the improvement of hospital services.* The King did not die until he was 91 and Frederick outlived him by less than one hundred days, leaving Victoria Louise a grieving widow in a somewhat hostile country. However, she continued her work with charities and reform movements and lived in Prussia until her death from cancer of the spine at the age of 61.

---

*Like her mother, Victoria Louise was a great admirer of Florence Nightingale (see pp. 99–111). When in London, the Crown Princess would sometimes visit Florence and discuss matters of health reform with her.

These letters begin during the period when Bismarck was urging the King of Prussia towards war with France. While Queen Victoria's upbringing had left her sympathetic to Prussia, the schemes of 'that terrible man', Bismarck, and the suffering incurred by them soon caused her to withdraw her (very private) support. She was grieved by the way these international antagonisms divided her extended family. Although her warm and trusting relationship with Victoria Louise was never at any real risk, she had to stand by miserably while other near and dear relations opposed each other across the battlefield.

The Queen had written to Victoria Louise on 25 January 1867: 'Unlike you I hate politics and nothing but the strongest sense of duty makes me talk about them.' The Crown Princess replied:

2 February 1867

You are quite mistaken if you think I like politics. I should prefer never to hear a single word about them. But I feel a deep interest in the cause of liberty and of progress – on each and every ground, and in all things; and wherever they are concerned I feel my zeal and my interest kindle, and can get very excited. I know no greater pleasure than to discover a like feeling in others, to hear and to have discussion on this subject and to relieve my feelings by giving vent to my enthusiasm for this cause. The course of daily, political events or rather diplomatical small-talk – I think the greatest bore in the world. I love Germany. I glory in national feeling, and I am ambitious for her greatness, unity and happiness. I am anxious that Fritz's endeavours to promote this end may some day be crowned with success, and that dear England may sometime or other look upon us as fit to share her position in the world – not only by the force of our arms, and the military talents of our nation but by the development of our freedom and our progress in civilization. I do not know whether this is being fond of politics. It is more a feeling of the heart than of the head, and consequently a woman's *point de vue*. All interests me that can lead to this result – every branch of science, art and industry, and I should like to help to push on and give all I possess to make the conditions of my fellow creatures (more especially my countrymen) better in every way, to raise them each individually. You see with me the desire is not to meddle with or to direct things which are not my business – I am far too lazy for that – but to try and add my little might to all great and good purposes gives me pleasure, and not for the effect it may produce for myself but for the inward satisfaction it causes. I think this is a part all women may take in politics and the one they are most fit for. Besides which I enjoy hearing clever talk and conversing with them – and I know you like it too.

The Queen wrote on 17 April: 'I fear there is great dishonesty on the part of Bismarck – who makes a proposal to one person and another to another. Still

I hope and pray that so dire a calamity as a war between France and Prussia may be averted.' The Crown Princess replied:

20 April 1867

What you say of Bismarck may be true but I do not think he is in the wrong for once in his life. The aggression comes from France – and it is there they wish for the war and not here. For my part, if the peace cannot be maintained I think it better the war should be now than later – horrible as it is. A war with France will be a very different thing from a war with Austria but if our honour is at stake – for the sake of Germany we must not hang back. That is my feeling and Fritz's and most people's here – not the Queen's [*Fritz's mother, Augusta*]; she fancies that anything is better than war now or war at all. I think the great united empire of Germany will never consolidate itself in peace – before France is not reduced to a second power on the Continent. I consider that as desirable for England as it is for us Germans. But please do not betray me to anyone – this is my own individual opinion and may be worth nothing. I trust and hope that England will not be against us and with France, and assist in dismembering Germany. I dare not think of such a possibility.

Queen Victoria wrote back immediately:

24 April 1867

With respect to what you say regarding the present critical state of affairs, I must say I am surprised at it! The Queen is quite right in wishing for no war, and that is what every woman should do. She should not only wish for it, but should do everything to prevent it. In the present instance it is not France or the Emperor who wish for war – quite the contrary; and I repeat it again – it is Bismarck who has for the last eight months encouraged the Emperor to believe he could get Luxemburg without difficulty.

I can really also not understand how you can say that that proud old state [*France*], which has ever belonged to the Great Powers, which Prussia has only done within the last century, should be made a second-rate Power! She, who stands on a par – or at least next to us – in the advancement of civilisation! I am sorry you should say such a thing. I am afraid the time may come, when Europe will wish France to be strong to keep the ambition of Germany in check.

Those who lightly encourage war, will have to answer in another world for the souls of many innocent lives who have been sacrificed.

Three years later, during the Franco-Prussian War, the Queen wrote to her daughter:

30 August 1870

I should be sorry if Paris were to suffer much, on account of art and its beauty. No one knows where the Emperor is. What will the terms of peace be? If only the French would give up this needless struggle! It would save such thousands of lives! People think it would be far wiser if Germany were not to ask for Lorraine and Alsace because peace would not be lasting if the French had, after so many years, to give them up. Morier is of that opinion and told Fritz so – who seemed to concur. But will Germany and the army ever be satisfied without them? What do you think, dearest child? I am so anxious for the power, unity and permanent security of Germany and Europe. Lord Halifax who is here, is a staunch supporter and admirer of Germany! He is very clever and sensible.

After Prussia's victory, the Crown Princess wrote to Queen Victoria:

30 January 1871

. . . Do not fear that my poor head could be turned by 'so-called greatness'. First of all to my mind an English woman and your daughter is far greater than any foreign Crowns, though I do not say so here. Then the greatness here is tremendous hard work. I do not think there is a greater slave than the sovereign, and with my love of ease and liberty, my fondness for travelling, and following up my favourite pursuits, the golden chains of the future – heavier than those which weigh uncomfortably upon me already – have nothing very attractive! I have a passionate love of liberty, and an idea and a passionate wish to see the ideal of a free and truly cultivated state become a reality. For this end I would suffer much and give up much – one must however have a cause to which to devote oneself and for which to live. Oneself – one's own comforts are too small, too narrowing and paralysing to all one's capacities – 'Man grows with his higher aims' says Goethe and I firmly believe that little interests cripple the mind.

A few months later, with hostilities between Germany and England mounting, the Crown Princess wrote to her mother:

4 March 1871

A thousand most tender thanks for your dear and kind letter by messenger. I am sure it must give you who are so generous, kind and just, pain to think of the animosity growing in England against Germany, but it is no use shutting our eyes against facts, and that it is one I do not doubt. It makes your position often trying, I am sure; but I can understand what that position is; you must not in any way allow yourself to be separated from your own people – the first people in the world, for I may say so to you, and it is every day more my conviction. How much I have suffered from the feeling between the two nations I cannot say! How at times unkindly and unjustly I have been used! And how many tears I have shed!

The Queen replied:

8 March 1871

Beloved and darling Child,

Your dear, affectionate and beautiful letter of the 4th touched me deeply. We have indeed both had most painful and trying times to go through, and I fear have still to go through – but I rejoice to see that you understand my duties – cruel as they are. With time and patience and a wish to go on in a conciliatory line, I hope and trust that we shall yet see a good understanding return and finally be established between our nations.

Calamity Jane to her daughter Janey, 1880–1902

Martha Jane Canary Hickock (1852–1903) lived and worked in the age of the American Wild West. She gained fame as a nurse and notoriety as a woman who flaunted almost every traditional expectation. She worked as a mule-skinner, a scout, a gambler, a prospector, a stagecoach driver, a show-woman; and she was the only woman worker on the Northern Pacific Rail-road. She also had more traditional women's jobs as a cook, a prostitute and a wife.

In 1877 she began keeping a journal in the form of letters to her daughter, Janey, who was then 4 and living in New York in the care of an old family friend, Jim O'Neil. Calamity Jane was an occasional guest in the O'Neil household, but Janey never knew that the exciting woman who told her all those stories was her mother. She never knew that Wild Bill Hickock, who figured prominently in most of the stories, was probably her father.*

'Legend' is a word which crops up regularly in writings about Calamity Jane. Between the legends she generated about herself and the legendary quality of most of the information we have about the Wild West in general, it is not possible to know precisely what she did or did not do in her fifty-one years. There is, however, a fair amount of consistency in accounts of *how* she did it: she was mannish in her dress and pastimes, and generally wild in her behaviour. She lost several jobs in show business because of her drunkenness and boisterousness – and this sometimes forced her to turn to prostitution to survive.

---

*It has not been clearly proved that Bill Hickock was Janey's father. Until these letters came to light in 1941, any liaison (legal or otherwise) between him and Calamity Jane was largely discredited by historians as wishful thinking on Jane's part.

No one claims to know how she acquired her name, but she was known as Calamity Jane long before she met Wild Bill Hickock, performed in Buffalo Bill Cody's Wild West Show, or worked as a scout for General Custer – if in fact she ever did any of those things. It depends on whom you ask.

September 1880

Janey, a letter from your Daddy Jim came today and another picture of you. Your birthday is this month, you are 7 years old. I like this picture of you . . . Your expression [is] exactly like your father's . . .

Your picture brought back all the years I have lived with your Father and recalled how jealous I was of him. I feel like writing about him tonight so I will tell you some things you should know. I met James Butlet Hickock, 'Wild Bill', in 1870 near Abeline, Kansas. I heard a bunch of outlaws planning to kill him. I couldn't get to where my horse was so I crawled on my hands and knees through the brush past the outlaws for over a mile and reached the old shack where he was staying that night. I told him and he hid me back of the door while he shot it out with them. They hit him, cutting open the top of his head and then they heard him fall and lit matches to see if he was dead. Bill killed them all. I'll never forget what he looked like with blood running down his face while he used two guns. He never aimed and I guess he was never known to have missed anyone he aimed at, I mean wanted to kill, and he only shot in self-defence. Then he was quite sure. I nursed him several days and then while on the trip to Abeline we met Rev. Sipes and Rev. Warren and we were married. There will be lots of fools doubt that but I will leave you plenty of proof that we were. You were not a woods colt Janey. Don't let any of those pus-gullied [erased] ever get busy with that lie . . .

Don't let jealousy get you Janey. It kills love and all the nice things in life. It drove your father from me. When I lost him I lost everything I ever loved except you. I gave him a divorce so he could marry Agnes Lake. I was trying to make amends for the jealous times and my spells of meanness. If she had loved him she would have come out here with him but she didn't and I was glad to have him again even if he was married and she was so far away. I always excused our sin by knowing he was mine long before he was hers. A man can love two women at one time. He loved her and still he loved me. He loved me because of you Janey.

January 1882

. . . You will have to excuse your mother Janey, she knows she's queer and half baked. I am going to see you soon now but I got to get into a poker game and win $20,000 before I can go to you. I am looking after a girl and boy and I must tell you, Jackie went off to

Alaska. These two are older. The girl, 16, the Indian boy, 18. I am going to take them East with me when I go to see you if I win the poker game . . . The boy wants to attend a medical school and the girl wants to be an actress. I will give them both their chance if I win and I shall win.

Darling Janey

The poker game is over. I won my $20,000 and paid back the $500 I borrowed from Abbot to start with. Will tell you more about Abbot later. I am so excited over winning for now I can go to see you in style. I want to look like something once in my life. Becky and Jimmie will go to New York City with me. They are so stuck on each other it is a shame to see them part but I think a few years apart will give them both different ideas of this mess called 'Love'. They will find out one can live in this old world without love or without a home of any sort. This is the last note of mine in this album till I return to this country [*the West*] again which may be never. Good bye till then.

After her visit:

30 May 1882

O Janey I did hate to come back here. Why couldn't I have stayed with you and Daddy Jim? Why didn't he ask me to stay? I was so in hope he would, but darling your mother is a misfit in a home like you have – or what can be wrong? I had such a lovely time there. Why can't I ever be anybody worthwhile? I likely will end up in the poor house in my old age. I am so discouraged. One consolation I shall always know you are alright and I thank God for your Daddy Jim. I gave him $10,000 to use for your education. There will be more in that old gambling tent for me when Luck again comes my way . . .

I hope you will think of me sometimes and of the things I told you, so you would remember the woman your Daddy Jim called Jane and of the man I told you about we called Wild Bill Hickock, and you said, 'What a funny name' and when I showed you his picture you said, 'He isn't handsome like my Daddy Jim.' There is nothing in this world quite so wonderful as the faith a child has in one they love. When you said your prayer that night to me you added, 'God bless Jane Hickock and that man who was shot in the back wherever he is. Bless him because Jane loved him.' I wondered how you know that I loved him.

Good night little girl and may God keep you from all harm.

1884

. . . Becky and Jimmie finished their training but they both forgotten me in the excitement of their careers. They fell out of love also. Becky is a good actress in New York. She is becoming famous and never thinks of the woman who gambled all night to get the money

which put her on Broadway. That is gratitude, Janey . . . I am going to
get a job of some kind. For awhile I worked in Russell's saloon. Abbott
got me the job. They want me to drive stage coach again. For when I
worked at Russells the good virtuous women of the town planned to
run me out of town . . . [*she describes the incident*] Now that's
Deadwood for you, and when you come out here, if you ever do Janey
and any of them stick up their nose at you because of your parents and
if they bury me beside your Father you move our bodies to Abilene
Kansas or where ever you wish to on the other hand if they treat you
decent. Remember Janey I want you buried beside us when ever your
time comes to cross the great divide. I'll never live to be very old Janey.
I can't stand this awful life very many years. I sometimes think I'll be
married again and then the thought of being tied to one man's shirt tail
sickens me. I wish things were different and I could live on through the
years knowing I would someday have you with me, but you will
marry sometime and you may be an old woman before you ever learn
who your mother really was. When you come here Janey there are a
few people I call friends I want you to look up.

This is all for this time you know I love you darling.

Always your Mother
Jane Hickock

October 1890

The years are going fast. So many things since I wrote last in this
book. More than anything I cherish my visit to see you and your
Daddy Jim. He is such a fine man that Jim O'Neil and I am so glad you
have such a nice home. I am driving a stage coach these days . . . some
mighty awe full experiences I've had since I started this kind of work.
Rev. Sipes and Teddy Blue Abbott got me the job. They seem to think
it was better than a saloon hostess. You see your mother works for a
living. One day I have chicken to eat and the next day the feathers.

10 May 1893

Coulson isn't as prosperous as when I first began writing this diary
but we still have Junction City and Billings. You should be here in this
country. Billings is some lively town. It supports about fifteen
hundred toughs.

These are hectic days – like hell let out for noon. These human para-
sites prosper, both men and women . . .

Located near the Yellowstone is an inferior spoke in the wheel. In its
basement are evil dirty smelling poorly lighted dens small vile and
dangerous where a trap door opens directly into the river to
accommodate those who just can't take it. More often they are robbed
and dumped in because the gang think they're spies or stool pigeons. I
am telling you this because I want you to know the sort of world we
have here . . .

25 September 1891

. . . This is your birthday. You are 18 years old today and a letter came from your Daddy Jim, dear old Captain. I love him so Janey. He has been such a wonderful father to you. It makes my heart ache to think of all the years he has gone on without his wife. Why does God let such things happen? Sometimes I wonder if there really is a God.

I did a most crazy thing. Some time ago I married Charley Burke. He got me in a weak moment and we were married. He is a good man, honest and on the square, but I don't love him dear. I am still in love with your father Bill Hickock. But Charley is near my own age, dark haired, blue-eyed. Marriage isn't all a romance either. We were married down by the river under a clump of cottonwood trees. Janey the sunshine crept softly down between the tree branches seeming to spread a glory of radiant light about the group of friends gathering there. The sunshine was like a benediction. Of course I cried. I'm always bawling. I know you are enjoying your trip. I envy you. Goodnight dear.

25 July 1893

I am leaving next week to join Bill Cody's Wild West Show. I suppose you will wonder what I will be doing up there. I ride a horse bare back, standing up, shoot my old Stetson hat twice before throwing it in the air before it falls back on my head. I will do all kinds of tricks on horse back shooting stunts and soon when the show gets East maybe you and your Daddy Jim O'Neil will be there to see me. Of course you won't know who I am but I will know you are my own little girl, although you are grown up . . .

It is a good thing that you don't know how your mother has to live out here these hectic days. I mind my own business but always remember that is one thing the world hates is a woman who minds her own business. They are telling awful things about me. None of it is true. Every man I ever speak to I'm accused of being an immoral slut. Just because I took several different young boys under my wing to help them while sick like the Stewart boy and Ben Greenwugh the tongues wag. I like to hope some day you may know them too Janey.

These other women who talk about me have bastards and shot gun weddings. I have nursed a number of them during child birth with my only pay a kick in the pants when my back is turned. They know what I know about them and they are trying to find extenuation for their own sins by lying about me. They are pot bellied, hairy legged and look like something the cat dragged in. But they wag their tongues behind my back. I wish I had the power to damn their souls to hell.

I suppose now that I am joining Buffalo Bill's Wild West Show they will know for sure down deep in their hypocritical hearts that I am bound for hell . . .

1896

Dear Janey,

. . . O Janey the years too soon have robbed me – yes the years have robbed me of you. I wanted nothing else but you all these years. Perhaps some day after you have lost everything you have ever loved and are an old woman yourself – then perhaps you will know how I feel. Ten more years of hardship will be my finish. Your Mother is going down hill. If you ever marry and have a little girl I am going to steal it. I need a little Grand Daughter. She would be my most precious possession.

You will hear lots of lies I have told concerning my own affairs. It is better so.

1898

Winter is here again and I am down here on the Clark Forks for awhile. This life is a long hideous nightmare. This country is beautiful but I am growing to hate it because it has taken from me everything I ever loved. It took Bill from me, it was the cause of having to give you up. It has wrecked me this country. I am not old Janey but I feel as though I have reached the end of my rope.

April 1902

Dear Janey,

I guess my diary is just about finished. I am going blind – can still see to write this yet but I can't keep on to live an avaricious old age. All hope is dead forever Janey. What have I ever done except to make one blunder after another? All I have left are these little pictures of you and your father. I can't go on blind and the doctor told me yesterday that in two months I would be absolutely blind. O how I wish I had my life to live over . . .

I hate poverty and Dirt and here I shall have to live in such in my last days. Don't pity me Janey.

Forgive all my faults and the wrong I have done you.

Olive Schreiner to her mother Rebecca, 1896

Olive Schreiner (1855–1920), author and feminist, was born on a South African mission station, the ninth of twelve children (five of whom died in early childhood). Her parents, Rebecca and Otto Schreiner, were both missionaries of deep fundamentalist conviction. Their relentless emphasis on sin gave Olive, from early childhood, an intense conviction of her own wickedness, and her self-doubt was reinforced by her mother's stern and undemonstrative personality. In one of her letters to her husband, Olive recalled two occasions of being beaten before the age of eight:

They did me such immense harm that I think they have permanently influenced my life. They made me hate everything in the heavens above and the earth beneath . . . It is all as vivid to me as if it had happened two hours ago, and the bitter wild fierce agony in my heart against God and man . . . the deep resolve I made . . . to spend all my life in helping weak things against the strong.

Rebecca's strictness took its toll on everyone in the family. Olive's brother, Theo, wrote to their eldest sister, Kate, when she married, that their mother's conduct had been 'unnatural and unmotherly . . . I am so happy that it is over, and that you will never more be subject to such tyranny as you have experienced in your lifetime'.

The Schreiners were poor and Olive's father started a small business to supplement his income as a missionary. When she was 11, her father was declared bankrupt and Olive was sent to live with her elder brother's family; she never again lived with her parents. During adolescence she began suffering bouts of 'chest illness' (the asthma which plagued her for the rest of her life). She moved from family to family and received very little formal education – only about a year in a school run by her brother – but she occasionally met visitors who introduced her to European books and she read widely in anthropology, theology and science. At 19 she began working as a governess in various families, teaching and caring for children and writing novels in her spare time. In 1881, at the age of 26, she went to England with the intention of studying for a career in nursing or medicine. She had already written three novels, which she took with her, hoping to get them published in England: *Undine; Story of an African Farm*; and an unfinished version of *From Man to Man* (still unfinished when she died, and published posthumously). *Story of An African Farm* was published in 1883 under the pseudonym 'Ralph Iron'. It was widely acclaimed and her identity was soon discovered.

Olive's health was too poor for her to pursue a regular course of medical study and her interests shifted to the social and political issues being discussed by her new acquaintances, Eleanor Marx, Havelock Ellis and Edward Carpenter. She became involved in the Men's and Women's Club, a group committed to the study of relations between the sexes. She soon became known as an outspoken feminist and was often invited to lecture; she was also asked to write an introduction to Mary Wollstonecraft's *Vindication of the Rights of Women*, into which she attempted to gather the result 'of my whole life'. During this period she began her friendship with Havelock Ellis which was to endure, mainly through letters, for the next thirty-five years. Their correspondence was one of her chief intellectual and emotional outlets: they communicated their intense feelings for each other as well as conducting lengthy discussions and arguments on her political work in England and South Africa and on their changing concepts of human sexuality and psychology. She also conducted an extensive correspondence with

Constance Lytton* and with her two closest friends in South Africa. Throughout her adult life, her most revealing letters were written to her women friends and to Havelock – the least honest ones to her mother.

Olive returned to South Africa in 1889. She had long claimed that she was unsuited to marriage, but in 1892 she met Samuel Cronwright, a farmer and politician, and they were married two years later; she did not change her name but he changed his to Cronwright-Schreiner. They had one child who died within twenty-four hours. Three more pregnancies all resulted in miscarriages.

Olive seems to have been miserable for most of her life, despite intermittent professional recognition. She always deeply regretted not having children. She was often alone for long periods, unable to go out because of her painful and incapacitating asthma. There were several times when she was ostracised because of her radical political stances (she stood up for the Boers against English imperialism, for Black Africans against white racism, and was a pacifist during World War I). She also suffered a setback in 1900 when she discovered that a major piece of research on women, on which she had been working for eleven years, had been destroyed when her home was looted during the Boer War. Throughout her life she was often too ill to work and was greatly frustrated by not being able to undertake or complete work to which she felt committed.

In their revealing biography, *Olive Schreiner*, Ruth First and Ann Scott† have 'tried to understand her illness and unhappiness as an expression of the split between her own needs and the reality of what was possible for women in the cultures in which she lived'. In an era so hostile to women's freedom, it was difficult, even for a woman of Olive's passionate disposition, to live a full and active life – and almost impossible to maintain a good self-image as a woman while doing so. The conventional feminine stereotypes narrowly defined a 'good' woman as one who was content to be idle and subservient.

In addition to the social and political limitations on Olive's development, distress from her early life, so dominated by guilt and self-hatred, continually undermined her attempts to realise her potential. One would never guess, from the tone of Olive's letters to her mother, how profoundly unhappy their relationship made her. With the exception of the letter below, she preferred to keep their frequent letters to uncontroversial topics such as the weather and the books they read. Rebecca was not always so obliging and, in a letter to a close friend, Olive blamed one of her miscarriages on unhappiness caused by a hostile letter from her mother and family. Like Florence Nightingale,** Olive sometimes claimed that she had no mother, although her mother figured prominently in her life well into adulthood – however unhappily. All

---

*See pp. 197–200.
†See pp. 370–82.
**See pp. 99–111.

of Olive's novels have characters who reflect her miserable childhood: she portrays a horrifying degree of human unhappiness and the mothers in her novels are uniformly cruel and/or destructive to everyone, especially young children. Even in her political writings on the Boer War and World War I, there are recurring metaphors of cruel and unloving mothers. Yet her writing is poetic and richly inspiring: she somehow maintained a vision of a world in which compassionate values would prevail, and women and men could achieve deep love and friendship based on equality and mutual respect.

Olive Schreiner is best known for *Story of an African Farm* and for *Woman and Labour* (1911) which was the 'bible' of the feminist movement for some years. In *Woman and Labour* she argued that all of society would benefit in every material and spiritual way if women were allowed to participate fully in paid labour and if men shared completely in domestic work.†
She once said that she most wanted to be remembered as the author of *Trooper Peter Halket of Mashonaland*, a short allegorical novel in which a British soldier in South Africa is confronted by Jesus Christ and forced to understand that Black Africans suffer as human beings.

Olive spent six weeks writing the letter excerpted below and it is the longest letter she ever wrote. It was written shortly after the Jameson Raid, a plot for a British takeover of the Transvaal Republic. The scandal of Cecil Rhodes' complicity in the Raid forced him to resign as Prime Minister of the Cape Colonies (now South Africa). Rebecca firmly believed that to be anti-Rhodes was to be anti-British; although Olive and Rhodes had been friendly in the early 1890s, they had always had profound political disagreements and Olive had stopped speaking to him long before the public disgrace of the Raid:

1896

[Dear Mother]
During the last six weeks I have been very unhappy, not knowing whether to answer your letters on political matters or not. Would it not, my dear little mother, be much better to drop all references direct or indirect with regard to politics between us? During the last fifteen years, both in England and here, my work and my interest in life have been mainly political, yet I do not think six times I have, in all these years, mentioned politics to you, because I felt you were not sympathetic to my view; and I believe that where, with regard to either *religion* or *politics*, parents or children, or even brothers and sisters,

---

†She was ahead of many feminists in her day in her broad view of women's liberation: at a time when suffrage still seemed the main issue, she argued that the basis of women's inequality was economic and could only be challenged by women being allowed to enter the workforce and become financially independent. She was also one of the first women to write openly about the possibility that women might enjoy sex – if only their relationships with men could be free and equal rather than based on financial necessity.

are not agreed, they should avoid these subjects. I have held this all my life. The tender love existing between mother and child and brother and sister need surely never be ruffled by these things . . .

Dear Mother, I have no time for long political discussions; can they be of any use when we are at the opposite extreme in regard to our views of what is for the good of the country? You must not feel pained if I do not take notice of what you say . . .

Dear little mother, are there not hundreds of fair and beautiful things we can write of, leaving politics out? I have surely as much right to be on the side of the Transvaal Government as you have to be on that of Rhodes: have I not, little Mother?

I used to feel it so bitterly when people would insist upon attacking you on your change of religion,* but surely, surely, politics need far less to divide a mother and daughter.

You have said in your two letters that I was allowing Cron [wright] to warp my mind and degrade my character. I can only think that you refer to the fact I am in politics opposed to Rhodes. Now, dear little mother, I will just shortly tell you the whole story of my relation with Rhodes . . .

This all happened long before I ever met Cron or knew that such a person existed: how then can he have had anything to do with my political opposition to Rhodes?

So far from my having opposed Rhodes more since I was married, *it is only the last two years* that I have taken *no* part or interest in political life, and, except that one little pamphlet on the political situation, *I have not touched* politics . . . Since Jameson's Raid I have had letters from people asking me to write and send wires containing my views, and I could have made much money, of which I am in much need. But I attacked Rhodes frankly and fearlessly and endlessly when he was in power, and therefore I can afford to be quiet now . . .

I have never read to Cron the things you have said of him in your letters to me. He has loved you so whole-heartedly and loyally that I couldn't wound him so. Never in one instance has he said one little disloyal or unloving word of kith or kin of mine . . . If he had ever said one little word or done one little ungenerous thing towards you I could tell him what you say of him, but I *can't wound* another person so. Whatever your views with regard to politics or religion, it would make no atom of difference to us. Cron's favourite brother is strongly against the Transvaal Government and for the Chartered Company, but do you think that makes any difference in our feeling towards

---

*This refers to Rebecca's conversion to Catholicism. Olive had become a freethinker even before she left home, at the age of 11.

him? Do you think I could love you one dot more if you were on our side in this matter? Do you think I would ever *care one straw what your political opinions were*? . . .

Goodbye, my own little Mothie. You must not mind if I don't refer to politics again.

Your little daughter,
Olive

The Personal Is Political: Twentieth-Century Liberation

The early decades of the twentieth century brought new opportunities and dilemmas to women. Suffrage continued to be the crucial issue,* but other political struggles gained in importance. The right to establish clinics offering women information and access to the means of contraception was hard-won; women's desire to control the number of children they bore was seen by many people as a moral and social calamity threatening the values of home and family – and raising further unsettling questions about the proper role of women in society. Women became increasingly involved in political campaigns over other 'personal' issues, such as divorce laws and the Married Women's Property Act (which so concerned Florence Nightingale in 1867 and was still a cause for Edith Summerskill to fight in 1964);† and the unprecedented mass mobilisation of World War I had the effect of opening up (at least temporarily) many new areas of work and responsibility in every sector of industry and national life. Women became plumbers, boilermakers, bank clerks, electricians, bus drivers, and carpenters.

As a result of the groundbreaking efforts of the nineteenth-century pioneers, women in the twentieth century have had from the start a wider range of options in their personal lives. The very notion that women might want to engage in activities other than marriage and motherhood was not in itself so alarming: women who were dedicated to their pursuits outside the home did not necessarily assume that they would appal their families nor did they all end up as spinsters. (All but two of the women in this next section were married to men who at least tolerated their dreams, and often gave vital encouragement and support.)

Many women today who were not brought up with the expectation that they could or would have to think and act effectively outside the domestic sphere, still describe the old battle against self-doubt and a lack of confidence when they take on challenges. The painfulness of this struggle is very real. But we do not see in most twentieth-century women's letters and life stories

---

*Woman suffrage was won in 1919 in the United States; in 1918 in Britain for women over 30 who were property owners (or married to property owners), and in 1928 for all women over 21. Women in France were only given the right to vote in 1944.
†See pp. 99–111, pp. 10–12 and pp. 185–8.

the same degree of inner conflict over their feminine identity. Unlike many of their sisters in the first section of this chapter, the women whose letters follow have not been literally paralysed by their conflicts. They can be proud of their strength.

Crystal Eastman and her mother Annis Ford Eastman, 1907–09

I shall have so much to tell you all the rest of my life . . .

Annis to Crystal (1899)

. . . no one really knows how passionately I love you . . . I simply can't imagine my life without you.

Crystal to Annis (1907)

*Introduction by Yvette Eastman**
These samplings from over five hundred letters (1892–1910) were written by two extraordinary women who were mother and daughter and were also the closest of friends. Max Eastman* described it best:

> The great love of Crystal's life, never replaced by any man or woman, was our mother. I have never seen or heard of a friendship more perfect than theirs. They asked no greater happiness than to be together; in separation they wrote to each other constantly, as often as twice a week; and yet, each rejoiced with admiration in the outgoing career of the other. No wish to retain, no glimmer of possessiveness, filial or parental, ever marred the sweet, tranquil, confident, life-enhancing flow of their friendship.

Annis Ford Eastman, AFE, (1852–1910), born in Peoria, Illinois, was the first woman to be ordained in the Congregational Church of New York State. From the time she was a high school girl, she had the conviction that women 'ought to be something', and she aspired to the power to achieve her goals. In his profile of her, Max wrote, 'When Susan B. Anthony came to lecture in Peoria, this ambitious high school girl introduced the famous suffragette and did it with so much eloquence that, according to the clipping in my possession, her speech was the "talk of the town".' Later, in the pulpit, she is described as having self-possession, a thrilling voice and a remarkable gift for speaking directly to the hearts of her audience. Her daughter Crystal

---

*Yvette Eastman is the widow of Max Eastman (1883–1969), youngest son of Annis Ford Eastman and the Rev. Samuel E. Eastman. He is remembered as one of the best-known literary radicals and one of the most dominant figures in American cultural life between 1912 and 1923. He wrote 34 books on art, science, poetry, philosophy, humor, aesthetics, journalism, Marxism, capitalism, socialism, psychology and two volumes of autobiography. His *Enjoyment of Poetry* is generally regarded as a classic, as are *The Sense of Humor* and *Enjoyment of Laughter*. He translated Trotsky's *History of the Russian Revolution*, was publisher and editor of the radical journals, *The Liberator* and *The Masses*, and with his sister Crystal organized the American Union Against Militarism and founded the Men's League for Woman Suffrage. He was a leading spokesman for the feminist movement. Max and Crystal remained close throughout her life and they often worked together. (Y.E.)

described her as having an eager active mind and tremendous energy. She was preeminently an initiator:

> Life was never dull or ordinary where my mother was . . . her sermons were not old fashioned sermons about the bible nor new-fashioned sermons about politics and reform. They were, I think, about individual life and they grew out of her own moral and spiritual struggles. For she had a stormy troubled soul capable of black cruelty and then again of the deepest generosities. She was a humble, honest, striving person, always beginning again to try to be good.

It appears that the 'stormy, troubled soul' stemmed in part from the emotional conflicts, stresses and frustrations of a nineteenth-century marriage to which – with her sensitivity, intelligence, humour and awareness of her own intellectual gifts – AFE found it impossible to subordinate herself. Disillusioned by the sexual intimacies of marriage, she was torn with self-reproach and Christian remorse. Her devout husband, whom she met when he was a divinity student during her year at Oberlin College, was unable to comprehend her problem, and she struggled to make herself worthy of him.

In 1886 Samuel Eastman's failing health forced him to give up for a time his career as a preacher, and AFE took over as the family's head and its main support. In 1900, she and her husband became joint pastors of the Park Church in Elmira, New York. They tried to make it a place where Christians of all creeds or no creed could feel they belonged: a home church. It had a fully-equipped kitchen, a free library, swimming pool, billiard tables, dancing hall and children's playroom with a stage and the complete fittings of a theatre. At Park Church, they became part of an intellectual circle that included Mark Twain, and it was AFE who was called upon to prepare Twain's funeral oration. On that occasion, as on some others when she happened to be indisposed, her sermon was delivered by her husband. She must have had conflicts about this. In one of her letters to Crystal she refers to her 'pain over father giving my sermon', and then to her 'victory over it'. She asked Crystal whether she thought it 'wicked to let your work go to another's credit?' (to which Crystal replies in her letter of 6 March 1907 below).

In the summers, AFE was the moving spirit behind a community of idealists who owned cottages in Glenora, on Seneca Lake in upstate New York. The four families involved erected a common dining hall, hired a cook and shared expenses as well as the work. On Sunday mornings the whole hillside would gather in the Eastman cottage for an informal service – a hymn, a violin solo, a poetry reading, a word of prayer. In Crystal's memory, there was no conflict between her mother's public role and her role as homemaker. 'We children loved her cooking as much as we loved her preaching,' wrote Crystal. 'She was all kinds of a devoted mother, the kind that drags you to the dentist to have your teeth straightened, or rubs your chest 'til you cry for mercy if you have a bad cough.'

In search of an intellectual definition of the Christian faith, AFE attended Harvard University late in her career to audit lectures by noted philosophers and doctors of divinity. In 1907, at the risk of losing the pastorship at the Park Church, she succeeded in changing the old creed from Trinitarian to Unitarian. While the issue was still in doubt she wrote Crystal that she would accept any job 'that includes a glimpse of you every day.' Later, she wrote more reflectively: 'I wish you *cared* more about it all. I wish you went to church, you and Max. That's weak and foolish, I know – you must live your own life. I suppose it is from a longing that what we are doing is real and necessary. If I had been better, you would have loved the church more.' This uncertainty about the 'realness' and 'necessity' contributed not only to her decision in 1910 to leave the ministry but also to consult Dr. A. A. Brill, one of the first Freudian psychoanalysts in the United States. In that same year she began to address women's suffrage meetings and to consider a career in education. Before that year was out, she died suddenly at the age of 58 of a cerebral hemorrhage.

Crystal Eastman achieved national and international importance as an activist in causes ranging from social reform to anti-militarism to women's suffrage and equal rights. She and Max were among the leaders of the first counterculture in modern American history.

Crystal graduated from Vassar College in 1903. She earned a Master's degree in economics and social science from Columbia University and a law degree from New York University and was admitted to the bar of New York State in 1907. She first achieved recognition directing an inquiry into the causes and economic and legal consequences of industrial accidents. After the publication of her book, *Work Accidents and the Law*, she was acclaimed for her contribution to labor law and industrial safety. As a result of this pioneering study she was appointed to the Employers' Liability Commission by the Governor of New York State – the only woman on a Commission of fourteen. She organised and directed the New York branch of the American Association of Labor Legislation and was in the forefront of the suffrage, peace and radical movements of the time as organizer, executive and journalist. She was co-founder of the American Civil Liberties Union whose reason for being at that time was to protect the rights of conscientious objectors in World War I. As war approached, she focussed all her energy on opposing US involvement. She founded the Women's Peace Party of New York and helped set up the National Women's Party which later became the Women's International League for Peace and Freedom.

Shortly after her mother died, Crystal married Wallace Benedict of Milwaukee but the marriage was not successful and ended in divorce. In 1916 she married a British pacifist, Walter Fuller, by whom she had two children, Jeffrey (1917–70) and Annis (1922–81). She spent the next several years between the United States and Britain where she worked in various feminist causes and wrote for American and English journals and papers (*The Nation*, the *New Republic*, *The Christian Science Monitor*, *Equal Rights*, *Time & Tide*, *The Liberator*). On both sides of the Atlantic, Max recalled, she fought social injustices 'with a humor which kept her belief in the coming triumph of freedom and decent human relations from becoming fanatical'.

Like her mother, she was a magnetic person and a magnetic speaker, force-ful, dramatic, inspiring. When she died of a kidney ailment at the age of 47, one of the letters Max received was from Frances Perkins who was then Secre-tary of Labor: 'Crystal made her contribution to the welfare of the human race, and it was a fine one. But I think the contribution she has made to her friends – to me and other women like me – has been even greater and perhaps more permanent. She was a great human being as well as a great public servant.'

Crystal to her mother:

6 March 1907

Dearest,

The laundry has just come – Wednesday at noon. However, the things are all right. The cake was in time for my dessert, and I think it is the best you ever made.

Oh, you will never know just what it meant to me to have it come today! I have been feeling lately somewhat lost and stranded, as if I couldn't tell where or with what people I belonged. You know, as you go along you keep discovering weaknesses in the people, or the move-ments, or places, that you were once altogether in sympathy with. Your thought turns from one stronghold to another, and it seems to be the same with all. On top of it, perhaps causing it all, is a sense of your *own* miserable inefficiency. Well, after awhile you keep saying to yourself, almost subconsciously 'where, – with whom, can I cast my lot, – and feel that my whole heart and soul is in the throw?' This in a poor way describes my state of mind since Sunday. Perhaps, you are wondering what this has to do with the laundry? Can't you see? It came as a visible sign of *you*, of your realness, of your work, and thought, and love. And suddenly I knew that I belong to *you*. My lonely spirit was comforted; the world no longer seemed an empty place.

It is so clear to me, every little while, that my soul is not big enough to get along without a very personal reason for existence. You will be the person for a long, *long* time yet. Won't you?

Well, this is only one of the inevitable 'downs' that come to an ambi-tious person like me. I shall soon brace up and find my place again. And you must forget that I am ever blue, remembering only that when I am . . . the thought of you, or a letter or package from you can almost always pull me out.

On Sunday Max read me a wonderful letter from you, and then on Monday came a great, fat, luscious one for me. How I laughed over that civic meeting. And you with the shovel and the black eye, tragic as it almost was – in your telling of it all was funny. I can't think of you trying to shovel coal without laughing and crying and longing to hug you.

Oh, the unhappy people who have not you for a mother! My heart goes out to them . . .

The pink sample is *beautiful*. Exquisite and unique. I would love it, but it isn't at all the kind of dress I need – a thin, unwashable material like this. When I do need one and can afford to have it made, there is that lovely green filipino cloth. I'll let you decide, if you've got the eight dollars. Nothing could be prettier – and yet I don't need it – and shall need lots of other things.

Yes, I am eager to have Max write and speak, and he ought to begin now. He can certainly live on what he has if you pay the rent. He could do a little tutoring and still have lots of time to write. Perhaps he will soon find just the job that will fit in.

No, – Max was the one I wanted to marry always.

I don't think anyone thinks I am wonderful but you and Dr. Simkhovitch. They never act or look as if they did. They liked me at Vassar, I think, and that was all I wanted. Sometime I'll tell you my impressions. It would take too long to write them.

It has just occurred to me to ask whether you ever had printed that sermon you preached in the evening while I was at home? I want that to read to some people as soon as you get it in shape, and for myself I want to read it . . .

Some time ago you asked me if I thought it was wicked to let your own work go to another's credit. No, I don't. I think it is great – heroic – in this instance. It would be impossible for me I'm afraid. I suppose from a large social point of view, the all-important thing is the *progressive step* – not whose work it was, or whose name it bears. But we can't look upon the efforts of our lives as though we were God. I honor you for your attitude in the whole business . . .

Perhaps someday we shall have light on this sex question. It seems almost the question of life – next to immortality. And yet we, most of us, live as a rule regardless and forgetful of it for the greater part of the time. And isn't it blessed and beautiful that we do? And we are individuals, human-beings, besides being males and females? I guess civilization has meant enlarging the field of interest, more than anything else, after all.

I found these things in [Edward] Carpenter which express what I meant:

> For there is nothing that is evil except because a man has not mastery over it. The ascetics and the self-indulgent divide things into good and evil – as it were to throw away the evil; but things cannot be divided into good and evil but all are good so soon as they are brought into subjection. Let the strong desires come and go;

refuse them not, disown them not; but think not that in them lies finally the thing you want.

Don't think that I do not sympathize with and understand your feeling, especially in this matter.* Perhaps the truth lies between us, or perhaps there is no absolutely right way of looking at it. A different 'right' for different people, I guess that's it.

Goodbye, sweetheart, I am all happy and hale again from writing to you and reading over your dear letters.

Crystal

AFE's reply:

7 March 1907

Beloved –

Your letter is the fountain of many thoughts and of feeling sad yet hopeful which come from the deepest in me. I have been working this morning about the house with a not very efficient cleaner (my Alice, the wonderful, is sick) but all the time I have lived in that realest world where we are so loth to abide – the world of thoughts.

I know so well the mood in which you began to write to me. That passion for perfection! – it made Paul cry out, 'When that which is perfect is come – then that *which is in part* shall be done away!' But immediately the preciousness of 'that which is in part' comes over him – '. . . But now abideth faith, hope, love –' these best gifts which *never could have been* in the world of the perfect – of *any* perfect. This is what I meant in that first sermon after you came home – the one that helped another 'poor thing', but not you – then. Yes, we turn from one stronghold to another and so soon they reveal their fatal likeness. Last fall it was like a blow in the face to me to find at that Unitarian Conference – the very same narrowness and self-ness that I fondly hoped belonged wholly to the liberal-orthodox. Now and then we see an *individual* who *seems* complete – Dr. Gannet is such an one to me – but if I knew him better it might not be so. And then the despair of turning upon one's *own partialness*! I am one of the most *intolerant* of persons – the least able to take another's point of view with sympathy – you know *me* 'tho'! The pity of it is that you should find it out so soon! To part so early with the illusions of youth is sad – but it must be – you must pass on to the illusions of maturity – for I guess it is all illusion (not, thank God, delusion).

Since we are in the world of the unfinished, the imperfect, let us make the best of its opportunities and enrich ourselves with its faith and hope and love.

---

*They had been discussing sexual equality – 'this sex question' (Y.E.).

After dinner

How do people ever throw themselves, without reserve, into anything? I believe the wisest do not. 'A personal reason for existence' –
there *is* no other. Ideals and principles are no better than ghosts if they
are not incarnated and worked out in people. In loving you I love
every high and holy thing – but it isn't truth and justice and loyalty
and kindness that I love – it is *you*. I haven't much faith in anybody's
living for the mass – for humanity – without the strong affection for
individuals. That story of Gorky's is wonderful in its passion for the
people – but it is the growth of the one mother's soul that impresses
and helps you most. I think you must read it. Once a young girl – a
revolutionary – says to the mother – 'Goodbye Comrade.'

'Comrade!' said the mother when her guest had disappeared from
view. With a sigh she looked back to bygone days in which her past
dragged along flatly and unemotionally, a thin black thread! Imper-
ceptibly she grew conscious of her usefulness in this new life – a consciousness that gave her poise and assurance. She had never before felt
herself necessary to anybody. But now she felt that she was helping a
good work. It was new to her and pleasant. It set her head erect on her
shoulders. But when her son – the Messiah of the cause – comes from
prison and finds what she has been doing to spread the gospel – even
teaching herself to read – he says, 'Thank you for helping our great
cause. When a man can call his mother his own in spirit also – that's
some fortune!' The mother laughed. Her heart was still leaping with
joy. She was fairly intoxicated with beatitude. She could love the great
cause thro' him . . .

Ah! We *need* each other. I'm glad the tho't of me so often helps you –
it is because I am not too near – you forget my fatal weaknesses and
only know my love and my aching desire to be *with you where you are*
in all the heights and the depths. You said the true word about good
and evil – 'a different right for different people'. That's what I tried to
tell the people last night – a different right for the same person at different points in his career, so we grow as our standard lifts – or our
standard lifts as we grow. Yes – yes – it is beautiful that we are human
beings as well as male and female. I shall take that tho't and the one on
the meaning of civilization as the enlarging of the field of interest – for
the foundation of a lecture on the Home, for Rochester next month. I
have never had a richer letter than this of yours in suggestiveness and
inspiration. At first it made me sad – but now I am comforted and
lifted up.

I will send with the next laundry both sermons (neither are printed
but they are readable . . .).

                                                                [Mamma]

P.S. It is a wonderful letter and feeds my soul.

25 June 1907

Dearest,

I am twenty-six years old and about twelve hours. (A picture of the morning I was born as you have described it, just flashed through my mind). A street organ is playing some haunting gay tune down on the street somewhere, and I can hear the sound of the children's feet as they dance. The city is really marvellous on a summer night. Everyone is out. Mothers and fathers and babies line the doorsteps. Girls with their beaux, standing in the shadows, or gathered in laughing groups on the corners. And children, thousands of them everywhere, little girls playing singing games in the middle of the street, and boys running in and out, chasing each other, throwing balls, building fires, fighting, laughing, shouting. Oh it is wonderful – this human nature with its infinite capacity, and unending desire, for joy. Let someone only strike up a common dance tune on a wheezy street organ, and, though it be the hottest, dirtiest street, and the weariest people in the land – you'll see the eyes light up and the feet begin to go – there'll be humming and singing here and there – and the little ones will dance their legs off. Isn't it beautiful?

And freedom, with all its long train of evils – is something – freedom to taste the common joys – to work, and fight and struggle, and die, with the others – after all it means something. Aren't there a great many different ways of looking at the world?

Your card was there in the box to cheer me as I started for the bar examination this morning. It's all over, and I'm not dead at all. In fact I feel quite lively, though it was quite an ordeal with this heat, and the bad air, and the long, long hours of it.

I hope I passed but I'm not a bit sure. I forgot many of the maddening little reasonless rules.

Goodbye, my darling – I'll be at home on Saturday.

Crystal

3 May 1909

Dear Magic of the Morning –

. . . I had a very good night with no alarums but some waking spells when I hoped you were sleeping in your little berth and blessed you in my heart.* If I have bettered years (a few of them) I owe it to Max's doggedness and your wingedness (don't let Max see this) and *I'll pay you back* see if I don't!

In the thoughts of the night I saw it all clear, the brave, *eternally right* choice you are making. If the *main contention* of the progressive woman is her right to a work of her own – a life work – then you are

---

*AFE is convalescing after an illness or an operation.

doing more to prove the rightness of that contention by making your way in a regular business – than you could do by the most brilliant success as a social worker or investigator for a few years before marriage. It would still be the old thing – a woman's work having no real meaning except the filling up of time before marriage. 'Thin foolish warring soul – Back to the ranks' I say to myself. God be praised that you are made of tougher fibre!

My heart is full of more things to say – more, more – but it is post-man time and I must call a 'reunion' – they are few now and very much occupied with their own matters – drat 'em! I am so glad to think of you with this cool fair day before you and no impedimenta in the shape of mothers.

Mamma

© *Yvette Eastman*

Helen Keller to her mother Kate, 1912–16

Like so many of her contemporaries, Helen Keller (1880–1968) felt that she must lovingly reassure her mother, who frequently became distressed by Helen's outspoken position on socialism, feminism and pacifism. Coming as she did from an arch-conservative Alabaman family (who had never quite reconciled themselves to the outcome of the Civil War and the abolition of slavery), Helen provoked an uneasy mixture of pride and shame in her parents, Kate and Arthur Keller.

Their famous daughter inspired wonder and reverence for her triumph over the total deafness and blindness which had struck her at the age of 19 months. Not only had she astounded the world with her mastery of sign language, reading and writing; she had also earned a Cum Laude degree from the prestigious Radcliffe College, at a time when most able-bodied women were still considered unfit to be educated. After taking her degree, Helen Keller divided her time between fund-raising for the blind and her own literary endeavours, which included journalism, essays and autobio-graphical writings. Her investigation into the social causes of blindness (such as poverty, malnutrition, untreated venereal disease and inhuman working conditions in factories), led her to conclude that profits were the enemy of the health and safety of working people – women, men and children alike. She therefore allied herself with the workers and pledged herself a lifelong enemy of capitalism. From 1909, when she joined the Socialist Party, her writings and other activities revealed her commitment to socialism.

Helen differed with her mother in almost all her views (except the suffragist cause, which her mother favoured). Even more astonishing, however, is the fact that she had strong disagreements with her respected teacher, Annie Sullivan Macy, who was neither a socialist nor a feminist. Helen was completely tied to Annie (or 'Teacher', as she was always called) from the age

of 7 until Annie's death, when Helen was 56. The dependence was absolute –
a condition impossible for most able-bodied adults even to imagine. In the
circumstances, it is remarkable that Helen Keller should have managed to
form unorthodox convictions, and to stand by them even under aggressive
attacks from outsiders. She clearly never doubted the continued affection
and care of both 'Teacher' and her mother and this seems to have given her
the security to speak her mind openly and with confidence.

Although Helen did not feel obliged to hide her political opinions from
anyone, she always gave particular consideration to her mother's feelings in
other ways, especially by acknowledging that Kate Keller should share the
credit with Annie, the 'miracle worker', for Helen's impressive record of
achievement.

The following letter was written on Kate's birthday; Helen, aged 32, was
increasingly involved in radical politics and often on the defensive about her
right to hold opinions on the 'outside' world:

11 October 1912

A happy birthday to you, dearest Mother, and many, many returns
of the day! How good it is to think of you visiting us again. It means
that you will be there to see something of my new and larger work.
Whatever success comes to me seems incomplete because you are so
often not at my side to be glad with me. But now you will have a
chance to realize more fully into what new worlds of thought, feeling
and aspiration I am entering, and see what new and fascinating fields
of knowledge and action are opening before me. This visit in
Washington is truly a flood of fresh experiences, impressions and
observations, and it is only a foretaste of what I am likely to have in
the near future . . .

A lady from England, Miss McMillan, called on me, and we had an
extremely interesting talk. She is on the Bradford School Board for the
deaf, and is deeply versed in all the problems of defective children. She
works for the children of the very poor, and she has succeeded in
putting some very important things through for their benefit. She told
me how very serious the conditions are under which the great majority
of the English people now live. They are so bad in fact that the average
child of the workman is threatened with lifelong invalidism. Miss
McMillan has established some night-camps where sick children can
sleep in the fresh air, receive proper medical treatment and physical
training and thus gain a better chance to escape the horrible influences
of the slum . . .

This brings me to something which gave me inexpressible
happiness. I shall henceforth be content, even if all the rest of my life
should be spent in pain and tribulation. It sounds incredible, and like
one of my daydreams. But I must needs accept the evidence of my

senses. Miss McMillan said to me that I had been a help to her in her work, that it was my education which inspired her with the idea of training those poor children in a new way. She thought: if my senses could be developed to such a high degree, what might she not do in developing the five senses of her many little pupils! . . . And [she] said, 'all this good has come to thousands upon thousands of unfortunate children because of your work.' She said these words calmly and paid me no compliments. Now, after hearing this, does Teacher not feel that she is truly a benefactor of mankind? Does she not feel that her travail of mind and spirit and body is being transmuted into the happiness and ennoblement of a generation of children? And you too, mother, you have a share in this beautiful work. For you helped me all you could in my first years, you kept me healthy and active, you strove to stimulate my mind, so that it would not be quenched in darkness and silence. How precious your motherhood is as I think what blessing you have helped to bring to mothers all over the world. Here is a treasure of comfort for you to lay up in your heart on your birthday.

By the way, almost from the first I felt sure of Miss McMillan's views on economic problems, and before she left she told me she was a Socialist. Isn't that a surprising coincidence?

With a heartful of love for you all, and with a bookful of news yet to come, I am,

Your affectionate child,
Helen Keller

At about this time, Helen felt obliged to leave the Socialist Party, which now claimed that socialism could be achieved through the ballot box. She joined the more militant Industrial Workers of the World (the IWW, or 'Wobblies') and openly lent her financial and journalistic support to the many strikes and mass demonstrations in the pre-war period. She steadfastly favoured militant opposition to the War, including a general strike, and regularly lent her name to protests against the drastic repressive measures taken against fellow Wobblies who were imprisoned for expressing their anti-war views.

Inspired also by the militant tactics of the English suffragettes, Helen now began to advocate hunger strikes and demonstrations in the American suffrage campaigns; many of her articles began to mention women's oppression as an example of injustice under the prevailing political system. But Helen fervently believed that women could not make meaningful advances under capitalism and her primary allegiance remained to a socialist revolution, which she assumed would pave the way for women's liberation, equality between the races, and world peace.

Kate Keller was not the only person to be disconcerted by her daughter's blunt political statements. By 1914 Helen was earning a substantial income as a public speaker: her pacifist speeches seemed increasingly treacherous as

World War I approached,* and she was warned by many people that she would have to curb her tongue or else damage her credibility and popularity. Helen did not yield to this pressure for many years. Once when a journalist offered to protect Helen's reputation by omitting certain sections of an interview in which Helen had been particularly uncompromising, Helen replied, 'I don't give a damn about semi-radicals.'

With her mother, Helen always spoke plainly about her views. For example, after a meeting with William English Walling, the intellectual leader of the Socialist Party's left wing, she wrote:

1 December 1914

Dearest Mother,
. . . He has just left and I am glad he came. For he is very interesting, and has wide experience in his work for the Revolution. Of course we discussed the War, and tried to think of some way to get hold of public opinion, so that another such war might never occur. Surely the world ought to take a day off and think. Surely all well-disposed people – philanthropists, pacifists, friends of the people – should get together at once and make a supreme effort to check the appalling waste of human life, arrest the swift retrograde of whatever civilization we have attained . . .

The war years, with the news of the Bolshevik Revolution, were the peak of Helen Keller's political activity. Helen and 'Teacher' travelled on the Chatauqua lecture circuit, demonstrating her progress in learning to speak and her proficiency and ready wit in sign language. Invariably she was challenged about her political views and, despite the pleas of the tour organisers that she should merely demonstrate her capabilities and offer inspiring platitudes, Helen was very ready to exchange political views with her audiences.

Around the time that this letter was written, Helen addressed a packed house at Carnegie Hall in New York, with a radicalism which created an immense uproar in her home town:

27 January 1916

Dearest Mother,
We were in Des Moines for a few hours Monday (we are to speak there tomorrow) and I was interviewed by a nice, cultivated young man from *The Leader*. I am sending you an editorial from that paper

---

*In this, Helen Keller is in good company with several other pacifist women in this chapter who courageously maintained their integrity in the face of slander and charges of treason from newspapers, co-workers and friends (see Olive Schreiner, Vera Brittain, Winifred Holtby and Lella Secor). Helen Keller tended to be more discredited than maligned: she was extremely well-loved, and newspapers who opposed her views tended to depict her as misguided, brainwashed, uninformed, and a puppet of the socialist or pacifist camps.

which may perhaps help you to understand why I am so deeply
interested in social and industrial problems that seem so wholly outside the 'limits of my personal world'. It seems the best explanation I
have found of my views and sentiments, over which I have often felt
puzzled myself. I am grieved to think of all the uneasiness I may cause
you, and I do long for you to see my heresies and heterodoxical 'nonsense' in the best possible light . . .

Helen's heresies and heterodoxical 'nonsense' at this point included frequent
articles on socialism, pacifism, civil liberties for strikers and dissenters, the
Russian Revolution, and birth control and other women's issues, which were
published in newspapers and magazines around the country. Her article,
'Why Men Need Woman Suffrage', which the New York *Call* published in
1915, was her longest and most forceful feminist declaration:

> . . . Women insist on their 'divine rights', 'immutable rights', inalien-
> able rights'. These phrases are not so sensible as one might wish. When
> one comes to think of it, there are no such thing as divine, immutable or
> inalienable rights. Rights are things we get when we are strong enough
> to make good our claim to them. Men spent hundreds of years and did
> much hard fighting to get the rights they now call divine, immutable
> and inalienable. Today women are demanding rights that tomorrow
> nobody will be foolhardy enough to question . . .
>
> The dullest can see that a good many things are wrong with the
> world. It is old-fashioned, running into ruts. We lack intelligent direc-
> tion and control. We are not getting the most out of our opportunities
> and advantages. We must make over the scheme of life, and new tools
> are needed for the work. Perhaps one of the chief reasons for the present
> chaotic conditions of things is that the world has been trying to get
> along with only half of itself. Everywhere we see running to waste [a]
> woman-force that should be utilized in making the world a more decent
> home for humanity. Let us see how the votes of women will help solve
> the problem of living wisely and well.
>
> When women vote men will no longer be compelled to guess at their
> desires – and guess wrong. Women will be able to protect themselves
> from man-made laws that are antagonistic to their interests. Some
> persons like to imagine that man's chivalrous nature will constrain him
> to act humanely toward woman and protect her rights. Some men do
> protect some women. We demand that all women have the right to
> protect themselves and relieve man of this feudal responsibility . . .
> Legislation made to protect women who have fathers and husbands to
> care for them does not protect working women whose only defenders
> are the state's policemen.
>
> Yet [woman's] peculiar knowledge [of family and social conscious-
> ness] and abilities are made the basis of arguments against giving
> women the vote. It is indisputably true that woman is constituted for
> the purposes of maternity. So is man constituted for the purposes of
> paternity. But no one seems to think that incapacitates him for
> citizenship. If there is a fundamental difference between man and
> woman, far be it from me to deny that it exists. It is all the more reason
> why her side should be heard.

For my part, I should think that man's chivalrous nature would cause him to emancipate the weaker half of the race. Indeed, it seems strange that when he was getting the suffrage for himself it did not occur to him to divide up with his beloved partner. Looking closer, I almost detect a suspicion of tyranny in his attitude toward her on the suffrage question. And can it be that this tyranny wears the mask of chivalry? Please do not misunderstand me. I am not disparaging chivalry. It is a very fine thing – what there is of it. The trouble is, there is not enough to go around. Nearly all the opportunities educational and political, that woman has acquired have been gained by a march of conquest with a skirmish at every post.

So since masculine chivalry has failed us we must hustle a bit and see what we can do for ourselves – and the men who need our suffrage. First of all, we must organize. We must make ourselves so aggressive a political factor that our natural protectors can no longer deny us a voice in directing and shaping the laws under which we must live.

By 1920, Helen Keller's speaking engagements were more or less free from provocative political observations. She spent the last forty years of her active life, until her stroke at the age of 80, promulgating her faith in the ability of blind people to be educated and trained for an independent life of useful employment. She travelled on five continents to promote these ideals and to make pleas for improved working and living conditions of blind people in the more than twenty countries she visited. She died of a second stroke at the age of 88.

Lella Secor to her mother Loretta, 1916–17

Lella Secor (1887–1966) was a journalist and peace activist in the United States during World War I. She was a co-founder of the American Neutral Conference Committee (later renamed the Emergency Peace Federation) and the People's Council of America. She later married and had two children; the family then moved to England, where she worked in campaigns for effective contraception and helped set up the Family Planning Association.

She was born to a staunch Baptist family in Battle Creek, Michigan, the youngest of seven children. Her father, an itinerant carpenter, drifted away from the family when Lella was very young. From an early age Lella assisted her strong and resilient mother, Loretta, in the various financial enterprises she embarked upon to keep the family from the poverty line. These included setting up a restaurant in California, working as a cook in a Wisconsin lumber camp, and, finally, starting a boarding house in Battle Creek; in this final, successful venture, 11-year-old Lella was made responsible for marketing.

Before she became involved in the peace cause, Lella moved through a variety of jobs, including a stint of pioneer farming on a 16-acre homestead near Spokane, Washington. Loretta wanted her to be a teacher but, for the most part, Lella worked for various newspapers, convincing editors that she could 'manage as well as a man'. While working as a journalist she became involved in peace work. She embarked on this new avenue almost by chance. A close friend, Rebecca Shelley, who was herself a peace activist, secured for her as yet uncommitted friend a reporting job on the Henry Ford Peace Ship Mission. The peace mission failed, but Lella herself returned to New York an ardent and committed pacifist. Within a short time she had teamed up with Rebecca as a propagandist and organiser for the cause.

It was at this point that the following letter to her mother was written:

26 March 1916

Dear Mother and All,

Christmas of 1915 will always stand out in a unique place in my memories. And one of the unique features was that I received not a single gift – gifts as we have been accustomed to think of gifts – except flowers. Instead I had the gift of Life itself – Life rich in new experiences and new visions and new dreams and new ambitions.

I suppose I shall never be able to repay all I owe Rebecca for having made this trip a possibility for me. I am experiencing again, as I did when I first went to Spokane, except in a much greater measure, that bounding, pulsing, thrilling joy of life within me; that old feeling of confidence in my powers – as yet not fully tried or tested – and the sublime sort of certainty that I shall be able to fight my way, however difficult the obstacles. Mr Sorensen in his last letter was kind enough to predict that 'some day you will be famous and great in the eyes of the world'. And someway – in a cool, matter-of-fact way, without thought of self-praise or self-esteem – I have sometimes felt that this might be true. And the reason why I think it might be true is because of my unwavering belief in the God-given powers which lie within us all, and which most of us have only begun to try out. There was a good deal of satisfaction, too, in his added statement that today, 'you are a great soul in the eyes' etc. etc. For after all, that is what I am striving for more than anything else in the world – to be a great soul; to experience life so fully that I shall be able to understand the joys, the aspirations, the defeat, the struggle, the discouragements of those around me. For I have come to know that in just such degree as one lives, and experiences, in just that degree one can be of the greatest service to mankind.

But I had no idea of delivering a sermon. Besides, the hour has come when I must be gone . . .

Heaps of love to all,
Lella

The next twelve months, until America declared war and the peace cause faltered, were some of the most hectic and exhausting for Lella and Rebecca – although suffused with the excitement and fulfillment of being so active in historical events. Lella's letters home tell of the organisations they helped to form and of what it was like to live month after month on two meals a day and very little sleep, working incessantly to obtain committed financial support for the cause. In one of the few letters she had time to write during this period, Lella is eager to make amends for her 'criminal neglect' of her family and sends her sisters a 'brief summary' of some of her activities.

The summary, like many of Lella's letters, extended to several thousand words; this excerpt describes her journey to the presidential nominating convention of the Democratic Party, during which she tried to get them to pledge support for the American Neutral Conference committee:

> . . . I feel almost that I have lived twenty years since last November. Certainly it has been the most strenuous and the most broadening nine months of my whole life. I really had a wonderful time in St Louis, though I carried the weight of my responsibilities so heavily that I slept only seven or eight hours during the four days I was gone. I found when I arrived that I was too late for a personal hearing before the resolutions committee which had already had its meeting. So I spent my first day with the aid of a stenographer, and a boy, in getting out the thousand letters [to the delegates]. It was a tremendous task, which I didn't finish until nine o'clock at night. Then I sat down to my first meal that day . . .
>
> I haven't any notion now of going off on a suffrage tangent. But I can stop to say this. I never realized how frightfully humiliating it is to be classed with imbeciles and criminals, until I lived in a state where woman is [not] accredited with human intelligence. Coming from Washington to New York has taught me a number of things.* Here women plead in vain for the decent conduct of children's homes and asylums – such frightful conditions have come to light lately – for laws which will protect the rights of the helpless. Politicians laugh them to scorn. Not so in Washington, where women have the power of the ballot behind them. If I were not so engrossed just now in stopping the war and working toward certain international ideals, I think I should be compelled to cast my lot with the suffrage cause.

This letter to her mother was written the same day:

4 September 1916

Dear Mother,

It is nearly ten o'clock, but I am not going to delay this belated letter another moment. I have just finished the final draft of a sort of 'heart' appeal which we expect to send out to thousands of people this week and next. I have put a good deal of time and thought on it, because I wanted to play on people's emotions. It is the only way that one can get money out of folks. From the beginning of our life as a committee I have contended that when the American people themselves were

---

*Before the Nineteenth Amendment was passed, Oregon, Washington, California, Montana, Idaho, Nevada, Utah, Arizona, Wyoming, Colorado and Kansas allowed women to vote in presidential elections. The state of Washington had given women full suffrage in 1910.

asked for financial support, they would give it. I have contended that we would get a more heart-whole response than we can expect to get from one millionaire in a thousand. So now the next few weeks will justify or prove false our contention. So far, our own plans have proved wisest on every hand, and I hope to be able to prove justifiable my faith in America.

. . . I almost believe that if I were to be at home, I would vote the Socialist ticket. They are for woman suffrage and they are for peace, whatever else they may stand for. I suppose that I might as well announce now that I am becoming quite strongly Socialistic in my tendencies. I hardly see how one can live in New York with all its bitter strife and struggle for a mere existence, and escape Socialism. I have not yet affiliated with their party, and I am not sure that I ever shall. But I do intend to study the matter somewhat exhaustively as soon as possible . . .

In spite of her evident commitment, Lella was still bothered by what she thought would be seen as neglect of her family. Although she was the youngest, she felt a sense of responsibility for all of them. When Loretta had to sell the family home, Lella took the opportunity to offer her emotional support (and even a place to live) but also to tell her mother – and reassure herself – that all the problems in Loretta's life did not arise simply out of the fact that Lella persisted in her own busy life, rather than rushing home to play the dutiful daughter whenever family difficulties arose.

In this letter she also replies to Loretta's insinuation that Rebecca, still the central person in Lella's life, seemed to have a 'snap' (i.e. easy) job:

Election Day, 1916

Dear Mother and All,

. . . You are at liberty, as I have told you before, to do exactly as you wish, and I do hope you will take advantage of your opportunity to make yourself happy. I am convinced that happiness rests with you alone. No one else can make or find it for you. I have worried a great deal about both you and Ina [Lella's sister], but I have come to feel that you must both work out your own happiness for yourself . . . it would be feeble folly for me to attempt it for you, as I have often falsely thought I could do, had I gone home . .

Rebecca and I are very happy together, though we see very little of each other because we are both so busy. We get along beautifully, because we allow each other absolute independence. We go off with separate friends at any time we choose, and in fact it is seldom more than once or twice a week that we even have dinner together. We show absolute respect for the individuality of each other. When we do have an evening at home, we feel that it is a rare treat. I am helping Rebecca as much as possible with her work, but I have come, as never before, to a pretty good realization of the limitations of my strength. I find I have very little vitality left, and for the most part I have to cherish it pretty carefully for my work at the office. I tire out so readily, and then I am likely to be good for nothing for days.

No, Mother, Rebecca has anything but a snap. I have discovered that all people, like Robert LaFollette and those who are giving themselves unreservedly to a cause or to promoting their ideals, do so only at the greatest cost to themselves. I have never seen such magnificent devotion and self-sacrifice as Rebecca has given and is giving to the peace cause. She has organized this big committee – of course I helped a good deal at the beginning – but in the main she may be said to have done everything herself, and she is now the life and spirit of the only movement being made in America to stop the slaughter in Europe. She gets a very modest salary when there are any funds, and when there are none, she goes without. Hers is purely a service of devotion.

At this late hour the election has not yet been settled . . . Everything hangs on the West, but I feel sure Wilson will win out, and I certainly hope so. I thought of you and Ina and Lena on election day, with your chance to vote . . .

Lovingly your baby,
Lella Faye

In a final, desperate effort to keep the United States neutral, Rebecca and Lella bought a full-page advertisement in the *New York Times* on the eve of Wilson's plea to Congress that America should join the fight to 'make the world safe for democracy'. Their advertisement was addressed to the 'Mothers, Daughters and Wives of Men' and they raised $35,000 overnight for the Emergency Peace Federation.

In April, 1917, America entered World War I. Lella, though resolved to fight on, was deeply disillusioned. Eventually her frantic lifestyle took its toll and, thoroughly worn out in body and spirit, she was forced to take a month's rest in a sanatorium. Although she resumed the fight immediately afterwards, at the age of 30 she had exhausted herself irreversibly and was never again able to work at the same furious pace.

In 1917 she married Philip Florence, a researcher on industrial safety; he had also dedicated himself at times to working for the Emergency Peace Federation. Lella had no desire to lose her independence and he asked her several times to marry him before she said yes.

She wrote to her mother while on her honeymoon:

1 October 1917

Dear Mother and All The Loved Ones,

. . . It was the first time Philip and I had ever had an uninterrupted bit of leisure, and we agreed not to do any work or to carry into our honeymoon any responsibilities from the outside world. It gave me an opportunity to get acquainted with the most charming, tender, thoughtful and delightful person in the world. I had always thought that marriage represented a distinct change in one's life, with always the lurking possibility that one might suddenly awake to the fact that the change was not agreeable at all. Instead I have found it just a delightful continuation of a rare and beautiful comradeship. I am convinced there are not many marriages such as ours. I suppose every bride thinks so. But my belief is based on something more than love for my husband. I have seen much of married people, and I have known much of marriage, but I have never known any union so sweet and beautiful, so spiritual and soul-satisfying as ours. I dwell in the sunshine of Philip's great soul, and my heart sings with happiness . . .

Boundless love to all,
Lella

After the marriage, Lella and Rebecca continued their political work, now joined by Philip. In 1918 they launched a new movement, The Young Democracy, founded on their longstanding dream of an international organisation whose aims would be international peace, freedom of thought and speech both in and out of universities, and 'economic democracy' for all people; their immediate task was to speak out against militarism and strive to protect the rights of conscientious objectors.

Lella gave birth to a son on Armistice Day, continued working for Young Democracy from home, and once again neared a complete breakdown from exhaustion: throughout their married life, Philip frequently had to intervene and persuade her to take rests when her health reached the danger point. After the birth of their second son (born in 1920 on the aniversary of Susan B. Anthony's hundredth birthday and named Anthony in her honour), Lella pursued a full-time career as mother, housekeeper and gardener; but after a year she began trying to get steady work as a journalist on New York magazines. Philip had difficulty finding a full-time job and they moved to England where Philip was offered a position as junior lecturer in economics at Cambridge University. Lella's mother died just before they moved, so there are no letters about her life in England.

In Cambridge (and later when they moved to Birmingham), Lella devoted her energies to family life, the world disarmament campaign, and women's rights. Her chief interest was the contraception campaign and she was well-known as a dynamic administrator in both the Cambridge and Birmingham Family Planning Clinics. She died of pneumonia following a stroke at the age of 79. She had managed to remain active in politics throughout her life, just as she had said she would in a letter written to her mother at the height of her idealism:

28 October 1916

. . . It has been my efforts for peace which have given me most of my broadening opportunities so that, while I have spent a great deal of time and energy, I have been amply repaid. I owe the peace cause a great deal just from purely selfish reasons. There will never be a time in my life again when I am not actively engaged in some big work which I think is going to better humanity, unless I am flat on my back.

Vera Brittain to her mother Edith, 1916–17, and to her daughter Shirley Williams, 1953

What mattered about a book was not its favourable reception from the public, but the quality and significance of the work put into it.
Vera Brittain, *Testament of Experience* (1957)

Vera Brittain (1893–1970), British writer, feminist and pacifist, was born in Staffordshire to Edith Mary Bervon and Thomas Brittain, a prosperous paper manufacturer. From an early age she rebelled against the provincial restrictions of her environment, and particularly against her parents' lack of interest in educating her. She eventually prevailed upon them to let her attend university (which they thought unnecessary for a woman), and in 1914 she won a scholarship to Somerville College, Oxford. World War I interrupted her university career almost immediately and dramatically altered the course of her life. Left behind in England by her fiancé Roland Leighton, her brother Edward, and their two closest friends, who all went to the front, she found her intellectual retreat at Oxford intolerable; after a year she left to enroll in the Voluntary Aid Detachment (VAD). Her next four years were spent working as a nurse in army hospitals in London, Malta and France – experiences which later formed the basis of her acclaimed memoir, *Testament of Youth*.

In the first letter selected here, she has just left Oxford and moved to London to work at the First London General Hospital: she writes to both parents in response to her father's suggestion that she leave her nursing work and return home. The second letter was written after a few months in Malta, and the third from a hospital in France where she nursed German prisoners:

[1916]

Thank you very much for your letter, the answer to which really did not require much thinking over. *Nothing* – beyond sheer necessity – would induce me to stop doing what I am doing now, and I should never respect myself again if I allowed a few slight physical hardships to make me give up what is the finest work any girl can do now. I honestly did not take it up because I thought you did not want me or could not afford to give me a comfortable home, but because I wanted to prove I could more or less keep myself by working, and partly because, not being a man and able to go to the Front, I wanted to do the next best thing. I do not agree that my place is at home doing nothing or practically nothing, for I consider that the place now of anyone who is young and strong and capable is where the work that is needed is to be done. And really the work is not too hard – even if I were a little girl, which I no longer am, for I sometimes feel quite ninety nowadays . . .

January 1917

[These watercolours] are for my study at Oxford if ever I get there again, and even if I don't I can't imagine myself without a study if I am alive. I would rather do without a bedroom and sleep on the sofa in the drawing room than without a room to myself where I can have a fire of my own and not be interrupted by anyone . . . Your remark about the War lasting five [more] years makes me wonder if I shall ever go there at all. If it really does . . . I think we should all be dead by then, but if I am not I shall only be twenty-seven, and it would still be worth while . . .

It seems very hard that we should be the generation to suffer the War, though I suppose it is very splendid too, and is making us better and wiser and deeper men and women than our ancestors ever were or our descendants ever will be. It seems to me that the War will make a big division of 'before' and 'after' in the history of the world, almost if not quite as big as the 'B.C.' and 'A.D.' division made by the birth of Christ . . .

December 1917

The hospital is very heavy now – as heavy as when I came; the fighting is continuing very long this year, and the convoys keep coming down, two or three a night . . . Sometimes in the middle of the night we have to turn people out of bed and make them sleep on the floor to make room for more seriously ill ones that have come down from the line. We have heaps of gassed cases at present who came in a day or two ago; there are ten in this ward alone. I wish those people who write so glibly about this being a holy War, and the orators who talk so much about going on no matter how long the War lasts and what it may mean, could see a case – to say nothing of ten cases – of mustard gas in its early stages – could see the poor things burnt and blistered all over with great mustard-coloured suppurating blisters with blind eyes – sometimes temporarily, sometimes permanently – all sticky and stuck together, and always fighting for breath, with voices a mere whisper, saying that their throats are closing and they know they will choke. The only thing one can say is that such severe cases don't last long; either they die soon or else improve – usually the former; they certainly never reach England in the state we have them here, and yet people persist in saying that God made the War, when there are such inventions of the Devil about . . .

Before long, this impassioned humanity in the face of others' tragedy was put to the ultimate test. Vera lost all four of the men she loved: first Roland, in 1915, and last of all her brother Edward, who was killed just five weeks before the War ended. The effect on her was not only a devastating sadness; she was left with a feeling of indebtedness, a sense of guilt about the lives they had not been allowed to live: 'I ended the First World War with my deepest emotions paralysed if not dead. This would not have happened if I had *one* person left. It was Edward's death rather than Roland's which turned me into an automaton . . . It left nothing. Only ambition held me to life.'

A committed pacifist after the War, Vera returned to Oxford to complete her studies for a BA in Modern History. There she became a close friend of Winifred Holtby,* about whom she later wrote *Testament of Friendship*. Vera and Winifred moved to London after taking their degrees and there they began their writing careers in earnest. Their extraordinary friendship was to be one of the major influences on Vera's life; she was inspired by Winifred and the two women gave each other encouragement and practical help for many years. Even after Vera's marriage to the political philosopher, George Catlin (whom Vera always referred to in her books as 'G.'), in 1925, Winifred remained a member of the household until her untimely death in 1935, when she was only 37.

Vera described the challenge of establishing the sort of life to which she and George and Winifred were committed: 'The word "career" is a limited expression, suggesting a neat nine-to-five job of small significance; the real clash lies between the important human relationship of marriage, and every type of fulfilment – spiritual, intellectual, social – which falls outside the range of personal intimacy.'

For the first six years of their marriage, G. maintained his appointment as Assistant Professor of Politics at Cornell University, in Ithaca, New York. Since living at Cornell did not appeal to Vera, and they each respected the other's work, they evolved a 'semi-detached marriage', with G. teaching in New York and Vera writing in London, meeting as often as possible each year. They loved each other devotedly and eventually G. moved back to England, although he continued to travel and lecture abroad, later becoming Professor at McGill University in Canada. Their son, John, was born in 1927 and their daughter, Shirley, in 1930.

Feeling that she owed something to the men she loved who had died in World War I, Vera collected their diaries and letters and in 1929 began writing *Testament of Youth*. She finished four years later, in spite of the demands of two young children, and in the face of ridicule from some writers

---

*See pp. 165–9.

who felt that she was too young to write an autobiography. Later, she described her reactions to their criticisms:

> Now, inspired only by blind faith and the urgent need for reconciliation with the past, I gave up hoping for any real fulfilments, and wrote on in my few spare hours because, if I did not write, I might as well cease to live.
>
> I was writing, I thought, to try to console others who like myself had known despair – about the loved they had lost, perhaps, or their work's frustration – and to prove that this universal emotion could be overcome even by individuals whose courage was as small as mine. I wanted also to show that war was not glamour or glory but abysmal grief and purposeless waste, though I acknowledged its moments of grandeur.
>
> Finally I wrote to commemorate the lives of four young men who because they died would never make books for themselves, yet deserved as much as anyone to be remembered . . . nothing could take away the significance of that memorial and its challenge to the spiritual bankruptcy of mankind.

Testament of Youth was published in 1933: it was an immediate bestseller in both England and the U.S. and Vera became famous overnight. She travelled extensively over the next years, lecturing in support of the League of Nations, the Peace Pledge Union and the American Friends Service Committee.

During World War II, her unswerving pacifist convictions led her to condemn publicly the saturation bombing of Germany, with the result that she was vilified on both sides of the Atlantic and ostracised both in her work and in some of her friendships. During the war she wrote *Humiliation with Honour*, an eloquent treatise on pacifism and the persecution which pacifists suffer in wartime. Written in the form of letters to her son, John, she explained her realisation that 'even the humiliations which it involves can become assets which add to knowledge and increase spiritual power if they are regarded as experience obtainable in no other fashion.

Testament of Experience is a memoir of her life from the time of her marriage through to World War II and her post-war peace work, culminating in a long-desired trip to India in 1949 to study the principles of non-violence with disciples of Gandhi. She continued to write books and lecture on both feminist and pacifist issues until her health failed in 1966; she published twenty-six books in all. Towards the end of her life she wrote:

> From the end of the First World War, I had seen my work ever more clearly as an attempt to enlarge 'the consciousness of humanity'. It had not brought me any special reputation, but I believed that it had played a small part in the mental revolution through which I had lived. The real cause of the two World Wars had been political unconsciousness; the too-slowly diminishing failure of the mass of people in all countries to perceive what was happening. If the peace-makers could extend, however little, this power of realization, they had accomplished much of their task . . .
>
> I remembered . . . the distance that I had travelled from the 'little girl' whose Staffordshire father had not thought her worth educating.

At least, I reflected, in the long struggle against heredity and temperament I had not wholly failed. Thanks to G.'s magnanimity, to the self-discipline demanded by my creed, and to the talent for writing with which, through the grace of God, I had been endowed, I had always been able to escape from ancestral impulses and become myself . . .

Shirley, I believed, would no more find marriage an end in itself than I had done, but in the process of becoming a complete human being she would not meet with the criticisms, the obstacles, and the traditional assumptions which handicapped my generation. Except for a period deliberately set aside for bearing and rearing children, the luxury of 'checking out' at will from the world's work into private life would soon be as little expected from wives as it had always been from husbands.

Shirley (now Shirley Williams, MP) worked as a waitress and farmhand before going to Oxford, where she became the first woman to chair the Oxford University Labour Club. She did post-graduate research on American trade unions, lectured in Ghana for a year, worked as a journalist on the *Daily Mirror* and *Financial Times*, and served as General Secretary of the Fabian Society, before being elected to Parliament at the age of 34. She married the philosopher Bernard Williams in 1955 and they had a daughter, Rebecca; the marriage ended in 1974. From 1976 to 1979 Shirley Williams served as Secretary of State for Education and Science. In January 1981, she broke away from the Labour Party and became one of the four founders of the new Social Democratic Party; later that year she became the first MP to be elected as an SDP candidate.

She declares that: 'Unlike my mother, I am not a feminist.' Being a Roman Catholic and a politician committed to social reform while accepting certain traditional values, she does not always see eye to eye with the women's liberation movement. She voted, for example, against the liberalisation of both the divorce and abortion laws; but she supports equal pay, positive discrimination for women in certain aspects of employment and in her own party, sex-blind education in which girls are encouraged to do technical and scientific studies, equal treatment in taxes, social security, promotion and recruitment, and many other issues which favour women's equality. Her book, *Politics Is for People*, makes little specific mention of women and this reflects her position of 'resent[ing] all inequality, not just the inequality of women. Women should be treated like other people.'

However, in spite of being in some ways as different from her mother as Vera was from her own mother, Shirley does not hesitate to acknowledge Vera's influence on her. She wrote to me in 1981:

'In my view one of the most important elements of a mother/daughter relationship is that daughters are likely to feel that they must justify themselves to their mothers, who in many ways can be the keepers of their conscience . . . her relationship with her mother tends to set the tone of relationships that a woman has with other women throughout her life.

'My own mother was someone whose integrity was difficult to live up to; it was so great . . . [It] involved total commitment to her own sense of humanity which went as far as condemning saturation bombing of Germany during the Second World War, which . . . was hardly popular and led to her being, to some extent, isolated until the war ended.

'But I remember her also in many other ways, as a person who loved walking and who loved nature and who loved long conversations on literary matters far away from politics. It is those periods of peace together that are in many ways the essence of a good mother/daughter relationship.'

The following letter from Vera to Shirley was published in 1953 as the Dedication of *Lady Into Woman*, Vera's historical survey of twentieth-century struggles for women's liberation:

1953

My Dear Daughter,

I owe you much gratitude for the title which you were resourceful enough to suggest.

You were right to propose a form of words which implies that the democratic movement described in this book has not been concerned exclusively with sex equality.

Not only has the sheltered 'lady' of the Victorian epoch become the self-sufficient 'woman' of today; the political and social changes of the past half-century have brought her close in experience and understanding to the millions of women in all past ages who were never sheltered and always had to work.

You will find that I have not attempted to be soberly impartial about the emancipation of women, past, present, or future; with Canon Raven I believe it to be more significant, and more beneficial, than any great constructive change of the past fifty years. But I do not expect every reader of this book to agree, for the backwoodsmen are still with us.

Up to date they have hardly troubled you, but unlike many of your contemporaries you do not regard the women's movement as a bygone issue. Even from your brief experience you know that it is continuing, and still has far to go.

When you were growing up you sometimes suggested, as you had every right to do, that certain aspects of your upbringing might have been better. But you have had three advantages which you do, I believe, acknowledge as likely to be of special service to you in your life and work.

First, you owe to the Infant Welfare movement in general, and the Chelsea Babies' Club in particular, the vital energy and powers of endurance which have enabled you to show that the physical inferiority of women was a myth based upon faulty training and a traditional expectation of feminine weakness.

Secondly, you have been free from the implanted sense of inferiority that handicaps so many women by undermining the self-confidence which is the basis of all achievement, both masculine and feminine. You were deeply desired as a *daughter*, and it was always taken for granted by both your parents that your education and opportunities would be equal to your brother's. The women of your family had sought these benefits before you. Your paternal grandmother was a pioneer suffragist; your mother grew up with that eager generation of young feminists who were the first to inherit the freedom won for women by women. You have repaid us both by making a full and early use of your heritage.

Thirdly, you belong to a household in which a woman's work has been constantly in progress, and professional standards obeyed with the same sense of obligation by a wife and mother as by a husband and father. You have never been made to feel that the profession adopted by a woman is somehow less important than the one chosen by a man, or that her failure to do as well as she is able would be condoned and excused because of her sex.

My work, it is true, has been more interrupted than yours, I hope, will be; for I belong to a generation in which most families still took, and take, for granted that a woman's vocation should be laid aside for parental illness, the troubles of relatives, and domestic trivialities of every description.

I could have written much better if I had been interrupted much less, and should have proved altogether a more effective person had I not been obliged – and not only in my youth – to spend time and energy in learning to believe in myself and my purposes despite the enervating influence of an Edwardian childhood.

That you, who have been spared that particular battle, will live to see women ascend to heights of achievement hitherto undreamed of and make your own contribution to this future stage of a great revolution, is the constant and joyful hope of

Your Mother

Winifred Holtby to her mother Alice, 1923

Winifred Holtby (1898–1935), novelist, journalist and political activist, grew up on a farm in Yorkshire, the second daughter of Alice and David Holtby who were both from long-established farming families. She had a warm relationship with both her parents throughout her life; although they came to differ with Winifred on virtually every issue of political and intellectual interest to her, she always maintained close contact with them, journeying home from London almost every weekend during periods of family illness and distress. Alice Holtby was a powerful figure in both her family and her community. A long-standing member of the local county council, she was the first woman to be appointed Alderman in her county, and Winifred greatly admired her mother's competence. Because she was so accustomed to viewing women as capable and active, Winifred admitted to being shocked to discover upon her arrival at Oxford that women there saw a need for a feminist movement.

When she was 18, Winifred worked for a year as a volunteer nurses' aid and then, in 1917, began studying for a degree in Modern History at Oxford. She left Oxford after a year and enlisted in the Women's Army Auxiliary Corps (WAAC) against the wishes of her teachers and parents. She then served in France for a year until the Armistice. She returned to Oxford to complete her degree course and there met Vera Brittain who became her closest friend.* From 1920, she and Vera (and, later, Vera's husband and two children) shared a home in London.

Although Winifred's greatest desire was to write novels, she had a relentless sense of family duty and a strong political conscience, so her literary efforts were constantly interrupted. In addition to being summoned frequently to Yorkshire to nurse sick relatives, run errands and, in general, play the role of dutiful daughter, she often worked more than full-time to promote the causes of pacifism, feminism and racial equality. In an obituary of her, Rebecca West said that Winifred Holtby 'belonged to the elect of the War generation, who were deepened and dignified by their experience, but not perturbed. There was no trace of hysteria or self-pity in her hearty loathing of war.' Winifred travelled extensively in Europe and South Africa lecturing for the League of Nations Union, and after a six-month trip to South Africa in 1926 she began working to promote trades unions for black South African workers and to focus the attention of the British public on the horrifying effects of racism. Vera Brittain wrote in *Testament of Friendship*: 'her months in South Africa struck a more formidable blow against the artist in her than any other adventure, for they provided the social reformer with an overwhelming programme of wrongs to protest.'

Winifred Holtby was considered by many of her contemporaries to be the finest journalist in London. She contributed regularly to the *Manchester Guardian*, the *Yorkshire Post*, the *News Chronicle*, *Daily Herald* and *Good Housekeeping*. When she was only 28, she became a director of the popular weekly, *Time & Tide*, and for the rest of her life she was also a regular contributor to that prestigious journal.

In between her services to family and friends, her political activities and her career in journalism, Winifred Holtby wrote six novels, two plays, a collection of short stories, a critical study of Virginia Woolf, and a history of the women's liberation struggle in the twentieth century. Her last two novels,

*See pp. 159–165.

Mandoa, Mandoa! (a satire on imperialist attempts to bring 'civilisation' to Africa) and *South Riding* (a complex and loving portrait of her native Yorkshire), were both great critical successes and *South Riding* has never been out of print.* *South Riding*, which was awarded the James Tait Black Memorial Prize as the best novel of 1936, was written in the last two years of her life when she was in almost constant pain and under heavy medication for high blood pressure. She completed this classic novel only a few weeks before she died at the age of 37.

This letter is a fragment found in Winifred Holtby's files after her death. The salutation was missing, but it was almost certainly addressed to her mother. At the time, Winifred was campaigning in the general election for a Liberal Party candidate in Bethnal Green who strongly supported the League of Nations Union:

1923

. . . I do want you to believe that however impulsive, tactless, weak and conceited I may be, I am trying to live up to the light which I see, and because I would not have you think that the light is all darkness, I want to try and explain a very little. I do not know quite wherein you think I am losing my soul, but I rather gather it is probably about these things.

The Church, for instance, because I don't go any more. This is the result of a long process of thought which began when I was in France. At Oxford I read a good deal of the history of the Church, of the way in which creeds were built up by men – generally of no great education or enlightenment – at times of hot controversy . . . I learned how year by year the original teaching of Christ became more and more set about with interpretations and symbols until the real meaning over and over was lost, and instead of His universal spiritual kingdom of God arose exclusive sects, at first one, then three, then hundreds, each claiming to be the receptacle of the true faith without which man cannot be saved.

So I said, 'I have loved the Church. Its services are beautiful. I loved its symbolism. Its historical association with martyrs and saints inspired me. But it is bloodstained, not only with the blood of martyrs but of heretics. It is darkened by superstition and fear. It stands between the world and the thing I long for most, the coming of the Universal Kingdom of God. So I will not take its sacraments nor support its organisation.'

---

*Three of Winifred Holtby's novels have been reprinted in the Virago Modern Classics series: *The Land of Green Ginger, Anderby Wold* and *The Crowded Street. South Riding* is published by Penguin.

Then there is selfishness. Dear heart, when I say that I want 'to get on', do you really think I just want fame? Don't you know that when I am in Bethnal Green I have a strong temptation to throw aside this climbing and to do what I always used to think I would do – just work in the slums among the poor people? But I believe that would be a coward's way of service. I believe that service lies in this – that each of us should use in the highest way, to the very widest possible extent, the abilities or powers they have been given. I believe that to be content with humbler service, when one is able to stand greater responsibility, is only cowardice.

Some must lead, and by their abilities are they chosen, and to ladle soup in a slum kitchen when one should be defending Justice as a King's Counsel, or Truth as a writer or philosopher, is blind sacrifice, which may even be deliberate cowardice and fighting away from the light.

I do not know what path I shall take. I do not know whither I am being called. I may do many things that seem to you selfish, heartless or blind. But here at the beginning of my journey I want you to know this, because I love and honour you and count upon your love more than you will ever know. I may not go the way that you would have me go. I may say and do foolish things, I may even in the end get nowhere, teach nothing, have helped nobody and have failed myself. But this you *must* believe, or you may be hurt and disappointed a thousand times, and I shall not always be able to explain.

As I see the light, so will I act, if I have strength and courage. I look each day for further light to see problems more clearly, to try my best to deal with them. By preaching Peace I am trying to find that Kingdom of God which Christ taught. By writing I am trying to put down something of the truth as I see it. And remember that in my very first book I said that with the seeing of new light, much that was beautiful and good in the old has to suffer – that the truth is not all good, that it is taught most often by unworthy prophets, that it comes with cruelty and often with injustice. And yet, 'there shall be no contentment but proceeding'.

My second book is to be this – That each of us must act by the light as we see it, choosing deliberately our path and accepting full responsibility for our own actions, looking for neither reward nor praise, nor even recognition. For by acting alone with his face to the light, the spirit of man expands towards his God, and seeing the light and yet refusing it – that is what Christ called 'the sin against the Holy Ghost'. What my third book will be, I do not know. Whether I am right to write these things, I do not know. Whether I shall ever teach the things I see, whether I am seeing them aright, I do not know. I only know that I have seen a vision of pure beauty on the earth, of universal love, and of a spiritual kingdom, and though I am a thousand times unfit to seek it, though I know myself to be a coward, often to lie, always to shrink from unpleasantness, to dread unpopularity, to hate effort, yet I must go along the road I see. And if I hurt you on the road, if I act impulsively on wrong assumptions, my dear, you must know I do not want to hurt you, that I love you, that if in seeking for the light I do wrong, it is not because the light is wrong, but because my eyes are too weak not to be dazzled.

Darling, this may seem to you off the point. It does hardly touch the present sore place – and yet it does, for it just shows where I fail. I am a coward. I hate saying anything unpleasant to people's faces, especially when I love them. I find it difficult to be straight. So when I try, I work myself up to a false courage, am rude and defiant and say not what I meant to say, and often half defeat my own ends. But to try to be straight, to try to be honest, that I believe is to keep faith.

Forgive this long letter. I know it may not sound quite clear, but I do not believe that you will fail to understand. Always you have understood, and just because you do, I shall make still bigger demands upon your understanding, and do and say things that you may think wrong even, if not just foolish. You may think me selfish or inconsiderate. I may hurt you again. But still I count on your love, and love you. And if the methods I see are different from the ones you would have me choose, it is because my qualifications and abilities are different.

Unless you want anything explaining, I will not write again about this. I have tried to make it clear, but sometimes it is not even very clear to myself. Only I know that I have seen 'upon the road a light', and I would not have you think that it was only darkness.

Amelia Earhart to her mother Amy, 1928

Before she chose her legendary career as an aviator, Amelia Earhart (1897–1937) had considered devoting her life either to medicine or to social work. She grew up in Missouri and Iowa, the eldest of two daughters of Edwin and Amy Earhart. After she graduated from high school in 1917 she joined the Voluntary Aid Detachment (VAD) and worked as a nurses' aide until the Armistice. Unlike her friends, who were preoccupied with their hopes of good marriages, Amelia showed no sign of wanting to marry; instead, she kept a notebook of news items about women's achievements as they began to take over jobs previously reserved for men.

In 1919, Amelia attended Columbia University as a pre-medical student; but after a year she decided that she would not make a good doctor because she was more interested in the experimental than the practical side of medicine. She had been taking flying lessons during the war and, after leaving Columbia, took numerous jobs to pay for additional lessons. Despite the low ebb of her family's finances (her father had lost her mother's inheritance in a mining venture), her parents and sister bought her a small yellow biplane for her twenty-fourth birthday. She began reading the history of women in aviation and in her own flights was soon breaking altitude records.

Amelia returned to Columbia for a semester, went to Harvard summer school and held dozens of jobs before she found a social-work position at Denison House, Boston, which appealed to her growing interest in working for radical change. A friend of the family pressed her to marry him, but she refused because she was dedicated to her work and did not want to lose her independence. At the age of 29, while she was still working at Denison House, she was asked to be a passenger on a transatlantic flight aboard the aircraft *Friendship*. This was one year after Charles Lindbergh became the first person to fly across the Atlantic Ocean: Amelia would be the first woman. There was widespread enthusiasm for flying, and the presence of a woman, even as a passenger, was intended to focus worldwide attention on the *Friendship*'s mission – if they survived. It was a secret assignment about which she did not even tell her parents; she wrote them brief letters which she never sent (see below).

George Palmer Putnam (of the publishing family) was one of the backers of that pioneer flight. Three years later, he and Amelia were married – but Amelia insisted on keeping her maiden name. She had never been eager to marry and she detailed her reservations about the forthcoming event in a letter which she gave to her future husband just before the ceremony:

> There are some things which should be writ before we are married. Things we have talked over before – most of them.
>
> You must know again my reluctance to marry, my feeling that I shatter thereby chances in work which means so much to me. I feel the move just now as foolish as anything I could do. I know there may be compensations, but have no heart to look ahead.
>
> In our life together I shall not hold you to any medieval code of faithfulness to me, nor shall I consider myself bound to you similarly. If we can be honest I think the differences which arise may best be avoided . . .
>
> Please let us not interfere with each other's work or play, nor let the world see private joys or disagreements. In this connection I may have to keep some place where I can go to be myself now and then, for I cannot guarantee to endure at all times the confinements of even an attractive cage.
>
> I must exact a cruel promise, and that is you will let me go in a year if we find no happiness together.
>
> I will try to do my best in every way . . .

The marriage was a happy one and it lasted until the end of her life.

The year after she married, Amelia made her first solo flight across the Atlantic; and now, at last, she felt that she deserved her acclaim. She broke the record of the *Friendship* flight by more than five hours and was hailed worldwide for her courage, endurance and passionate spirit. Amelia Earhart made many more record-breaking flights: in 1935 she made a solo flight from Los Angeles to Mexico City, continuing on to Newark, New Jersey; that same year she became the first woman to fly solo from Hawaii to California. Her feminist convictions became stronger the more that she attempted and succeeded; she used her fame to promote women's equality in aviation, education, marriage and every field of human endeavour. She lived for awhile in a women's dormitory at Purdue University and counselled women students on their career choices, urging them to work even after they married. In *Last Flight*, the posthumously edited story of her attempted round-the-world flight in 1937, she wrote about her involvement in feminism:

> With these activities came opportunity to know women who shared my conviction that there is so much women can do in the modern world and should be permitted to do irrespective of sex. Probably my greatest satisfaction was to indicate by example now and then, that women can sometimes do things themselves if given the chance.

In 1936 she began planning her round-the-world flight; she intended to fly east to west, as near the equator as possible – a distance of about twenty-seven thousand miles. The biggest risks were that civilian radio equipment was neither sophisticated nor reliable and, as always, there were innumerable hazards of flying long stretches over water. She was warned by most friends and colleagues not to try it, but on 20 May 1937 she set off from Oakland, California, with her navigator, Fred Noonan. They followed a route through Miami–Puerto Rico–Venezuela–Dutch Guyana–Brazil–Natal–Dakar–Gao–Chad–Sudan–Eritrea–Karachi–Calcutta–Burma–Singapore–Java–Australia. They had travelled 22,000 miles in forty days when they set off from Australia to do the last and most perilous leg of the journey over the Pacific Ocean. They made the first 1,200-mile leap to New Guinea successfully; on 1 July they set off for Howland Island, a two-mile-long speck in the Pacific which was to be their last stop before returning to Oakland and accomplishing the round-the-world challenge. The last communication from Amelia came after she had been in the air for nearly twenty-one hours: they were somewhere over the Pacific with little fuel left and faulty radio equipment. After weeks of intensive searching, they were presumed dead.

In *Soaring Wings*, his biography of Amelia Earhart, George Putnam wrote about the letters which Amelia had written to her parents before her first transatlantic flight aboard the *Friendship*: 'In the papers she left behind I found two other letters, unopened and exactly as she had filed them, held together by a weary elastic band which had lost all usefulness years since. Clipped to the envelopes in AE's pencilled writing, was the bald notation: "Popping-off Letters" ':

20 May 1928

Dear Mother,
    Even though I have lost, the adventure was worthwhile. Our family tends to be too secure. My life has really been very happy, and I don't mind contemplating its end in the midst of it.

The letter to her father was equally brief and contained similar sentiments. It began, 'Hooray for the last grand adventure!'

Sylvia Plath to her mother Aurelia, 1956–63

When Sylvia Plath arrived at Cambridge University in 1955 to take up her Fulbright Scholarship, she had already achieved considerable recognition for her writing and was embarking on her first major adventure after recovering from her suicide attempt at the age of 20.* This new phase of her life was marked by two goals: to develop her talent as a poet and to marry and raise a family.

According to her mother, from an early age Sylvia had had a horror of getting married and cooking three meals a day. In 1953, after her first year at Smith College, she wrote to Aurelia from her summer job in a resort hotel: 'Boys live so much harder than girls and they know so much more about life. Learning the limitations of a woman's sphere is no fun at all.' It is also clear from her letters that she wanted to get married and have children. However, for the 1950s, she had set a very unusual standard for a mate: that her own creativity would be cherished; that she would have time to write; that she would be allowed to be strong.

Sylvia fell deeply in love with the poet Ted Hughes during her first year at Cambridge. She wrote to her mother after their first meeting: '. . . I will probably never see him again, but wrote my best poem about him after-wards – the only man I've met yet here who'd be strong enough to be equal with . . .' They were married in June 1956 and set out enthusiastically to create the ideal conditions for both of them to write poetry, encouraging and criticising each other's work. They settled in the Devon countryside, where they both managed to write, publish and win prizes. In 1958, Sylvia Plath won her first coveted acceptance from the *New Yorker*; her first book of poetry, *The Colossus*, was published in 1960. When the children were born, Frieda in 1960 and Nicholas in 1962, Sylvia and Ted looked after them in shifts so that they could each have either the morning or the afternoon to work uninterruptedly.

The idyll ended soon after Nicholas was born; Ted Hughes initiated the separation and moved back to London, leaving Sylvia and the children in Devon. Finding the isolation too distressing, Sylvia decided to move back to London with the children; they all suffered serious bouts of flu in one of England's worst winters, during which there were numerous power cuts, leaving them without heat or electricity and driving her deeper and deeper into despair. Sylvia Plath committed suicide, possibly by accident, on 11 February 1963.

---

*See Chapter 1 for information on Sylvia Plath's early life.

The first group of letters which follow were written while Sylvia was at Cambridge University and include the early stages of her relationship with Ted Hughes. The second group, following her separation from Ted, show Sylvia's efforts to cope with her grief, the demands of the children and her commitment to writing poetry. The poems she wrote during that darkest period are considered her finest work; they were published posthumously in her second book, *Ariel*.

6 February 1956

Dearest of Mothers,

 . . . In the last two years, we have certainly had our number of great tests (first my breakdown, then your operation, then grammy's), and we have yet been extraordinarily lucky that they were timed in such a way that we could meet them.

 I am most grateful that I banged up all at once (although I am naturally sorry for all the trouble I caused everyone else), for I can't tell you how my whole attitude to life has changed! I would have run into trouble sooner or later with my very rigid, brittle, almost hysterical tensions which split me down the middle, between inclination and inhibition, ideal and reality. My whole session with Dr. B. is responsible for making me a rich, well-balanced, humorous, easy-going person, with joy in the daily life, including all its imperfections: sinus, weariness, frustration, and all those other niggling things we all have to bear. I am occasionally depressed now, or discouraged, especially when I wonder about the future, but instead of fearing these low spots as the beginning of a bottomless whirlpool, I know I have already faced The Worst (total negation of self) and that, having lived through that blackness, like Peer Gynt . . . I can enjoy life simply for what it is: a continuous job, but most worth it. My existence now rests on solid ground; I may be depressed now and then, but never desperate. I know how to wait . . .

 My best love to all of you; keep well and happy for me!

Your own loving
Sylvia

9 March 1956

 It is a beauteous morning, and I have my windows thrown wide open to let the crisp, clear air and pale sunlight flood into my room. Song sparrows are twittering and chirping in the gutters under my windows, and the orange-tile rooftops are all sparkling in the light, which reminds me of the chilled champagne air of Venice, Nice and the January Riviera. I felt especially desirous of just hugging you and sharing this lovely morning, so, in substitute, I am writing this letter before I set out to the laundromat and my weekly shopping, and also sending you my two most recent, and, I think, best poems which I have written in the last weeks . . .

I'll be so eager to hear what you think of these: for myself, they show a rather encouraging growth. 'Channel Crossing' is one of the first I've written in a 'new line'; turning away from the small, coy love lyric (I am most scornful of the small preciousness of much of my past work) and bringing the larger, social world of other people into my poems. I have been terribly limited hitherto, and my growing strong concepts of the universe have been excluded from my poetry (coming out, I think, most interestingly in my series of *Seventeen* stories about social problems: Jewish question, sororities, etc., which I still admire!). Now, I am making a shift. The world and the problems of an individual in this particular civilization are going to be forged into my discipline, which is still there, but, if you will read the poem out loud (it's meant to be), you will, I hope, not be conscious of rhymes and end-stopped lines, but of the conversational quality of the verse.

'The Pursuit' is more in my old style, but larger, influenced a bit by Blake, I think (tiger, tiger), and more powerful than any of my other 'metaphysical' poems; read aloud also. It is, of course, a symbol of the terrible beauty of death, and the paradox that the more intensely one lives, the more one burns and consumes oneself; death, here, includes the concept of love, and is larger and richer than mere love, which is part of it . . .

Oh, mother, if only you knew how I am forging a soul! How fortunate to have these two years! I am fighting, fighting, and I am making a self, in great pain, often, as for a birth, but it is right that it should be so, and I am being refined in the fires of pain and love. You know, I have loved Richard [*her current boyfriend*] above and beyond all thought; that boy's soul is the most furious and saintly I have met in this world; all my conventional doubts about his health, his frail body, his lack of that 'athletic' physique which I possess and admire, all pales to nothing at the voice of his soul, which speaks to me in such words as the gods would envy. I shall perhaps read you his last letter when you come.

Well, overcome as he is by an intense, almost Platonic scrupulosity, he feels he must conquer the phenomenal world, serve two years in the Army, find a profession and become self-supporting and then and only then found a home and all the rest. So with all these large things, he leaves me, consecrated to silence, and a kind of abstract understanding in our own particular world of devils and angels. It would be a good thing if someone from this world could overcome his image and win me, but I seriously doubt that, however I seek, I will find someone that strong. And I will settle for nothing less than a great soul; it would be sinful to compromise, when I have known this. I feel like the princess on the glass hill; what possible knight could overcome this image? This dynamic holy soul which we share?

Well, the essence of my difficulty and torment this past term has been to realize that no matter how I wanted to escape the commitment, I cannot deny that I am captive to a powerful love which passes all the surface considerations of this world and reaches to what we can know of the eternal.

. . . I have changed in my attitudes: I parcel out the love I have, the enormous desire to give (which is my problem, not 'being loved' so much: I just have to 'give out' and feel smothered when there is no being strong enough for my intensity), in homeopathic doses to those around me; the little woman in the subway lavatory whom I changed from a machine into a person for a minute and hugged her; the crooked man selling malt bread; the little boy running his black dog which urinated over a pool of white swans; and all those around me. I am, essentially, living in two worlds: one, where my love is gone with Richard; the other, this world of books, market, and nice people. If I could meet anyone this summer, or next year, or next, I would be most happy to learn to love again. I am always open to this. But until someone can create worlds with me the way Richard can, I am essentially unavailable.

I hope you understand that all this is very private, and I am sharing it with you as I would the deepest secrets of my soul, because I want you to understand that my battles are intricate and complex, and that I am, without despair, facing them, wrestling with angels, and learning to tolerate that inevitable conflict which is our portion as long as we are truly alive. I am growing strong by practice. All the growing visions of beauty and new world which I am experiencing are paid for by birth pangs. The idea of perfect happiness and adjustment was exploded in *Brave New World*; what I am fighting for is the strength to claim 'the right to be unhappy' together with the joy of creative affirmation . . .

Love from a very happy Sivvy

After meeting Ted Hughes:

17 April 1956

. . . The most shattering thing is that in the last two months I have fallen terribly in love, which can only lead to great hurt. I met the strongest man in the world, ex-Cambridge, brilliant poet whose work I loved before I met him, a large, hulking, healthy Adam, half French, half Irish,* with a voice like the thunder of God – a singer, story-teller lion and world-wanderer, a vagabond who will never stop . . . Forgive my own talk of hurt and sorrow. I love you so and only wish I could be home to help you in yours.†

All my love,
Sivvy

---

*Aurelia Plath adds: 'and a good deal of Yorkshire farming stock too'.
†Aurelia's mother was dying.

29 April 1956

I'm so struck full of joy and love I can scarcely stop a minute from dancing, writing poems, cooking and living. I sleep a bare eight hours a night and wake springing up merry with the sun. Outside my window now is our green garden with a pink cherry tree right under my window now in full bloom, thick with thrushes caroling.

. . . I have written the seven best poems of my life which make the rest look like baby-talk. I am learning and mastering new words each day, and drunker than Dylan, harder than Hopkins, younger than Yeats in my saying. Ted reads in his strong voice; is my best critic, as I am his.

My philosophy supervisor, Doctor Krook, is more than a miracle! She took me on an extra half hour last week, and I'm *in medias res* of Plato, marvelling at the dialectic method, whetting my mind like a blue-bladed knife. Such joy.

Bodily, I've never been healthier: radiance and love just surge out of me like a sun. I can't wait to set you down in its rays. Think, I shall devote two whole weeks of my life to taking utter care and very special tendering of you. I've already reserved London and Cambridge rooms . . . We'll leave about the 22nd . . . for Paris, where I'll see you through your first two or three days and get all set up for you so you'll know what you want there, and then I'll take off for a month of writing in Spain on the south coast . . . doing nothing but writing, sunning and cooking. Maybe even learning to catch fish!

Ted is up here this week, and I have become a woman to make you proud. It came over me while we were listening to Beethoven, the sudden shock and knowledge that although this is the one man in the world for me, although I am using every fiber of my being to love him, even so, I am true to the essence of myself, and I know who that self is . . . and will live with her through sorrow and pain, singing all the way, even in anguish and grief, the triumph of life over death and sickness and war and all the flaws of my dear world . . .

I know this with a sure strong knowing to the tips of my toes, and having been on the other side of life like Lazarus, I know that my whole being shall be one song of affirmation and love all my life long. I shall praise the Lord and the crooked creatures He has made. My life shall be a constant finding of new ways and words in which to do this.

Ted is incredible, mother . . . wears always the same black sweater and corduroy jacket with pockets full of poems, fresh trout and horoscopes . . .

His humor is the salt of the earth; I've never laughed as hard and long in my life. He tells me fairy stories, and stories of kings and green knights, and has made up a marvelous fable of his own about a little wizard named Snatchcraftington, who looks like a stalk of rhubarb.

He tells me of dreams, marvelous colored dreams, about certain red foxes . . .

The reason why you must be at ease and not worry about my proud growing this time is because I have learned to make a life growing through toleration of conflict, sorrow, and hurt. I fear none of these things and turn myself to whatever trial with an utter faith that life is good and a song of joy on my lips. I feel like Job and will rejoice in the deadly blasts of whatever comes. I love others, the girls in the house, the boys on the newspaper, and I am flocked about by people who bask in my sun. I give and give; my whole life will be a saying of poems and a loving of people and giving of my best fiber to them.

This faith comes from the earth and sun; it is pagan in a way; it comes from the heart of man after the fall.

I know that within a year I shall publish a book of 33 poems which will hit critics violently in some way or another. My voice is taking shape, coming strong. Ted says he never read poems by a woman like mine; they are strong and full and rich – not quailing and whining like Teasdale or simple lyrics like Millay; they are working, sweating, heaving poems born out of the way words should be said . . .

Oh, mother, rejoice with me and fear not. I love you, and Warren, and my dear suffering grammy and dear loving grampy with all my heart and shall spend my life making you strong and proud of me!

Enclosed, a poem or two ['*Firesong*', '*Strumpet Song*' and '*Complaint of the Crazed Queen*']. I don't remember whether I sent you these.

> Your loving
> Sivvy

3 May 1956

I feel that all my life, all my pain and work has been for this one thing. All the blood spilt, the words written, the people loved, have been a work to fit me for loving [Ted] . . . I see the power and voice in him that will shake the world alive. Even as he sees into my poems and will work with me to make me a woman poet like the world will gape at; even as he sees into my character and will tolerate no fallings away from my best right self . . .

> Your own loving Sivvy

6 May 1956

. . . From despairing of ever being able to use our whole selves, our whole strengths, without terrifying other people, we have turned into the most happy, magnanimous, creative pair in the world . . . I have new power by pouring all my love and care in one direction to someone strong enough to take me in my fullest joy. (It is interesting to know that most Cambridge boys preferred me when I was sick with sinus and they could take care of me, because that was the only time they were stronger) . . . I am utterly at peace and joyously at my best with him.

I do hope you can meet him in Paris, mother; he is the dearest, kindest most honest man that ever lived . . .

much much love, Sivvy

10 May 1956

You will no doubt think I have gone utterly potty to be writing you so many letters, but I am at that time when a girl wants to share all her joys and wonders at her man with those who will understand and be happy about it, and I miss your presence more now than I did in all the hard times during the winter when I was unhappy, uncreative and discouraged about the course my life was to take. Please bear with my volubility at this point! I have no girl here like Sue or Marty with whom I can share my happiness (without their feeling secretly jealous, as do all girls who do not have that strong singleness of purpose which love brings), and I really long for a woman confidante . . .

Much love, Sivvy

'The following was written more than three years after her own breakdown when Sylvia, [now] married to Ted Hughes, was studying on a Fulbright grant in Cambridge, England. S. was the son of a dear friend. His mother had written me about his being deeply depressed and asked my advice about urging him to get psychiatric counseling' [*Aurelia Plath*]:

29 November 1956

I was most moved by your account of S. . . . I suddenly 'felt myself into' his state where he must feel, as I felt, only a little over three years ago, that there is no way out for him scholastically. I wish you could somehow concentrate on him – have him over alone for a weekend, get him to talk, break down whatever sick reserve and terror he has and even get him to let go and cry.

If you think you can, use me as an example. I'm sure he thinks that even though I went to a mental hospital, I never had any trouble about *marks*. Well, tell him I went through six months where I literally couldn't read, felt I couldn't take courses at Smith, even the regular program . . . Tell him I went back without a scholarship for my half year. I know only too well how it is to have nothing anybody says help. I would have felt almost better if people had not tried to be optimistic when I honestly believed there was no hope of studying and thinking. I am sure he is not that badly off.

Find out how his marks *are*. Is he in danger of failing? If not, tell him that (even in our competitive American society) while marks may get scholarships, people are judged by very different standards in life. If he tries to *enjoy* his studies (I assume he is now taking some courses he likes), he will be enriched throughout life. Try to give him a life-perspective . . . walk out in nature maybe and show him the trees are the same through all the sorrowful people who have passed under them, that the stars remain, and that, as you once wrote me, he must not let fear of marks blind him to the one real requirement of life: an openness to what is lovely among all the rest that isn't. Get him to go easy on himself; show him that people will love and respect him without ever asking what *marks* he has gotten.

I remember I was terrified that if I wasn't successful writing, no one would find me interesting or valuable.

Get him to see that he must like his work for itself first . . . tell him to force himself every time he does a paper or exam to think, 'whatever mark I may get, I liked this . . . I have discovered such and such. I am that much richer whatever the examiners may think.' Marks have no doubt become the black juggernaut of his life. Do not try to be over-optimistic, because that will only make him lose trust in you . . . Agree with him about the problem, even if it is dark. Start from the *bottom*. If he is not failing, tell him how good that is. If he likes *any* subject, tell him how important that is. If he gets despairing or frantic and thinks he can't work or think, give him some ritual phrase to repeat sternly to himself. Let him be gentle in his demands; tell himself he has as much right to work and be at Harvard as anyone . . .

Tell him . . . that I only want to share some of my own experience with him . . . that I thought . . . that my case was utterly hopeless.

Do ask him out alone and talk straight out with him. It is better he should break down and cry if he has to.

I think psychiatrists are often too busy to devote the right sort of care to this; they so seldom have time to get in deep[,] and blither about father and mother relationships when some common sense, stern advice about practical things and simple human intuition can accomplish much.

. . . When he dies, his marks will not be written on his gravestone. If he has loved a book, been kind to someone, enjoyed a certain color in the sea – that is the thing that will show whether he has *lived*.

He probably feels like a hypocrite, as I did – that he is not *worth* the money and faith his parents have put in him . . . Show him how much chance he still has . . . I wish you would give him as much time and energy as you can through this time. Adopt him for my sake (as the Cantors did me) . . . Show you love him and demand *nothing* of him but the *least* he can give.

Much, much love –
Your own Sivvy

Sylvia wrote frequently to her mother during the years of her marriage to Ted. She wrote about work, Ted, plans, friends, and the successes they had with their writing. After she received her first acceptance from the *New Yorker*, she reported gleefully: 'You see what happens the minute one worships one's own god of vocation and doesn't slight it for grubbing under the illusion of duty to Everybody's-Way-Of-Life!'

She provided graphic and joyous descriptions of giving birth to her children at home and her letters became filled with accounts of the children's developments. Her first mention of the break-up of their marriage was on 27 August 1962:

I hope you will not be too surprised or shocked when I say I am going to try to get a legal separation from Ted. I do not believe in divorce and would never think of this, but I simply cannot go on living the degraded and agonized life I have been living, which has stopped my writing and just about ruined my sleep . . . I have too much at stake and am too rich a person to live as a martyr . . . I want a clean break, so I can breath and laugh and enjoy myself again.

From then on, her letters were alternately dispirited and resilient: every faltering of gaiety was followed by an injunction to her mother to 'tear up my last letter'. Her children and her poetry gave her life a deep sense of purpose, but they were not an easy combination for a single mother, even for one so disciplined as Sylvia. By October, she had established a regime (which she followed until she died) of writing before the children awoke: 'Every morning, when my sleeping pill wears off, I am up about five, in my study with coffee, writing like mad – have managed a poem a day before breakfast. All book poems. Terrific stuff, as if domesticity had choked me.'

Her strength was taxed by the physical and emotional rigours of writing, full-time childcare and coping with the immediate loss of the man she loved. If we use her poetry of this period, rather than her letters, as a guide, she seemed also to be re-living her unresolved feelings of abandonment after her father died. But her depression lifted sporadically and many people believe that when she put her head in the oven, it was indeed a cry for help and she did not intend to die.*

24 September 1962

Dear Mother,

I feel I owe you a happier letter than my last one. Now that I have come to my decision to get a legal separation and have an appointment with an immensely kind-sounding lawyer in London tomorrow (recommended to me by my equally kind accountant), I begin to see that life is not over for me. It is the uncertainty, week after week, that

---

*For an account of Sylvia Plath's last months, written by someone who had known her for a few years and who believes that she did not want to kill herself, see A. Alvarez, *The Savage God: A Study of Suicide*.

has been such a torture. And, of course, the desire to hang on to the last to see if something, anything, could be salvaged. I am just as glad the final blows have been delivered . . .

It is a beautiful day here, clear and blue. I got this nanny back for today and tomorrow. She is a whiz, and I see what a heaven my life could be if I had a good live-in nanny. I am eating my first warm meal since I've come back – having an *impersonal* person in the house is a great help. I went up to Winifred's [*the midwife*] for three hours the night I realized Ted wasn't coming back, and she was a great help . . . Since I made the decision, miraculously, my own life, my wholeness, has been seeping back. I will try to rent [the house] for the winter and go to Ireland – this is a dream of mine – to purge myself of this awful experience by the wild beauty I found there, and the children would thrive. Quite practically, I have no money to go farther. I have put all my earnings this summer in a separate account, the checking account is at *zero*, and there are 300 pounds I have taken from our joint savings – just about the last of them – as Ted said at one point I could, as some recompense for my lost nanny grant, to build over the cottage. This is a *must*. Also getting a TV for a nanny. I can't have one live in this house or I could have no guests, and I do want to entertain what friends and relatives I have as often as I can. I dream of Warren and Maggie! I would love to go on a skiing holiday in the Tyrol with them someday. I just read about it in the paper. And then if I do a novel or two, I might apply for a Guggenheim to go to Rome with a nanny and the children. Right now I have no money but if I get the cottage done this winter while I'm away, I might sink all my savings in a nanny for a year. My writing should be able to get her the next year . . .

If I hit it lucky, I might even be able to take a London flat and send the children to the fine free schools there and enjoy the London people (I would *starve* intellectually here), renting [the house] for the winter, and come down here on holidays and in the spring for the long summer holiday. I feel when the children are school-age, I won't be able to afford this. Some lucky break – like writing a couple of *New Yorker* stories in Ireland or a play for the BBC (I've got lots of fan mail for the half-hour interview I did on why I stayed in England . . .) – could make this life a reality. But first the cottage then the nanny. I'll have to do this out of my own small pocket, as I imagine Ted will only have to pay for the children . . .

Took Frieda to the playground again today. She is talking wonderfully, says names. I'm getting her two kittens from Mrs. MacNamara next week and trying to go somewhere, on some visit every afternoon with them, to keep busy.

Lots of love to you, Warren, and Maggie.

                                                        Sylvia

16 October 1962

I am writing with my old fever of 101° alternating with chills back. I must have someone with me for the next two months to mind the babies while I get my health back and try to write . . . I need help very much just now. Home is impossible. I can go nowhere with the children, and I am ill, and it would be psychologically the worst thing to see you now or to go home. I have free doctor's care here, cheap help *possible* though not now available, and a home I love and will want to return to in summer to get ready to leap to London. To make a new life. I am a writer . . . I am a genius of a writer; I have it in me. I am writing the best poems of my life; they will make my name. I could finish the novel in *six weeks* of day-long work. I have a gift of an inspiration for another.

Got $100 'birthday present' from Dotty today; $300 from Mrs. Prouty. Thank God.

Very bad luck with nanny agency; a bitch of a woman is coming tomorrow from them; doesn't want to cook, do any breakfast or tea, wondered if there was a butler. Ten pounds a week. If I had time to get a *good nanny*, possibly an Irish girl to come home with me, I could get on with my life . . . I feel only a lust to study, write, get my brain back and practice my craft.

I have, if you want to know, already had my first novel [*The Bell Jar*] finished and accepted – it is a secret, and I am on my second. My third – the idea – came this week.

After Ted left with all his clothes and things, I piled the children and two cats in the car and drove to stay with a . . . couple I know in St. Ives, Cornwall – the most heavenly gold sands by emerald sea. Discovered Cornwall, exhausted but happy, my first independent act! I have no desire but to build a new life. Must *start here*. When I have my second book of poems done, my third novel, and the children are of age, I may well try a year of creative-writing lecturing in America and a Cape Cod summer. But not just now. I must not go back to the womb or retreat. I must make steps *out*, like Cornwall, like Ireland.

Please share this letter with Dotty and Mrs. Prouty. *I am all right* . . .

Could either Dot or Margaret spare me six weeks? I can get no good nanny sight unseen; I could pay board and room, travel expenses and Irish fares. I am as bereft now as ever . . . I must have someone I love . . . to protect me, for my flu with my weight loss and the daily assault of practical nastiness – this nanny sounds as if she will leave in a day or so – . . . has made me need immediate help. Know my only problems now are *practical*: money and health back, a good young girl or nanny, willing to muck in and cook, which I could afford once I got writing. The strain of facing suing [Ted] for support, with the cruel laws here, is something I need to put off just now.

I'm getting an unlisted phone put in as soon as possible so I can call out; you shall have the number.

The babes are beautiful, though Frieda has regressed; the pussies help. I cannot come home. I need someone to cover my getting to Ireland. I can't rely on any nanny at this short notice – I just can't interview them. Do let me know what you all think. The life in Ireland is very healthful; the place, a dream; the sea, a blessing. I must get out of England. I am . . . full of plans, but do need help for the next two months. I am fighting now against hard odds and alone.

xxx Sivvy

18 October 1962

Do ignore my last letters!

The Health Visitor came to see Nicholas and gaped at me: 'My, Mrs. Hughes, you've lost weight!' I told her I was up at 4 a.m. every morning, writing till the babies woke, and she looked concerned. I guess my predicament is an astounding one, a deserted wife knocked out by flu with two babies and a full-time job!

I love and live for letters,
xxx Sivvy

25 October 1962

. . . Now stop trying to get me to write about 'decent courageous people' – read the Ladies' Home Journal for those! . . . I believe in going through and facing the worst, not hiding from it. That is why I am going to London this week, partly, to face all the people we know and tell them happily and squarely I am divorcing Ted, so they won't picture me as a poor country wife.

Love to all, Sivvy

21 October 1962

Will you please, for goodness sake, stop bothering poor Winifred Davies . . . She is busier than either you or I and is helping me as much as she can and knows and sees my situation much better than you can . . . she came over this afternoon and said you sent her some wire to tell me to 'keep the nanny' . . . Please do understand that while I am very very grateful indeed for financial help from people who have money . . . and while I should be glad for the odd birthday and Christmas present from you, I want no monthly dole, especially not from you. You can best help me by saving your money for your own retirement . . .

I am even enjoying my rather frustrating (culturally and humanly) exile now. I am doing a poem a morning, great things, and as soon as the nurse settles, shall try to draft this terrific second ['third': A.P.] novel that I'm dying to do. Don't talk to me about the world needing

cheerful stuff! What the person out of Belsen – physical or psychological – wants is nobody saying the birdies still go tweet-tweet, but the
full knowledge that somebody else has been there and knows the
worst, just what it is like. It is much more help for me, for example, to
know that people are divorced and go through hell, than to hear
about happy marriages. Let the *Ladies' Home Journal* blither about
those . . .

I adore the babies and am glad to have them, even though now they
make my life fantastically difficult. If I can just financially get through
this year, I should have time to get a good nanny . . .

In *Letters Home*, Aurelia Plath describes Sylvia's last months:

> In December she closed the large house in Devon and moved with the
> children to a flat in Yeats's former home in London, where, for a brief
> time, she responded excitedly to the cultural stimulation of the city.
> Then the worst cold, snowstorms and blackouts in over a hundred
> years engulfed London for months; Sylvia fought off flu; the children
> had coughs and colds.
>
> In spite of all this, she continued the writing she had started in Devon.
> She began at 4 a.m. each morning to pour forth magnificently
> structured poems, renouncing the subservient female role, yet holding
> to the triumphant note of maternal creativity in her scorn of
> 'barrenness'.
>
> Feeling she needed a backlog of funds to prepare for the sterile
> periods every writer dreads, she had earlier sent out *The Bell Jar* for
> publication, stipulating that it appear under a pseudonym in the firm
> belief that this would fully protect her from disclosure.
>
> By the time the novel appeared in the London bookstores, she was ill,
> exhausted, and overwhelmed by the responsibilities she had to shoulder
> alone – the care of the children, the bitter cold and darkness of the
> winter, and the terrible solitude she faced nightly.
>
> Despite the strong support of her friends, her sure knowledge of the
> importance of her new writing, her deep love for the children, suppor-
> tive letters from her beloved psychiatrist Dr. B., the hope of a recon-
> ciliation with Ted, and endless offers from her family to help her
> weather the crisis – her tremendous courage began to wear thin.

16 January 1963

Dear Mother,

. . . I am slowly pulling out of the flu, but the weakness and tiredness following it have made me cross . . .

. . . I get strength from hearing about other people having similar
problems and hope I can earn enough by writing to pay about half the
expenses. It is the *starting* from scratch that is so hard – this first year
. . . How I would *like* to be self-supporting on my writing! But I need
time.

I guess I just need somebody to cheer me up by saying I've done all
right so far.

Ironically there have been electric strikes and every so often all lights and heaters go out for hours; children freeze; dinners are stopped; there are mad rushes for candles . . .

Love to all,
Sivvy

4 February 1963

Dear Mother,
. . . I just haven't written anybody because I have been feeling a bit grim – the upheaval over, I am seeing the finality of it all, and being catapulted from the cowlike happiness of maternity into loneliness and grim problems is no fun . . .

I am going to start seeing a woman doctor, free on the National Health, to whom I've been referred by my very good local doctor, which should help me weather this difficult time. Give my love to all.
Sivvy

That was the last letter Sylvia sent to her family. Aurelia writes of Sylvia's death: 'Her physical energies had been depleted by illness, anxiety and over-work, and although she had for so long managed to be gallant and equal to the life-experience, some darker day than usual had temporarily made it seem impossible to pursue.'

Edith Summerskill to her daughter Shirley, 1955

This letter was written while Shirley Summerskill was a medical student at Oxford University:*

1955

My Darling S.,
I am not surprised to hear that you find that the stock question of the anti-feminist is, 'Why have not more women achieved eminence in the arts and sciences?'

Personally I am astounded that so many have distinguished themselves despite the conditions which society has imposed upon them. I was going to say despite the handicaps from which they have suffered, but I am not going to class domesticity as a handicap. Domesticity and love are closely associated in the mind of a woman and the home cannot altogether be separated from the uncongenial chores . . .

I remember well, when you and Michael had certain childish complaints and I was compelled to stay in the House of Commons for a

---

*For biographical information on Edith and Shirley Summerskill, see p. 10.

long sitting, how my mind wandered from the speaker and I would creep out to phone Nana for the latest news.

Women have their physical and mental reserves of strength tapped every day by these demands on their very finest feelings – their unselfish love and devotion to their families . . .

The authorities on genetics are unanimous in agreeing that the male chromosomes are no more likely to carry the spark of genius than the female chromosomes. Now, I attach great importance to the environment in which a potential genius has his being. The male musical composers of the past had their patrons, who provided financial aid, and their little coterie, from whom they received praise and adulation which acted as a stimulant and an antidote to any feeling of frustration.

Imagine the young girl with the same flair; even her family would have regarded her as a freak who should be discouraged. For centuries the world of music was closely associated with the Church, from which women were debarred, and you should read Sophie Drinker's book *Music and Women* if you want to appreciate the struggle of women to establish themselves in this field. It has been impossible to quieten a naturally beautiful voice, even a woman's, because society has permitted her to sing to her children, and to express her joy and sorrow in life whether through lullabies to her children or laments for those she has lost. Consequently, the world has enjoyed the singing of many brilliant women.

Though we see some women in our orchestras today, and not even their male competitors will deny their competence, still it needs a leader of an orchestra who is also a feminist to allow women to play.

While Myra Hess as a pianist and Wanda Landouska, the harpsichordist, are outstanding, one wonders again how many potentially brilliant women have lost heart from the frequent rebuffs which they have encountered.

As I look at the pictures of you and Michael which Amy Drucker painted I often think of her life dedicated to her art, of her journeys to Tibet, to the Andes, to Ethiopia, and her complete absorption in her work. She defied the whole Victorian scene. Her chosen way of life was no doubt regarded as a gesture of defiance. I wonder how many of her day and age took the line of least resistance and painted little Christmas cards until some man came along to offer a home.

Some of our best literary work has been done by single and childless women.

When I was in Norway I was told that some of Norway's finest artists were women – single women who, as the curator of a museum told me, 'had more time for that kind of thing'.

Madame Curie was assisted and abetted by an efficient husband who supported and encouraged her and no doubt with a scientific detachment was completely indifferent to irregular and unpunctual meals.

Undoubtedly the time factor is of great importance in achieving success in any field. One must have the time or *make* the time. The only way to make the time is to be quite determined that washing up, cleaning and cooking shall not sap all one's physical and mental energies, and that these jobs shall be shared by the people for whose benefit they are undertaken.

A family tends to take it for granted that all household work will be done by one individual, the mother. Members of some families, male and female, while on holiday in a hostel, camp, or somebody else's home, find no hardship in helping with the household chores, making their own beds and cleaning their own rooms, yet in their own home they are prepared to exploit the love of a mother by allowing her to work unceasingly at menial jobs.

For any form of creative art, leisure is essential. However, despite handicaps women like Angelica Kauffmann in the eighteenth century, Mary Cassatt, Marie Laurencin, Georgia O'Keefe, Laura Knight and Ethel Walker in the nineteenth and twentieth, besides many hundreds less well-known who have shown their works in exhibitions in every capital of the world, have demonstrated their abilities as artists.

Women novelists in the last century and a half have been outstanding. For the most part they have achieved this without university or any other training, and without a library or study and the possession of a dutiful wife who is prepared to minister to their needs, type the manuscript and generally help in delivering the final masterpiece.

Besides the Brontë sisters there were Jane Austen, Fanny Burney, George Eliot, Mary Webb, Virginia Woolf and Mrs Gaskell among many others. While in other countries there were the Nobel Prize winners Pearl Buck, Sigrid Undset, Selma Lagerlof, Grazia Deledda and Gabriela Mistral, the poetess.

On the stage women have shown a genius for acting, but I must confess that this becomes second nature to many women who have learnt that to dissemble makes life very much easier in a world where they are subject to prejudice. Men wonder why women know their secrets. Women make people a study, and the male and his behaviour and reactions play a most important part in that study, which in itself enables a woman to conduct her life in a way which is most profitable to herself.

It is not surprising to women that Sarah Bernhardt, Duse and Ellen Terry could hold audiences long after their youthful attraction had disappeared. They were probably consummate actresses in their adolescence and the years only improve their skill and technique in the art of self-disguise. Only a woman can smile while her heart is breaking, can weep when she feels no deep sorrow, can evoke sympathy when she is thoroughly undeserving of it. Yes, men must find women difficult to understand, but they have made them so, because they have compelled them to use what are called woman's wiles to outwit their masters – and they generally succeed. For these reasons although women in this country were only allowed on the stage in the seventeenth century, they very quickly succeeded in establishing themselves in the world of the theatre.

In the sciences women have shown aptitude, but not a special liking. Women are attracted to those fields where human relationships can be observed, and the rather impersonal world of science and machinery does not have a great appeal. However, where science is combined with the solution of human problems, as in the practice of medicine, there we find women coming rapidly forward in a world which can fully satisfy the brain and the heart of intelligent women.

Over the centuries girls have been reared against this background of suppression and subjection. The stories of the male composers of music and poetry do not lead us to believe that they were tough, thrusting individuals, but highly sensitive creatures; many of them died young or were mentally unstable and given to fits of melancholy. It is interesting to speculate on what measure of success they would have achieved if they had been subject to the same prejudices and subjugation as the women of their time. A young girl with the same temperament and equal genius, denied encouragement, probably ridiculed and admonished for her efforts, stood little chance of developing her capabilities to the full. When she had written her verses or composed her music secretly, then who was to be the brave man who would defy public opinion and support the work of a woman poet and composer?

Nan Hunt and her 'spiritual mother' Bunny Flarsheim, 1974–78

Nan Hunt is a full-time writer and teacher of writing. She met Bunny Flarsheim in 1965, when Bunny was 69 and Nan was in her mid-thirties: the relationship became a unique source of mutual support. Nan adopted Bunny as her 'spiritual mother' and as role model for a positive kind of mothering which she could enjoy and pass on to her own daughters – Diana (then 15) and Erica (6).*

Nan writes:

'Estrangement, depression, and conforming close-mindedness were much of what I inherited from past generations of women in the family. I didn't want to perpetuate that melancholy cycle with my own daughters. One act of

---

*Nan's correspondence with Diana is excerpted in Chapter 2.

breaking through was my finding a surrogate mother in an older woman friend. Bunny's example of a wise, vital and emotionally honest and expansive life was one I had rarely experienced before in a woman. Her generous nurturing helped heal me. The strengths I gained in self-esteem, enhanced my ability to persevere in working through conflicts with my daughters.'

Miriam ('Bunny') Flarsheim was born in 1896 in Kentucky. She studied to become a teacher at Louisville Normal School and married Henry Flarsheim in 1916. They have five children, two of whom were adopted as adolescents. Bunny is a lay analyst and has worked with Elizabeth Kubler Ross, giving seminars to terminally-ill patients and to their families on how to cope with death and dying.

She writes about the background to these letters:

'Nothing I did ever pleased my mother. When I was a baby, she was so ashamed of how ugly I was that she had special caps made to hide my face. She used to say that tears rolled down her cheeks constantly as she pushed my pram. I did well at school and was popular with the boys – but nothing earned her approval . . . Perhaps here lies the reason for my prancing through life mothering gently and subtly all who come into my path – because everybody needs a mother all the time. Perhaps I get gratification out of giving what I never had.

'When I married Henry, life began for me – my real birth. He is the one exception to my "mothering" relationships. All our life together, we've wanted to bring out the best in each other. He has encouraged and stimulated me to do the best I can as friend, wife, mother, cook, therapist, lecturer, grandmother, great-grandmother. And I have done the same for him.

'I feel considerable pride and gratitude for what my life has yielded and continues to yield, still at the age of eighty-four. I am proud of my successes in several areas: mothering; investigating several careers; assessing my own values and having strong liberal convictions quite contrary to my extremely conservative background; having the courage to face my own feelings, particularly about sex and, after years of experimenting, feeling free and open and proud of my pleasure in sexual activity. In fact, in the past six years when I have been lecturing to a wide-range of people on the subject of aging, death and dying, I have talked considerably about older people's sexual activity. Perhaps because I am handling a subject right at the top of my mother's long taboo list, my enthusiasm for this subject matter has been greater than any other phase of my most interesting work.'

At the time when the following letters began,* Nan had been widowed for a year and was adjusting to the responsibilities of single-parenthood, full-time work and writing. Bunny was involved in Elizabeth Kubler Ross's 'Death and

---

*These letters are excerpted from hundreds written between Nan and Bunny since 1965.

Dying' seminars and was busy nursing Henry who was bedridden for several months following a stroke:

16 February 1974

Dearest Bunny,

I am typing and making a copy of this because it is meant to be an important letter to myself and to you. I have made a decision about my work and I will need your help. My daytime job has run out of funding and although the college dean keeps making noises about finding some way to hire me on special projects, nothing has materialized. I have problems making decisions, but much of the turmoil going on in me says that I don't really want to have to do busy-work any more. I am teaching two nights a week – which brings in a very minimal amount of $240 a month and I have a small amount from Erica's social security. On top of that I am doing some 'hack' work, free lance writing on 'how-to-do-it' books . . .

I am best at teaching, writing poetry, dramatizing poetry orally. Therefore, come what may: bankruptcy, poverty, or what, I am going to take the courage to spend at least 3 hours a day on my own writing . . . I have to spend a couple of hours a day on planning my classes (my contemporary lit. students are very sharp). I spend time on the hack work, time for Erica, time for the house and yard, time for Ray. I do not know how I've had the strength to also hold an eight-hour-a-day job in addition to all the other responsibilities and contacts . . . Ray & I cannot marry as yet because of the tension between Erica and him.* At first he put up with Erica's hostility, but it became so uncomfortable, he just wants to avoid her. So you can see that we can't have any kind of family life – otherwise it would be a great relief financially just to be able to share living expenses. He has arranged his work hours so that he can be here in the morning when Erica's in school.

Last night I saw and heard Anais Nin speak at an English conference in L.A. I took the courage to speak to her and ask if I could study with her . . . She said it should be possible in the fall if her health improves. Her speech moved me profoundly because it reaffirmed deep insights I've had about womanly creative powers. I must continue believing in them. The help I want from you is the moral support. Remember when I made the decision to study for a Master's: it was you who continually reinforced me when I wavered. My devil is self-doubt. Besides that, I let myself be distracted by subsidiary projects or by the pressure of other duties.

You say I am a towering woman and I should *be* that. I am glad you said that because, of course, there are many hours each week I feel full

---

*Ray is Nan's lover. Jim was Nan's second husband and Erica's father; he died of a cerebral hemorrhage in 1973.

of defeat and despair. Then I remember that line in your letter and I say to myself, 'forget all this self-pity crap and be what you are supposed to be, Nan!'

The emotional energy is there, but it could be drained away so easily because I am hypersensitive – like an open wound at times. Rejection absolutely devastates me temporarily.

It is not praise I want from you although honest praise is great food. I want from you the *demand* that I go on in spite of everything – high expectations of what I can do, and the insistence that I not be deflected from doing it. I told Anais Nin that when I read her diaries three years ago, I never dreamed that I would be seeing her in person twice. I also told her that she has been literally one of my courage teachers. You have been the other one.

I am dribbling tears and runny nose all down my face. This wrench of artistic determination can be rather messy. But the gist of all this is that I am not going to expend my energies any more trying out for jobs just because they are jobs and I need the money. I am going to concentrate on what I do best.

I was so relieved to hear Henry sounding just like he usually sounds. You sounded tired. I probably take your strength for granted as does everyone. You owe it to all of us not to expend your strength on trying to be good to others even though you are asked to all the time. I hope what I'm asking will not be a drain on you. Please, please rest and get pleasure and get solitude. I love you and if my will could keep you in the world with me for as long as I live, I would will it.

Love and sexy kisses to Henry, even if his doctor says no.
Nan

22 February 1974

Dearest Nan,

What a magnificent assignment for me! I'm so proud of you.

I wish I could be closer to you so that I could express to you the hundreds of feelings and thoughts which course thru me – about you. Like – why be afraid of failure – it's an experience one can learn so much from, like *free* yourself – no Ray – no Erica – no Anais Nin – no me – no Jim – no nothing just you – living transparently so that all of you is aware of all of you. *Of course* you are gifted. What a tragedy it will be if you inhibit yourself because of conventional, cultural, traditional points of view. This would not be failure – this would be unliving. Failure can be glorious.

The only part of your letter which worries me is your saying, 'rejection absolutely devastates me temporarily' and I know this is true. I'm grateful for the 'temporarily' but I have seen you allowing precious emotional energy go down your own personal sewer because someone disagreed about something . . . The whole world doesn't have to love you . . . I hope Ray can help you financially as well as give emotional support. I think you are probably most impractical. I can imagine Erica's feeding on that. Perhaps you & Erica could come to some sort of agreement about how much Erica can spend for everything & also I think it's time she is beginning to be able to be responsible for earning some money. Can she mow lawns, wash cars, as well as baby-sit?

You have given Erica a good, solid beginning in life with an assurance of more love than most people have. Jim loved her too. She is now exploiting your guilt & it infuriates me. What in Hell are you guilty of NOW – because that's all you can do anything about. If you are bamboozled by Erica's ridiculous criticism of you ('you sleep with Ray'), I really can't fathom this. What is wrong with this? What business is it of hers? She is black-mailing you & that's humiliating for both of you.

Anais Nin has freed herself hasn't she? Perhaps *this* is where her genius lies. I feel certain it is where you should begin to discipline yourself.

Elliot Jacques has written about *Death and the Mid-Life Crisis* – saying that from about 35 to 45 the most creative people . . . have had creative slumps & their creative force after about 45 is quite different, more tragic, more reflective, more sculptured instead of spontaneous, wild, more optimistic. I have been wondering if this is an issue with you & if feelings which are very depressed, desperate might be frightening to you.

Because I've been concerned for some time that you haven't been writing.

I am going to teach a course in 'Death and Dying' at the State University: 3 hrs a day, 5 days a week, intense, as perhaps such a course should be. I am thinking so much about it.

Although Henry has done superbly following surgery, I faced his death more realistically than I ever have and I surely learned – like my love, compassion, caring, sympathy was all so all-encompassing that I felt I would smother. Then came times when I hated him – what right had he to abandon me, to worry me, to disturb my rest, to demand so much. These were blessed times. I don't think I would have survived without them. I came from this hate-time back to him, renewed & even refreshed.

For me this time – I'll be 80 in April – is wonderful – although I'm often deeply depressed & hideously frightened. I wish I could decide when I will die – *not* because I am no longer exciting, productive, creative, intuitive, fascinating. The head of the psychology department where I teach said to me, 'Everyone you have touched, student and faculty, has been blessed.' And I know it's true. But I am also such a terrific bitch & I don't even mind . . .

Love,
Bunny

After receiving a copy of Nan's journal (written during her studies with Anais Nin), Bunny responded:

14 November 1975

Dear Nan,

I've finished *The Rose Confessions* – or they've finished me.

I know I start reading your work with a strong pre-disposal to like, admire, etc., it. Nevertheless, I think this work is superior to Nin's. There is some of it which loses me – e.g. p. 63 and 64. I see the relevance. But up to this point you were running and dashing and panting – and in these two pages, *for me*, there is a flatness.

But, Nan, I truly don't think I am sufficiently knowledgeable to be a wise critic. So *pay no attention to this* – unless you agree.

I can think of only *two* men I know, who would, could read Anais Nin. Yours may be a little more accessible to men because it is so naked. But there are plenty of women.

Think of yourself as the power and beauty you are. Kill the crap.

Much Love,
Bunny

21 November 1975

Bunny dearest,

. . . Your reaction to my manuscript is real nourishment to me. I'm taking a careful look at pages 63 & 64 which you thought flat . . .

As for men responding to Anais's and to my writing, I think attitudes are changing and men are becoming curious as to what women really feel and think. Previously, most men regarded women's mental and emotional processes as trivial, unimportant to their lives. Now that we are shaking things up, men who aren't too defensive, are taking a look at what we are 'all about'.

I remember Jim paid scant attention to what I was writing until he thought he was doomed to lose me. Then he went avidly through every notebook, poem and story I'd written to find out what I was really thinking about myself and him.

There is so much to ask you and tell you – love

Nan

After a discouraged letter from Bunny, reporting Henry's setbacks in health, Nan wrote:

11 September 1976

Bunny dearest,

The instant I opened your letter and saw the style of your handwriting, I knew something was different. Usually it is big and bold and slants across the page very spontaneously. This time it was smaller, careful and closely written . . .

When Henry fails, you can't bear it because it is part of you, your judgement and agility that is failing . . . But, oh how I understand your *outrage* at the idea of acceptance of death. The feeling of ageing and deterioration as a horror. Do you know I was trying to write about my old age for our dramatic production and I cannot, could not visualize myself old. I can see you and say that is the way I want to be when I am eighty years old, but I *can't* visualize giving up my feeling about myself as seductive, eye-catching outstanding and sensual. Knowing you are still that way reassures me . . .

Be angry at the obscenity of deterioration – at death. Why should you accept it? Just when you have learned so much – have grasped the preciousness of life. Why should you have to lose it? . . . You should live forever. I want you to be here for *me* and I will never reconcile myself to loss of you. I have never been willing to live on memories – so I understand why you can't. Making things happen – being active in the present, being able to be bitchy and a fighter. Of course you want that. I can't imagine you floating in some benign, ethereal state toward your maker. I hope you laugh a lot in the years to come, but when you die, I might expect to hear you say, 'Oh shit, I don't want to go!'

I love you immensely,
Nan

10 February 1977

Dearest Nan,

I have been – am – tired – bone tired – feeling tired – doing tired – I'm tired of being concerned about Henry. I'm tired of taking care of him. I'm tired of my many friends. Two long-distance calls – Colorado and North Carolina – desperate people – and one here (Penelope – suicidal) – too too too sensitive – all nerves exposed – plus *many* suffering in my Death and Dying seminars whom I helped.

But you come to me, my darling. Nurturing you, for some reason, strengthens me.

Very much love,
Bunny

1 June 1977

Bunny darling,

. . . This is an incredibly intense time for me. I am sleeping fitfully, having nightmares, learning from Jungian readings and analysis (I go once a week to the clinic for $13 a visit). I am struggling with my animus who has been a seedy, rheumy-eyed, critical old man who says to me, 'You can't do it, what made you think you could do it' – he pursues me in my dreams like a rapist but never touches me, yet I scream 'Help' and say, 'This is a violation of a human being!' and wake up still screaming. But I have identified him and confronted him in dialogue. This is my task, to turn him into an admiring Prince. I feel like this journey into my subconscious is the most important, dangerous, exhilarating, revealing trip I ever made . . .

After attending a 'Women's Success Teams' seminar for a week early May, I've been involved with a group of dynamic women who meet once a week to give each other moral support and information and contacts toward our goals. The director of that seminar said that writers get so much outside criticism and rejection that they should think only of writing for that person who loves them so much [that] 'they would think it musical if they *farted*!' That would be my Bunny, I thought, so I keep you in mind whenever I'm writing. Even if what I produce may not be worth much more than a fart – only sometimes.

Love to Henry and to you,
Nan

The letter below came fast on the heels of a bi-weekly argument in which Nan tried to persuade Bunny and Henry to participate in a television programme about their lives as they were growing older. Bunny had said that they were not well enough and Nan kept trying to persuade them:

6 October 1977

Dearest Nan,

My God, what a creature you are! How does Ray stand you?

Now sit down and listen to me. *I* think you have a choice – either fail now after two months investment of time, money, effort, etc. – or fail after infinitely greater investment of same. I am *81* years old – look 181 – feel 281 – act 381. If I were to try to put the way I feel in a few words – I'd say I'm tired of loving. Along with my resentment, anger, disgust, frustration, hurt for Henry – my loving goes right along – eating at me. There is so much in the real NOW which can't be aired. I wouldn't want *most* people I know to know my feelings. Hiding them is cheating and means jeopardizing the value of anything I do or say.

But mostly, Nan, what I have not gotten over to you is that I have not the *energy* to do many things. The thought of a camera's 'following me in some of my activities' scares the shit out of me. I *hardly* have the strength for these activities – without the added weight of the responsibility of trying to do a good job . . .

It is *impossible* to *imagine* airing my feelings about Henry's deteriorating. I'd kill anybody who mentioned it.

Perhaps you can use your script and get some actors – some of your interested friends to portray our lives, (or what you *think* they have been) . . .

Could I be better later? I don't know. This is fiendishly hard.

So – so sad.

Bunny

The programme about old age was dropped but Nan decided to write a screenplay about a battered wife based on her own history:

30 March 1978

Bunny darling,

. . . This is such difficult work. There is interest in my screen story, but I've been asked to do re-writing and re-thinking of parts of it. One person tells me my dialogue and scenes are great, another tells me the dialogue is too full of exposition, and another says the incidents are not believable – and so I go slightly crazy trying to figure out how to polish the script in order to make it saleable. Then I get angry and determined to write it my way.

Some days I feel like Sisyphus pushing the load up a mountain. Then I think: 'what if I just refuse to bear my burden?' – in other words refuse to write any more – what a relief! Then I know I would feel guilty until the end of my days for giving up.

This screen story is about Naomi who has no heroines – and she becomes a victim – a battered wife until she learns to become her own heroine – and save her life – it's a story of recognition of self and the first steps of growth into self-sufficiency. I'll send you the script when it's finished.

It takes too damm long. I have no time for fun, for reading, for talking to friends – every bit of time I'm not doing essential housework and appointments – I'm writing or typing. Being a writer is slavery – it's a compulsion. That's why I haven't been writing you lately and I seem too slow to catch on to craftsmanship. Here I'm 50 and the creative juices are supposed to be drying up by now, and I'm just beginning. Isn't this just foolishness on my part – to think I'll have time to develop into a noteworthy writer?

These are some of the doubts that I beat off every day in order to keep going. I sit down at the typewriter to revise a scene for the third time, and I swallow the bitter taste of self-doubt. I make myself do it with no real hope of it ever connecting with a producer, with money, or with recognition. I do it . . .

Yet my life is good in many ways. I have the love of many people . . .

It is a joy to see my two gorgeous daughters together. They are so fond of each other. Diana says she realized the best thing I did for her was to instill in her a feeling of self-worth. Yes, I'm glad I did that. I had to struggle so for my worth. You helped!

Love,
Nan

Matters of Life or Death

In most societies women have not been brought up to take an active part in public life, much less involve themselves in hazardous forms of political struggle. But against all odds of feminine conditioning, women from varied social and cultural backgrounds have chosen to take action rather than wait for someone else to fight injustice.* Written in situations where the pressure of events left these women of conscience little choice but to take action, the following letters show how they have tried to encourage and comfort those closest to them, and to explain why they felt it necessary to risk death rather than give up their cause.

Constance Lytton to her mother Edith, 1909

I am one of that numerous gang of leisured-class spinsters, unemployed, unpropertied, unendowed, uneducated, economically dependent on others . . .

Constance Lytton (1908)

Constance Lytton (1867–1923), suffragette and prison reformer, was the daughter of Edith Villiers and the Second Earl of Lytton, Viceroy of India. The family moved around between Vienna, Paris, Lisbon and India, and returned to England when Constance was 11. She was a sickly child but she became an accomplished musician and received a classical education at home. Her father died when she was 22. Constance felt as if she had 'adopted' her mother and she continued to live at home to care for her. After four years, her mother accepted a post as lady-in-waiting to Queen Victoria and Constance was free to do other work and to travel. She helped her aunt who was writing a series of books which sold very well, and gained a small income from her share of the royalties.

In 1906 her godmother left her a large sum of money without any conditions attached and Constance felt 'a strange new feeling of power and exhilaration'. She began to look for a public use for her inheritance. As she later wrote in *Prisons and Prisoners* (1914), 'commonly accepted channels of philanthropy did not appeal to me'; through her social research she had also formulated two precepts:

1) It is useless to try to help the lives of a community without consulting the individuals whom you hope to benefit and
2) [That] to benefit the life conditions of men does not necessarily benefit the life conditions of women, although their interests may be apparently identical.

---

*In addition to the suffragist movement and pacifist activities already mentioned in this chapter, women have been very active in the US Civil Rights movement, in union activity, in the anti-apartheid movement in South Africa, and numerous other Third World liberation movements. Throughout history women have fought political battles along with men, but often in the background performing the crucial unglamourous tasks.

In 1908 at the age of 41, she met two of England's suffragettes, Mrs Pethick Lawrence and Anne Kenney. Although she was in full agreement with the aims of the suffragettes, she was at this stage unable to accept their methods of confrontation. She moved closer to the cause through her interest in prison reform and her concern for the treatment which suffragettes received in prison. Later that year she heard Christabel Pankhurst give her famous speech in Bow Street Court, and this was the turning point for her commitment to the suffragette movement.

In February 1909, Constance Lytton took part in a deputation to the Prime Minister and was one of the twenty-eight women arrested amidst violent scenes. She was sentenced to one month in Holloway Prison where she spent most of her time in the prison hospital because of her heart condition. She objected to the fact that no other suffragette prisoners had such privileges and that she was getting preferential treatment because of her aristocratic background. She was imprisoned in Newcastle in October 1909 and went on hunger strike. After being examined by a heart specialist, she was released without having been forcibly fed. Three months later Constance resolved to make a test: cutting her hair and putting on spectacles, she disguised herself as Jane Warton – a woman of the working class. She was arrested at a protest meeting outside a Liverpool prison where other suffragettes were confined and sentenced to fourteen days' hard labour with the option of a fine. Her heart was not examined and on the fourth day of her hunger strike she was forcibly fed. This brutal procedure involved the prison doctor kneeling on her legs, forcing her mouth open with a steel gag and pushing a four-foot rubber hose down her throat. When he could not get her mouth open, he tried to pour food through a tube in her nose. At each of her three force-feedings Constance nearly suffocated; she vomited over the doctor who retaliated by striking her.

After a week in prison, during which only a few of the suffragette leaders knew of her presence, the Press Association found out and told her sister who secured her release. The Home Office denied that the difference in treatment given to Lady Constance Lytton and Jane Warton warranted an inquiry.

Constance was seriously ill when she was released from prison and, although she continued working with the WSPU (Women's Social and Political Union), her health had been permanently affected. She suffered several heart attacks and eventually a stroke in 1912. She returned home to be nursed by her mother. From then until her death in 1923 she was bedridden and partially paralysed, but her spirit never failed. She learned to write with her left hand, and it was during this time that she wrote *Prisons and Prisoners*.

Constance wrote this letter the day before she was arrested for the first time:

24 February 1909

My Angel Mother,

I don't know whether I shall post this to you or see you first. I want to have a letter ready.

Don't be startled or afraid. I have something to tell you which – with the help of recent presentiments – you, I know, are half expecting to hear.

If you ever see this letter it will mean that after joining the deputation I have been arrested and shall not see you again until I have been to Holloway Prison. For months I have been planning this letter to you, but now that the time has come, it is not any easier to write for that. Of course, my hope has been all along that I should be able to take you into my confidence, that I should have the perhaps all-undeserved yet heaven-like joy of knowing that though you could not share all my views, yet that you would understand why I held them, and, granted these, you would further understand my action and the great sacrifice which I know it means to you. My darling Muddy, you will never know, I trust, the pain it is to have to do this thing without your sympathy and help – with, on the contrary, the certainty that it shocks you and hurts you and makes you suffer in numberless ways. Hardly a day has passed but what I have tried to feel my way with you, tried to convert you – not to my theoretic views, difference there does not matter, but to my intended conduct in connection with them. Every day I have failed. If I decided to do this thing, absolute secrecy was necessary, for, the whole of these police regulations being arbitrarily ordered and special to the case, they would never arrest me, not, I mean, unless I really broke the law, if they knew who I was. Unless I had your sympathy and understanding, it was, of course, hopeless to count on your secrecy. I had two alternatives, to give up the plan, or to keep it and deceive you about it. I chose this last. For your sake I have tried never to tell you an actual lie in words. I have not done this, and that is, perhaps, why you have your suspicions. But to my conscience that is no easier. It was my intention to deceive you, and I have deceived you, and, for all practical purposes, successfully. Once the intention is to deceive, it seems to me not to make any difference how it is done.

You will be angry. If it could be only that. But you will be hurt through and through. As I write the words their meaning is acute in my mind and heart. You will hardly care to know, but I must tell you what has decided me to take this torturing step.

Prisons, as you know, have been my hobby. What maternity there lurks in me has for years past been gradually awakening over the fate of prisoners, the deliberate, cruel harm that is done to them, their souls and bodies, the ignorant, exasperating waste of good opportunities in connection with them, till now the thought of them, the yearning after them, burns in me and tugs at me as vitally and irrepressibly as ever a physical child can call upon its mother.

The moment I got near the Suffragettes the way to this child of mine seemed easy and straight. But I knew the temptation to think this must make me doubly sure of my ground. I have felt from the start that I could not take this woman's movement merely as an excuse for Holloway. I have waited till my conviction was genuine and deep at every point, and till the opportunity occurred for facing the police regulations in a way possible to my whole nature, temperament, conscience. There are several other things which the Suffragettes do, which I would not and could not do.

I finally made up my mind in about the middle of January, and soon after wrote to Mrs Pethick Lawrence. Enclosed is her answer. I had not recently been seeing them, or going to meetings, or in any way specially communicating with them. I took the decision entirely on myself, in no way consulted her nor asked her advice; even had they not accepted me in the deputation I should have joined outside.

About the physical discomforts part of Holloway, don't be distressed for that. These are already nothing to what they were. And I am such a muff, what remains of hardship will be wholesome for me – really 'reformatory' for me as imprisonment seldom is to others. If I could only know that you will help me face it, it would be nothing to me. It's my journeying after the hobby that sucks up my soul like a tide, my Nile sources, my Thibet, my Ruvenzori. If you, my splendid Mother, will only help me in spirit then the little spark of Sven Hedin shall not fail in me. I am no hero, but the thought of other travellers' much worse privations on that road will, I believe, fizzle up my flimsy body enough for what is necessary, and if only I knew you were helping me in your heart I should not, could not, fail, Muddy darling.

You can't forgive me now, but perhaps you will some day. Whatever you feel towards me, whatever I do, I shall still be always

Your most loving and devoted
Con

P.S. The account papers, tradesmen addresses, wages paper, are in the . . . desk on dining-room writing table. I expect I shall be away from you a month. The others will cling round you. If I were going on a trip abroad you would not resent the separation. In my little warm cupboard nest in Holloway my only thought of the outer world will be of you. I shall try anyhow to get back to you tonight.

Con

Hannah Senesh to her mother Catherine, 1939–44

Hannah Senesh (1921–44), a Hungarian Jew, was executed by the Nazis when she was only 23. Hannah clearly made a profound impression on all who met her – fellow parachutists or hardened Yugoslav partisans, dispirited fellow prisoners or Nazi interrogators. Her actions and her strength of character have made her a national hero and her poetry is still widely read in Israel.

Two major decisions in her life are marked in her letters included here, and both have particular bearing on her relationship with her mother, Catherine. The first, at the age of 18, was to leave her native Hungary at the outbreak of World War II, to become a pioneering farm-worker in Palestine; the second, four and a half years later, was to return to Hungary on a dangerous secret mission.

In emigrating to Palestine, Hannah was leaving her mother to face the anti-Semitism and uncertainty of that period alone (her brother, George, was then working in France, and her father had died when she was quite young). However painful the sacrifices on both sides, Hannah felt it imperative to go. Quite apart from the problem of discrimination against Jewish youth looking for work, she felt compelled by the challenge which Palestinian life presented, and by a strong sense of purpose – even destiny – which was repeatedly to guide her decisions. Once in Palestine, she wrote in her diary (23 September 1939): 'This is where my life's ambition – I might say my vocation – binds me, because I would like to feel that by being here I am fulfilling a mission, not just vegetating. Here almost every life is the fulfillment of a mission.'

Catherine, though sad, had not disapproved of her daughter's decision to leave; and later, when the situation in Hungary had deteriorated further, and letters from George in France had completely dried up, her main source of comfort and hope was that Hannah, at least, was safe in Palestine. Unknown to Catherine, her daughter felt increasingly conscience-stricken at the thought of what her mother was enduring alone. Although for the most part their letters to each other remained cheerful (no doubt to protect the other from the truth of what each was going through), Hannah wrote in her diary in August 1942:

How long will this go on? The mask of comedy she wears, and those dear to her so far away? Sometimes I feel a need to recite the Yom Kippur confession: I have sinned, I have robbed, I have lied, I have offended – all these sins against one person – I have never longed for her the way I long for her now. I'm so overwhelmed with this need for her at times, or with the constant fear that I'll never see her again. I wonder, can I bear it?

Hannah wrote to her mother shortly after her arrival in Israel:

December 1939

Dearest Mother,

Perhaps so far you've judged my letters to be superficial, Mother dear. After all, I'm almost always writing about what I do, how I live, where I've been. But I am sure you're waiting for an answer to an unasked question. After all, you made a sacrifice when you let me leave home, and I made a sacrifice when I parted from you. And now I'm sure you would like to know whether it was all worth it. Perhaps I don't have the right to answer this question yet. It really takes a good deal more time to make a decision, but I'll attempt to answer sincerely according to how I feel at this moment.

My answer, dearest Mother, is unequivocally, Yes. I won't deny that there are times when I would give a great deal to see you all for a bit, or at least to have the knowledge that you're all somewhat closer. But at such times I think that a year or two away from you, spent in fulfilling the very reasons for which I came, is not too long a period, and try to imagine how wonderful it will be when we can all be together again.

It was worth coming for the sensation of feeling that I am the equal of all men in my own country (at the moment this last is merely a feeling, not a fact), for that peaceful feeling with which one can walk down the street without wondering whether the person coming in the opposite direction is a Jew or not, and for the knowledge that the smallest matters are not decided by the criterion of whether one is a Jew or not.

However, this factor – that there is no anti-Semitism – may not even be enough of an answer. The most positive answer is that a healthy, new Jewish life is developing here, which one can best express by stating that in the Diaspora Jews were sad if they had no particular reason to be good humoured, and here, on the other hand, people are good humoured if they have no particular reason to be sad – as people are in most lands . . .

28 February 1940

Dearest Mother,

Distant . . . far away . . . One can no longer use old words. They have acquired new meanings with the new times. Today, when worlds separate next-door neighbours and the world's oceans are spanned by the love of united peoples – today one must be careful of the word 'distant'.

Perhaps the distance is great in miles, and borders have become insurmountable obstacles, but if I look at myself in the mirror and see my tangled hair I can actually feel your disapproving gaze upon me. If I meet someone for the first time the thought flashes through my mind, What would Mother think of him? If I do something I know is right, I know you, too, would approve, and I feel that our thoughts are meeting somewhere, perhaps midway, above the sea. I feel how strong and resilient is this unseen thread that binds us, and I feel how unnecessary it is for me to write about all this, for you actually know about everything anyway.

So is it possible to say we're 'far' from each other?

What am I sending you for Purim? Just these lines. And the fervent request to heaven: Let the time come as quickly as possible when we will again be together and letters and words will be unnecessary.

Since her conscience would not allow her to remain inactive, Hannah eventually signed up for an elite commando mission to aid Jewish emigration from Hungary. Of course, she could not inform her mother of this mission; she could only urge her to prepare herself for escape:

December 1943

Darling Mother,

I want to write about something important without any preamble. At the moment there is a real possibility for you to come and join me. I have taken all the necessary steps, and it's likely the journey can be arranged within weeks, perhaps even days.

I know, my darling, that this is very sudden, but you must not hesitate. Every day is precious now and there is a growing likelihood that the road will be momentarily closed, or that other hardships will suddenly arise. George will be here in the nearest possible future too. I don't know whether there is any need for further arguments.

Mother dear, be brave and quick. Don't allow material questions to stand in your way. In today's world that must be your last concern, and you must have confidence in us that here you won't have any financial worries.

I'm sure, my darling, there is no need for further discussion. I don't want to ask you to do this for us – do it for yourself. The important thing is for you to come. Bring what you want to if you can do so without difficulty, but don't let such things stop you even for an instant. I just can't write of anything else now.

I kiss and hug you. With inexpressible love.

During the rescue attempt, Hannah was captured by the Nazis. In a Budapest prison, where they tortured her, they also brought Catherine to her and threatened to torture and kill her before Hannah's eyes if she did not divulge the secret radio code they wanted. She did not yield (and Catherine was in fact spared). Yoel Palgi, one of Hannah's commando friends, later wrote in a memoir: 'Where did this girl who loved her mother so much find the courage to sacrifice her, too, if necessary, rather than reveal the secret that was not hers, that affected the lives of so many?'

By engaging in the secret mission and risking capture, Hannah had shattered her mother's hope. For this, Hannah wanted her pardon. She felt that she would obtain it only if her mother understood why she had returned to Europe, and how her conscience and way of life had compelled her to take the steps she had. Fearing for her mother's life, she could not use any of their brief meetings in prison to this end. Even her last long letter to her mother was cruelly withheld by the Nazis, despite Catherine's repeated requests for it. It was written when Hannah knew that she was about to be executed secretly (the judges at her trial had not dared to sentence her because the Allies were nearing Budapest and they feared reprisals); one might guess that it contained her explanations and final plea for forgiveness.

All that was left for Catherine was a scrap with a few undated lines which she found in the pocket of a dress after Hannah's death:

Dearest Mother,
I don't know what to say – only this: a million thanks, and forgive me if you can. You know so well why words aren't necessary.

With love forever,
your daughter

Hilde Coppi to her mother, 1943

Hilde Coppi was arrested by the Nazis in September 1942, together with her husband Hans, because they belonged to a resistance group in Germany. In prison she gave birth to a son, Hans. One month later her husband was executed. When her son was eight months old, Hilde was executed. She was 34 years old.

Hilde wrote this letter on her last day:

5 August 1943

My Mother, my dearly beloved Mama,
Now the time has almost come when we must say farewell for ever. The hardest part, the separation from my little Hans, is behind me. How happy he made me! I know that he will be well taken care of in your loyal, dear maternal hands, and for my sake, Mama – promise me – remain brave. I know that you feel as though your heart must break; but take yourself firmly in hand, very firmly. You will succeed, as you always have, in coping with the severest difficulties, won't you, Mama? The thought of you and of the deep sorrow that I must inflict upon you is the most unbearable of all – the thought that I must leave you alone at that time of life when you need me most! Will you ever, ever be able to forgive me? As a child, you know, when I used to lie awake so long, I was always animated by one thought – to be allowed to die before you. And later, I had a single wish that constantly accompanied me, consciously and unconsciously: I did not want to die without having brought a child into the world. So you see, both of these great desires, and thereby my life, have attained fulfilment. Now I am going to join my big Hans. Little Hans has – so I hope – inherited the best in both of us. And when you press him to your heart, your child will always be with you, much closer than I can ever be to you. Little Hans – this is what I wish – will become hardy and strong, with

an open, warm, helpful heart and his father's thoroughly decent character. We loved each other very, very much. Love guided our actions . . .

My mother, my one and only good mother and my little Hans, all my love is always with you; be brave, as I am determined also to be.

Always,
Your daughter Hilde

Rose Schlösinger to her daughter Marianne, 1943

Rose Schlösinger was born in 1907. Arrested by the Nazis in Germany on 18 September 1942, because she belonged to a resistance group, she was executed on 5 August 1943. Her husband, Bodo, an interpreter with the German military police, ended his life by shooting himself in a Russian farmhouse when he learned that his wife had been condemned to death.

Rose wrote this letter to her young daughter, Marianne, the day she was executed:

5 August 1943

My dear little big Marianne:

I do not know when you will read this letter. I leave it to Granny or Daddy to give to you when you are old enough for it. Now I must say farewell to you, because we shall probably never see each other again.

Nevertheless, you must grow up to be a healthy, happy and strong human being. I hope that you will experience the most beautiful things the world has to give, as I have, without having to undergo its hardships, as I have had to do. First of all, you must strive to become capable and industrious, then all other happiness will come of itself. Do not be too prodigal of your feelings. There are not many men who are like Daddy, as good and as pure in their love. Learn to wait before giving all your love – thus you will be spared the feeling of having been cheated. But a man who loves you so much that he will share all the suffering and all difficulties with you, and for whom you can do the same – such a man you may love, and believe me, the happiness you will find with him will repay you for the waiting.

I wish you a great many years of happiness that I unfortunately could have for only a few. And then you must have children: when they put your first child into your arms, perhaps you will think of me – that it was a high moment in my life too when for the first time I held you, a little red bundle, in my arms. And then think of our evenings of discussion in bed, about all the important things of life – I trying to answer your questions. And think of our beautiful three weeks at the seashore – of the sunrise, and when we walked barefoot along the beach from Bansin to Uckeritz, and when I pushed you before me on the rubber float, and when we read books together. We had so many beautiful things together, my child, and you must experience all of them over again, and much more besides.

And there is still another thing I want to tell you. When we must die, we are sorry for every unkind word we have said to someone who is dear to us; if we could go on living, we should remember that and control ourselves much better. Perhaps you can remember it; you would make life – and later on death too – easier for yourself and for others.

And be happy, as often as you can – every day is precious. It is a pity about every minute that one has spent in sadness.

My love for you shall accompany you your whole life long. – I kiss you – and all who are kind to you. Farewell, my dear – thinking of you to the end with the greatest love,

Your Mother

Mansoreh to her mother Leila, 1980

Owing to the political situation in Iran, Mansoreh (who lives in England) and her mother must remain anonymous.

21 August 1980

Dear Mum,

How are you? Navid and I are OK. I am just tired. Why haven't you written for such a long time? Are you still living with Mohsen [*her brother*]? Do you still want to go on living there?

I am writing this letter especially because I want you to come and live with us for awhile. There are many reasons for my proposal and many barriers too. First, the Home Office in this country. You may not get permission to enter because black people, Indians and older women are barred from free and easy entry. I call the Home Office a pig house. They really are. The other day I went there to get a letter for the Embassy. I told them I needed a letter for a residency permit. The woman said, 'You must wait till we see your records.' After waiting for five hours in a smokey, stuffy and crowded room, she called me back and said, 'We are sorry but the Home Office never gives such letters.' Walking out, tears ran down my face. There is nothing one can do about them. Like their Iranian counterparts, SAVAK, they are a law unto themselves. If you were rich, or on a business tour, you would be welcome.

The reason why I ask is that Vida [*her sister*] phoned me over the New Year and told me that your situation in the house hasn't changed much. All the arguments and the tensions are still there. You know the same things have been going on for four years now and Mohsen just takes advantage of you living there. He hasn't done a proper day's work in that time and how he relies on your earnings! The way he mistreats Shirin [*his wife*] (especially his worsening behaviour since the Revolution) and puts you two against each other. Then there is the jealousy problem: you as an older woman who has the strongest position in the family – first, by being economically independent and, secondly, as a mother in relation to your son. The other important element in Shirin's jealousy is, of course, your attachment to Omid [*their son*] and the close ties which have developed between you.

I think you are a support and a help in the family and for her. But unfortunately, the way the structure of our family system is so patriarchal and capitalistic, you are not seen as a woman friend, a sister, a comrade, but as a dominant woman, an interference and a threat. This is so painful – and it happens between women a lot.

This is all a painful reminder of my childhood when grandmother [*her father's mother*] lived with us. You as a young wife resented her control over your life, your children, and her status in the family and with her son. We really liked her and were spoiled by her; she always took our side and you didn't like it. Although she was devoted to us, did most of the housework, and supported you against Dad's violence towards all of us, you still felt that there was too much difference of opinion between you two, and that she wanted to dominate you. I realise that you have no desire to control or dominate Shirin's life. As I know you, you isolate yourself far more than necessary and you wouldn't interfere in their personal lives. But you, of course, want to be in the family, to be with your son and grandchildren. However, I think Shirin feels too insecure, too powerless and unsure of her life. All this is because her position as just a wife and mother gives her little satisfaction. Therefore it is understandable why she directs her dissatisfaction and resentment against you. There is no other constructive channel open to her and, anyway, what does the Islamic Republic of Iran offer to women besides more oppression, more degradation, more violence against them?

I think Shirin will be badly off and more vulnerable without you. But she will be in a better position to see the course of her life and you would preserve your self-respect and dignity.

I also think you should travel around, see the world, different places, different cultures, and meet different people, nice people – and basically enjoy yourself. You did say that you wanted to travel but you couldn't do it before. You cannot do it in Iran as happiness is forbidden to women. I think you deserve some happiness. You have worked all your life: at home under the bullying of Dad and in your job. You brought up four kids who grew up and left you and left you in the cold. Soon you will be retired with only the peanuts of your pension to support you (if by then the clergy don't cut it off as unnecessary for women).

You could choose to live with us. I must say that we are poor, but with you we will be rich. Or you could live with Shapor [*her younger brother*] if you like . . . He is desperately trying to get his degree and furnish his future career. Whenever he comes to see us he needs something, usually money, and uses me as an older sister to scrounge on. I hate him for it. I don't think you should live with him. I am afraid you may prefer the security of living with him, but I think he would use you too. You should stay with us for awhile and then we could travel around. We could go around in England, if you like, or in Europe – see lots of places, meet lots of people, have lots of fun. Despite the fact that we have very little money to live on, Navid and I have managed to travel quite a lot. We've discovered cheap ways of seeing many places. You would be amazed. I really feel you need it and it will be good for you and for me and, of course, for Navid. Better than the domestic life of sweeping, cooking, washing for that big family.

I know that you will probably say what you always said before: 'I am an old woman, my life is finished, I am just waiting for death to come and take me, and what the hell would Europe do for me?' You have been a defeatist and you have not enjoyed a minute of your life. You have been a lonesome figure all your life, never had a friend, never went to see a friend, never had somebody drop in to see you. I don't remember seeing you cheerful, except seldom when you read poetry or talked about your grandmother. I can just see your face reading this, tears running down your face because you feel bitter and betrayed. You are right too. We have not fulfilled your expectation as a mother because we have chosen to live our own lives. When I ask you to come to England it is because I want to give you the support and companionship you want from me.

Vida phoned me the other day and said that you have put the black chador on. You put it on before it became compulsory, as if you predicted it. You know that is why women witches were prosecuted throughout history: they foresaw the future, they sensed it. I protested to Vida and she said I was wrong. She said that one of your colleagues was stabbed in the Bazarre for walking unveiled and you don't feel secure in the streets anymore. How soon the bastion of the revolution, where we secured the victory of the revolution, became our torture ground.

Carry a knife or a gun instead of putting on the veil. Didn't you say that you loved the courage of your grandmother who slung the gun on her shoulder, mounted her horse and rode through the farms to guard them when the allies had occupied your home town? You have been knived all your life, you grew resistant to it. So many women have been and are still being knived. The newspaper recently reported a sack found on a street corner with a burned and mutilated body of a woman in it. Another report was of a man who went into a police station claiming that he had just killed his pregnant sister to save the family honour. He walked out free and proud. Aren't we being mutilated all the time? There is no end to it. We need the courage and the spirit of your grandmother, and other resistant women before her, to raise and piece ourselves together and become whole again, a hard, resistant whole. Don't you think we must? Is it worth fighting? You have fought in your own way throughout your life.

What I have tried to say in this long, laborious letter and haven't yet said is that I really want us to spend some time together, to be with each other – alone and free to move around and enjoy ourselves. To bridge this long gap which has existed between us all of our lives. To get rid of our past bitterness, anger, non-communication. I have so much to tell you, to ask you. What would you say to this? Perhaps you have other suggestions; anything which brings us together in a free and friendly environment is welcomed.

with much love,
Mansoreh and Navid

P.S. You know what Navid told me today? 'Everybody in the whole wide world is your family. You know why? Because I have a mother (pointing at me), you have a mother, your mother has a mother, and her mother had a mother and all goes on and on like this until the end.' He would love to see you.

Ten months later, Mansoreh reported:

'My mother phoned me and said that she is not allowed to retire this year. She has to work an extra year (I assume for the good of the revolution). But she agreed to come. We were glad.

'Recently, however, the Islamic Government introduced a bill which prevents people from travelling abroad and taking money with them. Members of the Shah's regime took billions out of the country. The Islamic system makes people like my mother pay for those crimes. This new law effectively bars her from travelling.'

Mairead Nugent and her mother Margaret, 1980

Mairead Nugent, a member of the Irish Republican Army (IRA), is serving a twelve-year sentence at Armagh Prison for women. She was born and raised in Belfast, the eldest of five children of Margaret and Fred Nugent, both from nationalist working-class families. Only 9 years old when the current 'Troubles' began, Mairead has hardly known her neighbourhood without soldiers, guns, tanks and barricades in every street. She was a good student, but when she finished school there were no jobs available and no signs of the political and economic situation improving. Mairead was arrested at the age of 17 and charged with membership in the IRA, possession of weapons and possession of explosives.

She waited eight months for her trial and no bail was set. She had to appear weekly before a criminal court (without jury), which she refused to recognise because she considers herself a prisoner of war. She had no lawyer and did not defend herself. When her trial finally came up in June 1976, her parents wanted her to have a lawyer, but they left it for her to decide. Her mother writes:

'I suppose we hoped she would not get such a severe sentence. But the judge she had was famous (or infamous) and after her case was underway a short time I felt like getting up and asking him to tell us what he would give her, and just cut short the farce. There was no jury. The judge called her a dedicated terrorist at the age of seventeen.'

After being sentenced, Mairead was allowed one visit a month. They were very costly and dangerous to make because the prison is 40 miles away in a Loyalist (Protestant) area; but her mother never missed one. After five years, Mairead was allowed certain privileges, such as buying small items in the prison shop: the first thing she bought was a thank-you card to her family.

Mairead would have been released on parole in 1982 had she not participated in the IRA's hunger strike in 1980. Three women and seven men went on the hunger strike, which was halted after a few weeks because they believed that the British government was going to make significant concessions to their demands.* Three months later, none of the expected concessions had been made and another hunger strike began. Twenty-three men joined the strike and ten of them died, including Bobby Sands, who became an MP while on the hunger strike. Mairead is now scheduled to be released in 1985, after serving nine years of her sentence. She will be 26.

These letters were written during the initial stages of the hunger strike. The first letter was sent through the ordinary channels of the prison censor:

29 November 1980

Well Mummy,

Received your's and Brid's [*her youngest sister*] letters earlier tonight and, as always, it was really great hearing from you again. I got the socks alright. They were lovely, good, thick wooly ones, just what I wanted. Tell Mrs M I send my thanks won't you? I did mean to sit down and write to C and S, though still have to get around to it.

Was really delighted at you going up to see [the relatives], Mummy. I suppose the news of the Hunger Strike came as a shock to them. How were they? We've seen today's paper with the released statement and names. I believe they showed our photographs on the TV news tonight, hope you'se had a good photo shown of me as I wouldn't like

---

*There were five demands: the right to wear their own clothes (the women had this right, but the men didn't); free association; a weekly visit; a weekly parcel; and no prison work.

to have anybody thinking I wasn't actually the 'beauty' I am ha ha.
Things here are sound, we are well prepared for Monday and I will be
okay, Ma, so don't you and Daddy be worrying as this is definitely
going to be one fight we aren't going to lose. Just keep cheery won't
you'se? As we will be here – there's no way our morale will be
daunted, we'll come through this winners! I will still be in the cell with
Rosie . . .

I couldn't get over Brid's wee letter, she's a lovely writer isn't she? I
was all chuffed with hearing from her, tell her I will write very soon.
You can tell everyone from me that we're still allowed letters and that I
won't really mind being 'plagued' down with a grossage of mail ha ha.

Well I can't think of anything else to waffle on about at the moment,
a sing song is about to begin, so I have to go before I miss my big
chance ha ha. Excuse the bad writing nib on this pen. Give my love to
all the family, Don't you and Daddy be worrying, I'll be sound, we'll
soon have our weekly visits to look forward to eh? Tell everyone I was
asking, thinking of you'se all.

lots and lots of love
Mairead
xxo xxo

Mairead's next two letters were written on single pieces of toilet paper and
wrapped in cellophane, then smuggled out of Armagh prison in the vagina of
a woman visitor:

Well, Mummy and Daddy
    As promised here's your few lines. Things have gone sound today.
We went over to the doctors this morning and he gave us a med-exam,
blood pressure taken and we got clean bedding even new potties. The
blankets they gave us are pure new wool, what do you think of that
eh? Nothing but the best ahem. I was taken out of Rosie's cell earlier
and put in to the double cell along with Mary and Mairead. The
morale here is fantastic. At the moment there is some sort of demo
going on outside of the jail. We don't think we'll be moved off this
wing until the end of the week or so. We think we'll maybe be sent over
to 'C' wing. We will be off the 'no wash' then, so I will be able to get in
my clothes.* Hope you are doing well. I will write to you through the

---

*Margaret explains: 'The "no wash" started when about forty male screws in full riot gear
(backed up by the female screws) made a cell search looking for uniforms. Some of the prisoners
of war were badly beaten. They got no food and were not allowed to use the toilets or even the
water in the kitchen for days. The women were not able to change into night clothes because the
male screws were kept on the wing. So when the screws finally said they could empty the pots,
the women refused. This became known as the no-wash protest. We parents were very worried
about the women's health, what with periods and the risk of infection. The women were locked
up in dirty cells twenty-three hours a day . . . I still find it bad to think about, especially since the
women on hunger strike lost weight faster than the men.' ('Screws': 'prison guards'.)

censor on Wednesday don't be worrying, everything here is going to be sound, hope you'se able to make out this writing okay. You'se know the crack yourselves. Give my love to all the family and tell everyone I was asking thinking of you'se all. Keep up tho chins – we're going to win, see you'se soon

lots and lots of love
x Mairead xx

Shortly after Mairead was arrested Margaret was diagnosed as having cancer of the womb lining; she was in the hospital twice in the period leading up to the trial. She wrote an article in a local newspaper about her medical experiences, thinking Mairead would not see it; but in the first weeks of the hunger strike it made its way into the prison. Margaret says:

'I prefer to talk about the cancer because it helps me and sometimes helps other women. But I didn't want Mairead to know because in there they can dwell on such things . . . Reading these letters you might think I had a perfect daughter and that I was the perfect parent – which is not true. We get on well, but we are too alike to agree all the time. We are very hot tempered at times and even since she's been in prison we have fallen out. But it doesn't last long.'

Dear Mummy,

I am sending this out today to tell about me having a visit this week, we are still in the sick, we won't be knocked off it until Monday. I couldn't get word out to you any earlier as L. hasn't been in, she is still on holidays. I sent a blank docket down to the front so anyone can come up any day, but if you can make it up tomorrow or Friday I'd love it. I want to see you, but I will understand okay if you can't get the day off work but I want to talk to you about that article on you having 'cancer' as that shook me up a bit – So will you, John, and Granda try to get up eh? And will you phone up the NIO* again and get onto them about me being unfit for punishment and say you want to know why I am still being punished etc etc? Well, a visitor is in so have to go here, take care

lots of love, Mairead xxx

have a good birthday will be thinking of you!

Margaret wrote to Mairead when the hunger strike began:

December 1980

Dear Mairead,

I think this is the hardest letter I will ever have to write. When you

---

*The Northern Ireland Office.

were sentenced you wrote us a beautiful letter,* thanking us for all we had done for you. It helped us to understand. So I hope this letter will help you as it is impossible to talk on a half hour visit without showing any of our feelings before the screws. When you decided to become a soldier in the Irish Republican Army I knew you thought of what you were doing then, not because others were joining but because it was what you believed was the only solution to free your people. I have always asked our family to think for themselves and believe you have done this. When on that visit you told us you were going on hunger strike and had thought it very carefully through, you asked us to support you in this as we had supported you through the four years you had spent in Armagh jail. We promised you that if you went unconscious we would allow no medical help to be given. God help you and us to keep that promise. You and your comrades are not alone in your terrible ordeal, as the world knows of your great sacrifice and nobody can deny that a person's life is the ultimate sacrifice. I love you very much and I will go anywhere, talk to anyone who will listen, go anywhere to try and save you and your comrades' lives.

Love and God bless,
Mummy

---

*This letter was lost, by a newspaper which had been intending to publish it.

PART THREE

We must live as if our dreams had been realized: we cannot simply prepare other, younger daughters for strength, pride, courage and beauty. It is worse than useless to tell young women and girls that we have done and been wrong, that we have chosen ill, that we hope they'll be more 'lucky'. If we want girls to grow into free women, brave and strong, we must be those women ourselves.
Judith Arcana, Our Mothers' Daughters (1979)

CHAPTER FOUR

Tender Rage

The Letters of Teresa and Kate, 1973–80

Teresa was born in Ireland during the Great Depression and her mother died giving birth to her. Teresa and her ten brothers and sisters were divided up between relatives in the UK, Ireland and the United States; she was often made to feel a burden and was shunted from one set of relatives to another. Her father was an itinerant farm labourer who rarely saw any of his children and Teresa felt that he resented her for 'killing' his wife. She felt neglected by him, but still adored him; when she was 12, he was 'killed in a work accident' (she later found out he had been murdered). She spent the next two years in a home and at the age of 14 went into domestic service. At 18, she escaped by joining the Army, and when she was 20 she married John, a railway worker. They have four daughters: Liz, Kate (to whom these letters are addressed), and Annie and Pat, who are twins.

Teresa continued working after she was married, usually as a helper in local shops. After Kate was born, Teresa became very worried about having more children: they did not have enough money to provide for a larger family, and her doctor had warned her that her health was poor and she might die in childbirth. Shortly after the twins were born, she had a nervous breakdown. She was subjected to a constant series of threats from her husband who called her a bad Catholic and said he would have the children taken away from her if she didn't 'straighten up'. The marriage deteriorated as he became more violent and Teresa became more listless and frightened. She stayed with him because she had nowhere else to go, very little money and a strong desire to keep the family together.

Kate is a writer, active in the women's liberation movement since the early 70s. She combines 'political' work with personal writing: fiction and pamphlets, poetry and crusading articles. She says, 'I want to work like this because to be a "pure" artist would be to deny what needs to be changed in this male-run world, right *now*. Equally, to be purely a politico would mean denying the deeper side of human experience: the human confusion and contradictions that neat 'n' easy slogans so often blur.'

She writes about the background to these letters:

'My mother's hard and miserable childhood goes a long way to explain why she refused to leave my father and so desperately wanted to give us kids a happy and stable background; it is something she refers to many times in her letters. It also probably explains why she can't bear to admit her failure. I think that her mother's death, and her father's rejection of her, also help explain her hatred of sex and of men. She claims she is only bitter against men because of my father, but I can't help feeling it goes back further than that.

'My political involvement is something she used to berate me for, but now she more or less accepts it. She has even come with me to abortion demonstrations; she has handed out anti-fascist leaflets at her work and contributes money for equal-pay strikes. My father simply despises me for my politics. He also thinks I'm a snob, because of my education. I think I was a bit of a snob when I was younger; I felt embarrassed about my parents' lack of culture and resentful that I didn't have the same material advantages as some of the other girls at my school. After a while, my education became a defence: I could beat my father with words. But neither of my parents can understand why, with my degree, I should still be "messing around" with politics and "weirdo" writing when, to their minds, I could be "making it" with *Woman's Own* or the BBC.

'In many ways, my mother is really quite proud of me these days; she praises my writing, although she worries about my financial survival. She also seems to have accepted that I may never get married – but perhaps anyway she'd prefer me to be a blue-stocking celibate. I hardly ever tell her anything about my sexual relationships. If I do, she tends to throw it in my face when and if they go wrong: I'm a "whore" to go with men in the first place and I should expect to get hurt. If that sprang from Catholic morality I would understand it somehow; but it comes from her bitterness and resignation, and that is what I hate.

'All this may sound desperately unfair on my mother, and as though I allow my father to get off scot free. That isn't the case; it's simply that my mother is the parent I know, the one I have loved and do love with a passion my father has neither asked for nor, I feel, deserved. To us children he was only a nebulous and oppressive presence, someone we never really knew, someone who never shared his emotions – he just shouted. So my mother gets my love; she was the one who gave us warmth, sheltered us and made jokes even when times were bad. But as the one I love, she also gets the fuller force of my anger and grief. In the end, I suppose what I most resent is her status as a victim; she taught us to be angry and to be bitter about men but she never said we could escape. She is a horrible warning of what we yet might be. I have to move away from her in order to let myself at least become free.

'I wonder where this vicious circle of deprivation, mother oppressing daughter, daughter oppressing mother, will ever end. Perhaps it will be my daughter's daughter before we're anything like free. I suppose I would like these letters published for the same reasons as I myself need to write: in order to break the frustration, the feelings of impotence. Perhaps other mothers and daughters may see themselves in these and that may help speed the change . . .'

'I was 18 when I wrote this, and in my first year at university. I wrote it after a particularly horrendous week at home, when my mother had found my contraceptive pills and called me "a whore who should be boiled in hot tar". She also jibed me with my breakdown and attempted suicides (I was 16 and 17 the two times I tried), found some of my writings and scrawled over them: "You should leave university and burn your books on madness and get yourself a job, then you'll find out what life's about. Or if you're still hell bent on suicide do it properly and at least save us the expense of your university fees."

'We somehow or other "made it up", but I then failed her by refusing to honour Mother's Day (card, visit, present, etc.). Strained phone call, then this letter from me. I'm surprised by the moderation of it – for all my talk of "the need to find my anger", it's oblique as hell. I never told my mother I was in therapy till just before I finished – my "disturbance" was something I was always deeply ashamed of.

'The self-destructiveness I refer to in my letter ranged from having done everything in my power to fail at school – attempting suicide, becoming pregnant, and having constant accidents. The leg-breaking incident refers to the time I managed to fall down stairs the week before I was due to start at university.'

8 April 1973

My dear mum –

I'm not sure that I should write this, as I'm still working out my feelings about so many things, and it seems premature and a bit threatening to commit myself on paper about how I feel about what is one of my most important and central relationships – that is, my relationship with you.

But I know that you feel hurt, and, as I don't want you to suffer, I want you to understand. If you could really understand what was going on inside me these days you would be happy for me. I don't expect you to understand though, but one day, when I've emerged on the other side, you'll maybe be able to understand and accept the changes in me then.

All my past letters of this kind – written after a row, a separation or whatever – have been in the nature of an apology. I think that's one of the reasons I couldn't bring myself to honour Mother's Day. Because I realised that, in the past, all my statements of love – be it on Mother's Day, your birthday, whatever – have always been accompanied by laborious apologies. For my behaviour, for not being a 'good enough daughter', etcetera. Why is love, for me, so bound up with feelings of guilt? It is because I'm trying to untangle that, and the many other mental knots which at present imprison me, that I've had to withdraw from you. I need some respite, time to think.

I'm quite certain that as I write this you're already angrily exclaiming: 'and so you bloody well should feel guilty!' which is an interesting illustration of the way you react to me. Because it's quite one thing to feel guilty over specific actions or sins, quite another to have grown up with a total, constant and overwhelming sense of guilt – guilt at merely being, guilt at being loved, guilt at wanting to be loved, guilt at wanting to love . . .

Yes, I want your love, but I realise now I also experience it as totally threatening. Threatening to my attempts to become independent, to find a security that's based within myself and not dependent on your approval. I don't have that security yet . . . Looking back, I think much of my self-destructiveness has expressed not only my hatred of myself, but my anger for having been made to feel so worthless and bad. Take my over-eating for example. What's that if not punishing myself, because I've grown up to be ashamed of my sexuality? You found my pills and called me names you've no right to call me, so I went on a binge because I don't deserve to/oughtn't to look attractive at all. I feel guilty then get angry for being made to feel guilty all over again . . .

It's in order to break free from this cruel and vicious circle that I have to move away from you . . .

I'm angry mum, and very frightened at times of my anger. But I realise that it's only by expressing my anger that I'll break free of the mental prison I've caged myself in, along with all my energy and the positive things about me . . . I have to find out what I feel, instead of always having to cloak my anger and suffering in your suffering, your problems. I'm tired of having to pretend the only reason I'm unhappy is because you're unhappy . . . I'm tired of having to pretend I was never really ill. Most of all, I'm tired of just feeling guilty.

. . . I doubt if you'll understand or believe much of this, but confident that one day you will – and that you'll also understand that I've never stopped loving you, very very much. And that I also never stopped believing that you love, and have always loved, me very much . . . You have suffered very much, and it is my awareness of your suffering that made me feel so bad at wanting to go my own way, in my politics, in my philosophy, in my lifestyle . . . but I have to do this, otherwise I would just be another emotional cripple leading a life I could not believe in. My shout of anger can also be my expression of love, believe me.

. . . You don't seem to appreciate that I've made many steps forward this year . . . every time you dismiss my beliefs as 'just another stage' and say 'you'll soon find out what life's really like', I have to retreat, to withdraw, because they are cruel, self-fulfilling prophecies, your lack of belief and trust in me. I have to retreat because I have to grow. One day, I hope you will be proud of me, and be able to believe that, despite today's pain and fear at my seeming rejection of you – I had to grow away in order for us to come together again – and that, through it all – I have never stopped loving you . . .

Kate

'My mother's reply is the nearest to an apology I've ever had from her . . . I find it very sad, and very moving – it still brings tears to my eyes':

11 April 1973

Kate, do you know the old song –

> You always hurt the one you Love (*we all do that*)
> The one you shouldn't hurt at all
> You always take the Sweetest Rose
> and crush it, till the Petals fall.
>
> You always Break the Kindest Heart
> with a hasty word
> you can't recall
> So if I Broke your Heart last night
> it's because I Love You most of all

Don't you think that's lovely – one of my favourites. I am too down-to-earth and practical by nature to be able to help or guide you.

Through your troubles I have often wondered if my Mum that I never knew helped me – more than I have been able to help you. In this great Universe there must be an unseen hand that guides me – or something.

As a child I used to go to my refuge when troubled, an old church called 'St. Mary's Star of the Sea'. I often went there in tears, my little heart overflowing with Love–hate–fear–revenge–whatever. The Church had a very high roof and way up above the Altar was an O-shaped window to let the sun's rays come through in the form of a Beam of light – whenever I knelt in that Church, little and very scared – that Beam shone on me, my eyes would follow it and there in the window would be my mum. I didn't go to Church because I was a Catholic or to Pray to God – I just spoke to my mum and asked her advice. On the way out I always kissed the statue of St Teresa (hence my confirmation name, Teresa). God didn't seem to come in to my little visits – other than that I always said to him, child-like, Why did you take *my Mum* away from me – I would have been quite happy at that time (not now) if he had taken someone else's Mum. After those long visits Nothing could hurt me – I used to race along the road light footed and singing like a Linty – happy as could be. I don't remember being sad as a child – I don't dwell on the past as being full of sad memories. I was a Happy Child – but in Life there has to be Sadness and Pain to make us appreciate Joy and laughter and vice versa. I believe – my Mum gave me strength of character – the courage to go on in the face of adversity and ever the optimist the belief that Tomorrow the Sun will shine. If it doesn't my Mum is still there, perhaps it is God through her – I don't know. I am just a crazy mixed up Mummy ha ha. But if only I could give you, here on this earth, what my Mum has given me in her death, I would indeed be very happy. Now I will turn to God or my Mum and ask them to Guide and Protect you in all you do.

Love from your down to earth Mum xxx
xxx

'This was in response to one of my periodic attempts to persuade Mum to leave Dad':

3 December 1973

Dear Kate,

Thank you for your letter. You are still the Dramatic, over-sensitive girl that takes everything very much to heart, it's nice to be like that but can be painful. I often wish I was hard hearted and selfish, able to feel only for myself and not for those around me. That way you are in a state of good health and can afford to be smug and superior with those around you who feel so much for others.

Your letter hurt me deeply. You are indeed entitled to your own opinions and I really admire anyone that has an opinion, really believes in it and sticks by it at all costs. A person like that can only be admired.

Your father and I are not happy. That's unfortunate but millions of people are unhappy together, so I don't see why that should upset you so much; on the other hand millions of couples are happy. I have never at any time tried to turn you off men. They are not all miserable childish creatures like your Father who has gone through life throwing tantrums and I was put in the position of trying to keep the peace, not for my sake but in the hope that my children would have the security of a happy home, a mother's wish to give her children what she never had. If I had not wished that so much I would have kicked your father's teeth in years ago and got some relief for my emotions and perhaps made a man of him at the same time. Anyway I do not wish to discuss your father. I cannot help feeling the way I do towards him, he has never given me any reason to love him, such as little acts of kindness or sympathy or tolerance. He handed over a pittance for housekeeping and everything else, and there his responsibility to wife and children ended. In any crisis – and there are many when you are responsible for a home and children – he either collapsed into bed till it was all over or, as his favourite expression goes, 'I'm not having this, I wash my hands of it', and out he went leaving me with kids and crisis.

I am not the bitter twisted person your Father makes me out to be. On the contrary I have been sad over the years. Sad that my children should be brought up in such an atmosphere, sad that your Father is such a weak man, sad when I saw what happened to your older sister, and in the Depths of Despair when I saw what happened to you. I have never in my life done anything to harm my children. I have said things I shouldn't have said under extreme provocation and at the injustice of it all, with your father sitting there smug and self-satisfied stirring it up.

You are 19½ now, Kate. You must face up to the realities of life; the main ones being that your father and I are not happy together – sad but nevertheless true. You, I, and no one else can undo the last 23 years; there could have been nice memories, there aren't. I love you as I love Annie and Pat and Liz. We have all had happy times together with lots of love and laughter, giving and sharing and that is what life is all about. Togetherness – not *I want* all the time. Now what do I write to help you? I don't think I can help you, much as I want to. There are only two things I can say to you.

1) That your father and I will live happily ever after – that is not possible.

2) That we will stop being hypocritical and get divorced, that is not practical, where would the money come from to keep two homes going?

Believe me, Kate, in all sections of society there are people living together and going their own way at the same time, purely to give their children a home. That is what I intend to do, live here, but separately. Perhaps your father and I may even become friends, something we have never been. For the twins' sake I am staying here, because I do realize that children do love both parents, but they will not go through the nasty cursing raving and tantrums that you and Liz had to put up with, I can assure you of that. And if anyone and I mean *anyone* upsets them with problems at the age of adolescence they will have to account to me for it, they are going to have a peaceful life till they are old enough to fend for themselves. I am strong enough now mentally and physically to see to that and I will never again be bogged down to the extent I was in the past, regardless of threats from any quarter.

Your father will still have the same freedom he has always had to come and go as he pleases, to hold the purse strings and to take good care of *himself* but he will not under any circumstances be allowed hysterical tantrums, so he really will have to prove his manliness – have some control over his emotions from now on.

If the time ever comes when I leave here, I go with NOTHING, there is nothing I want and I do not intend to ever be a burden to my children as long as I have my health and can earn my living. Then I ask nothing from anyone – when I don't have my health the State can take over.

All I want out of life is Peace of mind, just as you do. I love you and if I could die this minute to bring you Peace of mind I would do it willingly and I mean that from the bottom of my heart.

I appreciate very much that when you were younger you tried to help and got all upset when it didn't help; my heart literally bled for you and I hated the circumstances that led up to you being disturbed . . . All I ask of you now is that you don't get involved, have your own opinions, keep them to yourself and perhaps learn from what you see and hear, love or hate both parents 'but don't get involved'. I love you and my one wish for you is that one day you will meet a nice kind good-humoured man who will share your joys and sorrows. Liz got a good one and I thank god daily for that. I wish the same for you and the twins. I am not here for a free meal ticket, that I find laughable. You are welcome to come home – you will probably find a happy atmosphere now. Certainly *I* am not miserable but you must accept the facts of life, Kate. I have told you the position, who knows maybe time will alter that and perhaps your father and I will settle down to some kind of decent life together, time heals all, so they say, plus of course a willingness to make yourself a nicer person to live with.

Meantime Annie and Pat are my main concern, when they are 16 they will be old enough to stand up for themselves. I intend to protect them till then. That is a mother's role in life. Father can join in if he wants to, but they will not be hurt if I can help it.

I am sorry that you are still sad and sincerely wish I could help. If this letter doesn't help then I am sorry but there is nothing else I can do except to say that I do love you and want as I have always wanted, nothing but happiness for you. How it can be possible to want that so much, and be unable to achieve it for you – I really don't know.

You have your life to lead, please lead it with the assurance of my love behind you. I cannot offer you more than that and if that doesn't help then I am sorry and sad.

Must run, have to go to work and the bus service is hopeless so I walk now. If you want to come home please do, but I do not wish to discuss anything at all concerning all this. Lets just hear your news, hope and ambitions etc. Lets see you happy. That is all I want. Be happy. (You are old enough now to know if you want to be good or not. Ha ha).

> God bless and guide you,
> Your loving
> Mum

'Things smoothed out for awhile at the beginning of my second year at university. I was living in a house with three women I liked very much and they gave me a great deal of support':

4 October 1974

Dear Kate,

. . . Re: your peace of mind, Kate, glad to hear your present house mates are helping in that direction; it's the most precious gift anyone can have, if I could be granted one wish, it would be that *you* could find Peace of Mind. I have no ambition to win the Pools or be rich. Re: your state of mind, I feel really helpless, it's a horrible feeling being unable to help or even understand, for instance I cannot see how you feel that you have destructive powers . . . Kate, we all have our share of sickness even death, we all have our Joys and Sorrows, we all reach the depths of misery when we feel that life is not worth living, we all reach the heights of Joy when our World is perfect and life is Wonderful . . . When all is said and done all we can do is say what course of action is the best to take for *me* and if you are married and have kids you want what is best for them because you love them more than yourself. I sometimes wonder if being married and having a couple of kids would help you to a peaceful mind, never being able to jump in to any decision without first saying how will it affect my wee helpless lovable dependent children and believe me it may change your nature to a certain extent but having to go against the grain does strengthen the *character*. As I see life, it is full of injustices and all we can do is fight to the death for those you love, fight injustice as far as possible, don't envy anyone anything. Envy really is a disease, the World is full of Goodies and Baddies, and all you have to do is decide which you are going to be and then get on with life, they say that Right always prevails but like a lot of people I often wonder about that.

So my love, all I can say to you in the way of giving advice is Live your Life, do the things you have to do in your own future interests, enjoy all the physical pangs we all have to go through, love and the lack of it and sex if it is necessary to you. Be happy and spread your happiness around, it's amazing how that helps others, be kind and sympathetic but at the same time do try to be practical, we all have to be in the end and we all have to try to discipline our emotions. As I see it you are a very compassionate person, I am too and my very compassion for others has got me into trouble on more than one occasion so we have to have some discipline over our emotions eh.

Love,
Mum

'This is one of the letters never sent. It started off "jolly" and gradually got more and more defensive and angry. My parents were cross with me because

I wasn't going to spend my 21st birthday at home. I was just about to graduate and leave university for a job in another part of the country and was sad at leaving the women I'd been sharing a house with. I had been extremely happy in that house and along with the other women in the house I was up to my neck in the National Abortion Campaign . . .

'The last time I had been home was for my parents' 25th anniversary and the hypocrisy of celebrating it totally sickened me. I'd hidden that but the weekend ended in a huge row about politics. The row was about race as well as my manic involvement in the abortion campaign. I was told to study for my exams instead of wasting their time and their money on immoral causes like that.

'I'm very embarrassed by the boasting/defensive tone of the letter, but with all the insults and predictions of failure thrown at me I didn't know any other way to respond.'

5 May 1975

Dear Mum,

Please excuse what will no doubt be dreadful typing, but my hands are about to fall off through writer's cramp . . . hence the typescript.

. . . I'm terribly involved with the abortion campaign, and would like to see it through 'til at least the national demonstration is over. In my own peculiar political way, being able to devote myself full-time to something I really care about is the nearest I'll get to a rest. I suppose that sounds funny to you, because your vision of me is as the Horizontal Champ, always asleep or lounging around, which would sound rather funny to my friends down here, seeing as they're trying very hard at the moment to see that I slow down occasionally.

. . . At the meeting last night we got a very good turn out, about 200 (mainly women). An anti-abortionist tried to wreck the meeting, but got shut up by a very good woman doctor who told him what it's like trying to save the life of a woman who's been driven to the backstreets – and what it's like failing. To this he had no answer. I am full of anger and pain, dreading that this Bill should become law, dreading that there should be more tragedies like the one she tells us of. But I cannot show that pain, I have to be strong. I have to be organisational. We collected nearly £70, and, afterwards, a little old lady of about 80 came up and told us to keep up the good work; she had had nine children and five abortions, all 'do it yourself'; that was in the good old days. Again I want to cry, because an old lady of 80 cares enough to drag herself out into the night to our meeting, and because she has suffered; and because she touches me very deeply when she says we are fine young women doing a fine job, and that she hopes that even if she could not be free we may yet be. And I need the reassurance of this brave old lady because you get very tired when people agree but just bury their heads in the sand, because you get very angry and lonely when the anti-s get up and tell you that you are a murderer, because you care about women, because you dare to care about the living.

And afterwards I knew again that we are right, when a young man I know only by sight came up to me after the meeting and gave me two cheques; one for £100, which is for our branch of the campaign, and the other, for £200, which is for the campaign nationally. It turns out that he is adopted, taken from a children's home at 3 because his unmarried mum could not cope. He tells me his earliest memory is of his mum crying – and then finding that he was alone. In his words, 'My Mum didn't have a choice about having me, so I'd like it, for her sake, if other women could.' The money was from a small trust left to him by his adopted father.

I expect you're thinking I'm completely cracked to tell you all this, to which I can only reply that I guess most of the things that really interest me seem cracked to you, cracked, irrelevant or wrong. And if I haven't been very good about repressing it all for the sake of this letter, I guess it's precisely because this campaign, the work it entails, the kind of energy it calls for, and the feelings it arouses in me, mean that I've little appetite for anything else; the other women in the house and I took some time 'off' last night, to go to the pub, and still the only thing we could talk about was the campaign; what we do next, how we do it . . . God knows I hope that I should never need an abortion, but I cannot separate my fate from those of the women around me . . .

I feel pretty choked about leaving here, not just because I'm going on my own to somewhere where I know no-one, but because I'm leaving a house that's been very warm, very supportive and lots of fun, to go and live with god knows whom; and I'm going to miss the fun, the midnight dancing, the cuddles when I'm down, the laughter when we're all up, and the relief and joy in knowing that you're with people to whom you don't have to justify everything you believe in . . .

You'll just about forgive *me* for being a commie bastard, you'd like to see put up against the wall and shot, but not my friends, eh?* No, I haven't forgotten what Dad said that time, and I doubt I ever will. Considering it's me that's supposed to be so insensitive, I find that one hard to beat. But then maybe it's my supposed insensitivity that makes it easy for you to say things like that in front of me; commie bastards don't have feelings – right? Just in case you want to wriggle out of this one by deciding not to remember what was said, let me remind you; 'If I live to see the day when all these left-wingers are put up to a wall and shot, I'll die a happy man.' You were all sitting in the front room

---

*'NB: I was never a member of the Communist Party.'

drinking duty-free, and I was in the kitchen trying not to cry. And yes, I do have a chip on my shoulder, and so would you in my shoes.

. . . So, if you want to see me maybe there could be just a little effort from your side sometime, like maybe you could drag yourselves onto a train, or even go to the bother of using your car. Maybe the long letters could come from you instead of always from me. Maybe you could remember that phone calls and visits home come quite expensive on a grant of £600 p.a. Most of all, it would be appreciated if you were nice to me when I actually get there, like maybe you could make a big effort and tone it down when you get to knocking everything that matters to me . . .

Maybe we could even agree to differ, and you could just stop provoking me, and keep the technicolour details of how you'd like to see me and my 'sort' hanged, drawn and quartered to yourselves.† And then, with the time that's left, maybe you could try and take just a little interest in the life I lead. There's lots of things I could tell you about if you bothered to be interested, and occasionally took some interest beyond telling me not to squander my grant/get in with the wrong crowd/go to demos/fail my exams. Yes, if you expect a response from me, expect me to be interested in what you're doing, maybe you could show just a little interest in me as I actually am, as opposed to the person you think I ought to be.

'A few years later, on a more positive note . . . I was living in the country at the time, having won a writer's grant. I wrote this letter two days before I discovered that doctors thought my mother had cancer. All that summer we had been very close and this is a very loving letter. In its own way, it's as true as everything else, the bitterness and the hate. I do owe her a lot and love her.'

14 October 1977

Dearest Mumma,

Many many thanks for your loving letter, and for your gift, which touched me very much indeed. I could just imagine you fretting around the shops, looking for something to cheer me, and that moved me lots and lots. It duly hangs upon my 'study' (grand, eh!) wall, opposite my desk, there for when I'm feeling totally devoid of inspiration, chewing my pencil and thinking perhaps I should take up charring instead. Don't worry about not being able to get that picture you wanted for me, it's the thought that counts, and yours I know are always dear and loving.

I'm feeling all soft and gooey tonight, very peaceful and contented. I've been reading through all my old letters, diaries and things, and it is

---

† 'I really was addressing my father here.'

very good to see how much I've changed, how far I've moved from all the fears and hangups that used to beset me. At times I was also a self-indulgent bitch, but I guess I had to go through all that, work through all the mud and anger, to finally come out, something like shining, on top.

And feeling especially loving towards you; reading all your old letters, remembering all the hurts and misunderstandings we had, and you – and I – desperately trying to make sense of it all. Your love still and always there, even the times I was furthest from you, and the times I hit out and hurt.

And now? So much has changed between us these past two years. I feel our relationship has become very good and strong again, and I love you very much. As for your love, it is an anchor for me, keeps me warm and brave when the going gets tough. I think what we went through was indeed a lot to do just with the simple process of growing up; me having to pull away in order to come back, and you, as mother, having to let me go in order for that coming back. We have both changed and adapted, and now I feel we are friends as well as mother and daughter – and that is something precious and, I think, quite rare. All my friends envy our relationship, you know, and are very fond of you, admire you a lot, think you a great tough soft lady, gutsy and fun, big and brave . . . all of which you are! I am as proud of you as you are of me.

Now I'm older I can better understand how difficult it must have been for you at times; to let your child kick out and rebel, and make mistakes and get hurt a lot at times, but all the experience I've had has made me the person I now am, understanding more and trying to put all that experience to good use with my writing. I think one of the break points was when you realised my politics and life-style didn't mean I'd one day come crawling home with 3 illegitimate children/VD/heroin marks on my arm/a wooden leg/2 syphilitic parrots and 3 buckets of dung and call it 'Art' . . . though at times you may have been right to worry!

What seems so good to me now is how both our ideas have changed, it's not one-sided, and there are many things we can talk and care about and share, where once there would only have been explosions. Women's Liberation, and my not particularly wanting to get married, etcetera – now you see I can in fact take care of myself, you don't have to act the moralist, and now I'm older and wiser I can also see where my idealism did put me at risk. With society as sexist as it is, and men as piggish as they often can be, I can now understand how hard it has always been for mothers of daughters; it's the wanting to protect your child that makes the mother end up wielding the big stick. What a hard time mothers have of it, at times it seems no way you can win.

Dear Mum, I don't think I'm expressing myself as well as I want to

. . . you have had a very hard life, and your lessons have often been bitter; in turn you tried to hold me back when I went soaring for the clouds, I know now because you didn't want to see me hurt. It was wanting to go for the clouds that also made me need to break away and now as I come back, I want you to know how much I am aware of all I owe you, though at times I didn't realise it, or show gratitude. So many of the fighting qualities I imagined I personally invented came in fact from you; all your loving, and your strength, have been with me always, even the times I didn't know it. The rebel in me is in fact the rebel in you . . . it was only your sadness and tiredness quenched it; but it comes to life again, I hope, a little through me . . . I was so proud of you the day you came on the abortion demo – we had both come such a long way from the silence of when I was 17 – and proud of you taking those anti-fascist leaflets into work; I've told everyone about it, and they think you're great! Of course, there will be things we won't agree about, but you're right, in the end it's the same things we want, and that's the important thing.

What I'm also trying to say is that all the times I rallied and railed it was in fact because I desperately wanted your approval and acceptance, didn't want just to be the 'nutter leftie' . . . because my politics, and those of my friends, do in fact often put us beyond the pale; Dad's right, there are certain jobs I'll never now be allowed to have, there are risks we all take, and sometimes you feel desperate, up against the brick wall of something that is so much bigger than us.

It's the politics, which for me pervade all of life, that make me want to write . . . the desire to somehow be able to communicate and help to change . . . Did I ever tell you I want to sometime write a novel or play about you? There – fame and immortality!

There's a show on next week I particularly want you to see because there's an actress in it that I'd like to play you when and if I finally get around to writing that play . . . she's bloody marvellous, and has a beautiful sympathetic touch, lots of strength, and a quite similar, cocky sense of humour.

And now I want to write out something for you that I meant to send a long time ago, but don't think I ever did. I heard it last year, after seeing a play about mothers and daughters. It was a feminist play, and tried to show how mothers oppress their daughters, precisely because they themselves are so oppressed; and how in turn daughters oppress their mothers, themselves take them for granted the way society does . . . then those daughters too become mothers and the vicious circle continues . . . except, the play said, if we join together and fight the forces that have divided us, then mothers will cease to try to bring up their little girls as Well-behaved Young Women, and daughters cease to hypocritically want their mothers to be Model slave-like Mums . . . and just love each other instead. It was a very moving play, and made me think and feel a lot, and how, for all I could rant on about MY wanting to be liberated, I still hadn't properly understood YOUR oppression, part of me still colluding with you-know-who about how dreadful it was that you weren't constantly up to your neck in Omosuds, Angel Delight and whatever else it is that Super-mums are supposed to chain themselves to . . .

> Even some revolutionaries are lovers,
>   even some poets have babies . . .
> I keep on wanting everything,
>   and I want you to want that too.

Words from the play: poetry and motion sung/danced by women strong in their fragility, proud in their vulnerability as mothers, as daughters . . . let me stand up and be counted, every shiver, every shout! A beauty I was glad for, bringing tears in recognition; Mum I love you, Mum I'm glad I got away from you, Mum I *love* you and I wish you would come too.

Not anger, but sadness that I ever had to get away from you. What anger I have is reserved for those who taught you to be fatalistic, for those who encouraged us both to take taking you for granted, for granted.

And I remember my wanting to send you a copy of Gorky's *Childhood*, hoping that you would recognise yourself in the Great Mother; beautiful love, massive protector, my ever-smiling laughter learner. Just as I thank these women for daring their play, I thank Gorky for his mother; she brought me in touch with my love for you.

Like him, I too have had to fight from the worst lesson you ever taught me: the need to submit, a sad-eyed acceptance of 'this is how the world is'. Mother, my world must be how I make it . . . little as I knew it then, or you, my suicides were in fact my *love* for life; my wanting, oh, so much more than we as women were supposed to want . . . the journey through the stomach pumps taking me to where? . . . to here: standing now waving the manacles I have hacked away, delighted in my terrifying freedom –

And I remember now, too, all the good you ever taught me. For it was from you I learned to laugh, to joy, to give myself up to experience; no person has ever taught me as you have, to so grasp life. You showed me with your drunken tears, with your sad 40's songs, with your compassion, your girlish jokes and, yes too, with your hate. Short on book learning, deep in emotion, it's you who've kept me from falling in for too long with the intellectuals, those dried up pedants who imagine that to think is the same as to feel; the gut-gripping life-destroying bloodily glorious REAL thing . . .

But you, Mum, you're ready and you're real. Your one fault was in teaching me to reach out only to surrender; but I've reached out and refused to surrender. I'm glad you taught me to reach out, and I'm glad I've learnt not to let go; and some day I pray you will joy in my victory – yet so strange to you – and be proud of your part in making me a lady hungry for victories. Little as you now accept it, the most loyal I could ever be by you is to finish the tales you were not allowed to write, to do honour to the visions you gave me, by straining for their reality . . .

You know you wouldn't really have wanted a *Woman's Own* Happy Ending for me. I'm different, Mum, the 'odd one out' in our family: at times I've been the mad man, the betrayer and the freak. But, in reality, my 'differentness' is only my giving credence to the dreams you first lent me . . . this idealism against which you warn me, it's yours too you know.

– mine won't be an easy ride, mother, not ever, I don't think. Daily I pay the price for my 'differentness', for my refusal to conform. And there are times when I long to be anything other than what I am; to be able to be happily blind, to not see the suffering, to become one of those pink-varnished girls who stare adoringly up at their jail-keeper husband: blind, and partly dead, but accepted, oh accepted, *normal*.

But I have come too far, can never turn back now – and most times I am glad for that. I try, I fail, I sometimes even succeed; and I joy in my courage, even finding strength from that loneliness which has again and again become mine for my refusal to play the game. Because what I will not surrender is the free me, the one who is real, solid, blood, lust and all . . .

I want
    what I guess, I have always wanted;
    – I keep on wanting everything,
    and I want you to want that too.

Mum, if only you knew it, that's your song I'm singing: it's you who taught me the tune, and it's for you I'll carry on singing it – and for my daughters' daughters; through the age-old strength of women, one day our day will come . . .

You'd better not show this letter to Dad – hide it somewhere, he'd throw a bloody blue fit . . .

Nuff for now. Write soon, let me know when to expect you, wear a black leather carnation so I'll recognise yer.

> Much and much and lots of lots and love too
> 'normous piles of it
> your one and only loving
> Personal Genius,
> Kate

Two days after this letter was written, doctors became suspicious that Teresa had breast cancer. The violent rows between her and Kate's father intensified throughout this period. He threatened to leave her, forced her to sleep with him and accused her of being insane. She seriously considered divorcing him despite the state of her health. Kate took her round to see divorce lawyers, spoke to her on the phone every day, went to visit their friends to try to sort out alternative living arrangements should Teresa decide to separate. For two months they lived with this 'scare' and eventually the tests proved negative. Kate describes her reactions:

'This is the kind of thing I can't forgive my mother. For those two months I cried every single day, because I thought she was going to die and because of the worry over how to protect her from my father. Then, magically, every-thing is all right (till next time) and she still feels free (in this letter) to tell me the full details of their rows. It never seems to occur to her what grief and impotence that makes me feel. Having just written a loving tribute in the last letter, I was jolted back into the realisation that nothing had changed – the following two letters seemed to prove that.'

November 1977

Dear Kate,

I told your Father how I felt, in a quiet *very* strong way. He must leave me – or else. He didn't say a word – then in the middle of *Coronation Street* he leaped out of the chair in front of Annie – said 'not you nor *anybody* is going to get me out of here.' He did not *tell you* he was leaving etc. etc. I told him not to *start*, I didn't want to know.

I said to A. – you heard what your Father said – nobody is going to get him out of here.

She jumped up, said 'get your Divorce, do what you like the 2 of you' and left the room.

(What you call The Vicious Circle.) I told you I knew what his answer would be. I am only writing to tell you this so that you will appreciate that *I do know* what I am talking about.

His answer to me was a foregone conclusion.

Please – Please do not worry about me – get on with your own life, don't get caught in his web of deceit, weakness and nothingness.

I beg of you not to worry about me, if only I could guarantee that – even that would be a weapon against him, because he loves it, having us all churned up worrying about each other.

Since his little speech, he has taken the dog out for a walk, he is now home, asked me nicely would I like a cup of tea and is singing quite happily.

Hope you had a nice journey, and that you can settle down to write, that would be my Dearest Wish.

Much Love,
Mum

December 1977

Dear Kate,

Thank you for your letter. It cheered me up no end. Also for the phone call the other Friday. On that evening your Dad leaped out of his chair at 8 o'clock, collected his wee bag full of empty Coke bottles and I thought Oh Christ – here we go again – lemonade, big spender. I said I didn't want any – that did it, he said he would get pissed by himself and for three hours the air was Blue. I got the usual old guff about how the daughters I loved have spent years pleading with him to leave me – owing to me being sick in the mind, but *he* couldn't leave me because A) he is the loyal type and he made up his mind to make the best of me and B) he was worried about leaving his children in my care. He was roaring with laughter telling me he had put in his resignation and was leaving his job on December 31st and once he got that gratuity in his hands, life was going to be all women and gambling, I would get nothing out of it. All the people I think are my good friends, he said, have all advised him to leave me. I thought it all over for two days – not having said one word that evening – on Sunday night I said to him very quietly – 'You are not going to do what you said you would with your gratuity and savings – I sweated blood all those years for you, to save and see that *you* never went without anything.' I said, 'you just try it mate and I'll get a heavy mob [*Kate's feminist friends*] on to you, that will leave you so that you won't look in a mirror for the next twenty years and you tell me just one more time that I'm sick in the mind and I'll kick your teeth so far down your throat that they will come out the other end.' I banged the table saying '*do you understand*?' He was literally shaking like a jelly. Since then he has been very nice and I'm almost certain his shouts about leaving the job (my fault) were a come-on to get his own way. Anyway as I said, everything is now very pleasant. I think he knew who I was referring to when I said I'd get the heavy mob on to him. (Who else but my Friends ha ha – all coming with their Banners to support poor little me and hit him over the head with them.)

Let's be truly thankful he's being nice at the moment. It's almost 3 a.m. and I have to be up at 7:15.

Oodles & oodles of love to you,
Mum

'This is probably the most explicit and honest letter I've ever written to my mother. It's addressed 'To *Both* of you', by which I really mean her, because she never allowed that my anger might be against her, not just my (undoubted) pig of a father.

'The "Christmas incident" referred to in this letter is something I never intended to talk about. Last Christmas Eve they both got drunk and my mum got into bed in my room in order not to have to sleep with him. I pretended to be asleep because I didn't want to listen to her problems anymore. Half an hour later my father came into the room, climbed into the bed and after a cursory battle of words, got his Christmas fuck.

'I couldn't let them know I was awake because I didn't know how I'd look them in the face the next day, or they me. All I wanted to do was kill them/kill myself. Eventually I did tell them. I never meant to, but about four months later they had another of their drunken fights in front of me and I just started screaming at them. All they could say of that horrible Christmas was, "We thought you were asleep." I wrote this letter because I felt that by their feeble excuses they had completely denied the significance of the incident.

'I hate my father for his rapes, I hate my mother for her submissiveness and I hate them both for making me a party to their sordid and destructive war.'

April 1978

To *Both* of you,

You can poison your own lives if you want to – just leave me out of it. You were adults long before any of us, and Annie and Pat aren't even that yet, but we've grown up *tainted by you* at every turn. You have no idea what you have done to your children, to our sexuality, to *our* hopes for happiness. If ever you do think about it, it's to blame the other. I told you about Christmas and neither of you even had the grace to look ashamed – that you made me party to your sordid rituals, your non-stop never-ending bloody war. You won't make it up, but you won't part; stop fooling yourselves that it was 'for our sake'. Is that why Liz and I left home at the first bloody chance at 16? All you've managed is to put us up on the crucifix with you too.

You want me to watch you bleed, be covered in your blood, clear up the mess, but you'd die rather than take any advice I've ever given. I'm just supposed to sit here and listen passively, listen to the same, same, *same* fucking stories – and do nothing. Every time I come home its the same. If I get angry I've 'betrayed' you, I'm taking sides (and all our lives you have both wanted us to take sides – don't say you never wanted us 'involved', we've never been given any *option*), maybe I should just pretend that I'm not human, I'm just a listening-machine – pretend that I don't have feelings, that it doesn't make me unhappy, that I don't fucking worry about it –

AS I'M SUPPOSED TO

– but neither of you want help, you want collusion. You want never to change, you don't dare to change, but by God you'll hang your children with you.

Liz, Annie, Pat, me – we can't all be imagining it. You've poisoned our lives, and I think it's time you knew that. If I've survived at all, it's no thanks to either of you.

'After the "Christmas incident" letter there was great tension but no real rift occurred until some months later when things came to a head over my little sister, Annie, who had a miscarriage. She was then 16. I had supported Annie through seven weeks of "I want an abortion/I'm going to get married/I'm not going to get married, I'll have it adopted/I'll keep it . . ." Quite deliberately, neither of us told our parents. I had my sister on the phone three times a day and was constantly taking her to counsellors, talking to her boyfriend, etc. By the supreme irony of ironies, I had found out that I was also pregnant (this time through contraceptive failure, not self-destructive risk-taking). I never told Annie about my pregnancy because I thought it would make her feel guilty about depending on me. I intended to have an abortion and did not want her to feel influenced by my own choice. In my case, the man concerned was not someone I wanted to have a child with. He was, in all fairness, as helpful as he could be, but the whole experience was very traumatic for me. Catholicism doesn't die easily. I did not tell my mother about my abortion.

'Annie miscarried while I was having my abortion. I had to rush home at my mother's command, to be interrogated as to whether or not I had known anything about my sister's pregnancy. This had to be completely denied, because it wouldn't have been worth trying to explain to her why neither of us had dared speak. Far from showing the "compassion" she claims to have shown to my sister, I had Annie round in tears after drunken accusations of being "a wee whore who deserves what you get, letting a man do *that* to you and I bet you enjoyed it. No man'll ever go near you again . . ." Etc., etc. (Sober she can be compassionate; drunk she's a vicious bitch.)

'While trying to recover from my own abortion I had my mother constantly on the phone complaining about my father/her wayward daughter. I finally lost my temper and said she was selfish. She wrote me one letter and then we didn't speak for several months:

August 1978

Dear Kate,

Re: our telephone conversation I have 3 points to make – 1. I regret having married your father but, having done so and being ever the optimist, always think – things will be better tomorrow – they never were and by then it was too late to do anything about it and no where to go and no one to help. I was brought up on the principle – you have made your bed now lie in it.

My second regret is not having had four kids but having spoiled them so that they grew up to be wayward, to go their own way – regardless of the pain or suffering they caused the only person who cared – their mother.

3rd regret is that after 20 years of misery, hard work – no drip dry clothes, washing machines, hoovers etc. in those days, as I said after 20 years of despair and worry with no light at the end of the tunnel I then took to the bottle, a very degrading and shameful experience, just one more guilt to have on my already over-worried mind – Drink has never been my scene – for 20 years of married life I had never gone out for a social drink, I could count on one hand the times I went to the pictures or anywhere else, except when I was taking the children. When I did hit the bottle I did it as a choice of 3 things. The bottle, a mental hospital or suicide, that's how low I was. I was too proud to let any B[astard] drive me in to a mental hospital especially a weak B. Suicide though, I contemplated. I couldn't do it for many reasons – at that time it was against my religious beliefs – I still had some then – I can understand that a person committing suicide is not a coward but a person in deep despair, however I do still think it is a selfish act with no thought for the people that are left behind, leaving them with the feeling of 'Was it my fault? Where did I go wrong?' and having to carry that thought with them for the rest of their lives. For me suicide wasn't on. I wouldn't leave the kids I gave birth to, loved, pampered and comforted – to face an uncaring world, without my hand to guide them. Seems I failed but it wasn't from the want of trying.

So the bottle was my choice – not to have a nice social drink (I don't even like drink) but to get utterly sloshed – to drown out the whole ghastly business, apparently it didn't do that, all it did was to bring the unhappiness to the fore and jumble up all the worries and doubts. I guess we all have them in our subconscious. For anything I may have said or done in drink that you have found offensive, I Sincerely Apologise. I resent the circumstances that led up to me hitting the bottle. I have given up the booze now and am feeling better for it . . .

. . . Don't blame me for the state you got into. *I told you nothing in those days* – you saw it all for yourself and your father sneaking around having quiet little talks with you or hysterical tantrums – don't blame me for his weaknesses . . . I tried to shield you all from the unpleasant realities of my particular circumstances. *I have never used you* as you insist. And you can take it for granted that I will never use you or tie you to me in the future. I have spent too many years of my life standing on my own two feet and if the day arrives when I cannot do that I sure won't turn to your father or my home to provide anything . . .

I wanted one thing in my life – A Happy Secure home for my children – that's the only thing I ever wanted and I fought all the way along the line – against impossible odds to make my own dream come true. I didn't achieve that – Complete and utter failure. You said I am selfish, think of no one but myself – I don't think you can honestly believe that. I doubt if your sisters would agree – even your father would disagree with that . . .

When you were young you hated me because you firmly believed I wanted you to marry and give me a grandchild. I had more than enough to cope with your laugh-a-minute, kind father and four wayward daughters. Then when I went to stay with Liz that time, my first proper holiday in years, when I came back you could cut the hatred in the air with a knife, Daddy had told you what a bad wife and Mummy I was. You blame me because you went from wanting to be a nun to being boy-mad – now it seems I am to blame as you cannot relate to men. *I* am not a manhater – *I* know there are kind loving men in the world – also some real Baskets – the same applies to women. I have never by word or deed encouraged you to love or hate either sex. Tying you to me – one great fallacy that has never been my ambition and if it was that's another ambition I didn't achieve. Eh, poor me – I'm feeling sorry for myself. The blood tie that seems to worry you – sorry I cannot do anything about that – that resentment could work both ways. *I* – thank God – face up to the realities of life – wish you and your father could do just that and not use me as the whipping boy for your mistakes. You are kind hearted and you do mean well – where I'm concerned I guess you just get too emotionally involved and you quickly lose patience. Your father, he's just emotional. If you ever take on a husband look for three qualities KINDNESS, PATIENCE, and a good sense of humour. If you find one like that grab him. If you ever have children then you will know what life is all about. Me self-righteous? More than likely – but with good reason. Hoping you are well and happy.

your new enlightened
Mum

'I didn't write for a long time. When I finally did, my letter was very angry. I told her about my abortion; how unhappy I was in my *own* life. I said that the reason I had not been in touch was that I was tired of always having to put on a cheerful and sympathetic face no matter what my problems, so that she could unburden herself on me. And that I just didn't want to know the intimate details of my parents' marriage, my mother's hatred, my father's sins – because I found it hard enough already to survive. I tried to make her realise that every time she made me party to their war she re-opened old wounds in *me* and that all of us, particularly Annie, had a right not to suffer any more.'

December 1978

Dear Kate,

Your two letters received and understood. I'm amazed at your anger at not hearing from me before – I received your first letter on Thursday and your second demanding a reply on Saturday. You took *3 months* to answer mine. I spent 3 confused days and sleepless nights answering your letter, but I will not post it for the simple reason that I am fed up justifying myself to all and sundry. I am full of guilt complexes – I am tired – weary – confused. (I really don't want to know anymore).

I am sorry that your life has been Hell.

I am sorry that mine was. It's a vicious circle.

You're 24. I am 48. You can try to erase the bad memories and live on your good ones. Everyone keeps telling *me* to erase the bad memories, the only difference with me is that I knew there would be no good ones to follow . . .

Re: my nastiness in drink and my convenient amnesia – the amnesia is genuine. I drink for oblivion, not for pleasure – unfortunately. After years and years of being told by him what sluts my daughters are and them coming in at all hours of the night, me sitting here waiting for them, in despair – the fears and worries of a mother. Yes it all comes up with the whiskey. If your father has shown loving qualities to you and you love him – *no one* – but *no one* could take that away from you. Your father would welcome you with open arms now. Life is not going his way. I am not his wife in the true sense of the word, – he is never going to forgive me for that. If I stay I am going to spend what's left of my life with heavy silences, sudden leaps out of the chair to go to the pub or the dogs, and the constant reminder 'you're not my wife'. No, I don't have your father's love, Kate, so don't get hurt, jealous or angry on that score. If he has any feelings for Humans – I could go so far as to say I am the one he feels for, but I would put it this way and say I am the one he needs. To lean on.

No doubt you know I have applied for a divorce yet again – make allowance for me Kate. I have no love for your father. That is a fact of life. I cannot help it. But even now I am not going in for a divorce lightly, he really does need me. *I* am confused hurt and angry that his behaviour makes it necessary. Re: Annie – I may have destroyed your and Liz's lives. But Annie's *no*. She is the total opposite of Pat, who is the only one of you who has never given me cause to worry. She is a spoiled little girl in every way. Annie admits she has never had any fear of telling me things, but has been ashamed to tell me. Fact of life – wayward adolescents never like to tell their MUMS where they have been naughty, they will tell anyone else but not MUM. Annie tells me all about her love life – its very amusing so we laugh together about it. It is tragic, so we weep together. Susan and Fay (her friends) have to be in at a reasonable hour, they wouldn't defy their parents over that, their mothers don't sit up all night with their stomachs churning – their minds confused with worry and fear . . . Annie is a hard wee nut, don't get taken in by her tears, she can turn them on at the touch of a button. You take life too seriously as I do. Must run – I'm not dressed yet and have to get to work.

[Later]

Hoping this letter helps you in some way and doesn't confuse you still further. Had to rush this A.M. so didn't get this finished. You said every child needs both parents. Don't you think every mother knows that – for years you have been telling me to leave him – then you tell me that – which I already know – because I am a *responsible thinking* person. How many women walk out on their husbands – most of us stick with it for the sake of their children and so we get blamed for that. How many men think of their children? When they want to go, Honey, they go – with no thought to who will suffer. They are not all like that but unfortunately many are and whatever *you* say it is still a man's world. Annie said to Dad last week – 'Dad if you are unhappy why don't you find somewhere to live and leave Mum and us here' – Dad's answer, as it has been all through the years – 'no, no, no, no, no – this is my home and here I stay.' I had a traumatic experience with him two weeks ago* – which I will not tell you about as you would only be angry and worried – it finally made me realize that no way can we stay together and this time I am getting the divorce for my sake. Also since that experience I have trotted round the streets every night, looking for somewhere to stay (still not wanting to leave the twins with him if possible). But at the same time knowing that, if necessary, Annie at least would kick his teeth in as she would not put up with his tantrums, like I do, sitting quietly in my little corner trying to look as though it is all going over my head – it may be – but it sure takes it out on my stomach. I am 48 Kate – Please don't try to tell me what life is all about – I was trotting the streets searching for rooms for us when Liz was a baby in arms – before you were born – and things haven't changed. At the age of 48 I have had to trot round many streets and go to many doors. I have given up now. The last place I went to on Friday night (having been to three others) a small single room – very clean – nicely decorated. With a for sale notice up so it would only be a short term stay anyway. Friday was a cold dark rainy windy night and there was me all dressed up in my pretend fur coat and my wee dash of lipstick – wet, windswept, and so alone, like a drowned rat. I looked at this room – thought it's nice and clean I'll take it. The owners are a young couple about Liz and Tony's age. The room contained a clean single bed – a nice table – no chairs – a very old fashioned black painted scratched wardrobe. A small electric Belling cooker, a very small wash basin and an electric kettle provided. I was told the rules of the house – £50 deposit plus £14 per week, there was one electric fitting, to be used only for the kettle, under no circumstances was anything else to be sneaked in and run off their electric or they would be very cross. *If* I had visitors they were to be orderly and out by 11 p.m. I stood there feeling like a little waif in my wet fur coat and felt like a child being spoken to by people that were only as old as my own children – they weren't too happy when I said I wasn't out *all day*. I thought, Oh God, what will I do during the hours I'm *not* working?

---

*He tried to strangle her.

Walk the streets? So there was me at the age of 48 standing in that little
room, thinking this is what it comes to – I've brought four kids up –
built up a home and worked hard all my life, to end up here. This
house will have to be sold when the divorce goes through – where do
we all go then? No, Kate, it is not easy.

I got home – feet like Charley Chaplin, having walked a good few
miles, dripping wet, tired hungry and disillusioned. Where was your
Dad? Sitting in his chair – in the warm – munching an apple. Smug and
Self Satisfied as ever. It's going to really hit him very hard when he has
to find somewhere as he is friendless, he's not adaptable, he likes to
keep to his routine. And what will he do with his share of the money
from the house – he'll gamble it all away – I have no feelings for him –
he is not an easy person to live with – but he has been my husband for
28 years and he is the father of my children – I wouldn't like to hurt
him – he can hurt me and get pleasure from doing so – but I'm just not
made that way. He's a weak man, he will crack up, I don't really want
that on my conscience. But there you are one of us has to be bloody
miserable and I've had my share. You obviously misunderstood when
I said Annie and I always say we'd better not tell Kate about anything.
That was not meant in a derogatory way, purely that we know how
upset you get, that you would worry. I even look at Rover and Tibby
[*the animals*] and think where will they end up, I would not like them
to be parted after all this time. If only we could be hard that would
solve some problems.

Mum

'The image of my mum trailing the streets really touched me – the sheer economic hardship and humiliation of divorce for a middle-aged woman without money. The letters I wrote then have since been destroyed. Despite my
sympathy, they were very angry and full of accusations that my parents were
still ruining my sisters' lives. I was feeling particularly distraught because
Annie had just taken an overdose (referred to in the next letter as "Annie's
little caper"). I told Mum how upset Annie had been after she'd been accused
of being a whore while she was still ill from her miscarriage – and that I
thought this was connected to her suicide attempt.

'My mother's ability to delude herself still astounds me. I think she
honestly believes that she never did involve us in the war and she certainly
forgets what she says when she's drunk. And even though she had filed for
divorce again, I saw no reason to hope or to believe what she said about it
being real this time.'

February 1979

Dear Kate,

Don't get upset over this – you have forced me to tell you. I have
taken it so long I can take it till the divorce comes through . . . Have
reread your letters yet again and wish to clear up two points. Re:
Annie's little caper – as that is what it was meant to be – she had

arranged for her boyfriend to pick her up – she was begging for his love. If I had not got a mother's instinct (she gave me no reason whatsoever to think she was going to do that – she ate a good meal and we had a laugh and chat about her boy friends), and gone upstairs and for some reason decided to give her a little shake – she would have been a gonner. All the worry and stress I suffered – Alone – The Thanks I got for that was Hmm you're some Mum – you didn't look very far for the tablet bottle. Six of us searched the beds, under the beds, the drawers, the bathroom and my medicine cupboard. She had hidden the empty bottle behind the mirror. Re: me automatically assuming that your dad told you – I know him – and as I didn't tell you and Annie didn't – who else could have done? Your father my dear is a devious calculating character. Annie's boyfriend told him on Wednesday that the doctor had been here on Tuesday evening. Your dad said to me on Saturday – What's this I hear about the doctor being here on Tuesday, making out he had just heard the news – is that not pretty deep? Needless to say he was at the dog track while it was all going on and why did I not tell him when he came in? Perhaps he would have comforted me, ha, ha, ha, – I didn't tell him because we would have had a big tantrum and he would have told me once again what he thought of my daughters and it would be all my fault. Did he or Annie tell you I locked him out last Saturday? No I had not been drinking – in fact I rarely drink – because I know now that's what your dad wants me to do – if I do I am giving in to him yet again – once more he can take advantage and at the same time be the great martyr. He wins all round – but he can't now because I haven't drunk for ages – he has lost another little hold over me, so he resents me for not drinking. That Bitter Woman he is always on about could never be as bitter and unforgiving as he is. The reason for locking him out was because of the worry over the traumatic experience I had with him – my nerves already wrecked with Annie's experience – he's angry because I won't give him money towards a new car. Why should I – I never set foot in the car. I decided to check up on his betting. He had spent £70 in one week, I didn't check any further or I would have really blown my top. Him really grieving because I wouldn't give him money and him spending like that. When I asked him why – it is my fault – what else can he do if I won't 'be his wife'. He has to gamble because he doesn't get sex and it's against his religion to have another woman. Can you figure out his way of thinking? He's so serious with it all that I sit here thinking he must be right and how can I be so wrong. I am only telling you this because of your accusations against me.

Mum

A few weeks after writing this letter, Teresa did, finally, leave her husband. She filed a divorce petition and then, using her own small savings and some money given her by Liz, her eldest daughter, went to stay with her sister in America. Noreen lived in a small fishing town, having moved there with her husband many years before. It was a wild and beautiful place, and Teresa loved it. She was made very welcome, and stayed there three months, in order to 'think things through' and recover from the especial tension of the previous few months. When Teresa did return to England, she found herself a live-in job in another town. She has not seen her husband since she left him and does not want to. After two years' separation, she was granted a divorce on the grounds of her husband's cruelty.

For Kate, the final break-up of her parents' marriage was both traumatic and liberating, triggering off emotions she found strange, painful and unexpected. Shortly after the divorce was made final, Kate wrote:

'When my mother finally did leave, I could hardly believe it. We had been through so many false starts and half-escapes before. The months before she left were terrible – her drinking, him ranting, and sometimes physically attacking her. And I, of course, getting an earful of it whenever I went home or talked with Mum on the phone. But I had reached the point where I could no longer sympathise, or didn't want to, because sympathy meant pain, and a sense of impotent, helpless rage. By this time, I also felt that, if mum ever was to leave, then that was something she would have to decide and organise on her own. Certainly my efforts in the past had never given her the impetus or courage to go. I realised that any decision – if it was to be a real and lasting one – would have to come from her. So my lack of involvement was, partly, tactical. But it was also self-protective, as my own life at that time was in a pretty bad way. I just couldn't take any more.

'I was worried about her future, but I also felt relieved and glad for her, and proud of her. What I hadn't reckoned on was an almost infantile sense of desertion: my mummy had left *me*. Her leaving my father meant that I no longer had something even vaguely like a family home. Even though I did not often go there, because of the tension, somehow just knowing that you've got a family home is reassuring. Both my parents used to tell me that it's families who rally when the chips are down, whereas friends will let you down; that blood, even acrid blood, is thicker and more reliable than water. Now I felt that I didn't have any family, or a home. I knew that I could never fall back on my father, if in need. At 24, for the first time in my life, I felt really and truly on my own.

'Six weeks after my mother left, I had my second and – I hope, believe – final breakdown. I got drunk, slashed my wrists and took a huge overdose. Before I lost consciousness, I remember wanting to ring my father, to tell him how he had hurt me, what his lack of love, his derision and cruelty, had done to me. It's strange that I've so often lashed out at my mother, in person and in letters, telling her how *she* has damaged me, when I've so rarely, if ever, really told my father what he has done. Perhaps I'm frightened; perhaps I feel there is no point; I don't know. To this day, I don't think he has any idea how his children feel. And he certainly didn't find out from me that terrible night because, of course, I didn't ring him. Or make any desperate suicide calls to anyone else. I was alone in my flat, it was night-time, and I really should have died. It was only (as I see it) a miracle – an unexpected midnight visitor – that saved me. In the hospital when they asked for next of kin, I refused to name my father who lived only 3 or 4 miles up the road. The only kin that mattered, I said, was my mother. Even if she was 3000 miles away . . .

'I still haven't told my mother about this last, and most nearly successful suicide attempt. I'm frightened that it will make her feel guilty and that she shouldn't have left. I know she feels guilty about the twins, who were only 17 when she went. Pat is OK, living in a bed-sit and soon to be married, but Annie has gone from the proverbial bad to worse – twenty jobs or so in a couple of years, and easily as many boyfriends, if you could call them that. I know, and Mum knows, that Annie feels angry at having been 'left' at such a young age.

'So I certainly don't want Mum to feel guilty about me . . . What I would like is for her to feel glad: painful as that time was, I think it signalled the start of my finally getting free from the ghosts of the past, the scabs and the wounds. I went to the pit all right, but when I started to clamber out, there was only one way I could climb: up and out and away. When you've been to the bottom, there really is no place else to go. But I did more than just "survive"; in the two years since my parents broke up, I think I've realised, at last, that I have the possibility and the *right* to be happy. Something snapped, something changed; I no longer had to be my parents' umpire, healer, or the guilt-ridden inheritor of the family wounds.

'What I started to discover at 24 was, finally, how to be happy. The crippling psychic bond between myself and my parents, with their terrible marriage, was finally broken. And for that I can never thank my mother enough. Perhaps then, it's time I tried to tell her: that in setting herself free, she set her daughter free with her.

'Given the suicide attempt, perhaps that's hard to understand. My relief at my mother's escape was real. But my subconscious reaction was, I suppose, sadness and anger – no matter how irrational – at being "deserted". And, of course, good old Catholic guilt: perhaps it really was my fault that my parents' marriage hadn't worked. After all, I had wanted them to split up for years. Certainly my father took care to make sure I felt that our relatives were blaming me: I was the left-wing women's-lib nutter and, minus my influence, Mum would have stayed where she was and never even imagined that she was unhappy. Ludicrous as such allegations were, they still upset me. All during our childhood Dad had told us that Mum only ever cracked up because we kids were so bad. And Mum, without meaning to cast blame, had many a time told me that it was kids that caused most of the problems in a marriage, put husband against wife. Maybe, then, I should just never have been born; and wiping myself out, at 24, was some kind of belated apology.

'Of course there were other factors involved in my breakdown. My life generally was in a mess. Since I could remember I had been trying to alleviate other people's suffering: first, my family's and then, as I became more politically involved, the whole goddam world's. But it hadn't occurred to me until that night that I too deserved to be taken care of – and, therapy cliché or no, that the best person to start caring for me was myself.

'For too long, guilt and anger had seemed to be the main factors of my life. And a terrible, terrible loneliness and sense of hopelessness. Looking back, I can't believe how relentlessly hard I was on myself. In the year leading up to my mother's separation I had had an abortion, become homeless and was penniless because I gave most of my time to politics and not to my own writing. I kept falling for awful men and had also surrounded myself with the kind of so-called friends who, far from giving me nurture or support, seemed set on knocking whatever small successes I did have in getting my work published. Writing was "bourgeois".

'It wasn't just them. Of course I was never a total victim. At that time I felt very unloved, but I think that I was also in some ways unloveable. Somehow I still had some good friends of old, and they rallied round after I cracked up. But most withdrew while I was in my most crazy and paranoid phase. I guess I was pretty hard to take. People who hate themselves, and blame other people for that self-hate, usually are.

'What the suicide heralded was the start of my saying "no more" to guilt and to the kind of insane political purism that says it is heresy to learn how to survive. I now have a nice flat; have begun to earn reasonable money without, I believe, compromising in what I write; have built a whole new circle of friends and I am very happy in a relationship with a man. He is no perfect anti-sexist but he does give me emotional shelter, understanding and fun – and most basic of all, a great deal of love.

'I still find it difficult to understand how and why the incredible changes of the past two years have taken place – but I know it has a great deal to do with my parents' separation. I guess that somehow, while my mother stayed with my dad, I felt almost duty-bound to suffer and to fail. Had I been happy, that would have felt like a betrayal of my mother, a mockery of *her* pain. I don't and can't lay that at my mother's doorstep. I genuinely believe that she wanted her children to be happy. But for very deep and complicated reasons, I felt that if I had achieved even relative freedom from oppression and trauma, that it would have been a rebuke to her, a taunt, a desertion. Perhaps that is the same tension which underlies much of the purism and griping within the present-day women's movement; the suspicion that any woman who achieves happiness or success in personal, political or work life, must have done so by selling out: other women, political principle or, as in my case, even my own mother.

'I'm still fully aware of the weight of male oppression and how hard life is made for women. I'm not trying to say, "Look, I did OK, why can't you?" I know that private, individual "solutions" to sexism are not enough. I know that my carefully nurtured happiness could be jeopardised tomorrow by my being raped by a stranger in the street, by losing my flat or earning potential by not being able to get my writing published because, in these conservative times, it's too "way-out", too female, too radical. Whether individual women want to admit it or not, we *are* sisters, if only because our fate depends on how *all* women are judged and treated. Commitment and loyalty to women are fundamental to my life. But I'm glad I finally realised that the oppression of other women, be they my mother or any woman in the street, is not something that I should feel so guilty about that I deny any chance there is of my finding and carving out just a little happiness, just a little freedom, for myself.

'Jews who came through the Holocaust speak of experiencing "survivor's guilt". That makes sense to me. As a daughter, I felt that as long as my mother was a victim, I had to be one too. When Mum finally left Dad she was giving up female martyrdom; she was waving farewell to that womanly "virtue" of self-sacrifice, deciding not to be so hard on herself. And, Jesus! – if she could escape that bondage, then so could I.

'On the most simple and everyday level, my parents' separation meant that I could now bury the past. I no longer had to arbitrate or feel divided about my loyalties. When either of them start up about the other – which they both still do – I now feel free to say: "it's over, that's finished and I don't want to know anymore." Before, I could never do that.

'Once my parents split, and I no longer had to take sides, I could afford to admit my need for my father's love. I could cry for what he had never given me and mourn what love we had shared but lost. Until the twins were born and my parents' war began in earnest, my father and I *had* been friends. I was his surrogate son, his working-class hope; I was his kid who was going to achieve what he had not been allowed to. He, the farm labourer's son who had won a grammar school place but had not been able to take it up – he had taught me his love of nature, of history, of literature. Even though he came to call me a snobby commie, a do-gooder queer, I was his kid, his hope. And until I started to take sides in the war, he did encourage and love me.

'I don't think I was wrong to take my mother's side. I don't know what else I could have done. But now I can understand my father more. His failings were partly a product of his society and his times. In his own way, I believe that he loved Mum and us. But it still hurts me that my father doesn't seem to care about me. I want his love and his blessing and I know I'll probably never get either. I get on much better with him now that my mother no longer comes between us – and now that I'm sufficiently mature or secure enough that I no longer feel the need to throw my 'outrageous' political beliefs at him just to provoke a reaction. There's a kind of tacit peace.

'What seems important to me is to be able to acknowledge what I wanted, and miss. You cannot recover from a hurt or loss unless you mourn it. My sense of loyalty to my mother, along with my feminism, made it difficult for me to admit how much I did once love my father before the "war" and how bereft I felt at losing his love.

'In the name of feminism I can analyse and despise the way he treated my mother – and me. But despising and hatred never rid anyone of sores.

'In order to get free of my father's judgements I have had to face up to my love for and need of him. Admit to what I did get from him, even if it was only a little, and mourn what I did not. Give him the place he has in my heart, as the father who taught me the names of plants, of working-class rebels; who read me *The Secret Garden* when I was 6; who taught me to play table tennis because I was sad when my goldfish died; who loved me for sharing his love for the mystery and beauty of the Catholic religion; and who wanted me to get to the grammar school because I was bright, I was going to do what he had never been able to do. All this is as true as his hypocrisy, his cruelty, his later coldness.

'I now find it far easier to relate to men. I no longer automatically see every man as my father in disguise, as necessarily being cold, judgemental and cruel. When my parents' marriage ended, my world enlarged. Until then my father had been the only model of manhood I really knew. Sure, I had boy-friends, but the spectre of Daddy always dominated. How could I find a good man, if my mother had not? And how could I deserve one?'

None of the letters that Kate wrote to her mother during this period of re-evaluation survived Teresa's upheavals during the divorce. Kate describes them as 'the letters of an embittered daughter who had at last begun to discover forgiveness and hope':

'I remember one where I said, "There is no victory in bitterness." I wasn't talking about bitterness as something one should not feel because it is "bad", inhumane, or unchristian – but that it hurts, distorts and damages even the person who feels it. Anger, I know, is very important to revolution. When I first realised, at 18, that I had the right to feel angry about how my family, class, sex, and religion had imprisoned me, I found the key to protest, pride and change. I did not have to be what I was born into; I did not have to pas-sively accept every hurt and indignity levelled at me. My anger gave me the courage of certainty. Yes, I had the right to change my own life and to fight for women generally. But anger, for all that it has been a rallying cry of both the therapy and radical movements of the Seventies and Eighties, is not all that a human being needs, no matter how oppressed they are. Bitterness never hurt the oppressor and being consumed by hate never made anyone strong.

'I began then to understand why, in my politics and personal life, I have often sought out and identified with people more oppressed than myself. The knowing cynicism of the left intelligentsia is easy to feign, and even fashion-able. But the revolutionary potential of bitterness is over-rated. Yes, it can politicise you, but it doesn't help you to survive, be happy, and feel capable of effecting change. People who have really known the depths of oppression and despair cannot afford the luxury of total hatred. It does not sustain or inspire anyone and it does not keep us warm. I have talked with South

African blacks who have been imprisoned for their opposition to apartheid, yet still find time to talk to whites like me – who even talk of feeling pity for the policemen who arrested them. Pity that anyone could be so blind, so stupid, so afraid. "If I only experienced hate, I would go mad," one of them told me.

'I knew what he meant because, as a woman fighting and trying to survive sexism, I have been driven by hate and its corollary, despair. I am not arguing for "turning the other cheek" or understanding your oppressor so much that you acquiesce in being a victim – but I finally learned that hatred is not the same as genuine pride, genuine autonomy.

'After my nervous breakdown, the two people who helped me most in my moves toward recovery and learning how to survive were people who themselves knew what hopelessness and oppression are like: they were both politically active and both escapees from violent, slum backgrounds. Both these people were, and are, very important to me. They didn't spit on my attempts to make a living wage, build a home, find some stability and happiness. They knew what it felt like to be at the bottom and that oppression is only glamorous in the eyes of voyeuristic or puritanical radicals – those who, mostly, have something to fall back on (usually Daddy) when slumming loses its appeal. To Mae and Tony, I give thanks for teaching me how to survive.

'I also thank my mother for believing in my writing when no one else did. Now that I've achieved a measure of success in the "real" world it's easy to find people who tell me I'm brave, daring, innovative. They weren't around when I was "the artist in a garret" – or, in reality, in a damp basement. When I had no money and my mother almost none, she helped support me. When I had no self-confidence, *she* believed in me. And when she did advise me to write for *Woman's Own*, to give the punters "what they want to hear", it was because she was concerned about my own material survival, not because she scorned my visions of how life could be, and should be. And now that I begin to be "successful" and don't have to worry so much about how I'll scrape together next week's rent, and begin to have an audience for what I want to say, my mother's happiness and pride in me touch and sustain me far more than the admiration of people who didn't want to know me when I was down. As I wrote a good five years ago, before I had any real hope of finding an outlet for my writing, "Mum, if only you knew, it's your song I'm singing."

'I think that my mother does understand this now. Her life is not perfect by any means and her escape has only been partial. Life as a divorced woman of 53, especially when you are "unskilled" working-class, and trying to survive during a recession, is not easy. I'm not sure that my mother will ever find what could really be called happiness. And maybe my own present happiness will not last. But as my mother's daughter, as the child of a time which is somewhat kinder to women, I at least believe that I have the *right* to happiness and fulfilment. And if I do not always have those, it will not be for want of belief. My generation is probably the first to throw out the idea that a woman's lot is to suffer.

'But in trying to eliminate self-pity, I don't think I've buried my rebellion. I do not accept how men often behave in the name of normality or their "rights", but I do think I begin to understand them. And there is an incredible relief in that understanding. In a strange way it gives you power. It means that you do not take men at their worst face-value, that you have not totally assimilated their most aggressive propaganda. I begin to understand the vulnerability and fear that can lie behind male supremacy. If I were raped tomorrow, I would not weep and cry over the possibly miserable childhood of the man who violated me. But I don't think that I would allow that man, all men, the ultimate chauvinist victory: the descent into believing that all men are necessarily brutes, *all women inevitably victims*. As I have moved away from the ghosts of my parents' marriage, I have begun to believe that another way for women and men to relate might be possible.

'I may well find that, whatever my hope, I may still end up as "a woman alone" in a world that still only values women insofar as they are tied to men. I don't want that, but I think I could cope with that now, in a way I never could when I was so consumed with fear and hate of men. I don't apologise for that fear and hate; men have given women every reason to feel these. But I am not going to allow such emotions to dominate my life. In the end, the truly independent women are those who get on with their lives, whatever limitations men have put on them. That may be life as a lesbian or as a woman trying to create good, caring relationships with men – against all the odds. The real achievement is in not allowing men and the brutality of the male system to limit and define our dreams.

'I know full well that men continue to run the world and to dominate and hurt women, as my mother was hurt. But there is a world of difference between knowing that, and being so paralysed by your knowledge that you can't even fight. Paralysed because, as in my case, that was all I *ever* knew. I grew up with male brutality, I grew up with female victimisation; I didn't need to read any books to discover and understand those. What I didn't understand, and couldn't even guess at until Mum broke away, was that any other way might be possible.

'It has not all been easy for Mum and I still worry about her a lot. What I don't doubt, and I know she doesn't doubt, is that she did the right thing in leaving – right for herself and for her daughters as well. The following letters which she sent me from America still move and inspire me; they are so free in tone, relieved, and outward-looking. For me, they were a real gift.'

18 April 1979

Dear Kate,

Guess it's time I got around to writing, as you will appreciate I have not had much spare time since I arrived. Surprise, surprise, I have just got a letter from your Dad declaring his undying love and asking me not to go through with the divorce – written on the morning of the 11th, the day after I left. I still can't figure out the way that man thinks.

Thanks for the lovely card you gave me at the airport, I have the cards and your photos on my dressing table. I'm having a wee laugh to myself thinking that the first letter I get from home has to be from the person I least wanted it from. I wonder how the old homestead is looking now that *that* woman who sat in the chair all day isn't there – your dad had some cute little sayings Eh, I wonder if he is pondering over them now. I won't answer his letter – but I still do feel sorry for him – wish I didn't. Annie and Pat will be feeling a bit lonely now that Liz has gone, I wonder how they are coping. What are you up to now? Are you still keeping busy? . . . I have just walked down to the foot of the garden to look at the sea – quite fascinating watching the waves pound up and away again, it's very pretty and frightening . . .

Lots of love, take care,
Mum

26 April 1979

Dear Kate,

Thank you for your long interesting letter which I received yesterday and for the birthday card today . . .

Re: Sally [*a friend of Kate's*] giving birth – had to laugh at you having sympathy pains – how she of the compassionate Heart suffers eh. Pleased to hear that the birth went well, that Sally had kind and considerate people with her, that must have made all the difference. It made me think back to all my births. Liz a breach birth and me in Birmingham alone, having been away from that fair city for a number of years. Your dad was in the Army still and it was many years later that the thought occurred to me that the Army got compassionate leave for births – but not him – he didn't ask for it – he came home six weeks later – I wonder why? I know the answer to that. During yours and the twins' births he and I weren't speaking so I was in the usual state of tension and trying to put on a brave face, with a smile and a joke. My God where did I get the courage and stamina to put up with that for 29 years? Have no fears re the divorce not going through this time. My God when I think of those 29 years my blood runs cold – how I didn't end up in a mental hospital or become a confirmed alcoholic I'll never know. Even now he has no idea, he asked me in his letter not to let my foolish pride stand in the way of withdrawing my petition for divorce. I ask you? He said he was missing me terribly, the letter was posted the morning after I left. I feel great pity for him – no love – liking – no hate. I'm glad I came away, otherwise the possibility was always there that I would have given in again through a mixture of sheer compassion and weariness, my spirit was indeed crushed and no human being should do that to another. Your dad asked me on the telephone if I had written to give him an answer, I said no, he said why, so I just said I was still thinking about it, I don't want to say anything till your cousins here have had their holiday in England – otherwise he could be very unpleasant to them – not being the most pleasant person at the best of times.

. . . They have been really good to me and I know my daughters will return their hospitality. They are dying to meet you all . . . Aunt Noreen is very proud of your politics and says you've to get a move on with your novel as she wants to read it . . .

She's really thrilled as they all are that I have come here. Your dad really mixed it up for us and put you kids against her like he did with all my friends – he sure is a queer individual, all he wants in life is me. Hmm.

Love and Blessings,
Your ever loving Mum

1 May 1979

Hello again.

. . . Well, how is Sally and our wee baby now, thriving I hope and how is the Mum, does she still have that feeling of pride and wonder and thinks that no one else in this world has ever accomplished such a feat before? – its a great feeling.

Re: your maternal instincts – what can we do about that – that's something Mummy can't help with eh. Wish you could find the answer my love. I guess you're setting your sights too high re: a man my Love. I don't think one like you are looking for has ever been made ha, ha, so what do we do in life – do we have to compromise? Your solicitor sounds nice, being intelligent, funny and having a good career are certainly three assets. Has he got Heart – is he mean with money Ugh – if so he would be mean in his relationships – take a lesson from your mum and watch out for that little bug – that's my one dread in life that one of my kids would marry a mean person. Is he kind and sympathetic to your feelings, if so grab him, ha, ha. I don't know if there is such a thing as the great shining love we romantics dream about, but I think love could grow if the man and yourself have good qualities, so if you don't get really serious with your solicitor, give it another two years and who knows a knight might come riding along in shining armour. Don't be afraid of men or marriage, you young ones can get away from both and I think men have more sense now than to put the shackles on eh.

I haven't been to the shops in town yet, will get a wee pressie for Juliet [*Sally's daughter*] – nice name . . . Here's hoping it brings her luck. However, having a baby outside of marriage must have pitfalls (having babies inside marriage has pitfalls!) What will the child think – not having a daddy like everyone else in school – and is it true that to have stable children you need to have two parents to make them feel

secure? With two parents they can also feel insecure. I guess I don't
have the answers to life, my Love, so I cannot advise you. Anyway
give Sally my Best Wishes and here's hoping all works out well for her
and the wee one.

Lots and lots of love from your loving mum xxxxx

15 May 1979

Dear Kate,

I have just been round to the PO and received *Spare Rib** – thanks.
Have just found your little letter and like you am disturbed at what's
been said re: my family breaking up my marriage – That's a giggle and
who told you I said that? Never in my wildest dreams has that thought
ever crossed my mind and you must know that. Aunt Noreen and
your dad have had long conversations on the phone; she is genuinely
worried about me, at my age and after 29 years of marriage, breaking
up – what if I get ill and have no one to look after me? That in itself is
the laugh of the century. If I was dying all he would do would be to
jump into bed with me. For so many years my mind was confused re
your dad as a human being, but now I am much more relaxed and
however much I think, I still cannot find a good point in him. So we
had a roof over our heads (provided through his job) and he gave me a
meagre allowance every week and stood by my side waiting for me to
beg for it – he gave me nothing and took 100%. When I was down he
kicked me and when I was up he made a point of getting me back
where I belonged – DOWN – I was strong and he was weak and the only
way he felt a MAN was to take. I am still not anti-men, Kate, there are
many good men in the world, I picked a number out of a hat and with
my luck in raffles I drew the wrong number ha, ha. I know lots of
unhappy women, don't we all, but what I have found in nearly all
cases is that fathers never blackmailed their wives through their kids
or their kids through their mother, that most men do allow their wives
to be ill and even if they don't show a lot of sympathy at least they do
accept that the human machine they married can break down under
stress now and again. Unfortunately I married God and all I can say is
God forgive him. Let's face the fact, my kids did keep me tied to your
dad – not their fault – I had no money and nowhere to go, sure I could
have cleared off on my own – but I love my children and no way in this
world would I have left you with him – it's not your fault I stayed – I
stayed because I loved you all and to protect you. It was nerve
wracking, mind wracking and I sure wouldn't want to go through that
again . . .

love,
Mum xx

---

*A women's liberation magazine published in England.

16 May 1979

Hello again Kate,

After a sleepless night, worrying about you worrying about being blamed for the divorce. Got up this A.M. feeling as though I had been put through a wringer, took one of Aunt Noreen's tranquillizers and spent four hours on the phone trying to send you a telegram, finally got through and guess you will understand the message, you should have it about now, that is if you're at home. I'm surprised really that you and Liz should feel bad about anything your dad says as its the old, old story, we've been through all that cross-talk for years, what I've supposedly said about you lot and what you lot have said about me, and all of us afraid to speak out openly – and while we were all worried, confused and unhappy – he was smug and superior – his superior days will soon be over. As Aunt Noreen and Uncle Bill chatted to dad again on the phone the other day, no doubt you will be hearing the old story again, they felt so sorry for him they promised him they would try to talk me into going back – he told Noreen she was welcome in his home at anytime and for as long as she wanted to stay – different to what he said to me, eh – if I brought my sister there he would soon show her the F'ing door – he's pathetic. I never want to see him again. He's a nasty mean vindictive little man and I couldn't take that anymore. So, my children – you, along with the pets and even the nuns will be held responsible for the divorce. Accept that, as he will never accept the responsibility – who cares. What you girls do as regards your dad later on is up to you, but like I said I never want to look on his surly face again, listen to his martyred whiny obscene voice again. I felt a bit better after I got the telegram off, so as its a nice sunny day, I took the radio down to the beach, also Peter the poodle. I listened to Hot Line – that's something to hear, there are elections here next week, so the Women's Lib are calling in everyday asking the politicians what stand they are planning to take on abortion etc. etc. and the things they say! One of them was beating about the bush and the girl said to him, 'Are you a chicken or a fully-fledged Hen – for God sake man stand up and be counted.' He hummed and hawed again, so she said 'You're still Chicken, John, and for my money you can get off the air and go and play with your yo-yo' ha, ha. The Women's Libs are demanding to know all the Churches' and MPs' policies on Homosexuality, Lesbianism, Abortion and the word Obey in marriage – you would be right in there with them. I was thinking if I can find out where they are I'll send them *Spare Rib*.

I read the *Spare Rib* down on the beach, you know that's the first time I've ever been able to read it without my nerves being jangled, having to hide it and all that, it's the first time really that I've read it all through, really enjoyed all items, even the one on Maggie Thatcher . . .

If you talk to the twins, do tell them to clear out if dad goes funny when he finds I really am going through with the divorce.

Love you all,
MUM

18 May 1979

Dear Kate,

I heard on the radio that the Women's Lib were having their annual Council in a nearby town tonight. Said to Aunt Noreen I was going – she thinks I'm mad and says there's no way I can get there. I got a bus, Aunt Noreen was worried silly about me, you would think I was a two-year-old and she swore blind they would not allow City Hall to be used for such a purpose. Anyway away I went as I wanted to find out how it is compared with ours in London.

They have women's councils here and don't get together too often as some of them are further apart distance-wise than from here to London. I had a chat with them all after the meeting, told them all about you and said that you would send out some back-dated *Spare Ribs*. I gave them the one you sent me. They are also interested in your writing. They are having a big convention in October and were thinking of asking Erin Pizzey out or Germaine Greer. I was to go to lunch at the Women's Centre today, the council are all flying back home tonight . . . (Uncle Bill was going to bring in his pick-up truck from work and take me into town and leave me there for the afternoon, unfortunately the pick-up chose today to break down. He rang and told me to get a taxi and he would pay for it, but it was a bit late then to bother . . . they were both sitting at home worrying about me, but dad made me independent, eh.) Neither Aunt Noreen or Bill believe in Women's Lib – so we had a good argument about it, but they admired me for going into town by myself and going amongst the strangers ha, ha. The weather is lovely so I've been sitting down by the sea reading the Women's Lib literature.

Lots of love,
Mum xxxxx

Teresa returned to England after three months and got a job as a cook in a holiday camp; the first part of the letter which follows was full of details about her twelve-hour workday, her workmates and the pride she felt in giving up alcohol, supporting herself financially and living an independent life:

November 1979

Dear Kate,

. . . Would love to have a chat with you about your marrying and having children. I married and had children and that was a right muck-up. To have well-adjusted children they need lots of love and security. When I married if I could have forseen what the future held for me and mine – I wouldn't have gone through with it. I'm not trying to put you off – there are happy marriages and I am no man hater. *I don't want one* – but I can enjoy their company.

I do think of you a lot, I do worry about you. I would like to see some improvement in your life – whichever way it goes. I would like to know that you are happy. That's all most mothers want out of life is to know their kids are happy and believe me, many Fathers have a lot to answer for even in this day and age. Your friend Alec seems a nice guy, but then I only met him once. Don't jump into anything too quickly – it's a very big responsibility bringing babies into the world. Just don't ever marry a mean, aggressive, vindictive type like your Dad – that's all I ask.

He seems to have been playing Santa Claus ever since I left him, being nice to all and sundry and throwing his money around. Racing around like a blue-arsed fly to socials and dances with his girlfriend. I pity him, I think he will marry her, because he needs someone, but I think he'll pay dearly for her services and quite right too. I think that both of them are trying to pull a fast one on each other, each working out how much the other has, ha ha.

Dad will have another 10 years of fatherhood ahead of him, bringing up her daughter and I can't see that. Am I being vindictive now? Not really – I regret the day I ever met him but I wish him no harm. I'm too happy in my new found freedom and in congenial company where I'm appreciated – I can't worry about what becomes of Dad. He'll probably marry her and say it was to get a roof over the twins' heads. He'll blame someone for his actions – he is so way-out he'll convince himself that *you* need a home to go to. So you can go to Mama Edith [*the new girlfriend*] ha ha – just think, you'll have a stepmother.

Seriously, she may be a very nice person. If she is, I hope she puts a boot up his arse and starts off the way she means to go on, otherwise he'll revert to type (Gestapo). Dad may have to sell the house, so he'll probably think he's on to a good thing since her mortgage has probably been paid off. I can see him weighing up the advantages in his tiny little mind – when the disadvantages arrive he'll blame us.

All I can say is that if she is a nice person I feel sorry for her and if she's not then they deserve each other. You wondered if I would feel hurt if he married again – Definitely not, Kate – she is more than welcome to the man I knew – he may change?

7:20 a.m. Here I am, up and raring to go . . . I have enclosed £50 for you to treat yourself – don't mention it to the family and don't waste it. I had thought of getting you a radio alarm clock with it, but will leave it to you now.

Must run, have to iron my overall. Bye bye – God Bless – Take Care. Write soon if you can and give me all your news.

Lots of love,
your own wee Mum xxxxxxx

5 February 1980

Dear Kate,

Thank you for your two letters, it was good to hear all your news. Yes it really was a great surprise to open the door and see Annie there. I think she looked quite thin and as you say, she doesn't say much but I think she is having to put up with a lot of stick from your dad over Rover and on the numerous occasions when Edith walks out on him – it's all Annie's fault etc. etc. I have never in my life known or even heard of a grown man that plays on his *children's* emotions the way he does and always has done. If he does that to his own flesh and blood, what is he going to do to Edith's little girl. I dread to think of it.

Fortunately Edith is in a different position to what I was in, she has got a home and some kind of an income. I had four children, nowhere to go and no money – no help from the State.

Believe me, I wouldn't go through that again if I could go back 20 years. I made the mistake of always thinking things can't get worse so they must get better – alas they never did. As a Women's Lib I am pleased for Edith that she at least can make a choice. I hold no grudge against her and I'm sure if things were different I would like her.

I am still trying hard to get a place of my own – there's nothing like your independence and your own front door. I have been in touch with every organization and advertise in a shop window . . . I have just written to the agent about a flat for sale – that's all I want really – perhaps I could borrow from the bank if it is a reasonable price. But I must get a roof over my head and it would be a place for you and the twins to come to when you want a break from London.

I do love it here and I don't think I would see much of you if I did come back to London. After all, you do have your own lives to lead. I got your dad off my back last year – that was the best move I ever made. No regrets whatsoever – no nostalgia. There are no nice memories to get nostalgic about. However, I will not feel the full benefits of all that till I have my own house.

Did you feel traumatic about your broken romance and how did it come about? Was it just his good looks you fell for? Believe me, looks are only skin deep. He has problems, don't we all. You hold out for the best, Kate – Looks, money and a willingness for them to see to your every need, not vice versa. There's just got to be one like that somewhere – I bet right at this minute there's one like that running around looking for someone like you. One day you will bump into each other.

Re: your friend using our letters for her book – by all means do so. I do have your letters somewhere in cardboard boxes and plastic bags. I think they have been up in Liz's loft with other things belonging to me. I had a quick shin up the ladder to have a look but there's so much up there I doubt if I'll ever find them. The letters I used to get from you while I was at home I had to hide them and eventually destroy them as however innocent, they caused aggro. The really hurtful ones I did destroy. Contrary to what your father always said, I do not thrive on bitterness. I would much rather forget the nasty parts and only remember the good parts. He made sure with his moaning and whining that I didn't forget the nasty parts. Divide and Rule. I've got away from all that now thank God.

You're not really naive enough to think your dad would enquire about your welfare on your visit home. He has always lived in a little world of his own. I'm alright Jack – pull up the ladder. The world consists of layabouts, leeches on society, long haired weirdos, girls using abortion as a form of contraception – all on *his* taxes. Women's Libbers are nutters and should be hosed off the streets. Raped women ask for it. Men are entitled to their Conjugal Rights, their freedom and their money, after all, they go out to work.

A hard day's work would kill your dad. He would shit himself if someone lifted their hand to him. He's a physical coward. He was born ten years too late, he would have reached the exalted rank of Commander in the Gestapo had he been in Germany during the War. He is made of their kind of stuff – whatever that is – all round weakness, I think.

He's a fortunate fellow getting someone like Edith second time around – it's more than he deserves. No, I don't find it weird, Kate, thinking about them – I do obviously, if only out of curiosity. My thinking I can sum up by saying I feel sorry for him – because no way can I see him not reverting to type. I feel sorrier for her because unless she puts the boot in at the start she will certainly have a heavy cross to bear. I feel sorrier still for her daughter, I just can't see that working out, however nice he is being to her at the moment. I have no feelings of jealously, hurt or pain (I had the latter two for 29 years) because he has someone else. I have everything to gain – I have my freedom, I go to bed every night and Thank God every morning that I don't have to see him, listen to him, put up with him. And besides all these Blessings, I am coming to make my life complete now, all I want is a little home and the peace of mind I would never have had I stayed with him. I would like to think my kids were happy and settled in whatever makes them happy, be it a job or marriage. That's what life is all about –

giving and wishing happiness for others. Don't have any worries about me, Kate.

I wrote to Margaret Thatcher about the Abortion Bill and have watched every programme on TV.* You get some quite good ones in the afternoon. I also watch question time, it's on quite late one evening each week. Naturally last week's dealt with the abortion issue. Two left-wing, quiet-spoken young ladies answered questions from the public. I was most impressed by them and am sure they must have converted many of the audience to their way of thinking.

I listened to a TV programme about soldiers trying to leave the army as conscientious objectors. One was a marine and one an officer – they couldn't take the brutality of the British in Ireland. The marine was just put in prison. The officer got a quick promotion to Captain and an office job with the Ministry of Defence. He recognized that as a form of blackmail and both finally got out through a civilian organization called Stand Easy. I had never heard of it – neither had they. They heard about it purely by chance. It seems Stand Easy send out leaflets to the military telling them how to go about being discharged.

A remark from the film, *Airport*: It's better to come from a broken home than to be in one.

I watched *Panorama* and could have kicked the set in when it was said that people must take the responsibility for their actions [*this was another programme about abortion*]. What responsibility were the men taking? How did you get on at the anti-Corrie rally at Westminster? I was boss-eyed looking for you on TV. Were you one of the ones that made it into the holy of holies? [*A group of women stormed into Parliament.*]

I have read the *Spare Ribs* and noted with interest the letters on abortion, also read the one on Ireland which was very good . . .

No, Kate, I wouldn't want you to tell tales to Edith – she must have her own thoughts. Why did I leave at the age of 48 after 29 years of marriage? I had to give up my home, my family, my job and my friends at a time of life when I should have been able to say Thank God the kids are grown up, now I can take life easy. It's not been that easy, having no home and still worrying about the kids . . .

A letter from your dad's solicitor last week said your dad has £3,000 in the building society and £400 in the bank – I wouldn't believe your father if he told me today was Sunday. I also asked him to check on the insurance policies your father had for £1,000 each. Your dad denies

---

*At this time Kate was heavily involved in the Campaign against the 'Corrie' Amendment to the 1968 Abortion Law. The amendment would have made it much more difficult for women to get safe legal abortions. It was defeated in March, 1980.

having any insurance. If he hasn't got them now, he did have and he must have been having a damned good time on them. So I want to know when they were cashed.

The worm has turned at last and why not.

Have just heard on the news that a nine-year-old child has been killed in Ireland in a battle with a Saracen tank. Did I tell you the tale about the soldier I met on the train coming back from London last time? He described with relish what he would do to any kid that threw a stone at him – my blood went cold when he described in detail what the latest gun does. He was due to go to Ireland on January 4th and I wonder how he is getting on there. Here's hoping no kid throws a stone at him. I hope they have a thorough investigation into that child's death. Liz is anti-IRA – we've had a few words on that subject and no way will she even try to see their side.

Did you have a nice weekend with your 'flame'? He's quite a character eh, but as you say, not to be taken seriously.

Did you manage to get an overdraft? I have enclosed £20 – guess it will come in useful when you get back from France. I can send you some more later if you can't get an overdraft. What extras I can screw out of your dad can go to my kids – they also deserve a share for having to put up with his mean nasty ways. So cheer up, you'll be in the money sometime soon I hope. I still don't know if the house is up for sale or not.

Must close now and get something to eat. Hope all goes well with your work in France. Do give me a ring when you get back and let me know how you got on.

Bye for now
God Bless
Take care
Lots of love
Mum xxxxx

CHAPTER FIVE

Children

Having Them

If you get pregnant at this point, you may be sure that you will never get over it as long as you live. Your husband is crowing too loud. If he succumbs to the temptation, don't believe he loves you. If he destroys your beauty you may take it as proven that his affection is not of sterling quality.

Madame de Sevigne to her daughter (1672)

You have probably repressed the time I said I never wanted to have children because I never wanted to be a mother like you, but now I want you to know how much I respect and admire a mother like you. I hope I've somehow inherited those qualities too.

Susan to her mother Pauly (1979)

If you ever have children, then you will understand what life is really all about.

Teresa to her daughter Kate (1977)

The issue of how to raise children can often be a touchy subject, especially between mothers and daughters. Throughout history, childcare practices and notions about what children need have varied greatly. In the past there has not even been agreement among philosophers, scientists or families about whether children need love and affection – a fundamental question which, today, virtually no one would question. However, there still seems to be doubt and argument about most aspects of child-rearing – a debate which now encompasses issues such as the importance of seeing mothers as individuals with their own needs and the value of re-thinking the role of fathers in everyday childcare.

For countless generations of women, having children at all was not a matter of choice, but a completely taken-for-granted fact of life. The choice we have today due to the widespread availability of contraception means that our experience of womanhood is significantly different from all previous generations of our foremothers. There have, of course, always been a few exceptional women who remained celibate and some who were sterile, but in many cultures womanhood *means* motherhood – with scarcely any choice in the matter. Even today, plenty of people still consider it 'natural' for women to want children, and unnatural, vile and selfish not to want them on a full-time-forget-everything-else basis. This makes it very difficult for women to admit their ambivalence about having children.

Nonetheless, social outrage about women who are childless by choice is possibly not the main reason why women hesitate to discuss this important decision with their mothers.* I've talked to many women about why such discussions are difficult even to imagine. One thing which most women mention is that their mothers, despite whatever hardship they have endured, seem genuinely to feel that their daughters would be missing out on one of life's most rewarding experiences if they decided not to have children. Their mothers' sadness (and certainty) about this makes it seem unlikely that they could have an open discussion. A further stumbling block is that a mother may feel that having children is the most important thing she has done in her life. Her daughter's doubts about doing the same may be seen not only as a de-valuation of motherhood but as a direct criticism of her mother's life. A woman's negative feelings about motherhood may also be interpreted as negative feelings about her own childhood and the way she was mothered.

One woman openly said that her mother's regrets about having children were the major obstacle to any discussion of the issue: neither of them could bear to talk about the fact that her mother had had virtually no choice about having children and that she was sad about the things she hadn't done in life as a result of being so tied down. Several other women mentioned their mother's martyrdom and lack of independence – without actually saying that the desire to avoid talking (or thinking) about their mothers' sacrifices was the main reason they have never discussed their ambivalence about wanting children.†

There are women today choosing to have children, who do so with a commitment to challenging the traditional concept of the dependent, self-sacrificing mother, and with a desire to offer their children an example of how women can enjoy work and other activities outside the family, yet remain tender, generous and loving.

When women with children talk about working outside the home, it

---

*I assume that this difficulty exists because when I specifically asked for letters on this topic, none arrived – and when my editors on both sides of the Atlantic set out to try to fill this obvious gap, they too were unable to discover any letters. A non-letter was the closest we could come – and that was discovered by chance at the eleventh hour. (See also *Why Children*, an excellent anthology on the decision about having children, in which nearly all of the 18 women included in the book mention that they thought about their mothers while deciding, but none of them said that they seriously considered discussing it with her.)

†Women have written very little about the negative aspects of their experiences as mothers, but there is massive evidence in the statistics about child-battering and in the high consumption of tranquilisers and alcohol among housewives with young children, that there are women whose needs are *not* met by full-time childcare in isolation from the adult world. Whether they want to or not, they are likely to abuse their children emotionally and/or physically – even though they may also love them very deeply. Mothers who feel alienated and frustrated by not being able to do things which feel important to them, often end up playing the role of martyr; with the best will in the world they are not capable of producing independent, spontaneous, guilt-free children.

usually provokes worried and negative responses about 'maternal deprivation'. The obvious person to fill the gap when a mother goes out to work is the
father of the children; however, for numerous practical and emotional
reasons, many men are still reluctant to consider exchanging full-time
employment in the Real World for the less prestigious and financially
unrewarding job of raising children. The practical obstacles (such as the fact
that men generally earn more money than women and part-time jobs are
scarce and usually badly paid) are so compelling that the emotional
stumbling blocks to men's willingness are rarely confronted. Apart from the
lack of prestige because it is women's work, and the loss of power in not being
seen as the main breadwinner, men have been raised to see women as
sympathetic and tender nurturers; they have not been raised to see
themselves that way. Those qualities which are needed in childrearing are
threats to conventional notions of masculinity. Yet even with all these
difficulties, shared childcare is still attempted by some families, not only for
the sake of giving women 'time off' – but to enrich the father-child
relationship and to enable men to develop valuable human qualities which
have often been discouraged in them from the time they were boys.

Involvement with children is potentially one of the richest of human
experiences: a wholehearted sharing of childcare responsibility between men
and women could profoundly alter our views on womanhood, manhood and
childhood. A new chapter in the history of childhood is being written by
parents who are creatively challenging masculine and feminine stereotypes in
their own lives and encouraging both their daughters and their sons to look
beyond conventional roles.

Alice to her mother Mary, 1982

Alice lives in London, where she works full time as an arts administrator.
Since turning 30, she has found the decision of 'motherhood or not'
unexpectedly difficult to handle. For some time she tried to sort out her feelings in a letter to her mother (a slightly artificial exercise since her mother
lives just around the corner): she was never able to finish a single draft. She
also found herself peculiarly good at *not* raising the topic in conversation
with her mother, with whom she discusses most things.

Finally, she wrote an open letter to herself about her dilemma. Ironically,
she decided that this at last was something she could show to her mother – 'as
a letter to both of us':

August 1982

I have come to the conclusion that only a poet could tell you
adequately what it is we women feel who are, so far, childless by
choice. I have tried countless times to decide finally whether or not to
have one – and also to discuss it fully with my mother. In vain.

The very thought of motherhood releases a kind of melancholy in me and I am sidetracked into remembering my own lost, happy (so I believe) childhood. My mother says her fondest hope for me is that I will one day have a tender, teeming household of my own.* On the other hand, she has also been known to recommend that I stand my ground as a thoroughly modern spinster – all things to all people, exciting 'aunt' to all children, good company for friends and still free to be my own woman.

I share her ambivalence exactly.

The men in my life include several wonderful brothers, an adored father who died in my early twenties (before he could fall off any pedestals) and, after many false starts, a true lover with whom I could in principle have children, if we both wanted to enough. He, however, already has some, and we both have full-time careers.

The reasons for procrastinating (still, at thirty-three) are legion, I'm sure, but they include:

— a primordial terror of dependents/ce;
— guilty foreknowledge that I couldn't possibly be as generous and exciting and genuinely parental as my own father and mother;
— greed, I suppose (loss of earnings);
— insecurity (loss of status through work);
— fear of the general practical consequences (in spite of endless evidence that all things are possible);
— jealousy (including a wish to hang on to my own child-self);
— affection for the numerous family I already have: it is hard enough to make space to love and look after them properly, particularly my mother whom I love deeply;
— anxiety about my temperament, one half of which seems to need the intellectual challenge of the workplace (and guilt about that too);
— sorrow and anger that so many women of childbearing age and nurturing temperament are forced to choose between work and love, rather than combine them.

I yearn to be free enough to spend all the time in the world with the people I love, before they grow up, grow old and die. As we always thought we could when we were children. Sometimes I think I should have children precisely in order to defy time and reclaim the hearth. Maybe that is what all mothers do . . .

By intuitive semaphore, my mother and I have in fact discussed this often: she knows it all already, she was there once too. She wants me

---

*'She interrupted her own professional career (as university teacher and social worker) to have children.'

to be happy, I don't want to hurt her. Perhaps it is too close to the bone for both of us?

Jenny to her mother Linda, 1982

At the age of thirty, Jenny* finally resolved her protracted ambivalence about wanting to have children. Once she had written to tell her mother her decision, it took her over a month to decide to post the letter:

14 January 1982

Dear Mom,

The news in this letter feels so good that I almost wanted to say it on the 'phone the other day – but I felt that I wanted to write it so I could explain everything slowly and enjoy it for longer.

One of the reasons I was so anxious to get back and talk to Jim is that I realised, after we had decided to live together, that I wanted our commitment to each other to include having children. I felt very happy about my own clarity because I have felt terribly unclear up til now about whether I wanted to have children or not. Now I know that I do – though not at least for another year. I felt very apprehensive about saying it to Jim, though. Because he already has three kids and he's been raising kids since he was 18. But I finally screwed up my courage on New Year's Day and said what I was feeling. Most happily he said yes he does want to have children with me and we both smiled and cried for hours. It feels amazingly sure and good and right. The sweetness of this time is simply awesome. I never thought that anyone as sensible as me could imagine thinking and saying such commitments with a man I've known for such a short time. But the certainty is rock solid and so much part of the sweetness . . .

Somehow I just really wanted you to know about this decision. I suspect (though you've never actually said) that you have worried that I didn't want to have kids – and that you probably thought it was because I had so much childcare responsibility when I was only little. To tell you the truth, I don't know why it was so hard for me to know what I wanted. I didn't ever feel certain that I didn't want kids. But I just didn't know. I knew I would decide eventually – but I didn't have a clue what would tip the balance.

I guess what finally tipped the balance was reading *The Mermaid and the Minotaur* by Dorothy Dinnerstein. That was over two years ago and it was the beginning of me seeing the positive side of the arguments. Before, I had mainly seen it in terms of a loss of freedom, less time to do other things, etc. Dinnerstein's book is about the crucial

---

*See also pp. 62–4.

importance of changing society so that fathers participate fully in infant and child care. Not just for the sake of liberating women, but for the effect it will have on the infant's psychological development. And for the effect it would have in humanising men. And how it would change the way men view women, the way that children view women and men, etc. It is a very revolutionary concept and I felt excited at the prospect of being part of all that. It made it seem possible and even necessary for me to continue working and doing other things, and it made such positive arguments for men to take active responsibility for helping children grow up. Without having so much fear of being burdened with the entire physical and emotional responsibilities of raising kids, I could begin to explore the excited and joyful feelings I have when I think of having children.

Some weeks later – and I still haven't posted this!

. . . What keeps running through my head is to wonder *why* you and I have never talked about whether or not I wanted kids. What were we so afraid of? It has clearly been an issue for me and I'd be surprised if it wasn't also an issue for you. So why have we not spoken? We're supposed to have such an 'honest' relationship.

I haven't, I guess, because I was afraid of hurting you if I said I didn't want kids. And I guess that you haven't spoken because you feared hearing what I would say, or because you feared we might disagree – or you might disapprove of me even thinking that I might not want them. I know that you don't like to show disapproval or criticisms of me. I know because you never do it. I'm sure there must be things I do which you don't like or disagree with – but you never say. Even on a subject as important as having children, you never expressed any opinion on the matter. I very much appreciate you letting me get on with my life and all the support you give me and all the praise. It has been invaluable to have you tell me I'm wonderful so often in my life. But I feel strong enough now to get on with my life no matter what you say – I would really like to know what you honestly think about things – even if it is negative. We are very different people; sometimes our values are the same and sometimes different. I have finally given up wanting all of our values to be the same or wishing we were more alike. I am happy for us to be different. I would like to hear what you genuinely think about this important decision I've made and why we've never discussed it before.

love,
Jenny

Isa Kogon to her daughters Cindy, Nan and Betty, 1980

Isa Kogon grew up in New York and California. She was, variously, a
mother/executive-secretary/politician/artist/actress until 1974 when, she
says, 'I chucked it all and headed for the woods. My three daughters I didn't
chuck. I saved them from the horrors of Los Angeles and watched them grow
into lovely, capable young women.'

At the time when this letter was written, Isa was living with Joe, her
husband of two years, and her 17-year-old daughter Betty on a small farm in
a backwoods logging community in Washington. Her two older daughters,
Cindy and Nan (aged 22 and 19 respectively), lived nearby with their
husbands and were both expecting their first babies:

1 December 1980

My Dearest Daughters:

How long it's been since I've sat up here at the typewriter and shared
my thoughts with you. I don't like these long absences, for the
cobwebs collect and dust covers everything. My time at the typewriter
is sacred to me, and I've missed it greatly during the work of summer's
harvest.

How often I hold mental conversations up here with you girls!
There's still so much to share with you, so much to teach, so much to
let go of. Sometimes I just talk to you in my head. Other times I come
up here to sort out my thoughts on the typewriter, or, like now, to give
my annual mother rap!!

I think this letter may become my Christmas message to you for I
may not be with you this Christmas. The traditionalist side of me will
be hell-bent on getting home in time. But my need for space from
motherhood and responsibility is so great right now, I might just stay
at my brother's for more than two weeks. I might even travel with
him, if we can stand each other that long!

You know, it's funny – when we were kids I felt so replaced by my
brother, I resented the hell out of him. After all, I was the only child
for seven years. I think I even blocked out most of the happiness of my
youth, and only remembered being replaced by my brother. That and
my mother's brainwashing to 'grow up and be somebody'. The more
she pushed, the more I rebelled, and that's why I never forced you
girls. I wasn't going to be that kind of parent!

But now I know the things I know, and after these many years of
letting go and working it out, Ted and I have actually come to like
each other! I even came to like my mother, once I understood where
she was coming from. How unfortunate that she never shared with me
until she was near death. So many things I never knew . . .

Believe it or not, I don't always lecture you in my mental dialogues,
or pen heavy stuff for posterity. Sometimes I need to let you know
how beautiful you are to me – all of you – and how much pride I feel in

you. And so I come to my private sanctuary and record a moment in time, a moment when you were elsewhere and I needed to share with you.

(Why is it sometimes easier to put it on paper than to grab you and tell you this? Is it because you each pushed me away once for a time, and now I tread lightly? Or is it because, believe it or not, my dears, I too have a shy side and can't always show what I feel. My mother wasn't able to show her affection, as was her mother before her. I think I'm more open that way, but sometimes I do have to resort to paper.)

There was a time last summer, right around her birthday, when I got to missing my mother real bad. I came upstairs to work it out on paper. I'd like to tell you about that now.

I had been thinking about the new life in each of you, Cindy and Nan, and the other young women in the valley who are pregnant. It seemed significant, having lost three friends that past winter, that three new lives would enter the valley next winter. What comes around, goes around, right?

The last time we had had a baby boom of any significance was the summer I was laid up with my dog bites, and that triggered some heavy reminiscences. A friend had come to visit one day, bringing with her three red roses, which led to thoughts of my mother, Rose. I was delirious with infection by then, and I thought my mother was dying. Then I thought it was Aunt Kitty who was dying, for she had once been a strong mother figure for me.

Much later I reflected on ego shedding and letting go, for that's what death thoughts usually symbolize – one's need to let go of something, to change something.

When my mother did finally die five months later, I was ready to let go of her. I had sensed her death just a few days before. That didn't lessen the pain, but I was prepared spiritually.

As I stood there that afternoon, looking at my own rose bushes I had planted in memory of my mother, and filled with daughter thoughts and memories of my feelings that summer of my accident, I realized I was now dealing with letting go of you too! Not preparing for your death, mind you, but for your growth. For the new roots you were sinking, and for the new wings you were spreading. And I rejoiced in silence as I realized you three beauties were blooming too! A great wind came up then (on the hottest day in August!) and I felt my mother's pride too, as well as the reassurance that I wasn't just daydreaming idly.

I went back to the typewriter to explore my feelings further, for I wasn't really sure about how I felt about your impending motherhood, Cindy and Nan. On the one hand, I was concerned about your following in my footsteps – having children early –

because EVERYONE SAID NOT TO. On the other hand, I wasn't so sure that was such a bad idea! So I tried to get in touch with how I felt about you two as prospective mommies. And mainly, about how I felt about ME in preparing you for such a giant step.

Basically, I felt good about what both of you girls are doing. And I understood the desire for some semblance of permanence with a mate, for I never tried to harness your sexuality once I saw it begin to develop. (I might have laced you into Victorian corsets and preserved you for higher education, and other vicarious thrills!)

When you came to me at age 17, Cindy, and said you were ready to create your own living space, I respected that decision, for you weren't running away from home.

When you and Bob allowed me to talk you out of getting married, Nan, to wait a while and see how you felt later on, I respected you for heeding my suggestion.

Well, children do come of such arrangements, so the notion of marriage and motherhood, even so early, didn't really bother me. Especially since I did see you shopping around a bit first, and finally choosing men of integrity I too admire.

The fact that all of you can cook a meal and stoke a stove doesn't go unnoticed either. I feel much pride in your homemaking skills, for your home is where your heart is, and there's much warmth in your homes. Even your little space, Betty – it reflects the warmth and gaiety in your soul!

I also felt good about what I'm doing with my life, and what I've already done, so I couldn't very well object to your following suit. As I told you last night, Bet, we're the kinds of people who create change. For us, that means tapping into our own instincts and following our own inner directions. But this also means being receptive to everything around us, for what we need to learn comes to us when we're ready to learn it. Right now, two of you need to learn how to can stringbeans and have babies, obviously, for that's what you're doing. And I can't see suggesting you get a Master's in biology first!

I had some self-doubts too, though, I confess.

I wondered whether I'd made it plain enough that you always had choices – options.

Did I instill in you the self-confidence to lead as well as to follow?

The night you left that wild party, Nan, the night of your accident, you showed me that you were your own person, and a strong one at that. I admire you for that action.

I wondered too whether I'd told you that man–woman relationships can be based on passions only, if that is what's mutually satisfying to both partners – but that they're best when there's mutual trust and respect. And better still, when there's love.

Did I also tell you that love takes many forms? That it's easy to confuse emotions and fall in love too easily, too fast . . .

One of my prized possessions is a slip of paper from a Chinese fortune cookie that says: 'You are doomed to happiness in wedlock.' That sorta sums up me and Joe, doesn't it? We fight and ego-trip each other, we sulk and go our separate ways . . . But we have something special and we know it, for it's based on deep respect and admiration for each other.

I hope I showed you that loving means letting go too. Letting go of NEEDING to be loved, and simply loving. It's somewhat like the way you girls tend your plants. Their response is born of your initial actions. Love blooms that way too. When we love, we become loved.

Once I completed my criteria for impending motherhood, I decided you were definitely ok – all three of you – because there really wasn't much we hadn't worked out already. And that meant I felt ok about who I was, and how I influenced my daughters with my being. Therefore it had to be ok to become a grandma at age 42! I was even eager for the experience! The chance to sing to a babe on my lap again . . .

By the time Abby Rose [*Cindy's daughter*] was born, I was geared up for the experience. It was one I shall never forget either. I was so proud of you, Cindy, for your strength and your endurance.

I'm equally proud that both of you girls chose natural childbirth over the usual options, and I'm eager to share in the experience with you too, Nan. (I know your strength is equal to Cindy's – not everyone climbs out of a canyon in the middle of the night when a truck's just landed on her head!) You have my word that I will return from this latest flight of fancy in time to see my grandchild enter this world. (At least now I'm prepared for a purple baby!)

My pride in you, Betty, has nothing to do with babies – please spare me that joy a while longer! I love you and feel pride in you just because you're you.

Mostly, I think I feel a special gratitude that you chose me to be your mother. And on that note, I shall go cook a chicken and cluck some.

All my love,
Isa

Jessie Bernard to her unborn child, 1941

The first of these two letters was written by sociologist Jessie Bernard to her unborn child when she was six months pregnant. She wrote the second letter when her daughter Dorothy Lee was one month old:*

---

*Biographical information on the lives of Jessie Bernard and Dorothy Lee appears, with other letters, on pp. 20–4 and later in this chapter.

4 May 1941

My dearest,

Eleven weeks from today you will be ready for this outside world. And what a world it is this year! It has been the most beautiful spring I have ever seen. Miss Morris (a faculty colleague) says it is because I have you to look forward to. She says she has noticed a creative look on my face in my appreciation of this spring. And she is right. But also the world itself has been so particularly sweet, aglow with color. The forsythia were yellower and fuller than any I have ever seen. The lilacs were fragrant and feathery. And now the spirea, heavy with their little round blooms, stand like wonderful igloos, a mass of white. I doff my scientific mantle long enough to pretend that Nature is outdoing herself to prepare this earth for you. But also I want to let all this beauty get into my body. I cannot help but think of that other world. The world of Europe where babies are born to hunger, stunted growth, breasts dried up with anxiety and fatigue. That is part of the picture too. And I sometimes think that while my body in this idyllic spring creates a miracle, forces are at work which within twenty or twenty-five years may be preparing to destroy the creation of my body. My own sweet, the war takes on a terrible new significance when I think of that. I think of all those mothers who carried their precious cargoes so carefully for nine long months – and you have no idea how long nine months can be when you are impatient for the end – lovingly nurtured their babies at their breasts, and watched them grow for twenty years. I think of their anguish when all this comes to naught. Your father thinks parents ought to get down on their knees and beg forgiveness of children for bringing them into such a world. And there is much truth in that. But I hope you will never feel like that. I hope you will never regret the life we have created for you out of our seed. To me the only answer a woman can make to the destructive forces of the world is creation. And the most ecstatic form of creation is the creation of new life. I have so many dreams for you. There are so many virtues I would endow you with if I could. First of all, I would make you tough and strong. And how I have labored at that! I have eaten vitamins and minerals instead of food. Gallons of milk, pounds of lettuce, dozens of eggs . . . Hours of sunshine. To make your body a strong one because everything [depends] on that. I would give you resiliency of body so that all the blows and buffets of this world would leave you still unbeaten. I would have you creative. I would have you a creative scientist. But if the shuffling genes have made of you an artist, that will make me happy too. And even if you have no special talent either artistic or scientific, I would still have you creative no matter what you do. To build things, to make things, to create – that is what I covet for you. If you have a strong body and a creative mind you will be happy. I will help in that. Already I can see how parents long to shield their children from disappointments and defeat. But I also know that I cannot re-make life for you. You will suffer. You will have moments of disappointment and defeat. You will have your share of buffeting. I cannot spare you that. But I hope to help you be such a strong, radiant, self-integrated person that you will take all this in your stride, assimilate it, and rise to conquer . . .

Eleven more weeks. It seems a long time. Until another time, then, my precious one, I say good-bye.

Your eager mother

24 August 1941

My dearest daughter,

Now that I have held your earthy little body in my arms and felt that voracious tug of your hungry lips at my breast, the earlier letters I wrote you in the spring seem rather remote and academic. Now I am so completely absorbed in your physical care that the more abstract values in your development are crowded out . . .

During the first week of your life I was impressed with your positive attack on life. You showed no negativism at all. You nursed with much energy, although there was little milk for you . . . I wanted very much to nurse you completely, but alas I did not have enough milk. So we compromised. I nurse you and then give you a bottle. So far you have shown no objection. Your positive, experimental approach showed up again the other day when we first gave you orange juice from a tea spoon. You took it joyfully, eagerly. No rejections. No objections. We were delighted with the ease of the new adjustment.

The first few weeks at home have been most difficult for you and for us. I am so terribly inexperienced with babies, I had to learn everything from the beginning. And even yet you baffle me completely. You are not at all a scientific object. A practice which at one moment will cause you to stop crying will have no effect at all the next time. You will be crying violently and then in an instant you stop and all is forgiven. It puzzles me immensely. I wish I understood you better . . .

You seem to have an insatiable curiosity about the world. You love to look at things. Your eyes open very wide and you hold your head up over our shoulders and drink in all the sights. I find you utterly adorable. I sit for hours just watching you sleep, or lie awake in your bed. Just the sight and touch of your little body gives me intense pleasure . . .

In about three weeks we will be moving out to St. Charles so that I can be near the College. I hope that by then you will have such a good adjustment that the move will not upset you . . .

I will write you again from time to time as I have the opportunity. Caring for you has absorbed me so completely that I have not been able to think or do anything else. I hope now, however, to get better control over myself. For your sake, as well as for mine. I must not allow you to absorb me completely. I must learn to live my own life independently, in order to be a better mother to you.

All my love to you, sweet daughter

Robin Morgan to her unborn child Blake, 1969

Robin Morgan was born in Florida in 1941. She grew up in Mount Vernon, New York, and wanted at the age of 6 to become a doctor and a poet. She says, 'the male-supremacist society destroyed the first ambition but couldn't dent the second': her poems have appeared widely in over- and underground publications, ranging from the *Yale Review* and the *Atlantic* to *Ms* and *Feminist Studies*. She compiled and edited *Sisterhood Is Powerful*, the now classic anthology of writings from the women's liberation movement, and has published three books of poetry, *Monster, Lady of the Beasts* and *Depth Perception*. *Going Too Far: The Personal Chronicle of a Feminist*, a collection of her essays from the early 1960s through to the mid-1970s, was published in 1978, and her prose study, *The Anatomy of Freedom: Feminism, Physics and Global Politics*, appeared in 1982.

Robin Morgan has been working in the women's liberation movement since 1967. She is married to the writer Kenneth Pitchford; their son Blake was born in 1969. She has recently edited *Sisterhood Is Global: The First Anthology from the International Women's Movement* (1983).

In *Going Too Far*, she wrote:

. . . They said we were 'anti-motherhood' – and in the growing pains of certain periods, some of us were. There were times when I was made to feel guilty for having wanted and borne a child – let alone a male one, forgodsake. There were other times when we 'collectivized' around children, and I found myself miffed at the temporary loss of that relationship unique to the specific mother and specific child. So much of the transition is understandable now. Since the patriarchy commanded women to be mothers (the thesis), we had to rebel with our own polarity and declare motherhood a reactionary cabal (antithesis). Today a new synthesis has emerged; the concept of mother-right, the affirmation of child-bearing and/or child-rearing when it is a woman's *choice*. And while that synthesis itself will in turn become a new thesis (a dialectic, a process, a development), it is refreshing at last to be able to come out of my mother-closet and yell to the world that I love my dear wonderful delicious child – and I am not one damned whit less the radical feminist for that . . .

We had chosen together a 'genderless' name for our child, whether it was to be a girl or a boy: Blake, because the name means 'bringer of light' or 'illumined one', and also for William Blake, the eighteenth-century poet and mystic who knew and was deeply influenced by Mary Wollstonecraft, as well as by Catherine Boucher, the artist whom he married.

I am touched, now, by the innocent false consciousness of this letter, the simple-minded views on oppression, revolution, sexuality, parent-hood. Some of the language reflects a striving to be 'hip', although a tug toward careful articulation is also present. Mostly, though, I am surprised at how deeply this letter still moves me, how much I recognize its sense of urgency, and how intensely I still validate what was happening there – in that woman's body, and on that woman's page.

9 July 1969

Dear Blake,

I've written you no poems or letters while carrying you these past nine months, and somehow feel I can write you now only because we know, K. [*her husband*] and I, that our labor with you has definitely begun, and so you seem finally very real, beginning your own struggle into the conscious universe.

First, I ask you to forgive us for having coalesced you via our genes from that whirling matter and energy that you were before. A planetary famine is likely within ten years; nuclear, biological, gas, and chemical warfare are all possibilities; our species is poisoning what little is left of the air, water, and soil that is our natural Edenic heritage, and it is moving out later this very month to land on (explore? contaminate?) our satellite, the moon. You are part of a population explosion which may well be alone responsible for the destruction of life on earth. Overbreed and overkill begin to be common everyday phrases.

Yet we have conceived you from our sex and love, from the blending together of our brief tissues, K. and I. I could cite excuses, some of which I believe and some of which I don't: our own egos, our curiosity about what our genes would produce, our callousness, our desire to make an ongoing revolution in our own lives, on and on. Perhaps none is the truth, or all are. Perhaps none is really relevant.

The fact is that you are now being born, a woman or a man, but mostly yourself, Blake for now (later you might want to change that name to one nobody has a right to give you but yourself), into a dimension we are all struggling to space out, to make freer, until we are ultimately free from it, into some new life or death – some meaningful way of living, or dying at least, in ecstasy.

Some people are arming themselves – for love.

Some people are refusing to bear arms – for love.

K. and I will be trying to find new ways to save ourselves and our sisters and brothers from suffering and extinction under the greedy powers of a few madmen, and you will be involved unavoidably in that struggle. But on your own terms, as soon as you know them and make them known.

We have no claims on you. We are your genetic mother and father, and beyond that, and more important, merely two people who will take the responsibility of you while you are still small and helpless, who will love you to the best of our ability, provide you with whatever tools of knowledge, skill, humor and emotional freedom seem to interest you, respect your own individuality, hope you dig us as people but hardly dare insist on that (only try to earn it) – and let go.

Of course, I already envy you. Despite the horrors that oppress people around the world, those people are rising up to fight for their freedom. You are born into the age of worldwide revolution. You will be thirty-one years old in the year 2000. You may well travel to other planets. More prosaically, you have one hell of a groovy father, which I never had, and in some ways I trust him more with you than I do myself. I know you two will have crazy beautiful fun together. I have to get my ass in gear so I can join in.

If you are a woman, you will grow up in an atmosphere – indeed, a whole Movement – for women's liberation, so that your life will be less reflective of sexual oppression than mine, more human.

If you are a man, you will also be freer; you will not need to live a form of stereotyped masculinity which is based on the oppression of the other sex.

If you are a woman, you will be free to think – unlike so many women today. If you are a man, you will be free to feel – unlike so many men today.

K. and I are trying to be humanly unisexual, or pansexual. Join us?

If any of us survive these next decades on this planet, you will live to make a society where people share and love and laugh and understand each other. If none of us survive, it won't matter, because then we'll be free. Meanwhile, we can play with each other, and create poems and colors and songs and orgasms together, and learn to fight not so much for what we believe in as for what we love.

Dear Blake, I love myself right now.

Dear Blake, I love K. so very much.

Dear Blake, I love you, even though we've not been introduced.

Dear Blake, leave my body behind you quickly. K. and I, together throughout labor and delivery, will work hard to aid you in your struggle toward light and air and independence.

Dear Blake, welcome to the universe.

Dear, dear Blake, goodbye.

R.

Nan Bauer Maglin to her daughter Quintana, 1980

Nan Bauer Maglin was born and raised in the suburbs of New York City in a middle-class Jewish family. When Nan was 34, she and her husband Arthur decided to adopt a child, having been unable to conceive despite consulting fertility specialists for over two years. They went to an agency which finds homes for Colombian children and after a year of waiting and bureaucracy they flew to Bogota to meet their ten-day-old daughter, Quintana. She was delivered to them in New York when she was two months old.

Nan is an active feminist and teaches English at the City University of New York. She has published numerous articles on teaching and literary criticism in feminist, academic and radical journals. She is now divorced and is striving to create a new family structure with a man who has three children, one of whom is adopted.

In 'Awaiting Quintana: A Journal of Adoption' she wrote (nine months before Quintana's arrival):

> Many of my friends, like me, now past thirty, want children and do not know why or how they can still be feminists, be strong, be active, be independent. Many want little Quintanas, seeing in our daughters a new tribe of women. Often I believe that Quintana will rebel, marry at fifteen and settle in Queens – determined to be the 'total woman' to her husband . . . I have many worries and fears, but I look forward to being a mother, having a family and sharing childraising with Arthur's brother and some of our friends – perhaps.

Arthur's brother was killed a week before Quintana arrived, making the first months with Quintana very painful. Nan's other plans for shared childcare did not come to fruition for reasons which she describes in the letter below. Initially, disillusionment and resentment accompanied the spoiled hopes for radical solutions to the nuclear family; and then, three years later, Nan wrote to Quintana this letter about the revitalisation of her ideals after a visit to Cuba with a group of nine children and eight adults. Fittingly, the last entry in her adoption journal had been, 'I hope Alice Walker's description of the relationship between parents and children in Cuba will apply to Quintana and myself: "I envied his children, all the children of Cuba whose parents are encouraged and permitted to continue to grow, to develop, to change, to 'keep up with' their children. To become *compañeros** as well as parents." '

8 July and 24 December 1980

Dear Quintana, My Compañerita,

Quintana, three years ago I wrote a journal-letter to you, for you, of you and me. At that time we had just adopted you from Bogota, Colombia and I needed to understand that overwhelming experience. I wanted you to have a record of the events and our emotions surrounding those months so that someday when you will need and want to understand your adoption, there will at least be my words for you to use. Although I have sporadically kept a journal since then, I have not really written regularly nor seriously; 'the events since 10 September 1977 when we waited anxiously outside the sliding doors of

---

*'Compañero' means comrade; a 'compañerita' is a young woman comrade.

Immigration at Kennedy Airport, expecting each bundle to be you, our daughter, carried by a Colombian social worker, have not been preserved, on paper at least.

I have not written for many reasons: I think the life of a mother (as well as a full-time teacher) is too busy to take time out for creation and reflection: also, I was living our life rather than watching it. Moreover, while the pre-adoption seemed extra-ordinary, your life with me seems ordinary, in the sense that you are my daughter and I am your mother and the fact of adoption is no longer relevant . . . Our ties seem so deep, coming from some faraway dark womblike place, that they can be no different nor less than those of the biological parent. There was, I think, another reason I did not write. I did not want to deal with some of the really painful events surrounding your life with us. My journal holds up two hopes, hopes to transcend the threesome I feared you, me and Arthur would become. Neither hope survived your arrival.

I had hoped that Phil [*Arthur's brother*] and Jeff would be an alternative family for you. The journal already records some ambivalence on their part; we will, however, never know if their ambivalence (like my own) would have been worked out in the process of parenting. Ten days before your arrival, Phil was killed – a New York City event. His death, and your coming – too close. The same people who came to the funeral came the following week to see you. I could not feel the joy; I could not wake up; I wanted so desperately to lie down; Arthur wanted to go off somewhere by himself; instead we had a demanding three-month old baby on our hands. Looking back, that year was such a terrible one.

Whereas death took away one chance for expanding the nuclear family the other chances were sabotaged by practical and emotional difficulties. This is too complicated to lay out fully in a letter; it is in a sense the story of coming of age in the Sixties, drawing bold radical and feminist dreams that are now shrinking in the Eighties. Because of our busy lives, our jobs, our house, the solidity of the family, we were unable to incorporate Carolyn, someone who seemed to want to be intimately involved with you. I met Carolyn about two years before your birth; we were in a women's group together. She a lesbian, myself a heterosexual, both wanting to cross boundaries, participate in other lifestyles. And so, Quintana, when you appeared, she was there. In those first few months, she took you to meetings, to sleep at her house (she lived with other women); before I felt secure enough, she took you on your first outing on a cold late Autumn day. But it did not last – neither of us understood our real needs and motivations; there was tension and lack of clarity between the meaning of friend and of family; there was resentment over our different availability and ability to give and take; there was resentment over our many differences. So Carolyn disappeared. It was no one's fault really. While it was a very personal, individual situation, it was (and is) also a social problem, one which we could not work out. What has happened is that my world of friends has changed. They now look a lot like me: white, middle-class, professional, radical, feminist, with children. I need their support, but I mourn the closing off of difference in my life.

Quin, I write now not really to confront the last three years, but because something extraordinary has happened in our lives: we went to Cuba together and I want to share our trip with you because already you do not remember those momentous nine days. I want you to *know* this place, unlike the many places you and I have visited which have probably already disappeared from your awareness. Cuba is more than a place to visit; it is a place that poses real questions about the way we live – meaning we, our nuclear family and our daily life – meaning we, the people and government of the United States. This letter, then, is one way to make memorable your experience, like the picture scrap-book hopefully we shall make for you, Daniel, and Micaela – the three-year-olds who were there, and yet not wholly there. And, of course, this letter is also a small way to preserve the experience for myself and a means to share it with others . . . It is not to give you a day-by-day account of our trip; rather I write to tell you that you were there and that Cuba, like your adoption, forces us to imagine the many different possibilities for you (and thus for everyone). I think of you growing up in a white, middle-class, professional, Jewish-by-origin family in Brooklyn, New York, USA. You were born poor, I presume, in Bogota, Colombia, to a woman we know nothing about. What will your life be like in the United States? What would your life have been like growing up in Colombia? What could your life be like growing up in Cuba?

To write at length of your three different lives would include too many statistics and too much speculation. I do not know, for instance, what the public schools will be like in three years when you begin PS 321 on our corner; I do not know if nuclear plants and chemical wastes will so pollute our environment that you will have no time even to define yourself. I expect the tensions in our lives will get worse as we try to survive New York City in a time of a move to the Right and a desperation among the poor as the class differences get more damaging. Nevertheless, I do know that you will be growing tall (you are already quite tall: what would the nutrition in Colombia do to you?) and strong and self-confident in America: you must learn to laugh and to struggle and to think; you will take karate lessons as well as dancing; you will watch TV but will also sing folk songs and learn Spanish; you will discover the pleasures of your body and come to honor those who have laid theirs down against oppression; you will buy me cards for Mother's Day but will march on International Women's Day.

In Colombia you would have had your people, the culture and religion of your birth. If your family had been well off, you would perhaps have had a chance, but women in Colombia, as my student Mildred Fajardo wrote in her journal, are still condemned to the life Virginia Woolf imagined a sister of Shakespeare's would have had. She would get little or no education; she would sew until and throughout marriage; if she escaped domesticity, she would be mistreated, manhandled and raped, discriminated against, ending her life in suicide, despair, or insanity.

There is no comparison between the life you would have had in Colombia as a girl or woman, and the life you would have in Cuba. In Cuba, the life for women is unlike any Latin American country (except Nicaragua where the Revolution promises to give all women and young girls the opportunity to learn, to develop, to use their abilities). In Cuba, although the rhetoric is still far ahead of the reality, I was impressed by many of the things we saw. The lack of consumer goods is a genuine problem, especially for women with young children, but what is promising is that the emphasis there is not on material accumulation but on sharing and service. I was impressed with daycare (especially compared to that for which I pay highly for you here); I like the emphasis on work. Quintana, will a factory adopt your daycare center? Will you have a work-study program, with your school being responsible for contributing to the economy? In the US we pay for young people to go to summer work camps . . .

I was impressed with the emphasis on collectivism from the corral (a group playpen) to shared birthday parties for all the children born in the same month. I am concerned about what you are not getting in this country which children in Cuba have the benefit of: at age four, learning about 'our friends the Guerrilla Fighters' and singing songs about peace; at age six, joining a mass organization like the Young Pioneers where you discuss issues such as apartheid in South Africa, how to participate in the literacy campaign in the countryside, and how your school ought to be run.

The Cubans repeat often that 'Children are the Revolution' and the entire society seems to feel responsible for raising children; there you would have a sense of not just one mother, neither the mother of your genes nor the mother who nurtures you exclusively, but of a collective committed to you. And you would have a commitment to them – which could give you a rich sense of yourself and give a sense of meaning to your whole life.

No, I am not a rosey romantic. For instance, we were told at the Cuban Women's Federation (FMC) that only women can train to be daycare workers and that it is 'abnormal' for men to work there and do such things as dance with children (meanwhile, our men were dancing with the children, entertaining them so that we could attend the meeting). This one statement and the real discrimination against gay people* contradict the emphasis in the Family Code to give women equality, to eradicate machismo. Even if Cuba has come a long way, certainly there is much to struggle over.

I write this now because you are too young for us to attempt to figure out these days, this country, our values together, the way that some of our friends on the trip, such as Susan and her eleven-year-old daughter, Ragan, have begun to talk and think about it all. Our dialogue will have to wait. I write so that you will think of those days and speculate about the future for yourself and other niñas and niños. In Cuban liberator Jose Marti's words: 'Children know more than you would think, and if you let them write what they know, they would write great things.' You know of Cuba from this letter; from my journal and your album you know that you come from Colombia; and you do know Brooklyn. I wonder what you will do with your knowledge.

Elaine Marcus Starkman to her daughter Naomi, 1976

Elaine Marcus Starkman was born in 1937 and was raised in Chicago. Married at the age of 24, she had three children in three years. Before her marriage and during her first pregnancy she taught elementary school in the Chicago Public Schools.

After the Six Day War in 1967, she and her husband moved to Israel with their three young children. Two years later, faced with the dilemma of returning to the United States or raising their children as Israelis, they decided to return home. Shortly after her return, Elaine became pregnant with her fourth child, Naomi, to whom the following letter is written. After Naomi's birth Elaine began her career as a writer.

Elaine is the author of two books of poetry, *Coming Together* and *Love Scenes*, and a translation of *Hannah Senesh*, a play about the poet-parachutist of World War II.* Her work also appears in *The Woman Who Lost Her Names: Selected Writings by American-Jewish Women* (1980) and *Ariadne's Thread: An Anthology of Women's Diaries* (1982). She is co-editor of *State of Peace: An Anthology of Women's Poems*. She lives in Northern

---

*According to some more recent reports, the discrimination against gay people has somewhat abated, possibly in response to the discontent expressed by the 1980 'Meridel Exodus'. Gay artists are now having their work performed, published and exhibited, which marks a significant change in policy. It remains to be seen whether this new spirit of tolerance will extend to all homosexuals.

*See pp. 200-4.

California, where she teaches adult classes in autobiographical writing and
writes for literary magazines.

She writes about the background to this letter, written just after her thirty-
ninth birthday, when Naomi was 6:

'I was a foolishly idealistic young woman when I married. My whole
approach to sex, contraception and childbirth was extremely naive.

'I was overwhelmed, unprepared and shocked at the responsibility of rearing three small children. Yet at the time I felt I had no other option. My
husband wanted children more than I; I felt I had to please this mature man of
such serious character. Months passed when I thought the endless demands
of motherhood would gobble me up, that I could no longer maintain the
integrity of my inner life: to question, to learn, to teach, and to try to understand life by writing.

'In the early years my husband always helped with the housework and the
children. Back then people used to tease us; for many years I was ashamed of
the fact. I also felt indebted to him. Having several children close together
was an acceptable fad of the early 60s. I'd hoped that as soon as they went to
school, I'd resume studying or teaching.

'When we returned from Israel, we faced both a culture shock and sense of
loss. Confused about the direction in my life, all my earlier plans evaporated
into thin air. We'd talk about having a fourth child to make up for that loss –
as well as the loss of millions in the Holocaust, including members of my
husband's family. To my own shock, I simply got pregnant again.

'Although this fourth pregnancy was hard on me, I instinctively knew that
after this last child I would have proved my worth to the utmost. I decided
not to have an abortion. After Naomi was born, a kind of creative power was
released from me; I began to open up and write seriously; I began to better
understand myself as a woman. I wanted to write about my feelings which I
was sure many other women had experienced as well. I wanted to write on
my own terms, which I believe I've done.'

'Letter to a Last Child':

31 October 1976

Dear Naomi,

You're gone on the school bus; I step into the house filled with
demands, reluctant to finish chores, anxious to get to my desk, the
meaningful part of my day when you're not here. Gone. All that's left
is an image of a six-year-old who's left her toys and books scattered
about the bedroom floor. No, I haven't taught you to love, what I
can't love, the rigors of housework. Still, you're a happy child, not so
different from Kathy and Kristy whose mothers are far better
managers than I. Yet what are those dark rings under your eyes? Have
I put them there? What are those monsters you saw hanging in your

closet last night? Refractions of your mother's rebellion in a town of house-keepers?

You've run down the hill, ragged mouse-brown hair flying in the wind. Will it ever have shape? Your sturdy legs pump as fast as they can while I stand here alone flooded with sudden warmth, a warmth that comes to me late. Because at 39, you're the child of my under-standing. Is it only now that I am capable of accepting motherhood unlike my early 20s with your now half-grown brother and sisters?

At the corner you met Kathy and Kristy, both with blonde hair and blue eyes and neatly matching outfits that mimic their mammas'; you wait at the bus stop looking at them awkwardly, swinging your Raggedy Ann lunch box with dry peanut butter sandwich, urban child of Jewish parents, brown eyes wide, thin lips spurting forth family secrets so that you can be like them: 'My mamma yelled at my brother this morning;' 'I got a fancy costume for Halloween tonight. My neighbor gave it to me. My mamma doesn't know how to sew.'

Your body twists and turns and opens itself to a benevolent world that holds out-stretched arms and smiley faces. Later when you come home this afternoon and drop your sweater on the floor, study your-self in my bathroom mirror, you'll ask, 'How comes I don't got blonde hair?' As if she were asking about her lineage and those lost relatives before America. 'Because your Grandma had dark hair; not everyone has light hairs.'

'But Kathy does; Kristy does. My sister does.'

'That comes from the *other* Grandma.'

Soon the big yellow bus will return and I'll have accomplished nothing. I'll come out from my room to watch its cavernous mouth belch you out with grime and fumes. Watch you trudge up the three blocks, my stomach unknotting as you arrive. For my world isn't benevolent. Any moment an evil hand can reach from around the corner, a disease rise within, a young driver screech out of the court mowing down your young life, punishing me for being a wicked mother, leaving me without a small child to keep at center.

How I worry when I love. I never wanted to give myself fully; I held back so I wouldn't be hurt, so your siblings wouldn't consume me when I was just beginning to know myself.

But with you, I think I've found that self. What pleasure in your growth, the unwanted, fourth child, watching you hold that fat red pencil, drawing that monster, erasing the paper until it is full of holes, drawing pumpkins and witches, forehead wrinkled with determination.

'Halloween's for everybody; it's not Christmas or Easter,' crooning to Barbie and Ken as you have them make love, biting the tiny white scar under your lip, the one from dancing in the tub three years ago.

How that dance irritated me. I didn't feel sorry for you, only myself because your fall kept me from doing what *I* wanted – something's always keeping me from doing what I want – I had to take you to the doctor and skip the lecture I was planning on for months.

How strange that my sense of mothering comes to me so strongly on Halloween of all days. I'm reliving my own childhood watching you. I've at last overcome my fear of goblins, my fear of both differentness and conformity, my fear that this ultimate female role would destroy my goals I've so desperately clung to.

But I've allowed you to nourish me as I've nourished you. I've allowed that bond between mother and daughter to gradually grow, to reach beyond the limits I've always held. Not that I didn't love your brother and sisters – how they overwhelmed me – but with your birth, the child whom I didn't want but at last proved my worth so that I could say, Enough, I myself began to bloom. Is this my tie with you? That I've finally learned becoming a mother will not change my love of learning, my desire to write?

Those angry months before you were born! Legs wrapped in bandages, I blamed your father for my getting pregnant, as if I didn't have anything to say! I blamed him for my wanting to please him! When I thought of abortion he said a new life would replace all those from his family lost in the Holocaust. Who could argue with that? I didn't have the strength.

Besides, I had no plan that year. I thought I might teach again but I couldn't. Why was I so anxious when I had so much to learn? I wasn't ripe enough to internalize the experiences I'd gathered.

I cried up until the last minute. What if you had a birth defect from my not wanting you? What if I didn't love you? All that weight I'd gained! All the hair that fell on my comb! I had created a life but couldn't control my own.

You came on a cool rainy June evening. Not until the last minute did I believe you were here. With your birth some primitive joy was released. Like tonight on Halloween when witches come forth. But it was spring then, not fall like today; it was *Shavuot*, the holiday of First Fruits. We gave you an old name, Naomi, that all your friends mispronounce. At the sight of your long legs and dark hair, all my fears died, and I wrote a poem to you, and I write this now and know why.

Love,
Your Ema

Mrs Colbert to her daughter Jane, c. 1930

Jane Colbert Friday Scott was the eldest of five children. Her father was an attractive, ambitious, difficult man who loved his wife; but they argued constantly. He made a fortune in steel alloys, lost it in the Depression, and made it again. Unable to show his positive emotions, he was loved and feared by his children – who loved their mother passionately, despite the fact that she had left the family when Jane was 14, taking only the youngest child with her to Florida.*

Jane's daughter, Nancy Friday, wrote in her bestselling book, *My Mother/ My Self*:

> When my grandmother wrote this letter, I doubt that she intended to return to my grandfather. I don't think that her leaving him was a false gesture, but a desperate last alternative . . . She saw only separation ahead and clearly wanted to give her eldest daughter something to help fill the void.

c. 1930

My darling Jane,

When you read this I want you to do it with an open heart. Forget the things that have been said – the thoughts you may have had, and try to remember only the better, more beautiful phase of life. When I am not there with you, it is going to be your task to try to help the little ones to see things. Try to guide them in the right way. This is your work and your duty.

To me motherhood has been the most beautiful thing in my life. The wonder of it never ceases for me – to see you all developing from tiny helpless babies into big strong girls and boys, to see your minds changing with your years and to remember that some day you will be grown men and women. It is overwhelming.

All my life as a child I looked forward to the time when I would have children of my own – and in spite of my so-called talents or urges toward other things, underneath was that spark which had to burst into flame sometime. And when I held you, Jane – my first baby – in my arms, I had the greatest thrill I have ever experienced. I felt almost saintly, as if I had really entered heaven. There is nothing else in life like it. And anyone who receives such a blessing should be eternally grateful.

I am telling you this, Jane, just so you will understand my love and feeling for you. Always remember this and as you grow older, think of me sometime and try to understand what I am trying to convey to you.

My heart is full, but I could not write the things I feel in a thousand years. Love each other and be good to daddy and he will take care of you. This is the hardest, bitterest moment of my life, leaving you, but I cannot do anything else. I cannot see through my tears. God bless you all,

Mama

---

*Mrs Colbert returned within a year, and died two years later of sleeping sickness.

Letting Them Go

I long to put the experience of fifty years at once into your young lives, to give you at once the key of that treasure chamber every gem of which has cost me tears and struggles and prayers, but you must work for these inward treasures yourselves.

Harriet Beecher Stowe to her twin daughters (1861)

In theory, it is a cause for celebration when a daughter or son can begin to make their own decisions, test the skills they have been acquiring since infancy, stop depending on their parents for everything and begin to trust their own judgements. In practice, most people describe adolescence as a nightmare. Parents of both daughters and sons acknowledge great conflict between their feelings of protectiveness and their desire to help their children take the necessary risks to discover their capacity to survive independently.

It is a notoriously difficult time for mothers and daughters, who must negotiate new boundaries of involvement in each other's lives. In many families, 'growing up' has been particularly fraught where daughters are concerned – not least because women in our society have not been expected to grow up, but to remain dependent and in need of protection. But as women come to be seen as capable and autonomous adults, the task of being a good mother to an adolescent daughter can be viewed in more complex and positive ways – and not merely as a ceaseless hair-raising battle to restrain and control her frightening impulse to test out different ways of being.

In her groundbreaking study of changes in the way women view motherhood, Signe Hammer uses the term 'enabling' to describe aspects of mothering which 'encourage a child to grow and develop as an individual in her own right'. The mothers whose letters appear in the next section have experienced some of the challenges and rewards of independence in their own lives, and can explore new ways of relating to their daughters' struggles to leave childhood.

Jessie Bernard and her daughter Dorothy Lee, 1954

By 1954, Jessie Bernard was a single mother, reluctantly deciding to send her 12-year-old daughter, Dorothy Lee, to a Quaker boarding school in Philadelphia.* In *Self-Portrait of a Family*, Jessie wrote:

> I wasn't altogether sure in my own mind whether I would be sending her away for her own benefit or for mine, to give her practice in coping on her own in protected circumstances or to save me from the issues of adolescent rebellion . . . A copout? You might well call it that. My uncertainty about the decision . . . meant that the moment she expressed a desire to return [home] for high school I reneged.

---

*Further details about their lives appear in Chapter 2, and also earlier in this chapter.

6 November 1954

My darling,

I have been doing a lot of hard thinking since I saw you off on the bus at noon today. I have concluded that a Friends school was a mistake for a girl like you . . . It may be that the atmosphere of the school is not good for you, not nourishing enough emotionally. I feel very bad about this. I mean about my judgement in this respect. Please let me know if you think you should return here next semester. I would be inclined to say you should. It bothers me that you have doubts occasionally about my love for you. It disturbs you terribly if I disapprove of you, which suggests that you are not sure about my love. And I have become convinced that your acne is a psychosomatic reaction to all this. I feel certain that if I had you here with me for a month it would clear up completely . . . You make a perfect adjustment wherever you are; you are at ease with everyone. But your unconscious rebels and takes it out in symptoms – skin in your case. It distresses me to no end to think that I made this mistake . . .

I can't promise to write every day, but I will be sending you waves of love all the time so that you should feel them all the time. OK? Don't try to be such a perfect girl, darling. Do the best you can without too much anxiety or strain . . . We think you are pretty terrific just as you are. I think we can see that you get a good education right here at home. We all love you terribly.

Mother

In a letter accompanying her permission to reprint their correspondence, Jessie admits:

'One reviewer commented on this letter that it was reassuring that I had my "moments of self-doubt." Moments? More like months, years, even decades. I still have them. The children all turned out well. Still, whenever life deals any one of them even a relatively mild blow, I find myself wondering what I might have done wrong, something that brought on this misfortune. It is utterly absurd, as they have all at one time or another reminded me. Dorothy Lee once set me back on my heels when she told me that my constant guilt trips about my mothering practices were a sign of enormous arrogance. Who did I think I was anyway, God? . . .

'I was almost doctrinaire in my insistence that Dorothy Lee be autonomous, her own woman. This policy was not wholly a matter of principle; it was in part a matter of self-interest, to relieve me of some of the responsibility of motherhood . . . I was anything but a possessive mother. I did not relish the exercise of authority. We are told nowadays that children need and want limits, that they do not want too much freedom. I think I still vote for freedom. It is possible that the children of the Sixties were given too much freedom, so that any authority at all became galling to them. I still prefer thought-through challenge to authority to supine acceptance of it. Dorothy

Lee's ability to stand up to me pleases me as I read her letters now, however dismaying it may have been almost thirty years ago.'

They argued about the usual things: clothes, money, friends, school. The following is Dorothy Lee's reply to Jessie's demand that she spend less time with older girls and more time with friends her own age; she wrote it when she had been at school for about two months:

[1955]

[Dear Mother]
    . . . Your present decision makes me very unhappy . . . I hope you change your mind . . . for this is something I feel very strongly about and if necessary I will fight you. I am sorry. I love you very much and I hate to fight with you but here I think you are wrong. It's my life and I want to have some say on how I live it. I always want your help but you don't have the right to say who I run around with. Love you very much.

Dorothy Lee

Dorothy Lee, now in her forties, comments:

'As I look over my relationship with my mother it seems to me we were playing a kind of game. She admitted she liked her work as much as she liked me and my brothers, that her intellectual and academic preoccupations were a kind of escape from having to deal with us. So the game on my part was to find ways to blow her cool, to make her drop her impersonal, abstract stance, to stop her from taking refuge in the scientific and rational realm. Take money, for example. She needn't have worried about being penurious. I had everything I wanted. But I knew that it was the unexpectedness of requests for money that bothered her. If she were properly prepared she was usually willing to grant almost any request. But if I sprang it on her unprepared she would be floored. So I had to learn when to spring things on her – to make her angry – and when to prepare her for them. I became quite good at it.'

Money remained an issue until Dorothy Lee married.* When she first went away to school, Dorothy Lee and Jessie had had joint accounts; after many blow-ups (such as the letter which follows), Dorothy Lee made the suggestion that Jessie simply send her a certain amount of money each month:

[1955]

[Dear Dorothy Lee]
    You make it quite difficult for me ever to rebuke you about anything because you immediately ask if I love you. The fact that I am angry doesn't at all affect the fact that I love you. But you do do the craziest things. As you know . . . I had just assumed that you were

---

*See p. 24.

sensible about money. I never went over your checks to see how much you were spending . . . But when my checks began to bounce and I found myself almost $100 short it was extremely embarrassing and annoying. It is extremely bad to get the reputation for making out checks that bounce . . . When I found myself so short I checked your checks and found you had spent $120 in January. Just imagine that! I just don't understand how you could do such a thing . . . I hope you will keep a careful account of your checks and never, never do such a thing again.

Judy Green Herbstreit to her daughter Teri, 1979

Judy Green Herbstreit was born and raised in a small town near Dallas, Texas, the eldest child of a middle-class family. She was a full-time mother of three children until she and her husband divorced in 1978. Judy had enjoyed being a Brownie leader, Sunday School teacher, chauffeur to music lessons and homemaker, but was forced to go to work to support the children: Teri Lynn (15) John Travis (11) and Kirk Edward (7). This left many of the major domestic responsibilities on Teri's shoulders; after three years she packed her bags in a rage and left home.

Judy now uses her maiden name and works as vice-president of marketing for her second husband's package design company. Teri is studying for a degree in International Business at Ohio State University.

Judy explained the background to the letter below, which she wrote immediately after Teri left:

'When I realized that my husband could not be happy – no matter which job he took (ten moves in fifteen years and his jobs were all very good ones) – I stopped believing in him. It was the most painful time of my life. I could no longer give him my full support. It scattered me terribly, mentally. My purpose was gone. After several years of hurts, confusion, depression, turning to others, psychiatry (one long trip to a mental ward from being despondent enough to want to die), we were divorced.

'I was not a college graduate. I had not worked for years. I was almost a total basket case. And I had three shattered children to raise. I was very frightened. But I had a purpose again: Raise those kids! Feed those kids! Clothe those kids! Survive! . . .

'After a few low-paying jobs, facing sexual harassment from the manager of a company and getting fired for reporting it, applying for other jobs and many rejection notices later, I got my first real job . . . selling Cadillacs . . . commission only. I really loved it. I loved it even though the men on the floor greatly resented the first woman salesman. (They went through my files when I wasn't there; many of them were stolen. I felt personally attacked.) It made me hurt and angry but I still liked my job and loved my customers.

'Teri had been raised with me at home and she was not prepared for her tripled responsibilities; she hated it when her brothers wouldn't co-operate. We were all tired. I was very upset with her for not realizing how much I needed her help. (I was on commission only. If I didn't sell, we wouldn't eat.) I had moved them to a more expensive house (one of my gutsiest moves) so they could have better schools; I wasn't there to give them attention and I at least wanted them to have the best school system we could find. I was working hard to take care of them and I couldn't even get their co-operation. I was furious. I had spent years of my life on these children and I was outraged that they wouldn't give me support too.

'When I had worked all day and came home to a torn-up, messy house with kids watching television, I would scream at them. Teri was doing the bulk of the work that *was* being done, so she would be upset. At least, she felt, *she* was trying.

'Teri never returned after she left but we have re-built our relationship and she is working to pay her own way through college. I'm so proud of her. She's fighting a big battle to get through. I think she'll make it – and she's getting invaluable experience for being out in the world. She will have such a great head start over where I was . . . thank God.

'I know the battles "not only to survive but to prevail" are far from finished, but I can't help feeling victorious somehow, even with the sadness that is always there. I am very happy to share the situation with you because many other women today are facing similar situations. Perhaps it will give someone else courage to know they are not alone (though they may feel so).'

[1979]

Dear Teri,

It is difficult to grow up. It is very difficult to leave your home. It is not only hard on you, but on your family.

Perhaps, from your perspective, your feelings are justified. Let me tell you my feelings.

Children are a mixed blessing. They are a tremendous source of work, time spent, money invested, pain, joy, sadness, pride, closeness. You often wonder if they understand – or care – about the things you give them while you do without – the nights you bake all night to give them happy memories – the fears you have for them because they *do refuse* to understand that life is not really going to be a 'take' situation when they get out in it – as it is *now* while they are safe in the growing years.

I believe growing-up-years of safety are vital to a child. (Maybe I'm wrong) . . . Some parents protect their children long past the time when they are ready to make their own way in the world – to work as well as play. This makes children dependent and soft and makes parents feel strong and important. It makes me feel disgusted and sick because it is a manipulative thing to do. Some parents never protect their children and throw them into life's challenges very young without much preparation. If the child survives this it will be strong but it may know little about love and supportive feelings and attitudes – sharing and caring.

Remember the saying I used to keep on the refrigerator? 'A mother is not a person to lean on but a person to make leaning unnecessary.'

When the day comes for your child to leave home, you want them to be able to say, 'Mom, I'm ready! I can do it, Mom! I'm going to fly on my own.' It hurts when your child says, 'You don't love me. You don't want me or understand me. I'm getting out of here. I'm leaving *you!*'

You *are* ready to go, Teri. I assure you you *can* fly. It is time for you to do it. I don't think it was wrong for you to leave, I only wish you had chosen another way to do it. But, that was your decision. (Remember, it is as disgusting to be a manipulative *child* as it is to be a manipulative *parent.*)

You have mountains to climb – without me. I don't even know your world, I don't know your mountains.

You have my love. You have my support and my encouragement. (I cheer good.) You have me believing you can do what you *want* to do – whatever it is. That's all I can give you now. I've done the best I could do as your mother. I know I've failed you sometimes, it is unavoidable in raising a human being – especially when you are only a human being yourself, and you are still climbing your own mountains.

The best thing you can do is believe in yourself. Don't be afraid to try. Don't be afraid to fail. Just try again. Just dust yourself off and try again. (Remember the guy – Billy Joe Armstrong – who told me 'Don't bother to dust yourself off – just get up and *go!*')

The last and most important thing to remember is:

Philippians 4:13, 'I can do all things through Christ who strengthens me.'

My love and thoughts go with you. My first child. My daughter.

Love,
MOM

Nan Hunt and her daughter Diana, 1974

These letters were written when Diana was 26 and Erica was 14 and living with Nan in Los Angeles:*

---

*For biographical details on Nan Hunt and her daughters Diana and Erica, see the letters of Nan and Diana in Chapter 2, and of Nan and her 'spiritual mother', Bunny, in Chapter 3.

9 September 1974

Dear Mama,

Erica and I had such a good visit, having her with us again simply reaffirms the deep love I have for her. And besides she's such a neat person, I think I'd love her even if she weren't my sister.

I've been wanting to write and try to tell you about my personal feelings regarding you and Erica. I'm afraid what I'm going to tell or rather talk to you about is going to hurt you, but I don't want it to nor do I think you should let it. The way I see it Erica is coping with her feelings of blame and hurt in the best way she knows how for her emotional survival . . . I think she'll be alright if you can just manage to leave her alone for the most part. She reiterated to me her indignant feelings toward you because of your (as she saw it) total lack of guilt for your involvement with Ray [*Nan's lover*] even though you know how much hurt and pain you caused both her and Jim [*Nan's late husband and Erica's father*].

Erica's feelings for you have really been numbed to the point where she finds it healthier to not feel anything [rather] than to feel hatred, which is probably what she thinks she wants to feel . . . down deep I don't think she wants to go to that extreme. She's very resentful and mad at you for what she views as your seemingly blatant lack of guilt for actions she thinks you should feel guilty about. She does not want to feel this way and she herself feels guilty . . . Then she feels like you are putting unrealistic demands on her affection toward you when you go through the normal motions of a loving mother, i.e.: asking her about her day, showing your love for her in physical demonstration. Therefore, she feels guilty because she can't unreservedly love you back in return. That would be going against her feelings in the first place.

I don't feel like I'm expressing myself as clearly as I would like to so I wish you would call me after you get this letter . . . Erica wants to stay with you in California and I think if you can try to just leave her alone as far as expecting any loving behavior goes, y'all might be able to at least live in peaceful co-existence. – Take care.

Much love,
Di

14 September 1974

Diana dear,

You are very perceptive about the situation between Erica and me. I agree that she is indignant because of my seeming lack of guilt. She is torn between hate and the old feelings of love-dependency. She feels she must disapprove of me for the sake of her father's memory – to condone me would be a betrayal of him. That is why I don't think she is going to be able to live harmoniously with me for awhile –

everything I do is wrong whether it is cooking the spaghetti sauce or making her a blackberry pie, to showing interest in her activities. She has to reject and criticize in order to punish. The question is, is it healthy for a 13-year-old girl to be allowed to punish her mother? I think it is destructive to her & destructive to me.

What are the answers to her insistence on my guilt? I could talk about how guilty I feel. I could have immediately punished myself by saying goodbye to Ray forever and punished him too. I could have sunk deep into depression, wished I could bring Jim back from the dead. I could have committed suicide to atone for hurting Jim. I could have begged Erica's forgiveness and fawned over her to try to make her pity and care for me.

None of these alternatives seemed either wise, constructive or honest to me. Nor did they seem like any kind of example to set for Erica. Guilt is a terrible and private thing. I do not think Erica should have to bear hearing about my dreams (nightmares) and regrets. I have talked to her honestly about my relationship with her father & with Ray – as honestly as I could and still keep Jim's memory valuable to her. I don't want to complain about Jim. You know all these things I'm saying to you – mainly it is for the purpose of organizing my thoughts that I write thus.

I now think that my fault lay chiefly in listening to my guilts & super-ego too much in the past. I tried to love Jim because I thought I *should*, I ought to, & I must do this & that. My deep feelings ran counter always to what I *ought* to have been doing and there was that strength in me, yes *strength* that resisted the dutiful way, resisted a luke-warm relationship, resisted household chores, resisted constant motherliness. At times I am the most maternal, domestic, wifely creature, but that is not all. I should have had the courage to choose just what I really wanted for me long ago before I had husband and children. However, I was too confused by all the whisperings of should & ought and the 'right thing', to know who I really was. I made the best of it – often rationalizing, sometimes breaking out in desperate flights of freedom to love affairs or to school or to career.

But, damn it, I loved you both, you and Erica – not because you were dependent, but you were people – part of my life. I can hardly bear living with someone whom I loved so dearly as I have Erica, and feel the vibrations of her resentment, hate, bitterness, criticism, etc. I am trying.

My determination has been to live in an emotionally honest way. To try to be tolerant of Erica but not allow her to brow-beat me. I have chosen to do what I *feel*; to be happy when I can and show it, to do constructive things and resist destructive feeling and actions. To be emotional when I feel emotional and not put on a damn façade of stoicism like Jim did which ate away his insides. I tried to love him because it was the reasonable thing to do and it didn't work. I did care for and feel deep friendship for him.

What example Erica will be able to take from me, I don't know. I have attempted to give value to courage, honesty, tolerance and empathy for people, acknowledging all the while that these virtues do not come constantly or easily – that I fail more than I succeed, but I do try. Therefore I think it no cause for shame to admit that you have been afraid, that you have deceived yourself and others, that your biases have blinded you, and that sometimes your own busyness & self-interest has blinded you to others' need of you. That is the human condition – but it is right to be *real* and not an automaton.

One of the problems between Erica & me is that she is repulsed by emotionalism . . . therefore, if she observes me being enthusiastic or tearful, or intense, she feels squeamish & skeptical of the realness of my expression. There is nothing I can say to convince her – eventually she will learn that it is consistently me – even though she may not like it, she may learn a tolerance and hopefully an affectionate tolerance someday.

I'm so full of emotion now, I can't write anymore but I felt impelled to answer you immediately from the top of my head. Thank you for being the concerned, loving person you are.

As always, love
Mom

Brooke Jacobson and her daughters Babette and Marlene, 1976

Brooke Jacobson spent the 1960s being a wife and mother and campaigning against nuclear arms and the Vietnam War. When her marriage broke down, she and her three children (Jeff, Babette and Marlene), chose to live collectively, inviting other friends to share their home. Some of these were women in similar circumstances who came together after separating from their husbands to help one another meet financial and emotional needs.

Brooke organised and obtained funding for a regional film centre at the Portland Art Museum and then set up an organisation of independent film and video makers, the Northwest Media Project. In 1976 she decided she needed a change and began discussing plans to move from Portland, Oregon, to Los Angeles. Her daughters were then 17 and 16. They had had years of experience in living with groups of people, not as children but as members of co-operative households, and they supported Brooke's decision to move.

Brooke now works as a lab technician in neurobiological research on ageing while she is earning her MA in Cinema History and Criticism. She also writes poetry and film criticism. Babette and Marlene work in Portland: Babette continues to take classes in science as part of a pre-Med programme, and has begun performing with a group of musicians; Marlene is an apprentice baker with a dream of having her own business.

During the years since Brooke's move they have all written frequent long letters, reporting the details of daily life and their goals for the future. These first two letters were written in the first six months after Brooke left; both Babette and Marlene were at school part-time and had part-time jobs:

October 1976

Dearest Brooke,

Probably I haven't said to you anything about what an inspiration you are for me. When I find myself in trouble I only have to think back on advice you have given and I say, 'now here's something solid'. I do that more and more lately. Especially now that I am thinking about school. You know Evergreen College sent me an application for admission and also a questionnaire. My first look at it scared me off. Well, I thought about it for a while and was amazed to find that I had a little courage tucked away somewhere. I thought, after all, it wasn't any worse than writing the letter to Adams Highschool or applying to Rogue for the horseshoeing program or any number of other things that you have encouraged me to do. I must stop and thank you now, while I am thinking about it. Actually the questionnaire is really neat. They send a little letter that says they want only students who are going to work hard and have an understanding of what the college is all about, and are willing to work within that framework. At first I was put off, but then I realized this was a chance to really outline my goals. As I began to do that I realized I *do* know what I want from them and pretty much what I want from myself. Not meaning to put myself down, just saying that some of my goals are not quite clear yet. What I want from school is a chance to bring all my ideas together and start constructing a base for learning. I want to start expanding in a way that I haven't in the past. I have come to think that I really am capable of dealing with academics. It might have been the reading of *Summerhill** that made it really clear to me. Neill says that his students had enough confidence that they didn't need to learn what they didn't want until they were ready and saw a need for it. It's true that I can do anything with some confidence. I have been feeling more and more confident in myself, and most things look easy. Not only do they look easy, they are easy. The point is that you concentrate on what you do know or can do, and the things that you don't know or can't do seem less important and can be easily dealt with when they come up – or maybe aren't worth worrying about. Not that I've conquered it all yet, but I have a happier outlook . . .

Marlene and I have made the decision to move . . . As far as I can

---

*Summerhill was an 'experiment in freedom' founded by A.S. Neill in 1921. This self-governing school was non-hierarchical: students and staff had equal rights and equal responsibilities for running the school.

see, nothing but money could stand in our way, and that won't be a problem. I finally broke down and gave Marlene and myself a big lecture. We've just gotten too irresponsible and lazy. We make up too many excuses and rationalizations. I'll have no more of it from myself or Marlene. From now on everything is going to work within the framework of getting things done. You might as well be doing something when you're unhappy; it gives you less to be unhappy about. There are so many changes to make and somebody's got to take control. I've decided to delegate myself that position because no one else is going to do it. Marlene will when she gets on her feet again. I may be a little arrogant, but I've decided to just play it as I see it.

Well – wish us luck
love
Babette

P.S. It's very early morning and lovely to be up.

September 1976

Dearest Brooke,

. . . I'm at my first class on the first day of school in the highschool completion program . . . I feel differently about school this time around. I want to really get into it and get to know people. I feel more capable of doing that now and it feels good. I have been doing Transactional Analysis and Gestalt Therapy. It was very hard for me to stay in touch with my feelings. I can't remember any of my childhood from 0–6. If you have any information that might be helpful, let me know . . .

The instructor in this class seems to have a good attitude toward learning. He is very easy-going. The class should be fun. Maybe I will get over my fear of talking in class, and also my fear of not knowing what I am talking about. I have so many fears and really want to overcome them all. I am so excited about it. Me and my self-development . . . I still don't know what I want to do in the future, but I don't have to make a decision right now anyway.

I have tried to write you three times before this. I have so much to say and I didn't know how to say it all. The YWCA has a stop-smoking clinic this term. I am going to do it. It is a $27.00 life investment I have made and happens one week in October. I have to figure out how to fit it into my schedule. I might have to take time off to do it . . . I have such a full schedule: piano lessons, counselling, school and work.

Well, this is all I'm going to try to write for now.

Did you get the birthday card we sent?

love,
Marlene

On the eve of her fifth anniversary of moving to Los Angeles, Brooke wrote a letter to Babette, now 22:

. . . A few nights ago I was going through my box of letters, now overflowing with five years of shared experiences and good wishes. I began, inevitably, to reread the contents. I was impressed all over again, as I read your and Marlene's letters, with how supportive and loving you were to me in that period of transition when I left home. As I think about it I know that the love was very old and deep, but I was most aware of it and glad for it in that time of creating a new life in a new city. The funny thing about this is that I still carry a burden of guilt – something I feel must be inherent in motherhood – which has to do with the notion that somehow, as a parent, I never took enough time or gave enough love or security to make your lives perfect. But the wonderful thing I see in reading your letters is that in spite of all that, here you both are, young women, seemingly far more conscious than I at your age, generating love, being supportive, evaluating every experience and gaining wisdom at every step . . .

Sometimes I want to forget about love and just stay with the business of writing poems or doing whatever needs to be done around me . . . As a mother I would like more than anything to be an example: I still look for some unique contribution I can make to this world. For you that may be veterinary medicine or singing or training horses – or all three of those. For Marlene it may be music or acting or something she has yet to discover for herself . . .

Best of luck and much love,
Brooke

CHAPTER SIX

Loving Women

*. . . sisterhood, like female friendship, has at
its core the affirmation of freedom.*
Mary Daly, GynEcology (1978)

The letters in this chapter are part of a long tradition of mothers and daughters writing to each other about how they love women. For centuries women's letters have described the joys of female companionship, the comfort and tenderness of women friends in times of distress and the durability of their close female friendships throughout their lives, even after marriage or during long separations. It is only since the early part of the twentieth century that the love of women for women has become somewhat of a taboo and mothers and daughters have felt that they must step gingerly around the subject.*

Even though the first person we love is a woman (our own mother), it is usually a surprise for a mother to be told that her daughter is a lesbian – that her deepest love and commitment is directed towards women and that she chooses to have sexual relationships with women; it may equally well be surprising for a daughter to discover that her mother is a lesbian. As girls grow up there is great pressure to switch our affection to men; relationships between women are seen mainly as competitive, catty, transitory and secondary. This denigration of women's capacity for loving friendship makes it difficult for us to value our bonds with other women and contributes to a negative image of what it is to be a woman: it does not help us to love and respect our mothers or ourselves. Loving women means reclaiming our appreciation of women, including our mothers and daughters. It means feel-

---

*See Rosenberg, 'The Female World of Love and Friendship in Nineteenth Century America', and Faderman, *'Surpassing the Love of Men: Romantic Friendship and Love Between Women from the Renaissance to the Present*, for numerous examples of correspondence between mothers and daughters, sisters and friends in which the love of women for women is celebrated.

ing proud to be a woman and taking delight in how strong, loving and courageous women are – and always have been.

The letters here are in many ways a departure from the earlier tradition of mother-daughter letters on the subject of loving women because today women all over the world are working and playing together in new ways in order to change the world – so that every woman can feel excited and hopeful about her own life and confident about the possibilities for fulfillment in the lives of her mother, daughters, friends and sisters.

Katy and her mother Marta, 1979

Marta was born and raised in Russia. She moved to England in the 1920s, and her first daughter was born there during the Depression. Her second daughter, Katy, was a 'mistake' twenty years later. Marta divorced her husband when she was 46 and Katy was 6; she married Alan, who became a loving stepfather to Katy. Alan died a year before these letters were written. Marta now lives alone but surrounded by friends, and is much depended on by her family.

Katy is now a doctor and works as a general practitioner in the north of England. She describes some of the changes in her relationship with her mother over the years:

'Through my increasing involvement in the women's liberation movement I was reconsidering everything about myself around the time when I wrote this letter. I eventually realised the necessity and found the strength to commit myself to joining a political party; I joined the Communist Party, knowing that there is no 'perfect' party but feeling that struggle from within is better than waving banners from the sidelines.

'This was difficult for Mum, even though she is always a staunch supporter and defender of the position of the Soviet Union because she realises that for the majority of people things have vastly improved since 1917. Although she is a socialist in many ways she cannot forget the horrors and bloodshed of the revolution and civil war which she lived through, and 'communism' is irrevocably associated in her mind with violent struggle, which is something she cannot come to terms with.

'These letters marked the beginning of us both trying to be more honest with each other. We have managed to become close friends. She now feels proud that she has come to a position of strength and independence, to an active enjoyment of life at the age of 71 – despite traumas in her early years. Since writing them two years ago she has come to accept me more for what I am and I hope I have become less arrogant. I now realise that, although my mother had custody over me, throughout my childhood she felt insecure because my dad constantly threatened to "take me away". My childhood was a tug of war which climaxed with me getting anorexia when I was seventeen.

'Alan was, in many ways, the love of my life despite the fact that I never saw a great deal of either him or Mum as I was away at school and lived with my dad for a lot of my childhood. I did not realise until later how much Mum felt excluded by the closeness between Alan and me. His death and Mum's courage and determination to survive made me suddenly notice her, as if for the first time.'

At the time when these letters were written Katy was helping to set up a Well Woman Clinic and was active in the struggle over abortion rights nationally and locally:

Mother's Day, 1979

Dear Mum

. . . I felt very close to you while I was living at home for three months . . . in fact in a way it was quite difficult to get over this feeling that one should be 'breaking away' from one's parents – at the same time it was really exciting to get on well with you because I feel you *are* an important person to me – quite apart from being biologically my mother. This feeling has grown in me because of my increasing involvement in the women's movement. This is because I now see women as important and powerful people and I see how much we have to struggle to get what we want. You have always been a very independent person and although you got sucked into marriage at 18 in the end you had the strength to defy society and social pressures and do what you wanted, i.e. marry Alan even though it involved personal hardship and humiliation at the time. The fact that we both loved Alan a lot will always hold us very close.

Also you have always made an effort to form your own opinions and stick up for them despite having had no formal education and moving in a world where education is all-powerful. Another thing I like about you is that you are very simple and honest and are not afraid to stick your neck out.

I suppose I was most surprised when I had my abortion last year that it was not me but *you* who was so sad about it, not because of the fact of the abortion but because you wanted to have a grandchild and I hadn't realised how my not wanting to marry and/or have children had affected you and even hurt you. I think you realised (as I did) that getting pregnant and having an abortion was for me a final statement about not wanting kids, about not wanting a one-to-one relationship with a man and about the way I want to live my life. Often one finds out about what one wants to do only by doing things one doesn't want to do!

In a way I have continually shocked you gently about the things I am involved with and the way I am but you have always absorbed it well and tried to understand, and I believe wherever my sexuality eventually comes to rest that you do not find lesbianism so awful and ghastly as when we first started talking about it.

Perhaps the only thing I blame you for is not fighting for me in relation to dad and my stepmother when I was in my teens. I see my anorexia as a kind of desperate protest because I really suffered for many years amidst a wealth of material comfort – but being torn apart spiritually and mentally. At the same time I know you were concerned and hurt by it all and were only trying to do what was best. *And* as I said before, even that has a really positive side because I feel much stronger having worked through anorexia and depression to discover what I didn't want in life (to be a deb, to marry someone with money and 'class' as my stepmother wanted) and to explore what I do want.

To be a woman alone is exciting and frightening but now in the women's movement I have many sisters and you are one who I love very much.

Love,
Katy

[1979]

[Dear Katee]

Your letter, dear Katee, is an admirable composition – or is it because this is what you want to get out of your system? Or perhaps such letters are something we all want to get out of our systems? Anyway, mine is – you know well how much I can't help my feelings towards you – you are my love child conceived when I was already old. You were a specially lovely baby (lovable and cuddly and so perfect). I was surprised! And it was love at first sight!! Accompanying this love was dreadful uncertainty, never knowing whether I would not lose you for ever – such were and probably still are the legal complications of divorce. It does not need imagination, just very simple psychology, to explain my attachment to you.

I understand your feelings. There is nothing more irritating than 'love' from the 'wrong' person, hovering over one, and breathing down one's neck – Even though I pretend to be indifferent or detached, instinctively you know, I worry about you.

I hated the idea of your boarding school – but against your Father, I had no choice. I did not want you to have a scientific career, but against Alan, I had no choice. Naturally, with my background, sciences and intellectual achievements were and still remain mysteries and in a way contribute to a further separation between us. You know how it was with me. I only learned to read when I was 11 years old.

That is why it hurts when I detect your arrogance – it makes me feel a third-class citizen in your very modern world; which quite a lot I don't understand and some of which I disapprove.

It hurts too when I think Alan never really understood how I felt about you, and nightmarish, when even being so close to a man it was impossible to explain oneself. But your clever and jealous stepmother realised that the best way to hurt me was to hurt you.

On one occasion when she had been particularly cruel to you and I was desperately upset, Alan said, 'Don't worry she will never win Kate over – behaving as she does'. He could not see that all I wanted was for her to replace me somehow so that you could be happy not 'tortured' – I say 'tortured' because that is how I was every time you were made to go to Scotland to be with them.

Now all this is in the past. Your life is in your own hands. My advice is better kept to myself. Again, I think it would only cause misunderstanding. It's good to think that we are not totally remote and still communicate reasonably well. Old age has its advantages. No way, over you or about you, can I be hurt as I used to be . . .

With all my loving
Mum

Sarah to her mother Elizabeth, 1980

Sarah was born and raised in England, in a Roman Catholic working-class family. She married soon after completing her degree at Bristol University and has been a primary-school teacher for the past twelve years. She writes:

'My mother sees herself as an ordinary housewife. Her husband's and children's needs automatically came first throughout her life and she lived vicariously through the lives of my brothers and myself as we progressed from school to University.

'I always assumed I had disappointed my mother by moving away from the small town I was raised in, and not producing her grandchildren in a cosy, conventional marriage. And then there we were, in the small hours, during her visit to my "strange" communal house in the city, discussing sexuality, dope-smoking and lesbianism. My mother is not an intellectual and the discussions were the more powerful because they were so personal, honest and emotional. I felt, in my 36th year, that I finally had to take responsibility for my life – I could no longer totally lay the blame for my difficulties as an adult on the way I'd been brought up and, as I saw it, repressed.

'Also, one of my "problems" had been in the area of sexuality, and to find my own mother looking to me for advice and support in an area I was so unsure about myself, really was a role reversal. My grandmother died tragically when my mother was just entering adolescence and this left her with no model for dealing with a teenage daughter – a fact I'd never fully appreciated.

'This letter represents my tribute to her for being who she is – and for the courage she has given me to be who I am despite the differences between us.'

Sarah's letter forms part of a longer correspondence, initiated by Elizabeth's request for some information on sexual problems following menopause.

Elizabeth's doctor had been singularly unhelpful, probably because of his 'inbuilt prejudice against mothers being sexual women' (which is how Sarah later described her own attitude). After the GP had told Elizabeth that she'd better learn to live with painful intercourse (perhaps for the rest of her life), she wrote to Sarah who had been active in organising local courses and discussions on women's health. Sarah replied by answering her mother's questions. She then wrote the following letter, wanting to tell her mother how moved she was by their dialogue. Two years later, she still hasn't sent it. She writes, 'Unfortunately, overwhelmed by the intensity of my feelings, and, more crucially, afraid of setting a precedent for a new level of intimacy between us, I wrote the letter only in my private journal, and was never able to find the courage to send it. The remaining traces of adolescent rebellion prevented me from allowing my mother to know how close she was to me at that time:'

February 1980

Dearest Mum,

I was very touched by your letter. For years I've paid lip service to the notion of 'sisterhood', whilst applying it selectively to women who were 'like me'. Now I feel closer to understanding that we're all (even our mothers) sisters under the skin.

I want you to know how much I value our new relationship. I feel a closeness and tenderness towards you in my new role of 'researcher on Women's Health' and supporter during personal difficulties, which is akin to 'motherliness'.

We're so alike, in many ways, which made the years from my adolescence onwards so fraught for both of us. Perceiving myself as no longer a 'teenager' makes me feel that I'm on the same side of the river as you now, having struggled across, refusing all your offers of help, or advice, along with your (and Dad's) over-protective measures, as I saw them. God help me if I'm ever faced with an adolescent daughter – I hope you'll still be going strong and able to remind me of my own rebellion.

I do think ours is an unusually honest family relationship – certainly for me, the only 'real' relationship with anyone outside my own generation. It's not so much that I have broken my self-imposed boundaries on suitable topics of conversation between mother and daughter. You not only didn't freak out when you heard about my experiences of extra-marital sexual activities (some bisexual), pot-smoking, abortion, communal living, psychotherapy, and sexuality (even masturbation!), but genuinely accepted and supported me in whatever my chosen activities because of your unshakeable faith in me. That did more to help me to come to terms with myself and my chosen lifestyle than any therapy.

I'd blamed you (along with religion) for my hangups for so long, that, when you suddenly gave me permission to be myself, with no danger of losing your love, I was thrown off balance. I marvelled at how matter-of-factly you dealt with all the mind-blowing information I was feeding you. It was as if I had to tell you my worst excesses in order to test your love for me.

When you applied the new level of interpersonal honesty to yourself and opened up to me about your sexual problems, *I* was the embarrassed one, with my inbuilt prejudice against mothers being sexual women. I'm impressed that you can be so open with me, particularly as you've had so much more sheltered a life than me. I'm proud of you, proud that you're the person you are, despite fears of repression from your own parents, that you're so receptive to the new ideas I blast you with, and proud that you produced me, the way I am, which is how *I* want to be (most of the time!).

love,
Sarah

Leslie to her mother Eunice, 1979–80

Eunice was born during the Depression and was married in 1955. She lives with her husband in southern California and works part-time as a salesperson in a department store. She has one daughter, Leslie, and a son.

Leslie was born and raised in southern California. At the time of these letters she was living in San Francisco, where she wrote poetry, fiction, journals and letters and taught a journal-writing class at the Women's Building while working full-time as a typesetter. She has since moved to France where she studies French at the University of Clermont-Ferrand and teaches English to adults and children. She is co-founder of the Mariposa Press, a small collective which emerged from the Feminist Writers Guild. Leslie comments on the letters below, which she wrote over a fifteen-month period:

'What transpires between mothers and daughters is such a telling indication of our awareness as women – in all the pain, anger and love. During the time these letters were written, I came out as a lesbian and became more committed in my writing and radical politics. All the indications of my changes lie as seeds in the first letter, becoming a reality later. That letter was written after a visit in which I had introduced my mother to some of my lesbian friends. All during that visit I was trying to find some connection between my life and my mother's; it was a frustrating meeting, the beginning of my awareness of the widening gap between us.'

4 January 1979

Dear Mother,

(How different it feels to address you only!

How marvellous it feels to address you only!) . . .

I have been reading a wonderful book in the last week entitled *Of Woman Born* by Adrienne Rich, in which she explores the complexities of being a mother, both in personal, artistic terms, and in terms of how mothers are viewed in this society. She speaks with a clarity that I find rare amongst women speaking of their experiences as mothers as well as their experiences as daughters. One chapter in particular – her chapter on mothers and daughters – speaks to the core of myself. I found myself taking notes, writing down certain sentences from the chapter, then writing about their relationship to you, and before I knew it, I had at least four pages of scribbled handwriting which has elucidated much of how I feel towards you, much about the complex, emotionally-charged, wonderful, painful relationship called mothers and daughters.

How to begin? Maybe with your visit a few weeks ago. I learned much from that visit about my false delusions, about my love for you, about the pain involved, about the patterns which we follow that have been reinforced for years in our relationship. In the last year or so, with my growing awareness of myself as a woman, I have also begun to examine our relationship, to acknowledge it, in ways that I had never been encouraged to do . . . I have recently met many women, women I could admire and identify with. To talk about our mothers, to write about our mothers, to *honor* our mothers, has been a great liberating experience.

But one that has also taught me honesty.

I suppose what I learned the most from the weekend when you came to visit is how different we really are, yet how alike. And how painful the differences are for me. From very early, when I was a teenager, I knew that I was going to carve a different life for myself. I knew I wouldn't be satisfied with marriage or children. At first, I was afraid that I was selfish, that I was doing something taboo, unspoken, unfeminine. I felt this acutely when I was in high school. To be the only woman in the school who held these values, the only woman who would dare speak up for herself, who knew that there was something 'better' out there, who refused to be defined by football coaches and cheerleaders, was very difficult (when I look back, I don't know how I made it through). And who could I turn to? Although you and Dad never discouraged me from speaking my mind, from doing what I wanted to do, I also didn't feel that someone was rooting on my side. Maybe you weren't aware of how difficult the struggle really was . . . And it was in high school that I first began to realize that one way for me to deal with all these complex emotions, all these struggles, was through art. For I am learning as a writer, that art is not only a certain way of structuring one's day – it doesn't only mean a book, or a film, or a pen and paper – it is an entire response to life. One filled with commitment, with determination, with beauty, with ugliness.

With struggle. For me, being a woman has not meant 'having it easy'. It has not meant passivity, vacillation, weakness. It has been full of struggle. The most courageous people I have ever known have all been women. And I don't mean courage in the sense of flying the first plane over the Atlantic, or climbing Mt. Everest, or becoming a military hero. For me, courage means being able to change the patterns of our lives, recognizing the faults and the beauty in our lives and always going beyond the limitations that others have imposed upon us. It means being black and poor and working eight hours a day, raising three children without any support. It means leaving Russia as a teenager and coming over to America by steerage. It means having an abortion when there are no facilities to make it safe, legal, recognized. It means giving birth to a child, alone. It means living the existence so many of us must live, day in and day out, doing what we can.

The possibilities for women's lives have expanded in the past decade as they never have before. It's still hard and far from perfect. But I am aware of the possibilities: I am aware of my own power as a woman, as a human being; I am aware of my potential to change the patterns around me; I am aware of my capacity to love, to nurture, to act. As Adrienne Rich has written, speaking of what a mother can do for a daughter, 'The most important thing one woman can do for another is to illuminate and expand her sense of actual possibilities . . . It means that the mother herself is trying to expand the limits of her life. To refuse to be a victim: and then to go on from there.' It hurts me, it pains me, to see you give up sometimes. It hurts because I know how it must hurt you. It hurts because I know you get very little support for yourself; you have always been so generous in supporting, in nurturing others. It hurts because you are my mother and I still look up to you as an example, for strength, for advice. And if after an afternoon's walk, after a phone conversation, I seem unusually silent, it's because I'm processing the pain, it's because I do not know what to say. What can *I* say? What advice can *I* give you? I, who have grown up in another decade; I, who am living a very independent life with plenty of women friends of different ages and backgrounds, who are transforming their lives and those around them? What advice can I give you? What can I say to you over the phone when you tell me about Dad's depressions or Aunt Ellen's bitchiness or your disgust with your job? So many times I feel myself lecturing to you, when I don't want to. Or else I will say something that will purposely shock you ('I will never have children' or 'I will never get married'). Like a rebellious child (do we ever get over our own adolescence?). But I think the first step for me is to not feel threatened, and I think I can do that by acknowledging the different life I have chosen for myself, and acknowledging it to you. Without harsh words, without fear.

I am learning to understand you, to love you, without having to *become* you. Without having to have a boyfriend, and pretend we're playing house, thinking that is one way to understand you and therefore, understand myself. I will never understand you through a man. Yes, men bring up certain patterns in myself that remind me of you: that nurturing, tolerance, that you have expressed with Dad for years that I admire, that I know I have the capacity for. But I also learn what I do not like in you (and how painful it is for me to even suggest that I may not like certain things in you; how different *like* is from *love*), and I have a harder time accepting those things if I do them unwillingly. I must be myself. And that means acknowledging what I have inherited from you, and acknowledging what I have inherited from others.

I love you deeply, Mom. And if it's been hard for me to show you my affection physically, it's because of what I had always thought of my body, what images I had been bombarded with in school. It has taken me many years to understand how I feel about my body and what I admire about a woman's body. I have always had difficulty in accepting the traditional role of women as fashionable, as images, as something to look at only.

And then there are times when I feel attracted to you, for you are my mother, for I lived in your body for nine months, for you held me at your breast, bathed me, fed me, changed me. There are times, like the last night when you were here, that I wanted to crawl out of my bed and into yours, to lie next to your body, feel its warmth, as I did when I was a child.

Mother, this is a new age for both of us. For the first time, we can be proud of being women, we can define ourselves anyway we want. We can struggle together. We have a long history behind us of grand-mothers, and great-grandmothers and great-great-grandmothers. We can change the lives around us by not expecting others to relate to us as they always have. We can find support for our new lives. We are beautiful. We are strong.

Mother, I love you, and may we always be able to acknowledge the mother and the daughter in each of us.

Love,
Leslie

'My mother replied saying how much she loved my letter and looked forward to hearing more. I wrote again, after a visit home during which I was still attempting to understand my mother and thus get a clue into myself. On that visit I also saw how much my father affects my mother. Lately I have felt more critical of him, of his self-brooding over his unhappiness at work; his lack of belief in himself; his inability to pull himself out of his own problems. His feelings about himself were always a burden to my mother and me. Yet, at the same time, he displayed a sensitivity, a love of solitude, of knowledge, of classical music, of humor, that I loved and learned from. He was always the tolerant one, more so than my mother. I wonder now, if he had spoken up more, would I have loved or hated him? Being partially invisible, he was not subject to the same criticism from me as my mother. He was not so easy a target.'

27 December 1979

To my dearest mother –

This morning I awoke with an image, a memory, of you in your blue leotard and tights, dancing in the living room the last night I was home. When I was watching you from the armchair, I suddenly saw a different Eunice. I saw you before you met Dad, before you had two children. I saw you dancing, before the onset of responsibilities, before the limitations of those responsibilities (even though they have brought you great joy, certain facets of yourself must have changed when you got married, when you had children). For once, I didn't see you as the parent or the wife, but as the woman, yourself, unfettered by any lack of confidence or distrust. You were yourself that night, dancing in the living room, joyous, spontaneous, full of life, smiling.

I couldn't tell you all of that then, because the event was so strong that I couldn't speak. I just sat back in the chair and smiled. It was only later, when I got back to Berkeley and wrote it down in my journal, that I realized its significance.

When I think of the things you have told me in the last year or so, especially concerning how you feel about yourself – your fears, your feelings of inadequacy, of not being as good as those around you – I think of this memory of you dancing. You must trust your dancing self more . . . the joyous self, the one who loves people (for I truly do believe you love people and you love being around them). Yes, I think Dad is different, his sense of achievement seems to come from a more private place, or else one filled with chores, tasks. Maybe these years of living together have dampened your enthusiasm in some ways. You and Dad have cloistered yourselves in the last few years, attending fewer and fewer social engagements, but I think when you do this, you are not getting in touch with your main strength, your own power.

It is frightening to get in touch with your power, to really acknowledge your strengths, to stop hiding from others. We were taught always to care for others before we care for ourselves. Even though this was never consciously said to me from you, I still picked it up from watching you as you picked it up from Grandma, who seems to be the supreme example in our family of someone who always needed the love of others but in a very dependent way. By being *needed* by them, she knew they would love her, but this prevented her from being herself, I think. I really don't think she was that way deep down and I believe this because I feel it whenever I go to visit her. I get mixed messages, one being how sweet and wonderful I am (the old Grandma, always praising, up to her old routine), but then the other message is go out and live your life and don't let anyone or anything stop you, goddamn it. I remember her telling me once not to get married for a long time and I was shocked. Even though I was never one for marriage, or at least not in the traditional sense. But for her to say that meant something – some realization that she has come to, which has nothing to do with Grandpa as a person because she knows he's wonderful – but has to do with what never was developed after she got married, some other sense of self that she sacrificed in taking care of everyone else. And then finally, it all caught up with her and her body reacted with a stroke. I think this is what happened on a deep level, and it's important for me to discover this, because I think I, too, have this 'martyr' quality in me, of pushing myself very hard, even of pleasing others for fear of being rejected.

That's it: the fear of being rejected, of being criticized, of failing, of falling flat on our faces. So we let others live for us, let them get all the criticism, the failure, but also they get all the praise, the experience, the life, while we sit and watch them.

We have to stop being spectators, Mother. We have to stop letting our kids, our husbands, our friends, live our lives for us while we remain the nurturers, the supporters. We need to live our lives too, to get out there, to trust our inner selves more, to trust our survival skills. (When I read oral histories of Jewish women who came over from Russia,* I am amazed. That is *our* history, these women survived. We have this in ourselves too). We have to stop being afraid of hurting others, of taking something away from them because we are strong, because we become assertive, because we become ourselves. And the thing is that if we decided not to sacrifice ourselves for someone, they probably wouldn't hate us. I think we are more afraid of being labeled a Bad Mother, a Bad Wife, a Bad Woman. Bad, bad, bad. That's how we are portrayed in literature, on television, in the newspapers. Only recently are women portrayed as anything other than sex symbols or mothers. But we have a strength that we were born with, a strength that has nothing to do with the role most women have in this society.

---

*'I really don't know much about these women who were my ancestors, except that they had to deal with tremendous difficulties in Russia – pogroms, emigration, etc. My grandmother's mother left Russia, came to New York, raised five children and died of a brain tumor. When I look at her photograph, I see a very sturdy yet unsmiling woman. That's all I know about her.'

We have just been brainwashed to believe we are weak, ineffective, stupid, clumsy, ugly.

I tell you all this, Mother, because the part that you are always telling me about – that Eunice who doesn't think she's worth anything – is not the Eunice I remember when I was growing up. You are really very strong, sure of yourself, confident, doing a million things, optimistic, able to give of yourself, to love others freely, to trust people enough to talk to strangers, and they knew you would listen and they would tell you their stories. You also were probably more sure of your role then – as mother and wife – whereas now, the mother role doesn't have to be as strong and I think this is what is confusing you . . .

I understand that you feel doubts about me: I think this is a difficult time because the times are changing and allowing new growth for me. Maybe you have a fear of me outgrowing you in some ways, of doing things that you want to do but haven't been able to. But you don't have to do it in my way, just like I don't have to do it in yours. As much as we are mother and daughter – and we are very much mother and daughter, each of us changing roles back and forth – we are also Eunice and Leslie, two individual women, with different ideas and strengths. If we can only stop being afraid of hurting each other, of disappointing each other . . .

I think you and I are really growing, that our individual growth is going to show in our relationship. Perhaps we can stop being afraid of being Bad Mothers, or Bad Daughters. You are my mother, sometimes you become my daughter. I love you very much. I believe in your strengths, I accept your weaknesses. You have given me a trust in the world, in myself, that I will always be grateful for, but that trust came from you, within you. You believe it in yourself too. It's time to mother yourself for a change, to not be so quick to comfort others when you need the comfort. If people aren't listening to you you should go where they care. You are worthy of yourself, of this world. You are my mother, sometimes my daughter, and I think of you this morning, beside the frosted window and the clear blue sky.

Love,
Leslie

'The third letter was written after another visit home in which I told her I was a lesbian. The visit was a very painful one and the anger I felt towards my mother startled me. I was also hurt by the irony that my deepest connections are with other women, yet this produced such a gap in my relationship to my first woman lover, my mother.

'The anger I felt after I came out was linked, I believe now, to the realization that I didn't have to be the good or understanding daughter any more. Up until that time, I listened to many of my parents' problems but this became increasingly difficult to do, especially when my mother talked about her reluctance to deal with my being a lesbian. I refused to feel that I was "disappointing" her or that there was a "cause" to my being the way I was (i.e., bad relationships with men, or that I was encouraged by friends to be a lesbian, etc.). I was also less willing to attend large family functions and my mother thought I was cutting myself off from the family . . . I found after coming out that I could accept my anger towards my mother; ironically, coming out has helped me to make the separation from my family, to let them live their own lives and me mine.

'My father's response to my lesbianism is not all that clear to me. He was the one who used to ask me why I never talked about men, yet when I came out to my parents, he was also the one to say, "I can see how two women can love each other as much as a man and a woman." He seems to have been much more accepting of my lesbianism – he encouraged my mother to go with him to a Parents of Gays meeting. Yet, he doesn't have the same emotional investment in my growth as my mother does. Underneath what he says, I don't know what he feels. Perhaps rejection. I don't know.'

5 April 1980

Dear Mom –

Sunshine after the rain, this illuminated valley, people walking their dogs, cars speed by the corner . . . it's nice to be back at this desk, back in my room with all its familiar things. I have the house to myself to relax, to think about what I have experienced in the last few months, to draw some conclusions (if any – really, there is only understanding), be prepared for the next round, Spring, a new roommate, my unemployment coming to an end, all these things . . .

Mother, to reassure you that I love you, that I don't envision breaking my tie with you. How could I? We have a very close relationship and there are bound to be ups and downs. We haven't fought much in the last few years and perhaps things are coming out now. It's only natural that there be anger or impatience. Maybe because we aren't used to it, it seems more jarring, traumatic. But I believe it's healthy for it to come out.

As for my life, well, it's my life, it's different from yours and Dad's and that's all there is to it. I made a choice, I will always be changing, trying new things, searching deeper within myself for meaning, that's what I've always done. With all the pain I've experienced in the last few months, there has been a lot of happiness too: learning that I'm not an island, that there is more to life than isolation, or this daily nine-to-five existence . . .

The trip down was a hard one for me. I don't think you nor Dad fully understood what I had gone through up here and it was probably mistaken of me to think you would, but I really needed a vacation. My skins were unpeeled and I was very vulnerable. Everyone has reassured me that coming home after coming out as a lesbian is not easy, will bring up a lot of emotions for everyone involved. I guess I just refused to bridge the gap between my life up here and what I grew up with. It's too hard on me, Mom.

I love you and Dad very much, you know that. I don't know if I would do it the same way next time, maybe I'll have to spend more time with my friends. I hope you understand this.

What separation and distance becomes apparent, much pain in this, remembering your tears and anger, that my loving women has brought up the gap between us, such bitter irony for we have always loved each other.

Wounds split open and the possibility for healing with time.

Love,
Leslie

Susan Abbott and her mother Miriam, 1980

Susan Abbott was raised in Massachussetts, the eldest of four daughters. Her father left the family when she was 4 and her mother has always worked full-time as a nurse to support the family. Susan now lives in San Francisco and works as a hospital clerk. Her poetry has been published in several feminist journals, including *Sojourner* and *So's Your Old Lady*. At the time when these letters were written, she was a student at San Francisco State University.

In deciding to have the letters with her mother published, she analysed some of the reasons for writing them and breaking ten years of silence on the subject of her lesbianism:

'I was prodded by a question Muriel Rukeyser had raised in her teaching at the Women Writers' Center seminar. She asked, "What is/was unspoken in your house?" She also spoke of the job of the poet, the writer, to say what is difficult, to voice the unspoken – and so I began to look closer at what those things were in my own life. I decided on a letter – because it would make me sit down and work out the best way to express it all. It was clarifying for me to write it first, and later talk about it with my mother . . .

'Part of me thought that if I could come out to my mother I would be able to say anything to anyone – that it would give me that much courage. Ha! That has not proved the case. There are still difficult things to speak of and in each individual situation the fact of having come out to my mother doesn't make it any easier . . . However, I now have an awareness and a willingness to take risks which her supportive response has encouraged.'

The letters included here are excerpts from much longer letters which were interspersed with family news, information about Miriam's job situation and financial difficulties, and the discrimination which she experienced as a middle-aged woman. Susan and Miriam wrote frequently during this time and quickly answered each other's points from the previous letter. When sending in the most recent batch of letters, Susan said: 'The way things are going, I look forward to her letters the way some people look forward to the latest installments of their favorite soap operas.'

23 February 1980

Dear Mom,

. . . Right now I'm in the process of writing my proposal and justification for the Women Writers' Center [which] I intend to develop while I do my MA. This is making me think about the importance of reading, writing and literature in my life, in the lives of other women, images of women characters portrayed, how they affect who we become, who we have become as a result of this – many of us lonely, isolated from each other. And this is what's so unnecessary, the loneliness, fear and trepidation we have of one another. In the past three or four years, writing a lot for college has gotten me more into the habit of writing for myself – to get over my fear of the word – what it will tell, what it will do.

. . . I've been excited by what I've seen in my classes focusing on women writing; each of us coming to voice, redressing lies, history, silence, so-called secrets, making the 'private' public – in attempts to help us out of our isolation from ourselves, each other.

I should tell you that in journal class the other day, we talked about letters (like this one); how relationships develop (or don't) through the exchange of letters. The speaker we had was specifically interested in relationships with our mothers vis-à-vis letters. We meditated for five minutes in class and then she had us write in our journals, a dictation: 'Dear Mother, what I've always wanted to tell, but haven't been able to . . .'.

I will be so brave as to continue with what I wrote in class: 'More often than not, I love you. I want to tell you about my writing. This is not a need to confess, rather a desire for recognition. I want to tell you more about my writing, about my subject matter, to send you these things. I will. You have asked that I'd tell you if I had anything published . . . I gulped because I had already done that and not told you. This letter may be painful for us both, but no less necessary . . . I am bored with myself in letters telling you how busy I've been with work and college. Surely there is more substance and depth and texture to my life? The same is true for yours. You have inquired about my writing. For the honesty and openness I search for in my own writing, it bothers me that I have been hesitant with you. This is so unnecessary. I think I've had you up on the pedestal, "my mother". I don't like you up there. I want you at my level and much of this letter wants to address you at my level, from the heart.'

So much for what I wrote in class. Does it make sense so far? To continue with 'What I've always wanted to tell you, but haven't been able to . . .' – the unspoken between us, but what I think you know, is that I am a lesbian. Phew! That's said. And why was that so difficult? And why has this been the unspoken between us for so long? Would you guess how long? If you said ten years, more or less, you guessed right. But why this, the unspoken? I think of your scorn for Jane and Jim, the knowledge that they are carrying on a (presumably) sexual relationship outside of the bonds of matrimony. I cringe to think of your scorn at the knowledge that the loving relationships I carry on with women are not just outside with bonds of respectably acceptable 'marriage', but outside the commonly accepted *mores* of mainstream society. To acknowledge to your mother that you are a sexual being, especially with the good Catholic views we were raised with, is not easy, regardless of one's sexual preference. I also have hesitated to tell you this, outside of being scared shitless. I don't expect your approval (though it would be nice), any more than I expected it when I told you when I was moving in with Steven, but there will be your recognition of the fact now.

Who knows, maybe you'll tell me you're a lesbian too? Though I won't hold my breath waiting to hear that one. And why is this saying that I'm a lesbian to you so difficult? I remember telling my three closest friends when I made this discovery about myself – that was a two year process in itself . . .

Also I'm sure that we come at the word 'lesbian' from different angles; most dictionary definitions refer to love between women, but by 'love' they only mean 'sexual practice'. And I mean so much more . . . But why this letter? Why now? I'm feeling like this may be one of the more brave letters I've written, but it's long overdue. I feel like I've been pushing for honesty and intimacy in my other writings, why not here? You've asked about my writing and I don't want to hide . . . Not that what I write is great literature, mind you, but most of my writing assumes a love, a bonding between women. Much of my writing is political, mystical or erotic – which brings up the three things I have been taught to not speak about, ie. sex, politics and religion.

Also I should tell you, in case you haven't guessed – Deedee and I are lovers and that's been for quite some time now. And I feel that it will be that way for some time to come whether we live together or not. We are very close. I like our relationship. It is moving, it is tender, it is fierce. I've learned and grown a great deal in it; learned about what 'relationship' means, the give and take, the fights, the reconciliation, the willingness to work it out, not just run away when there is conflict, the realization of joy in our lives together, in each, in ourselves, the delight, the knowing of our cycles, of sexual passion, of abstinence, always the tenderness, and on top of that, the hows and whys of people's reactions to us – to the fact of women loving women.

Well, have I chewed your ear long enough? I could go on, but I'm tired and I've managed to get out a healthy chunk of 'what I could not tell'. Note that the first thing that came to mind is, I love you.

Along with some of my poetry, I'm enclosing some poetry of Muriel Rukeyser, who has influenced me greatly. My evolution as a poet and as a lesbian is finely intertwined. They are not separate . . . so that when you ask about my writing, my fuller self must be acknowledged to recognize either.

Write soon,
Love, Susan

1 March 1980

Dear Susan,

I received your epistle yesterday. The word epistle meaning, according to Webster – 'formal, didactic, elegant'. It certainly was all of those.

I too am relieved. Yes, I suspected for some time, as you implied . . .

When I visited you in San Francisco, Deedee had been away when I first arrived on Thursday. She returned the following Tuesday. I really enjoyed that first part of the visit. Tuesday night when I heard you ask Deedee if you could sleep in her room that night, I knew. I remember Wednesday morning being down at The Bakery for their speciality. I wanted to scream! I was so upset and couldn't say anything. I wanted to get on the next plane back to Boston that very day. Much of our activities centered around Castro St. – the gay center of San Francisco.

I had such resentments towards Deedee. The few times we were alone together she came out with what I thought were very unkind innuendos about you, I wondered how you couldn't see through her. When I realized how defensive you were about her I kept my mouth shut. But in one of our conversations that subject of gay came up. I remember her saying something about growing into it, with contacts, environment, etc. I remember saying at the time if you did grow into it, it was most likely innate or delayed reaction. Otherwise one wouldn't be that way inclined. The hormone balance in a human being is so delicate that it is not impossible to be a male in a female body and vice versa. I firmly believe it is inborn. The fact that you have such a beautiful relationship with one other person is what it's all about, whether it be male or female.

I was reading your letter at the kitchen table with Gram sitting across from me. I did not panic, over-react, etc. I related to her a synopsis of school and work and travel. I will carefully, not casually, bring up the subject to her. Right now she wouldn't be able to read the letter. I think I will let each of your three sisters read your letter and also Aunt Pat. They will understand much better than my telling them. Otherwise, unless the proper opportunity presents itself I won't blurt it out. At least now it will be easier, now that it is acknowledged between you and me.

No, I'm not a lesbian. I do prefer women relationships, but not to the point of sexuality. Right now, I'm a neuter. It would have to be some real relationship to get involved with a male sex thing. I'm almost positive your father was bisexual. Thirty years ago when I myself was not familiar with all the facets of this it just wasn't spoken of. The way our sex life went I know he got most of his experience in bordellos. No foreplay. He being my first I didn't know except from reading like *The Naked and the Dead*, a World War II story. So my body would demand other kinds of responses which were new to him. He was a womanizer, and *that* I couldn't handle. It was mostly street women. So possibly and more probably you had more of male hormones by birth. What are your thoughts on this aspect?

. . . This was the best time and way for you to tell me that you are a lesbian. I love you and like you say, being honest and real is much more important. Be good to yourself.

Luv,
Ma

12 March 1980

Dear Mom,

Sorry it's taken me awhile to respond. I feel like your letter and the questions you raised require more thought and introspection and I'm not abundant in the time to do them justice yet. Still, I want to thank you, acknowledge your response to my 'epistle'. Yours was quite elegant as well. It made me feel better. One friend of mine told her father she was a lesbian this week – his response was to get up, walk to the toilet and vomit.

As for your hormone theory – according to which, if my father were/is bisexual, thereby being a female inside a male body and you being heterosexual, a woman inside a woman's body – wouldn't I then have more female whatever in me? I don't subscribe to the hormone theory of lesbianism, nor do I believe/feel/think that I am a man inside a woman's body . . . You believe that homosexuality is inborn and I agree with you on that count, to the point that we're all born as sexual beings. I prefer the term sensual beings. I think that we're all born with the sensual/sexual capacity – and I mean in the pleasure sense, not in the reproductive sense. Now, as to what expression that sensuality takes in our intimate relationships – I believe is a matter of socialization and choice.

I don't quite understand your resentments towards Deedee and I don't know what derogatory things she may have said about me (though I know she says them from time to time). No, mother, alas, I am not perfect and the person I live with and love gets to see more of my imperfections than you do at present and so is in a position to make criticisms. Am I sounding defensive again?

. . . Peggy [*one of Susan's sisters*] called the Sunday morning after she had been over to your house and read my letter. I'm glad you shared it with her. It's funny she said she thought I was a lesbian, but didn't know how to ask, thought I might be insulted. Actually, it would have been one of the nicest compliments she could give me. Fear, on both our parts, kept us silent for too long. And once it's out of the bag, it's sort of like this whole other world is opened up to you. Who else is queer? Kids we grew up with! I'm not the only one – even in little 'ole Medford. In a way, it's finding out who and where your people are. The whole Roots number.

Love,
Susan

12 March 1980

Dear Susan,

Along with what I said to you in my last letter, I did not say what courage it took to write it. I did as I said I would: I let your three sisters and Aunt Pat read your letter before I said anything to them. They all agreed it was a beautiful letter – you are still Susan to us. I was finishing writing to you when Gram came down for breakfast. I read the letter to her – I had to explain what lesbian meant. I know, like me, she is sad, but loves you because you are the Susan we have known these past twenty-nine years.

Yes, I am sad. The Wednesday after I received your beautiful letter I picked up the book you mentioned, *Rubyfruit Jungle*. There was a piece in the *Herald* that morning about how they want to make it into a movie comparable to 'Cruising' but are finding it more controversial because of it pertaining to lesbians. So I read *Rubyfruit Jungle*. It was most depressing to me. The opinion of the general public towards lesbians has not changed, as Rita Mae mentioned in her story as of 1977.

If I want to know about you, I want to know through your writings. There's no comparison between you and Rita Mae's lifestyle as far as the beginning is concerned. There is enough written about lesbians in regular novels, fiction, that I have read. I'm not naive about what goes on between a dyke and her femme. You have placed yourself as being on the defensive about this position. It's not an easy life. That is why I feel sad. You will still be my Susan as I know and will always love you.

Well sweetie, write when you can. Be good to yourself,

Luv,
Mom

18 March 1980

Dear Mom,

I received your letter yesterday and I wanted to respond right away. I'm making the effort to carve out some time this morning. I feel responsible about this 'coming out' process and need to explore some of the questions/ideas you raised.

You say *Rubyfruit Jungle* made you sad. I read that book when it first came out in 1973. There were scenes in that book which had me laughing, in stitches. My sadness about the story came from seeing the ignorance and prejudice with which lesbians are treated by the mainstream of society (something I was becoming all too familiar with). As you say, my lifestyle and Rita Mae's are quite different, but I think we share oppressions of a parallel type for loving women. You say 'there is enough written about lesbians in regular novels, fiction that I have read. I'm not naive about what goes on between a dyke and her femme.' I would say that if what you know about lesbians is in 'regular fiction' – that none of them (what books specifically are you referring to?) tell the truth of who we really are. I think this is where my compulsion to write comes from – the need to tell, to educate, to further understanding about women-loving-women in a wholesome, pleasing way. Most 'regular fiction' is written from a sensational, 'look-at-the-perverts' perspective; to sell a book, to make a buck – and those books have very little to say about truth, about furthering understanding. Just the fact that you say you've gotten enough from such books to know what goes on between a 'dyke and her femme', isn't that about all they tell you? Just those two words – dyke and femme – the way (I think) you've used them – conjure up the roles 'male' and 'female', those rules most lesbians I know (myself included) are trying to break away from. What I want are egalitarian relationships; having had years of education observing and developing hierarchical relationships, this is not easy; but it is crucial to at least make the effort, the explorations, to create egalitarian relationships. You must realize (please try to imagine) that there is something so life-giving and pleasurable about being a lesbian, that the risk and censure of the cultural mainstream are small and insignificant in comparison. It has something to do with self-love.

. . . I'm glad that you've shown my letter to my sisters and Aunt Pat. And yes, it took a great deal of courage to write. I'm not so sure where that courage came from. It's amazing how brave we can become egged on by frustration and someone else's positive example. You said you had to explain to Grammy what lesbian meant. I wonder what exactly did your explanation entail. I'll tell you my bottom-line, lowest-common-denominator definition of lesbian so you'll know my point of reference: a lesbian is a woman who has an emotional and/or sexual or affectional preference for women.

As for the making of *Rubyfruit Jungle* – that attempt has been being made for years. But the producers, Hollywood script writers want to change the ending so that Molly Bolt either gets married or commits suicide. It would not do to present to the American public, especially women, that we can exist independent and happily without men as central figures in our lives. The lesson they would like to hammer home – the only good lesbian (read: woman) is a dead woman or a woman surrogate to a man. Rita Mae Brown would not compromise the integrity of her story, her life, the lives of other lesbians to pander to Hollywood to make a buck. She and some independent feminist film makers have been trying to raise the money to make the film themselves.

Take care. Write. Love, Susan.

22 March 1980

Dear Susan,

Received your letter today. While it is still fresh in my mind, I'm writing now. As for the explaining to your grandmother, I said it's when women love each other. The day Pat read the letter she read it at the kitchen table with Gram and me sitting there as well. When she finished Pat went on to say what a beautiful letter, etc. Gram interrupted very abruptly with the fact that Peggy and Steven were going on their super vacation trip. So other than what I've told you about what Pat said at the time we have not had the opportunity to discuss it again.

As for the fiction I read I've been wracking my brains for the title. I read the novel – as you say, a 'sensational' – by Harold Robbins. There was a movie made of that particular book . . .

When I was working as a night supervisor . . . one of the doctors whose children would be about your age stopped in to ask us this question. If two females were together did they interchange, or did one take one role and the other another (one a male, one a female?)? In books I've read is a dildo used? Does one use it or interchange? To be a little more personal, did you ever have sex with a male?

I think of you and the pj [*pyjama*] parties at the Cape when you were a junior in high school! How good you were with the Christian Doctrine children when you were doing that kind of teaching. Also how good a baby-sitter you were with your cousins. You would have been a beautiful mother! I suppose that is why the Catholic Church has such disapproval of homosexuals, although they are trying at this time to make room. The fact that it is for pleasure rather than procreation . . . I can see your identification with Rita Mae, it still makes me sad.

Write soon. Be good to yourself!
Love, Mom

28 March 1980

Dear Mom,

. . . Received your letter full of questions yesterday – some of the questions are confusing to me, the way you've phrased them. You say, 'In books I've read is a dildo used?' I can't speak for the books you've read, I don't know. I sense you asking me, beyond books, is a dildo used? Do I use one? Quick to focus in on lesbianism as sexual practice, aren't you? Personally I have not used a dildo – I don't go in for accoutrements in general, but that doesn't mean that others don't. That's a matter of individual preference. Also you bring up this phenomenon you call 'interchange' which is a new one for me. The way you speak of it I gather you mean an interchanging of male/female roles between two women. I think I already told you when you said that you knew from regular fiction what goes on between a 'dyke' and her 'femme' that I wasn't interested in roles and do not choose to act them out in any situation, including intimate ones. Also you ask if I've ever had sex with a male? The answer to that is yes. MY question back to you is what does that have to do with any of this? . . .

Ah yes, what a beautiful mother I would have made! That's still an option, though at this point a very unlikely one – mainly because I'm more interested in the work of writing, teaching at this point. I go back and forth on the issue whether to have a child or not, but I've been pretty consistently *no* for the last couple of years. Lesbianism does not preclude or exclude motherhood as you can well imagine . . .

Take care. Write. Love, Susan

A few months later, Miriam reported a conversation in which Susan's grandmother had said to tear up Susan's letter. Miriam replied that she couldn't tear it up because 'it is a classic'. Susan wrote back:

8 May 1980

Dear Mom,

. . . I hear your need, frustration, desire for someone to talk with, get another opinion, perhaps someone else who's 'been through it' . . . especially when those around you are mum, pretend it didn't happen. Besides, is tearing up that letter going to erase what I said, deny my existence, the meaning of my life? The letter may be a classic, but it isn't quite that powerful. Dispensing with the garbage does not mean that you did not partake of the substance it held. Bad metaphor, I know. I do not consider myself garbage, though the fact that my grandmother considers my letter, particularly that one, as something that should be torn up – a symbolic tearing up of me – does that not reflect that she views me as garbage?

One thing that has always stuck in my mind about Grammy – she often says when something's going on she doesn't like, 'If there's one thing I've learned in this house, I've learned to keep my mouth shut!' And aren't we all on the verge of suffocation from keeping it bottled up, from keeping our mouths shut, under the guise of politeness? When she says stuff like, 'Nobody cares what I think,' 'Nobody listens to me anyway,' that's all so untrue. I think it's her way of saying, 'I don't/can't/won't care what you think. You can't affect me. I am a rock.' It hurts us all – the withholding; this denial of information whether or not you agree with it. It is valid as a statement and sharing of experience. Besides just saying what you think/feel gives us all something to think/feel a little deeper about.

I appreciate your judgements on disseminating your piece of information further until you feel more comfortable in dealing with your own multi-faceted response, as well as reactions of others. If you are interested I think that the Homophile Community Health Service in Boston sponsors a 'parents of gays' rap group – they would at least lend a sympathetic ear to your concerns and maybe you'd meet some nice people.

Well, enough diatribe for now. It's late after a long day at college. Time to sleep.

Love, Susan

14 May 1980

Dear Susan,

I could have chosen not to say how your grandmother reacted. I'm sure if you walked in the front door tomorrow she would greet you with open arms. She still relates to you as when you were here. It is still difficult for me to see you in this other lifestyle. As I told you on the phone, I just want to know you through you, not someone else's writing, or meeting parents of other lesbians. Did Peggy tell you that Mary M. also is a les? Her mother is a nurse also. Even though we live so close I don't see her (mother or daughter) at all. Mary had a great sense of humor. She was the only daughter – her mother probably has more sorrow than I do.

It really is sorrow more than anything else that I feel. For you more than for me. The oppression = depression for me. Even though I know you yourself are a really great person. I thought you were going to be 28 when you received your 'piece of paper'. I remember saying at one time you would be thirty before you got 'it'. Well, you are getting 'it' before thirty.

Well I've got a job for the next few days. So I'll sign off for now. Write when you can.

Be good to yourself!

Luv,
Ma

23 May 1980

Dear Mom,

    . . . What is this, 'It is still difficult for me to see you in this *other* lifestyle?' Do you realize it is the same lifestyle, the only 'lifestyle' I have, and that is not something 'other' than recognizing what has always been there – sort of like Columbus 'discovering' America. I wonder what it is you are imagining about this other 'lifestyle' that you have such difficulty seeing me in?

    And when you *say*, 'You're still our Susan' – clearly I have been transformed into something other as well in your eyes. Especially when you tell me things like the fact that Mrs. M. has only one daughter and that one daughter turned queer, that her sorrow must be greater than yours. Does that have something to do with what you perceive as the socially and personally redeeming value of at least having other daughters turn out straight? And your equation that oppression = depression: feeling *sorry* for *me* so you say, because I'm oppressed, is downright oppressive. The sooner you stop feeling sorry for me, the sooner that oppression will begin to disintegrate. Also, who you kidding? You ain't going around feeling sorry for anybody but yourself. So get over it.

    . . . You say you could have chosen to not say how Grammy reacted – I'm glad you did say it. There's bound to be some stepping on each other's toes in this whole exchange, but I for one, am glad that it is taking place. So please keep writing – don't censor too drastically. After all, we're both trying to understand . . .

Love, Susan

1 June 1980

Dear Susan

    . . . As to your last letter and my not being consistent – I am playing the Devil's Advocate. That is how we middle-aged, middle-class feel about homos. I'm telling you all the negative things that have been prevalent especially for my age group. The reason I mentioned Mary M. is: do you remember her mother in church on Sunday? She was such a stylish dresser and socially very active. That kind of a mother would want a big wedding for her one and only daughter and all that goes with it.

    I can accept you as you are but I don't intend to know you more through other people. You say your lifestyle had been the same. I'm glad you're happy with it. With your telling me about your being a lesbian does give me a different dimension to your lifestyle I didn't know about. There's no way I can't think differently about you now that I know. I love you, you are a beautiful person. Maybe in your

work you can change my provincial way of thinking but right now I'm
still with the middle-aged, middle-class. I haven't tried to contact
other parents in this situation. I don't want to know about others – I
just want to know about you!

Luv,
Mom

13 June 1980

Dear Mom,

. . . Now as to you 'playing' Devil's Advocate – come off it! Sure,
honey, like I'm 'playing' lesbian. And I am very familiar with the sentiments of your age, race and class about 'homos' – as you so thought-
fully phrased it. It is altogether too easy to blame our circumstances
for our ways of thinking. There are many lesbians that come out of
middle-class circumstances who are of your age group – and there
always have been across and down time. The poem I've enclosed ('For
Each of You' by Audre Lorde) speaks to some of the issues you raised
in your letter (for me). The poem is a challenge I keep in mind when I
find myself taking the easy path – 'Do not pretend to convenient
beliefs . . .' I know that we don't grow up in a vacuum, we are
products of our environment, but we are nonetheless instrumental in
creating that environment, in making change. Pawning your beliefs
off on the fact of your age and class to me is irresponsible. You say that
maybe in my work I can change your 'provincial' way of thinking . . .
if it were only that simple. You need to ask yourself – what are you
willing to do to change for yourself? I am not in the business of per-
suading you, of converting you to lesbianism.

. . . As women, we have been *taught* to despise ourselves, our
bodies, our hearts and minds..Lesbianism is unlearning what we have
been taught to despise. It is learning that love of self and other women
– it is essential to my survival and my capacity to be a self-determining
person. What I'm getting to Mom, is that I cannot change your 'provincial' way of thinking for you. You must do that for yourself – if you
have any inclination to – and I believe you do . . .

Please write.

love, Susan

20 June 1980

Dear Susan,

. . . I agree I can't use age, class, environment for my beliefs about
lesbianism. Your development in this has come about from you. The
fact that you are happy with it and are gaining more in your goals
because of it. This is your style, you've developed to know and like
yourself – ergo self-satisfying accomplishments. Many people live and
die not knowing what they are all about. Knowing yourself is the most

basic. Also liking yourself. You can accomplish anything once you know that. You are on the right track.

. . . Look kid, I like you, love you because you're you.

Write when you can!

Luv,
Mom

Jackie Lapidus and her mother, 1975–76

Jackie Lapidus was born in 1941 in New York. After receiving a BA in History from Swarthmore College she spent three years in Greece in the mid-60s; she has been living in Paris since 1967. Now a magazine editor, she has worked as a public-relations correspondent, secretary, literary agent, teacher and translator. Active in the feminist movement, she is best known as a lesbian feminist poet. Her work has appeared in various magazines and anthologies in the United States and she has written three books of poems: *Ready to Survive, Starting Over* and *Ultimate Conspiracy*.

In the 1920s, Jackie's mother was one of the pioneers of the entry of women into the field of law. Discrimination against women lawyers was rampant, and it increased during the depression years of the 1930s. She managed to earn a living by legal writing and editing, an occupation which she pursued until Jackie was born. During the 1940s, Jackie's mother was a full-time wife and homemaker, taking delight in rearing her two daughters. She remembers this decade as a time when she was most at peace with the world.

At the onset of 'the empty-nest syndrome', Jackie's mother returned to college, acquired a doctorate, and began a new career – teaching law. When budget cuts forced her retirement a dozen years later, it was time to pioneer once more. Currently, she is learning about computers and their impact on modern society, including the issues of computer fraud, privacy and civil rights.

The letters included here are excerpts from much longer letters which discussed a wide range of subjects of interest to Jackie and her mother. This exchange began shortly after the publication of Jackie's first book of poems, *Ready to Survive* (1975), which includes a poem called 'Coming Out' in which she compares the love between mothers and daughters to the love which lesbians feel for each other. In another poem, 'Energy Crisis', Jackie explores her pain in heterosexual relationships, the exhaustion of giving and giving to men, and her renewal in lesbian love.

14 October 1975

Dearest Jax,

I have reread your poems many times. If they were written by someone else's daughter, I would be even more enthusiastic about them as poems. As expressions of my daughter's life and feelings, I find them rather sad. As though you have been 'picked, peeled, pitted . . .' by those who have been your companions. The 'Energy Crisis' poem was, of course, disturbing. Women can pick, peel, and pit just as well as men . . . and more dangerously. I bought ten copies of the book, planning to give them to my friends. Instead, I decided to sell them. By paying for a copy, they will read it more carefully as poetry – I hope. If I can think of any more people to sell it to, I will. I'm your business agent!

Mommy

1 November 1975

Dear Jackie,

I said it was more dangerous with women because of the risk of social stigma and personal attack and the consequent emotional anguish. You may know enough lesbians to think that the modern world takes it as a matter of course. Far from it. Most people find it unnatural and revolting. Certainly nature didn't intend it so, for the primary rule is the perpetuation of the species. So far as I am concerned, I feel that if people are gaited that way, OK, that is their business. But I can't see why anyone should want to cultivate it. It is one thing to like, be friends with, and work with women. It is quite another to spend 'wild, wet nights' with them. I *would* like to talk about it with you. I am not so sure I want you to write freely about it. Have you been reading about how widespread the opening of mail has been in the United States? It is outrageous and truly frightening . . .

We are happy that you are able to write while being happy. Stay that way.

Love from Dad and
Mommy

12 November 1975

Dearest Mom,

Pity you aren't handling the distribution for Hanging Loose! You're so marvelously efficient – owing perhaps to personal enthusiasm? Anyhow, bless you, I really didn't expect it.

. . . Now the lesbian question. I do, in fact, know enough lesbians – happy, stable women, in fact – to think that in certain milieux, including my own present milieu, it is indeed possible to avoid the social stigma and personal attack, and therefore the emotional anguish, that you mention. Furthermore, I think it can be avoided even under pressure (the anguish, I mean), if one feels comfy being lesbian and ready to defend one's right to choose. Sexual identity and orientation may be produced by cultural conditioning (and I think they are, in many more cases than those produced by chromosomes or whatever), but are still such very personal things that I honestly don't see what reproduction of the species has to do with it. There will always be enough heterosexuals around to reproduce the species; meanwhile, people do define the purpose and value of love and sex relationships otherwise: for communication, for pleasure – and any and all sexual relationships can give pleasure and assure communication between the individuals involved, whether they are heterosexual or homosexual. In this society of conflict between the sexes (on the basis of unequal power, unequal opportunities, widely differing human values), it is even possible that homosexual relationships can be more communicative and understanding than heterosexual ones, though I grant that not all of them actually are . . .

What I want, obviously, is a world in which all these questions of sex and sexuality and identity and orientation will find their proportional place in the culture and cease to obsess people, cease to provide a basis for categorizing people, cease to provoke controversy. What we need to cultivate is acceptance of other people's choices.

When you look into the reasons for a society condemning this individual choice (as it condemns individual choices in other areas), you find that: a) men are afraid of lesbians because lesbians are women who don't need men for sex, whereas the men still need or want women; b) men feel their power threatened by any woman who refuses to have sex with them, and lesbians are a striking case of this – not different basically from the heterosexual woman who refuses for other reasons; c) women's solidarity is subversive in general, therefore lesbians, being women who love women, are, again, a striking example of the general subversive category of women who identify with other women; d) women who do not believe in women's solidarity, or women who have won a precarious place in society by adopting male values, tend to belittle or fear the lesbian phenomenon which affirms women's values.

There is also another thing – what *is* natural? OK, there is certainly a reproductive instinct which now requires heterosexual mating.* But is mating the same as love? If you look at love, not mating, the basic love-instinct is the maternal one: mother/child. And the mother may love children of either sex, the children of either sex may love the mother. The primary relationship between mother and daughter is homosexual (and that is what my poem, 'Coming Out', acknowledges). The primary relationship between mother and son is heterosexual. These primary relationships may or may not be projected into the child's later life, depending on what happens during its education and cultural conditioning. Our society teaches boys to love people *like*

---

*This letter was written before artificial insemination device (AID) had been successfully tested.

their mothers, but forbids them to love Mama herself sexually. It teachers girls to love people *different from* their first love, their mother.

And this in the interest of preserving an assortment of institutions based on the male/female dichotomy, of which the basic one is the nuclear family, upon which the others rest. Reproduction is a quick business. The Amazons conceived their children in the usual way, with men, but did not bother to form heterosexual families or take their everyday pleasures with men. They certainly did not accept unequal pay for their work on the theory that they were 'unnatural', 'inferior' or whatever! You will probably now ask, 'What does equal pay have to do with sex?' To which my answer is, 'What does sex – of *any* kind – have to do with anything else?'

. . . I think there are various different sorts of lesbians: 1) the woman-identified woman, who identifies herself as a woman and loves other women who do so too; 2) the woman who wishes she were a man and imitates men; 3) the woman who hates or is afraid of men and is attracted to the nearest substitute, i.e. a mannish woman. The first category, nowadays, includes a lot of women who have never had sex with other women but who recognize that *any woman can* love other women . . . It also includes mothers and daughters who do not, generally speaking, have sex with each other! The second two categories cover the 'traditional' lesbian butch-femme stereotypes . . .

I also see why you aren't sure you want me to write freely on the subject. But *I* am not afraid of snoops, censors, criticism, disapproval, etc. I can deal with it, and am not alone in being prepared to deal with it – there's a whole movement, don't forget. If *Time* Magazine can write about homosexuality, so can I. If women who have a lot to lose can (or, to put it another way, a lot to defend, to build, to fight *for*), so can I. There are plenty of lesbians who prefer not to call themselves lesbians because they are afraid of the stigma attached to the label, and of being attacked or disapproved.

There are also plenty of women who, regardless of whom they sleep with, agree that lesbians and non-lesbians are different only in whom they sleep with, and otherwise identical *as women*, and should therefore seek to de-fuse the label by proclaiming it proudly (sort of like all the Danes in Copenhagen, starting with the King, wearing the yellow star to proclaim their identification with, and refusal to be set apart from, the Jews during the Occupation). Radical feminists take the same position with regard to prostitutes. We are all prostitutes, potentially – we are all living in a society which tries to make us sell ourselves to the male structures, and it hardly matters whether it's done for a house, a life-time fee, a yearly income, a monthly pension or scholarship, or an hourly or one-night payment. So, by analogy: we are all lesbians. Women can and do love women. The only difference between lesbian lovers and a close mother/daughter is the part of the body they touch. And is that how you want to categorize people, by what part of the body they touch to express love? Of course not.

So much for the theoretical matters. My policy on personal matters is that I don't answer any questions that are not asked, and I do answer any questions that are asked in the spirit of understanding. So I'll be really interested to see what you have to say about all this, and always interested to go on talking if you want to.

love,
Jackie

1 December 1975

Dearest Jax,

. . . About the lesbian question, I am simply not up to arguing the theory with you – it just depresses me too much. Theoretically you may be quite right . . . As a practical matter, things have hardly changed. My point is that this kind of sexual identity is just as much a cultural conditioning as the usual one, and I can see no point and much harm in your cultivating it. Life is hard enough without complicating it. I am not at all frightened about lesbianism for myself – I never considered it and never will. I am concerned that something hurtful may happen to you. You live in your own little world at the moment and do not understand how other people feel. Of course it would be ideal if the world accepted other people's choices. But in an ordered society there are some things that will always be regulated and the ideal is an idea, not a *fait accompli*.

. . . It is highly unlikely that at this late date I will get into any 'movement'. I can just about manage to get my work done on the book, take care of household chores, maintain some social contacts, get a bit of much needed physical exercise, and keep Dad and myself on our two – our four – feet. The biggest job at this moment in our lives is to STAY WELL.

Love,
Mom

5 December 1975

Dearest Mom,

Thanks for your letter and the $15 and your honesty and concern and sensibleness, which I appreciate greatly whether or not I agree with your opinions or react the same way as you do. For two very different women, I think we have a pretty good 'entente', don't you?

. . . At the moment I *am* satisfied with my life in Paris, in spite of the fact that my job bores me and doesn't pay a fortune. My real life is elsewhere – my poetry, my women's activities, my friends. I've made something here at last that is unmistakably *mine*, and am enjoying it. I have no idea whether it will go on forever or not. I do not make long-term plans, as I told you last spring – I can't – and see no point in doing so. I much prefer to be flexible and take life as it comes, and be firm on another level, namely, try to live my principles with as much courage and consistency as I can muster. I believe that this is worth the effort, and that it will not cost me anything that is really valuable to me. And that, of course, is the secret of commitment and compromise – it's right, both are right, if they are consistent with one's priorities and do not cost you anything you value more highly than what you choose. I value courage more than prestige, health more than money or aesthetics, political consistency more than social approval. I don't feel that I have 'given up' anything I really want in order to live the way I do, though some things I might have enjoyed have been requested, for the moment, to take a back seat and wait.

. . . Yes, I think a lot about you and how you feel about my choices. I know you aren't happy about them. You never have been. All my life, I've known you wished, rather wistfully, that I were somebody else with a different viewpoint, and for years it upset me, and now it doesn't any more, because if I have to choose between my own approval of myself and yours, I know I must choose my own, just as you choose your approval of yourself rather than mine. I reckon the best thing about my relationship with you is that we have agreed to disagree and still be affectionate and open to each other, n'est-ce pas?

. . . I agree that economic independence is essential for everyone, for women, but I do want to point out that there are many cultures today in which the women have economic autonomy and are still socially oppressed and tormented and attacked by men. Economic independence is necessary but not sufficient for true freedom. It must be fought for, yes, but the battle does not stop there, and my objection to the attitudes of the American middle-class moderates is that they still believe the battle stops there. I also believe very strongly that human equality and capitalism are incompatible, and that the women's movement, because it is working for human equality, must eventually disturb and oppose capitalism. I realize many women today must work for a bigger slice of the present pie, but *I* will not do so – I prefer to work to change the recipe. I consider that both sorts of effort are historically necessary for the whole shebang to get anywhere in the next few hundred years.

. . . I know the world does not accept individual choices – but I refuse to accept the world's attacks on my choices. I refuse to hold that the world is right, I refuse to loathe myself for being me. I refuse to loathe other women for being themselves. I refuse to hold that what anyone does with their genitals is a criterion of fitness for taking care of children, doing a job, or any other activity. And I will fight the law if it reflects injustice. Nothing hurtful will happen to my image of

myself. My self-image was in pain all my life until very recently, but
I have finally managed to make it coincide with the self it represents, and feel incredibly strong and sane and sure. Yes, dear, I *am*
content. And healthy, too, thanks to vitamic C and natural physical
resilience.

As for my sexual identity, well, I consider it is this: I am a woman,
and I love whom I please . . . I simply know I am a woman and am not
interested in labelling my capacities in any way that limits the possibilities. However, I think the lesbian label in its political sense – the
woman-identified woman, which means social identification, not
whom you sleep with – is important at this time, and so if anyone
wants to call me a lesbian, I say, sure, and don't care whom it disturbs.
It is meant to disturb *me*, and I am simply turning the tables by saying,
'why, no, it doesn't disturb me, why, does it disturb you?' and enjoying society's discomfiture. Fancy being able to upset the world by not
minding being called a woman who loves people like herself! It's the
world who's in trouble, not me. And if it attacks me, I shall defend
myself, and also, I am trying to make a life for myself that will allow
me as much freedom as possible, rather than have to give up my
choices in order to get along in the mainstream. I'm not interested in
living in a mainstream that has nothing to offer me except money and
prestige. Simply not interested. What kind of approval could possibly
be more important than one's capacity to love? This is not just theory,
but a matter of daily choice and action.

. . . As my 'Coming Out' poem has just appeared in the Amazon
Quarterly anthology entitled *The Lesbian Reader*, this is tantamount
to a public 'coming out', and I suppose it will startle, in certain
quarters . . . But I no longer see why I should hide facts from anyone.
Especially since I am so incredibly happy, feeling so energetic, getting
so much support from other women (both lesbian and straight), discovering so much about the myriad ways in which culture created by
women (lesbian and straight) is different from, and much richer than,
the patriarchal culture we have inherited. That poem is getting an
amazing response, by the way – it is going into another anthology, too
– precisely because it deals with the fundamental love-instinct
between mother and daughter.

Anyhow, one last word about being a lesbian – it does mean, as you
point out, that I'm going to take a lot of flak from society. But that is
all the more reason for straight women to support lesbians who are
also feminists and fighting these attacks: because *we are all being put
down as women*, and attacking the lesbians is attacking women's front
line. If you do not identify with those women in the front line, you are
in effect saying to the patriarchal phallocrats, 'don't hurt me, I'm not
like them'. But you *are* like them (us) – you're a woman too, and just as
likely to get shot at when the battle crosses the front line and moves

into the second and third and etc. lines where you, the straight mother, happen to be.

. . . About asking questions: Liz and I worked on getting you to not ask embarrassing ones to which you didn't really want to know the true answers. But we never wanted you not to inquire about who we were and what we did in the factual sense. I always wanted to share my self and activities with you, and the trouble came when it was clear you didn't *like* the person and the activities you were being introduced to. You did your best to be fair and not judge, but as my mother you sometimes couldn't help wailing or having migraines, and at the time a certain distance became necessary for both of us. Luckily, the society is catching up with me a little and the social approval you seem still to need will not be withdrawn from you as quickly now if you yourself stick up for your maverick daughter.

Love,
Jackie

5 January 1976

Dearest Jax,

I see that you have been telling your friends how interesting and openminded and lively and active we are. I am not at all sure that we are so openminded. We are resigned to the fact that our children do not listen to us, and do what they please. We accept it, and hope that they will not be hurt badly if they persist in breaching social norms. We would much prefer it if they could establish a happy family life. It is easier to write about it than it would be to talk about it, and the truth is that I am afraid to come to Paris by myself – not because of fear of travelling, of course, but the fear of not being able to get across to you how I feel about radical lesbianism.

Much love, despite my disagreement and despair,
Mommy

10 January 1976

Dearest Mom,

Compared to most other people's mothers, you are openminded – which does not mean you approve or accept everything, but simply that you try not to judge before the evidence is in. I know you don't always succeed, and that you do project yourself onto other people's situations, but then, who doesn't? I do listen to you, though I don't do what you wish I would. I try to understand your feelings and choices in the context of your personality and background and situation . . . I still want you to come, disagreement and despair notwithstanding. I'm a bit scared too, but the fact that you are willing to cross an ocean to see me in this context, counts for more than my silly fears. A—, whose mother is fear-ridden and conventional to an extent you cannot imagine, says she wishes her mother were more like you, and looks forward to knowing you.

Love,
Jax

29 January 1976

Dear Jax,

I decided to give our serious colloquy a rest. You *write* so logically. But I *feel* so logically, and we are miles apart. My only hope is that this is a phase through which you will manage to pass. I do have confidence in you in the long run, even though I can't approve of your short-term projects. The idea of visiting you is not altogether on the shelf, but I am letting it rest for the time being.

Love and kisses from Dad and
Mommy

Three months later, Jackie's mother visited her in Paris. She wrote when she returned home:

22 April 1976

Dearest Jackie,

. . . It was a good visit. I tell everyone that you look well and are happy, that you are busy with work and activities in the women's movement, and that you share an apartment with a friend. I may have to do some more explaining later, but for the moment there is no need to say more . . . I really have not had much time as yet to think over our conversations, but I do know that I am very happy that I made the trip, and that I feel better than before I went. We may be uneasy because of the direction your life has taken, but you do seem to be able to take care of yourself.

I want you to know that I appreciated all the attention you paid to my needs and comfort. I enjoyed my visit very much and came home feeling that I had had a vacation – something I had not even anticipated. A— is obviously a good person who cares a great deal about you and is easy to live with. The only thing that disturbed me was that you were so easily upset by her change in mood. I hope that in time you will acquire the 'inner strength' you want, and become self-sufficient so that little things don't bother you so much. Please convey my thanks to A— too. I was touched by her attentions. As I tried to tell her in my halting French, I am not afraid of her and you. I am simply afraid *for* you because I know the world better than either of you – or so it seems to me, with more than twice your years behind me.

Take the very best care of yourself. We love you muchly always,
Mommy

22 April 1976

Dearest Mom,

I'm still euphoric about our week together, immeasurably happy to
have reassured you about myself and to know, finally, who you are
and how you feel and why. I wish you could have stayed longer. I
hope we'll be able to get together soon, somewhere. It felt so good to
be talking and listening calmly, openly, comfortably after all those
years of tension, apprehension, reticence, and explosions. Sharing my
delight and admiration with the women in my consciousness-raising
group last night, I began to think that maybe this can only be done
when the daughters grow up, at least in the context of our present-day
society, since my being older put us on an equal footing in a way that's
rarely possible earlier. You seemed to think that, and some of the
women in the group remarked that they, too, found their mothers
easier to understand and be with, now that everyone was older. Anyhow, it was wonderful, and I hope you still feel as good about it as I
do.

It occurred to me, after you left, that in spite of the radical, subversive nature of my philosophy/commitment, I lead a very quiet,
sheltered, un-dangerous life (so far), and that there is very little for
you to worry about on the practical level – I could have spent more
time pointing this out! Well, I'm sure you saw and felt it. It made both
me and A— so happy to see you feeling good with us and with our
friends, especially since we all knew you hadn't expected to. A—
really appreciated the last evening's conversation which cleared the air
between you and her and reassured her that your reaction to her was
at least partly due to the fact that you and she have pretty much the
same temperament, the same sense of privacy and preference for not
talking much, the same extreme sensitivity requiring considerable
'defenses'. I am sure it's no accident that I love a woman who
resembles both my mother and my sister in some way!

I'm looking forward, eagerly, to a letter from you. Hope you felt
just as good after you got home, and comfortable about telling Dad
what you found and felt in Paris. I'll write to him separately and
enclose the letter with this one. Very best regards from all my friends.
A— sends the hug she was too shy to give you Tuesday night, and I,
oceans of love as always,

Love, Jax

26 April 1976

Dearest Jackie,

I did feel good about our visit after I got home, and comfortable
about telling Dad what I found and felt in Paris. So far as the rest of the
family and our friends are concerned, there is no point in saying anything more than that you are well and happy, that you have a room-

mate, that you are very busy writing, working and active in the Women's Movement, and (when they ask me about men in your life) that you are currently not interested in men. They simply would not understand. I too wish our time together had been longer, and hope that we can get together again soon. I agree that mother and daughter can communicate fully only when the daughter has grown up.

I would like to read all your work . . . As for the un-dangerous life – the danger depends on the climate of the society in which one lives. Did you know that the US Supreme Court just upheld a state law making homosexual acts in the privacy of one's home a crime? New York has a similar law, punishable by imprisonment for up to five years. Never enforced, of course, but nevertheless still there for future witch-hunting.

Please give my best to all the people I met in Paris. I really liked them all and thought they were extremely intelligent. It was a pleasure to be with them and listen to their talk, and I was very pleased that they were able to accept in their midst a grey-haired old conventional American who had come to Paris to look them over. Eventually I will write to A— to thank her for her many kindnesses. She did everything she could to make me comfortable and happy.

Love and kisses from both of us, especially ME.
Mommy

CHAPTER SEVEN

The Infinitely Healing Conversation

I no longer have fantasies – they are the unhealed child's fantasies, I think – of some infinitely healing conversation with her, in which we could show all our wounds, transcend the pain we have shared as mother and daughter, say everything at last.
Adrienne Rich, Of Woman Born *(1976)*

In the long and painful process of disentangling our own aspirations from what we have learned in our families, many women are attempting to re-evaluate our mothers' influence on our development. Using insights of the women's liberation movement to become aware of the conditions of our mothers' lives, we can begin to appreciate their strengths and weaknesses; we can understand their experiences, as well as our own, in the context of the systematic denial of opportunities for women to realise their full potential. It has meant being able to see our mothers as individuals with needs, desires, hurts and confusions of their own – not just as women who either gave or didn't give us what we needed and wanted.

However, as Kate says in Chapter Four, 'the textbook answers don't stop the personal pain.' This process of examining how our mothers affect our lives can open wounds about things that have happened in the past (which may also remain as patterns in our current relationships with our mothers and with other people). These wounds may need to be fully acknowledged in order to be fully healed.

Separation is the psychological term for the process of growing up and coming to terms with the fact that one's mother is a separate and imperfect individual who is not always available and who cannot and will not satisfy all of one's needs and expectations. It has taken me years even to begin to grasp the implications of this term which I've heard bandied about constantly since I started my research; endless probing of the concept intellectually has possibly only hindered my attempts (through therapy as well as through writing) to achieve emotional separation from my own mother. Many of the women with whom I've discussed this book have readily admitted that they too find the concept elusive. It is apparent that even women who feel very committed to notions of independence, autonomy and separation may have difficulty in coping with their feelings of dependence on their mothers and/or daughters, and find it devastating to acknowledge the reality of imperfect women who imperfectly meet our expectations.

Where the process of separation is most successful, the tendency to 'blame the mother' (or 'blame the daughter') virtually disappears: as two separate adults, both women want to take responsibility for the quality of their own lives. They refuse to use an unsatisfactory relationship with either their mother or daughter as an excuse for not 'living to the hilt'.

In the week before my deadline to complete the first draft of this book I wrote a letter to my mother about several issues which were upsetting me. It was not a letter about the book – but about issues which have long troubled me in my relationship with her. She lives in Texas and I live in England, so in the small amount of time we have together we tend to downplay our anxieties or unhappiness and concentrate on reassuring each other that life is going smoothly; it's what we've always done. As I finished the letter, a friend dropped by to see how I was getting on with my deadline. I confessed that I had just spent the entire day ignoring the deadline by writing this difficult letter and agonising over how my mother would respond. My friend interrupted and said, 'But you don't have to send the letter, do you?'

The irony escaped me until the next morning. Here was I, about to finish a book which has dominated my life for four years – a book which depends entirely on such letters having been written and received, a book which affirms the possibility of the relationship between a mother and daughter to be renewed and transformed through honest disclosure. By taking the risk of showing themselves more honestly and not revealing only what is most likely to receive approval, numerous mothers and daughters throughout this book have tried to know and care about each other as they really are, and to give up their fantasies of the perfect mothers or the perfect daughters who only live their lives to meet each other's needs and expectations. By openly admitting the ways in which they have been hindered and hurt by each other, they could more generously acknowledge the ways in which they have been helped to become the women they are.

Nonetheless, I was seriously attracted by my friend's suggestion that my letter was really for my own clarification and growth, that my mother should be left to get on with her life in peace and that she could uncover everything she wanted to know about our relationship by reading this book, whereas my letter might force her to see things which she doesn't wish to think about and I would have to live with the guilt of hurting her. It was quite a closely reasoned, compassionate little tirade, at the end of which my friend laughed ruefully that she sounded exactly like her own mother, but didn't I think it best to retire to bed with a hot water bottle and a little whisky to calm my nerves?

In the end, I sent the letter; but only partly because of the inspiring evidence from the letters in this book that such communication can be beneficial. I was able to send it because I see my mother as a person striving to grow and change and know herself, a woman who sees that the most difficult circumstances in her life have provided her with the opportunity to become the confident, self-accepting person that she is today. But mainly, I suppose I sent it because it was the only sure-fire way I had of discovering that lightning would not strike me dead if I admitted to my mother that she has hurt me and that sometimes I feel angry when I realise ways in which she has failed me. For years, I have declared my gratitude to her for her love and support, her courage and generosity and humour. Then, for one day, in that one letter, I talked about a more negative side – and I felt that lightning might strike me dead. In some way, I even wanted it to – because for me, the unseparated daughter, it seemed a terrible thing to admit and I felt awful.

In editing and analysing these women's letters, I have frequently had to remind myself that feelings of unforgiving rage and infantile disappointment are legitimate stages of separation and healing, and that anger and disillusionment occur in all good, strong relationships. No doubt because my separation from my mother is incomplete, these have been difficult lessons to bear in mind. More than any other letters in this book, those in this chapter have helped me to recognise that if the relationship is at all strong, the bonds will endure phases of stress. Not that expressing unbridled hostility will automatically bring positive results: many women feel that, while it is important to *admit* their feelings of hurt and anger (whether in discussions with their women's groups or with friends, in therapy, or in journals and unsent letters), it is not necessary to communicate negative feelings in their most one-sided and irrational form to either their mothers or their daughters.

A few letters in this book illustrate the fact that some mother-daughter relationships are not strong enough to benefit from the frank admission of differences or negative feelings. Because of the past they have shared, the difficult conditions in which women in our society must try to be good wives and mothers, and/or a mother's distressing relationship with her own mother, there are times when there is not a strong enough bond of love and compassion between a mother and daughter to enable them to survive confrontation. Yet, even when the relationship falters, recognising the extent of the sadness and anger is often the first stage for the individual mother or daughter to heal herself.

In relationships where there has always been some love and caring, why shouldn't they survive differences or confrontation? Why shouldn't they survive anything?

It is as if we imagine that there is a bond between us which would be broken if we expressed too many differences or if our pain and disappointments were made obvious. It seems there is a fear that if we aren't connected to our mothers or daughters in the way we have been (whatever that is), then we won't be connected at all.*

Of course, we can't know what that new connection might be. It might not be new at all; it might be an older, more sturdy bond that we don't even realise is there because we have come to rely so desperately on our imagined bond – the bond we invent and sustain by covering up certain truths about ourselves, about what it feels like to be a mother or daughter with our own particular ties and history.

Karen Blixen to her mother Ingeborg Dinesen, 1921–31

Karen Blixen (1885–1962) was the real name of the popular Danish writer, Isak Dinesen, best known for her memoir, *Out of Africa*, and for *Seven Gothic Tales*, a collection of short stories. She was born the second of five children of Ingeborg and Wilhelm Dinesen, who both came from wealthy land-owning families active in Danish politics. Karen's father committed suicide when she was 10 and her youngest brother was less than a year old. Thereafter, Ingeborg raised the five children with the help of her mother and sister; the daughters were taught at home by a governess, while the sons were sent away to school. Karen showed promise as an artist and, between the ages of 17 and 25, attended various art colleges in Copenhagen, London and Paris.

In 1913, at the age of 27, Karen left Denmark to marry her second-cousin, Baron Bror Blixen-Finecke, and begin a new life on a coffee plantation in the Ngong Hills, Kenya. She quickly came to love living in Africa, where life was so entirely different from the bourgeois existence she had left behind. During the following years she steadfastly defended her decision to remain on the farm against the insistence of her mother and numerous relatives that she should return to a more comfortable and secure existence in Denmark. The coffee plantation which Karen and Bror Blixen owned was continually on the verge of bankruptcy and the Dinesen clan pumped money into it fruitlessly.

In exchange for their financial assistance, her family expected Karen to allow them to govern her destiny in even the most private matters: her mother, aunts and uncles met in family councils and unanimously pressured Karen to divorce Bror, whom they disliked for his mismanagement of the farm and because during the first year of marriage he had infected Karen with syphilis.† After six years of marriage, much against Karen's wishes, Bror filed for divorce. During the next decade, Karen managed the Karen Coffee Company alone, until the Depression forced the Danish shareholders to sell

---

*From a discussion led by Luise Eichenbaum at the Women's Therapy Centre, London (March 1979).
†She was successfully treated in a Danish hospital during an eighteen-month visit home and was pronounced cured in 1916.

and she was obliged to return to Denmark to live with her mother.

During the seventeen years she lived in Kenya, Karen Blixen came to see her coffee farm and her relationship with the Africans who lived and worked on it as her 'life's work'. There she was occupied with farm business and with the affairs of people she cared about: she attended to medical problems with rudimentary first aid and soon became known to Africans for miles around as someone who could cure ills as well as advise them on bureaucratic matters, help organise schools for their children and intervene in local disputes. She also had her friends and social engagements and spent long periods painting and drawing the people and landscapes she loved. Karen had often said that, if she ever had to leave the Ngong Hills, life would be over for her.

Her misery at leaving Africa was compounded by the sudden death of Denys Finch Hatton, with whom she had fallen in love after she and Bror separated. For ten years Finch Hatton had visited Karen at Ngong, sharing her worries over the farm, her sympathy with the Africans with whom she lived and her outrage at the racist attitudes of the English; they both loved the African bush and enjoyed going on safari together. Neither had believed in marriage and they had maintained their independence through the many years of their love affair.

Devastated, she returned to Denmark and it was then that she began in earnest the work which made her famous. In the remaining thirty-one years of her life Karen Blixen, alias Isak Dinesen, wrote several collections of short stories as well as her acclaimed memoir. She was twice nominated for the Nobel Prize, although never awarded it. Despite many years of illness, at 73 she made a three-month visit to New York where she was fêted and enjoyed a busy schedule of writing and lecturing. However, she never returned to Africa and she died in 1962 at the age of 77.

These letters have been chosen from among the hundreds Karen Blixen wrote to her mother which provide fascinating accounts of her life in Africa. She wrote about the men she loved; about her concern for people on the farm; her financial anxieties; her illnesses; her unorthodox views on politics, race and marriage; and her feminism. The letters selected here mark decisive stages in her battle to become an autonomous adult and achieve psychological separation from her family (already being separated physically by thousands of miles). They begin during a difficult period in her relationship with her husband:

Autumn 1921

My own beloved beloved wonderful little Mother,

. . . Now I want to beg you earnestly that in future – perhaps for a year, but perhaps not for so long, – I may feel that I am able to write to *you only*, without any one else reading my letters. I am quite aware that the others take such a part in how my affairs are going, and in my joys and sorrows, that they will be hurt by this; but it must be like this for a time; for otherwise I have come to realize that as God is my witness it is utterly impossible for me to write . . .

Also it is impossible for me to reply to their letters in the way they would like. I am having a terrible time out here; I am involved in so many things, – both purely practical and also where my feelings, my life itself are concerned, – possibly by my own fault or perhaps quite by chance, that it is going to take all my strength if I am to get through them or over them; you are all well aware of this. I believe that I am going to get through; there may well come a time when I feel that I am the happiest of us all and that it will have been worth all the trouble. But as the situation is now, and as every day I have need of all the strength I can muster in order to manage things, I cannot enter into discussion about it with a whole crowd of young and older women and uncles and brothers-in-law and friends.

If I know that I can write to you alone, I will tell you everything I am thinking about; all my plans, when I have any, will be for you to hear, but I must be absolutely sure that you will not show my letters to anyone, without one single exception.

I love you all . . . but they are not to write about my intimate circumstances, for they do not understand them in the least, and it is merely upsetting to read and completely impossible to reply to . . .

I think my greatest misfortune was Father's death. Father understood me as I was, although I was so young, and loved me for myself. It would have been better, too, if I had spent more time with his family; I felt more free and at ease with them. I feel that Mama and Aunt Bess and the whole of your family, – and Uncle Aage when he was out here, – if they care for me at all, do so in a way in spite of my being as I am. They are always trying to change me into something quite different; they do not like the parts of me that I believe to be good.

You must not think that I am saying this as a reproach, the only person to reproach is myself, because I did not tear myself away before, and then because when I did tear myself away after a fashion, or anyway took myself away from it all, – I accepted help from you in order to do it. That is the one great mistake I have made in my life, and suffer and have suffered all the pains of hell for it. For otherwise what would it matter whether it rained or not out here, and whether land went up or down, in fact, what would anything at all matter? I should surely be able to manage somehow or other.

But it must be possible to manage it somehow, I think the best way would be by purchase, and I shall surely be able to get through these difficulties I have brought upon myself.

But, – if I can do it and make something of myself again, and can look at life calmly and clearly one day, – then it is Father who has done it for me. It is his blood and his mind that will bring me through it.

Often I get the feeling that he is beside me, helping me, many times by saying: 'Don't give a damn about it,' – about many of my shauries [*troubles*].

No doubt each one of your children thinks that he or she loves you most, and so do I. It is probably not true. But each one cares for you in his or her own way, and I think that there is something in the way that I love you that resembles the way Father loved you. For me you are the most beautiful and wonderful person in the world; merely the fact that you are alive makes the whole world different; where you are there is peace and harmony, shade and flowing springs, birds singing; to come to where you are is like entering 'heaven' . . .

These *are* difficult times for me, far, far more difficult than, for instance, when I was ill here. Your love and understanding are lights and stars shining and sparkling through them. And I have to take them in my own way; otherwise I will die of them, you must understand that. And I am sure you have the strength, little Mother, to keep this understanding in spite of others' condemnation . . .

When they talk like this, then listen to them and say yes and amen, but smile in your heart of hearts. Don't let them make you see it in their way; understand me, as only *you* can. And imagine that Father is sitting beside you perhaps talking anxiously too about this child of yours out here and saying that she has used up too much money and been improvident in many ways, but perhaps he might see some sense in it as well and would say: 'But she is brave, and she loves you and me more, perhaps, than any of our other children; give her a little more time, then you'll see that she will manage.' – Yes, talk about me to Father. It is really he who is responsible, for he deserted me and must have seen that things were not going to be easy for me.

But do not discuss me with the others; just let them say what they like, and let me write to you alone. For I love you so very deeply . . .

Your Tanne

25 October 1921

My own beloved Mother,

. . . I am going to beg you, dearest Mother, not to write to me any more concerning my marriage or Bror. Of course I know you do it with the best intentions; but sometimes even things done in this spirit can fail, and what costs you effort and pain to write, costs me effort and pain to read, and I do not think anything is gained by it other than my realization of how little you understand me . . .

My little Mother, you must not think that I am writing in anger or bitterness; but I think that this is the reason for even *you* writing as you do, and I do so deeply wish that it would stop . . .

There are two things that none of you understand: how different from you I am and always have been. What makes me happy or unhappy is completely different from what makes you happy or unhappy. I could live in conditions that you would think frightful and be happy, and in conditions which you would think perfect I would be miserable. And you cannot make judgments in advance regarding these conditions; you do not know and can never know what effect they will have on my state of satisfaction, and thus you ought to be careful about the advice you give; you might come to regret it most deeply. For instance, to me my illness was not such an enormous disaster, indeed, if I had not still been under your influence I would have thought it even less of one; but I was constantly aware of the sorrow it would cause you. I actually enjoyed being in the hospital, although it was a hellish cure. No doubt it would have been quite a different matter for one of the others. But not for anything in the world would I go back to the time when I had to go to Folehave for dinner every Sunday. You must not think this is written out of hard-heartedness. I would really rather leave it alone; but it *cannot* be avoided when you write as you do, and I think that you have written things to me now that have hurt me still more, and this is the only way that I can think of to put a stop to it from both sides . . .

Goodnight my above all else beloved mother

In 1925 Karen and Bror Blixen were divorced and in 1931 the farm finally went bankrupt. This letter was written as Karen was dejectedly making arrangements to leave Ngong and return to Denmark:

17 March 1931

Dear Mother,

. . . You must not think that I feel, in spite of it having ended in such defeat, that my 'life has been wasted' here, or that I would exchange it with that of anyone I know. I feel, like Aunt Lidda, that in fact it is astonishing how much, given my abilities, I have been able to achieve. Aunt Lidda did not say this as applying to me in particular, but to herself in comparison with Aunt Bess, who did not feel she had got what she should have had out of life.

Of all the idiots I have met in my life, – and the Lord knows that they have not been few or little, – I think that I have been the biggest. But a certain love of greatness, which could not be quelled, has kept a hold on me, has been 'my daimon'. And I have had so infinitely much that was wonderful. She may be more gentle to others, but I hold to the belief that I am one of Africa's favourite children.* A great world of poetry has revealed itself to me and taken me to itself here, and I have loved it. I have looked into the eyes of lions and slept under the

*Underlinings indicate Karen Blixen's use of English words within the Danish text.

Southern Cross, I have seen the grass of the great plains ablaze and covered with delicate green after the rains, I have been the friend of Somali, Kikuyu, and Masai, I have flown over the Ngong Hills, – 'I plucked the best rose of life, and Freja be praised,' – I believe that my house here has been a kind of refuge for wayfarers and the sick, and to the black people has stood as the center of a <u>friendly spirit</u>. Lately it has been somewhat more difficult. But that is so all over the world . . .

It is an irony of fate that we have had such good, early rains. When I think how often at this time of year I have gone outside gazing for the rain that would not come, it is strange to lie and listen to it pouring down now, and know that it doesn't make the slightest difference . . .

Give a thousand greetings to everyone, and all, all my love to you, my own beloved, charming Mother.

Your Tanne.

A few weeks later, Karen wrote to her brother, Thomas, asking for his assistance and advice. She said that she would prefer to kill herself if he did not think it would be possible for her to undergo some form of training which would enable her to work and become financially independent of her family:

> . . . But you must not think that I am frightfully depressed and see everything in a tragic light. That is not at all the case; on the contrary, I think that these difficult times have helped me to understand better than before how infinitely rich and beautiful life is in every way and that so many things that one goes around worrying over are of no importance whatsoever . . . It seems to me that it would in no way be terrible or sad if I, after in many ways having been more happy here than it is by far the majority of people's lot to be, – and there is not one single person I would change with, — were now quite calmly to retire from life together with everything that I have loved here. What I imagine a great many people would think of that: for instance, that it was terrible for Mother and so on, is something I cannot take into account. It may perhaps be just as hard for Mother to lose me as for me to lose Ngong . . .
>
> I am putting this so strongly in order not to express it too weakly and so give you a wrong impression. Summa summarum: I am no more acquiescent than I was before; on the contrary, I cannot come home with remorse and contrition no matter what has happened to me and what I have been doing; I still feel that death is preferable to a bourgeois existence, and in death I will confess my faith in freedom.
>
> There must always be one thing that is more important than anything else to a person and I think that for me this is freedom, or space. I cannot and will not live in a situation where I feel myself incarcerated . . .
>
> I know that I can die happily, and if you are in doubt, let me do that. Let me take Ngong, and everything that belongs to it, in my arms and sink with it, and it will be without complaint, but with immense gratitude to life.

Her mother, anxious to discover Karen's plans, opened this letter, although it was addressed to Thomas. She had had no idea what a bombshell it would contain and forwarded it guiltily to Thomas. The letter which she would have wanted to write to Karen, she wrote instead to him – a letter which demonstrates touchingly how she, as a mother, had resolved the issues of separation and autonomy which Karen had initiated in their correspondence several years earlier.

This letter to Thomas was probably the one which Karen most needed to receive. However, she had shielded Ingeborg from the full weight of her despair, and was prevented from receiving the benefit of her mother's comfort:

> . . . I was aware of the risk I was taking in opening Tanne's letter to you, – the chances were high that it would contain things that I ought not to read, – but it was such a great temptation to find out as soon as possible what plans she might be making . . . Anyway, it looks as if I have had my punishment by reading this letter, which was certainly not intended to be made known to me. But I shall give no more consideration to that, – the vital thing is that Tanne *must never suspect* that I have read it.
>
> As it happens I think it will be easier for you to know that I am aware of Tanne's plans and ideas. You know that for the whole of my life with you I have tried my best to understand you, and you may be sure that I understand what Tanne is going through now. For I have always known that the environment I offered her here was not suited to her character and talents, – this has caused me great pain, but it has not been possible for me to change it so much that it would make her happy. Perhaps she has not really been willing to make the attempt to find happiness in this environment; but no matter how much violence she might have done to her nature she would never have been able to feel at home in what she rightly calls a bourgeois existence, and so much of the value in her would have been wasted.
>
> I know, – and I know that you believe it to be true, – that I will be able to give Tanne complete freedom to do what she thinks is best for herself, – I will not hold her back if she thinks life is too hard for her, I will not for one moment put her under an obligation to 'be something' to me in these years, – when I wrote that to her it was mostly so that she should take it as the suggestion for an undertaking. The sole consideration for me is that she should live according to her nature, – I neither can nor will demand anything else of her. She has often caused me anxiety, probably more than any other of my children, but she has filled my life with so much love, so much festivity, I have been, – and am, – so proud of her, that whatever she may come to do I will always love and bless her. I would rather never see her again than that she should feel herself 'incarcerated'. I should know that in a life where she did not feel that, she would love me more than if she were caged in here at Rungsted.
>
> You know that when I first began to reconsider, after Tanne told me that you wanted to go to war, I was fully aware that it was necessary for you to have my complete approval and blessing before you went, – that was what I owed you, the only thing that I have been able to do for all of you is that, to try to understand and help you to follow your own natures. Whenever I felt something in you that was alien to me I was always afraid lest it should be impeded if I did not take the trouble to support it. Those rich years that I spent with Father taught me to

understand other aspects of life than those to which I was drawn. I have had so many qualms of conscience because I allowed Folehave to bear down on you with its loving but heavy weight to such an extent, – and naturally most on Tanne, to whom the whole of that atmosphere was most foreign. I make no excuses for it, – it arose from love, but it was wrong . . .

My own dearest boy, you must not harbor any hard feelings toward Tanne because she despises what I have to offer her, and perhaps, too, makes too great demands on us. She is cast in such a completely different mold, – and I am glad that I have realized in time that we were wrong in thinking she had changed. She has been through a hard school, but this in itself has not changed her nature, – the development that these years have brought her has not turned her into a more commonplace person than she was, and if we have thought so we have been wrong, I see that very clearly now, and I see that we mistook the situation chiefly because it would have been easier for us . . .

I have written this immediately after reading yours; I will put it aside until tomorrow, – perhaps I may need to rewrite it completely, I must sleep on it and see . . . You know that I love you.

Mira and her mother Protima, 1960s, and her daughter Rita, 1980s

Mira was born in the eastern part of India, the oldest child of an upper-middle-class family. In 1960, at the age of 20, she enrolled at the University of California to study Sociology and she has not lived in India since. She married an American student in her second year of university and after graduation they moved to another part of the United States, where both she and her husband took up academic careers. Their only daughter, Rita, is now a university student.

Manisha Roy, an Indian woman who also left her family in India to study abroad, explains some of the background to the letters between Mira and her mother:

'In India the custom and practice of writing letters among people within one's immediate family is a recent tradition. Partly because people did not travel away from the ancestral base very often, and also because most of the necessary communications took place by word of mouth and face to face. Women did not begin to be educated enough to write letters until as late as the early nineteenth century. Then mothers would perhaps write letters to their daughters who had moved away after being married into families outside their own villages and towns. But these letters would carry messages of a very ordinary kind – advice on health, advice for good conduct with in-laws and some small news about the family and the relatives. I suspect it was mostly among the educated middle-class and upper-class that even letters of this sort would flow. Writing letters to express one's emotional feelings and conflicts is still rare among both women and men, with the exception of literary men and women or people with unusual backgrounds. For example, the poet Tagore and the statesman Nehru both wrote letters to their wives or children which were later published. These letters carry information on great minds more than individual feelings and emotions; they have mass appeal because of their generalised contents. The very few mothers who are writers themselves may write a different kind of letters than ordinary mothers, but their numbers are small.

'When a middle-class ordinary mother writes to her daughter, the letters usually contain everyday mundane news and gossip and advice and concerns, over the daughter's health, etc. There may be subtle hints here and there to indicate some unspoken concerns and worries, but little is verbalised and most of this kind of emotional exchange goes on between the lines. Whenever some signs of open conflict arise – say for example, over issues of marriage or career – a mother may become more explicit in conveying her ideas and values which the daughter knows all along and is newly reminded of.

'The emotional intensity that binds a mother and her daughter is not only a bond between two blood relatives but also between a growing woman and her *culture*, her tradition and customs. An Indian mother is usually a fairly stable custodian of her social, cultural and moral traditions by the time her daughter is of marriageable age. Whatever conflicts the mother herself may have felt when she was younger, these would have been pushed aside and repressed and compromised by this time. Now, she must help her daughter to make these compromises, so that the family and the society can count on her. It is also her duty to offer this security to her daughter who, as a woman, will have enough to suffer from life anyway.'

These letters began when Mira, aged 20, had just arrived in the United States and was studying at the University of California:

1 October 1960

My affectionate Miru,*
    Since we have not heard from you yet, we are extremely worried. Have you reached your destination yet? Your father keeps telling me that you must be all right, otherwise we would hear from you. I would like to hear from you even if you are all right. Do write at least twice a week to assure me that you are not unwell. Things are very much the same here. The jeweler brought the first set of bangles back last week for approval. They look nice; if the wedding took place next spring, you will have to be back for the ceremony . . . We miss you specially on our shopping trips. Mira, what is it like there? Is it really as good as you and your father tried to make me believe? It's hard for me to know.
    Your grandfather (my father) once took me to Kashmir when I was 16 before your father and I were married. I wove fantasies about the

---

*Miru is the diminutive of Mira.

place with high mountain-peaks, snow, clean winding roads with beautiful people, beautiful trees and cool crisp air. But when we got there everything seemed different, although there were high mountain-peaks and winding roads and beautiful trees and people. It rained a lot and the people did not seem so nice or beautiful. I was very disappointed. I hope your dreams were not far from what you really found. Do tell me more about the place and the people . . . Things here are as usual. Mejho mashi [Protima's sister] is showing her first sign of rheumatism. Yet she does not stop going for two dips a day at the Ganges. Your father is constantly teasing her about this. Well, Miru, I must stop now. Someone is yelling from the kitchen as if the whole household is going to collapse. I know you would laugh, but do take a glass of milk every night before going to bed, please. By the way, I hear the Americans drink only cold milk, is it true? Be careful and take care of yourself.

Yours affectionately,
ma

18 October 1960

Respected Ma,

I realize I let two weeks pass before writing you. Hope you are not too worried. I sent a post-card to baba [Mira's father] from London which you must have received. It took me a while to get settled. I already started my classes and I am finding out that life here is going to be quite busy. Imagine my spending all my day and even evenings doing either studies or housework. I shop twice a week, but I may have to do it only once. Fortunately the fridge is big enough. Yes, three of us girls share an apartment, and so far I like my house-mates. They are both American and around my age . . . The university campus is just beautiful. I enjoy walking everyday from building to building and hear students chat or birds make funny noises. People here are very friendly and open. They even smile before they know you! I have already been invited by two students (both girls) and I enjoyed meeting their parents. But, ma, food here is really tasteless. I miss your cooking and grandma's mango pickle and Choto mashi's special spinach. Oh, well, I guess I shall get used to it all. I cook for myself only over the week-ends. There is hardly any time during the week . . . Classes have been very interesting so far and I am getting used to the American system bit by bit. I like the way the professors treat the students . . . There is so much I could tell you but I must make it brief and perhaps, write another letter next week. Please do not worry about me. I am taking care of myself and I feel very well. The cool air of autumn seems to suit me well, after the heat in Calcutta. Please show this to baba and tell him that I would write him separately telling him all about my courses and the professors, etc., later . . . Please,

please do not worry if my letters take a while to arrive. Remember, I am a big girl now and if I could travel around half of the world to be here I can also take care of myself.

How is your health, and baba's? Please give my respect to grandma, mashimas and pishimas. How is Uma? I think of you all and wonder how you all are. Ma, the life here is so different that sometimes I have to talk to myself in Bengali to think about Calcutta and you all. I miss you a lot. But, time seems to fly very quickly here. With respect and love,

Yours,
Miru

10 December 1960

My affectionate Miru,

You must have received all my letters by now. We have had only three letters from you in the last month and a half. I know you are busy, but I worry if I do not hear from you. Have you received the parcel I sent by sea-mail? I put some pickles and other 'goodies' together and requested your uncle next door to mail it for me. I did not want to let your baba know about this. You know how much fuss he makes over food parcels. He always gives me big lectures that food in America is a thousand times better and more nutritious. As if that is enough! . . . Uma's wedding date is now firmed up and it would be some time in February. Please plan to be here and do not tell your father that I suggested it. Everyone would be very upset if you miss this first wedding of the family. The future groom seems like a good boy and Uma and he met a couple of times when the two families went to the movies together. I think she liked him . . . Your Ghosh mashima asked me the other day if I was expecting an American son-in-law. Imagine her guts! I retorted, 'Of course not. Our Miru is as she was before and she would not do such a thing. She went to America to study, not to catch a husband.' . . . Have you made some friends? How do you spend your week-ends and evenings? Surely, you do not study all the time.

I have to end this letter and get back to the invitation lists. Mejo mashi and I have been digging out all the names of relatives to make a good list and not to leave out anyone. Most of our shoppings is complete except the jewelry. We do not want to pick them up until just before the wedding. It's not safe. Oh, Mira, you should have seen the diamond and ruby necklace! It is just beautiful! Write soon and remember the wedding date.

Your mother

This is the letter which Mira wished she could write to her mother in reply:

My dear ma,

With every letter from you I have an increasing feeling of a distance between us. I cannot explain it even to myself. On the one hand, I know why you are worried about my health, about my life and about my safety. Yet, I thought I gone ten thousand miles to get away from this protective love which makes me feel suffocated sometimes. It breaks my heart to tell you this and I can never bring myself to say so. What a strange dilemma! I read between the lines of your letters and sometimes I feel like screaming with frustration and anger. What are you fantasizing about my life here? In case I fall in love with an American or whoever, be sure I will do what I wish to do. If you think that you can dictate my life from such a distance, you are under some illusions. But, you know that it's not so easy for me to act the way I would like to. I do not know why. Even when some young men ask me out, your face and the rest (aunts, neighbours, all) appear in front of my eyes. What is this inner restriction? I cannot talk about it to anyone here and I cannot talk about it, least of all, with you. It's not just being free to mix with American men, in different things I feel a tug from behind. I wish I had some power to tear away from this tug and pull . . . I also wish I could do everything a good daughter is supposed to do, the way you brought me up. Believe me, it would be so very satisfying to be your good daughter who does not tarnish the name of the family or the wish of her parents, especially her mother. While I am in this interminable conflict, I seem to have no choice but to remain in this tension and confusion. I shall continue to try to please you as much as I can until some part of me gives way. I like my life here and yet I miss India, the family and most of all *you* so intensely sometimes. Sometimes, I feel I am walking in my sleep and this is a big dream after all. Is it really possible for me to close my eyes and finish my studies and be back exactly the way I came and everything would be just fine for ever. Oh, God, I wish I had some idea how to deal with these problems . . . I must sleep; there is a 8.30 class tomorrow. I am so tired.

Your loving and confused daughter

This is the letter Mira really wrote:

January 1961

Respected Ma,

It was nice to hear from you and get all the news. I am happy to know that Uma's wedding date is firmed. February is a difficult month for me. The classes would be in full session and it would be a loss of nearly three to four weeks of my work here. This break will really be hard for me and I am not so sure I really want to be there only for a wedding between two people who do not even know each other well.

No, don't worry. I am not talking about my choosing my own husband or anything like that. But, it seems strange to me when I tell my American friends the way marriages take place in our families. I seem to feel a bit embarrassed about it all. Perhaps, I am not making myself very clear. There are things I feel more and more strange about our customs and it's no point telling you all this. I know you will begin to see mountains out of mole hills. Perhaps, baba and I could talk about these things a bit better. At any rate, I shall try.

Thanks so much for sending the food parcel. No, I won't tell baba a word. I am waiting eagerly for it. The pickles! Even the idea makes my mouth water! By the way, please tell Ghosh mashima that Miru has not changed that much yet. And, suppose I do marry an American, is it really the end of the world, ma? I thought you liked fair-skinned tall men! (Well, I am joking.) Is Uma really happy about this match? I guess I should not say things like this at this point. Forgive me. This letter has been a bit confused and please don't read between lines, now. I must stop and shall write a longer one perhaps, this week-end. I must rush. *Pranam* to you and baba and greetings to all.

Your Miru

A week later:

January 1961

Ma,

This is a quick note to tell you that I am making plans to come in February. If I can finish some of my term-ending papers beforehand I may be able to come without feeling too guilty. It would be wonderful to see you all again. It would be good for me to be back in the family and taste all the good cookings of a wedding. Do you think I should bring a separate gift for Uma from here? Something she might like? Do ask her and let me know. I am terribly busy, but well. I take a glass of milk every night and feel wonderful every morning! The parcel is not here yet.

How are you and baba? I wrote him a long letter giving all the details of our university and life here. Has he received it yet? Please take care of yourself and don't go out everyday on errands. How is everyone? My *pranam* and love,

Miru

A year later:

4 January 1962

My respected ma and baba,

I am writing this very important letter to ask your permission to marry John – John Cohn whom I met nearly 6 months ago. John is two years senior to me and already has a part-time position in his depart-

THE INFINITELY HEALING CONVERSATION

ment which is biology. He comes from a good family; his father is a professor of biochemistry and he has one sister who is in music school. I met his family over the last Christmas and we got along very well. John is very interested in India and would like to come and visit you all as soon as the summer vacation begins. But I would like to come as his wife. It would be easier. We talked and discussed the matter over many hours, and this seems like the best way to do it. Please send your blessings. We would have a civil marriage and, perhaps, a Hindu one when we come, if you so wish. I know how disappointed ma would be otherwise . . . Please ma, try to understand that time has changed and perhaps, I have changed too. I love John and it is important that I marry him and it would be easier and more convenient for both of us to continue our studies when we are married. It's also less expensive to share the same living space . . . I am sorry that I had to break the news like this. I did not know how to do it any other way. Both of you gave me enough independence to allow me to think for myself for my life and this is a very important decision for me to make. Ma, I realize this is going to shock you. But, as I said, you do try to understand and I know that neither you nor baba would stand in the way of my happiness. Please write soon and let me know if you want to know anything more about John . . . We do not plan to get married until April or May just before the summer holidays.

Please accept my *pranam* and love.

Yours,
Miru

This was the reply from her mother after a week:

Mira,

Both your father and I are astounded by your letter. So Ghosh mashima was not so wrong after all! How can you do such a thing to us? We suggest that you come home as soon as you can and we will discuss the matter face to face. Your baba is sending you enough money for your trip. If marriage is what is in your mind, I don't see any point of your remaining in America. We could arrange a marriage for you here in no time. It's pity that all the effort and expenses for your trip abroad came to this. At any rate, I always told your baba that a woman's higher education comes to little. But, who listens to me? Now, he could learn some lessons. Please drop a line as soon as you get the money and get your air-ticket.

Affectionately yours,
ma

My respected parents,

John and I got married last week-end and used the money you sent me for a small reception we gave. I felt good that something arrived from my family for this important occasion of my life. I have to get married without your verbal blessings, but I considered the token money as your blessings. We still hope to visit you in summer and I would like to know if you so wish. My address will change from next week and I give it below. Hope your health is good and everyone in the house is fine.

With *pranam*,
Miru

This is the letter which Mira wished she had written:

Dear baba and ma,

I am even more astounded by your lack of understanding. I know you have feelings and hopes for me. How can you not be flexible enough to realize that I am not in your generation? You show no sympathy for my inner struggle before I decided to take this step. Perhaps, in your time it was not important to love a man or woman to marry. You loved later and loved slowly (or did not love, perhaps). I am in America, not India, and I am influenced by the atmosphere here. I take the responsibility of my marriage. If I make a mistake (I know it is always possible), at least *I* make it, not you. Marriage now-a-days does not have to be for ever. I love John and I am happy with him. If I have occasional doubts, these are my own. The security I lost when I made the step to come here is not going to offer me the security you had to protect your marriage. There are many others around you. I am alone here, so is John and many others. Unfortunately this is true and this situation makes us bold and perhaps, even, daring. I don't believe I could ever make you see this. Sometimes, I feel as if I am split in the middle. Please let me live the other half, at least now. My life and learning here go well with this step. I know many other Indian girls would not do this. Their love and concern for their parents and families would be paramount and they will sacrifice their desire to live a new life, to experiment perhaps. Even if it turns out to be nothing but only an experiment, let me go through it myself. I am a big girl now . . . Oh, God, I wish I could be freer to be happy right now. Yet the same nagging tag continues. May be, I should stay here for ever to erase this nagging pull from behind. Perhaps, John can help me do so. But he is so eager to go to India. I suppose I am alone after all, in this. Please try to understand the struggle within me and be with me. I need you for myself.

Love,
Your daughter

Twenty years later Mira's own daughter wrote to Mira:

June 1981

Dear Mummy:

This last trip to India with you has brought home to me a few hard facts – facts that I wanted to avoid seeing for some time. As you well know, you and I have had a few arguments and several days of tensions during the trip. As I approach my seventeenth year I suddenly ask myself where do I belong. I know this is the usual teen-age identity crisis, etc., etc. You came to this country when you were slightly older than I am now and married my father and admired the American life-style and tried to be an American as much as you could. I am born of you who is Indian and my father who is American. Of course, I am American. Except for a few trips to India I have little to do with India outwardly. But, I feel how much you would like me to become Indian sometimes. I cannot explain it with examples. But I feel it in my bones. The India that you never quite shook off your system comes back to you now and you want to see your daughter live it, at least partly.

Yes, mummy I know I am wrapped up in many superficial things, things my friends and peers indulge in and I can understand your need to protect me. But, I am part of them and in order for me to be accepted by my friends sometimes I do things which do not always please me either. I need their approval and I want to be like them sometimes. But, your good intentions to teach me those good Indian things then clash. Although I dislike the superficiality of my friends, I cannot move back to your life-style just because it is better (for you) or more ancient or deep. Let me live the life I am surrounded by and reject and suffer as I wish and as many of my friends are going through . . . While I understand your point, I must admit sometimes I really do not know how to communicate to you what I really feel. Words seem to fail on both sides. That's why I am writing this letter. Perhaps it will be a bit easier. Dad does not seem to be the problem in this regard. When I argue with him or reject something he wants me to do, I do not feel such ambivalence as I do when the same thing happens with you. Isn't it strange! Perhaps, I am a bit Indian under my skin after all. Although every time I visit India after the first two weeks of love and food, I begin to weary of all the slow sloth and all the rest. I ache to come back to my superficial friends with whom I do not always need to use even language. It's the communication that I feel is at stake between you and me and between India and me. Mummy, you did not have to grow up in America; you grew up in India and could keep a lot of nostalgia and good memories when you decided to reject India. When you criticize me, you never think that we were born in two different worlds and that makes a big difference between us even though I am your flesh and blood as you often point out, rightly.

My dearest mother, I cannot be protected by you. Forgive me if I remind you of something you related to me many times. You could not be protected by my grandparents (your parents) when you decided to embrace this culture along with my father. Nor can you protect me despite the fact that we are not separated by physical distance. Perhaps, we are separated by something else and I suspect, that is India.

I have never written a letter like this before in my short life. I feel good about writing this and I would like to hear what you have to say. Ma, perhaps, you and I still can be friends in this way that you and your mother could not be. Let's try. I love you.

Yours,
Rita

Fiona and her mother Kate, 1979

Fiona was born and raised in a small town in northern England to a family of mixed class: her father is working-class and her mother, Kate, middle-class. Kate is no longer occupied as a full-time mother; she writes short stories and has published one book of poetry. Fiona is a lesbian feminist, active in the women's liberation movement. She has a paid part-time job and shares the child care of a baby girl with three other women.

Kate describes her feelings during Fiona's painful adolescent years:

'In the past, my daughter and I had endless opportunities to talk and I was ever willing to elicit from her anything which might be troubling her, but there were occasions when I was completely at a loss and which caused me a great deal of pain. Frankly, I ended up by not knowing whether I had loved her too much or too little! I felt that she was sensitive but she sometimes showed all too little sensitivity to me, so I put it down to a love/hate relationship on her part which apparently many adolescents have. She seemed to take an endless time to grow up which was strange as she had such an independent nature when she was little . . . When she seemed to be going through hell, hating herself and everyone (save a few friends) including me, I told her quite frankly that it was she who was rejecting me. I had never and would never – could never – reject her. I loved her dearly and thought there would *always* be a bond between us. I loved her more than anyone else . . .

'I felt this letter was a vindication of my basic belief in her and in our unbreakable relationship – which had been damaged but not irreparably. I had always hoped we would get back. She has been the person closest to me.'

14 February 1979

Dear Mama,

I want to tell you a little of my inner life, the journey I am on, a journey which is very hard and lonely, but which sometimes gives me great joy.

I am a divided self, and my journey is to the centre of myself, to make myself whole. I am often in pain, pain at being a woman in a man's world, pain at being alone, the pain of my past, being belittled and seeing my mother and brother constantly belittled by a father whose only means of self-esteem was at another's expense – and what pain must he have blocked in his unaware, uncomprehending life. My pain of being dependent on one person for love and affection, my mother (because it is the mother's 'role' to give herself up to her family), who wanted to exist in her own right as an independent woman.

There are not many people who go on such a journey to heal themselves. Most don't get the chance. There are not many people who lead 'inner' reflective lives. I know that it is a journey that I shall be on all my life. Yet I know that one day I shall be whole. And what I want you to know is that I feel I have the strength to do it because, in spite of all the contradictions of family life, you loved me.

Some people are so damaged that they do not know it. Others know yet can do nothing about it. But I have been loved enough by you to know the extent of my self-alienation. And knowing it, I can mend it.

Not only did you love and nurture me, but I know it's from you that I learned or inherited a reflective way of being, which looks to nature for nourishment of the spirit, and also I feel that you are 'aware'.

I don't think I shall ever, in the 'normal' sense, be a 'success'. I am an outsider, with neither academic, marital or career status. They are of little importance to me. What is important, at the deepest level, is the peace I occasionally experience, the joy I sometimes find on my journey. I am alive and conscious of every moment, and I wouldn't trade my place with anyone else in the world. I want you to know this, I want you to know that you helped me to be here. You could say this is purely a daughter's acknowledgement of a mother's love. Thank you for being you. Thank you for striving. Thank you for caring.

love,
Fiona

23 February 1979

Dearest Fiona,

I was pleased and grieved to get your letter. Pleased that you wrote and with the tributes you paid me in it. Grieved to learn you still have a feeling of self-alienation.

From my experience I would say that most people, especially modern thinkers, have contradictions in their nature to deal with and often these are the most interesting characters. Self-awareness has a Janus face as it brings extreme pain and extreme happiness. Living with it and trying to guard oneself from *too much* of the pain is, I suppose, what the life-long journey is all about. Challenges to be met, situations to be accepted. Building defences, but not such impenetrable ones that they become stone, in which case one might be invulnerable to pain but also the bliss on the other side of the wall. If one did not suffer the pain I think the appreciation of the contrast of the ecstasy would also be lacking.

None of this seems to be very original and not, I suspect, new to you in any way . . .

I know that you will find your wholeness (or that *it* will find *you* unawares!!). Worldly success, by itself, is of little value.

Yes, I will always care very much and am glad to know that I have helped even a little. In the past I did have a sense of our both being in a wilderness of our own, but knew there was a lifeline there (between the two) for the asking/clasping. In your childhood you were all I had to make me happy.

Mum

Three years later, Fiona wrote:

'I have reached the end of the journey I described in my letter and I am no longer a divided person, alienated from myself or from the world.

'I am reclaiming more and more my capacity to think and to love, and I am taking great pride in myself as a woman, a lesbian, and a non-biological mother.

'The pain that I journeyed through was the pain of being mistreated because I was a child, because I am a woman and because I am a lesbian. I learned to understand that there is nothing inherently hurtful in any of these things, that the hurt comes from having our human rights, power and intelligence denied us as children, women and lesbians.

'I am taking charge of my life, and part of that taking charge is a re-evaluation of the relationship with my mother. I know that it is still growing, as we are both still growing, and I am beginning to realise what a deep and profound relationship it is. I think my mother has always known it.'

Chungmi Kim to her mother, 1980

Chungmi Kim, poet and playwright, is the eighth of nine children of one of the founding families in the city of Chong-Ju, South Korea. She received a BA in English from Ewha University in Seoul, then worked as an assistant to the Director of Korea Drama Center and as a producer/director for MBC Radio-TV in Seoul. After her arrival in the United States, she earned an MA in Theater Arts from the University of California, Los Angeles.

The awards she has won include the Harry Kurnitz Creative Writing Award for her play, *I Beg Your Pardon?*, and the first prize of the Open Door Writing Award from the Writers Guild Foundation for her screenplay, *The Dandelion*. She has written and produced a number of television programmes including 'The Asian Hour' and 'Korean Community in LA'. In

1980, she created and produced a poetry special, 'Poets In Profile'.

Her poetry collection, CHUNGMI – Selected Poems, was published in 1982. She is currently involved in developing projects for television and the theatre, while compiling her second book of poetry. She lives in Los Angeles, where she is an active member of Women In Film and a participant in the Los Angeles Actors' Theater Playwrights Workshop.

Chungmi writes:

'My mother in Korea has sacrificed her life for her family: husband and nine children. When I went to see her three years ago, she was bedridden in a state of apathy, incapable of her usual emotional response. And when I left ten weeks later, she showed a few drops of tears, her first since she fell ill. This is a tribute to my mother to whom I am most grateful.'

DAUGHTER/MOTHER DIALOGUE

Daughter:
I see your face
Mother
smiling
with a shadow behind
in the sunset.

The days of your youth
in your eyes
silently
unravelling –

Born a woman
half a century sooner
you were a warrior
in disguise.

Your heart filled
with love and courage
you taught your children
such optimism
that life was indeed worth
living.

At seventy seven
now
you sit against the wall
your back bent
your body shrunk in half.

Silent in apathy
you do not cry
for joy or sorrow.

And you have no questions
about my homecoming.

Tell me
Mother
what has taken your soul
away
so cruelly?

Mother:
Nothing matters.
Nothing –
in this life.

I'm waiting
for my life to be taken
away.

Daughter:
Why, Mother?
Why?

Mother:
A bride of seventeen –
I was married to a man of
    thirty
chosen by my grandmother.
The first, the only man.

He was proud as an eagle
with a temper like a thunder
    storm.

Daughter:
Did you love Father?

Mother:
I bore him four sons
he was proud of.
I bore him five daughters
he was indifferent to.
Together we built
a nest of wealth and
nurtured our children
with words of wisdom.

I taught you to respect
your Father.

But nothing matters
any more.

Daughter:
What anguish do you
      remember
most
Mother?

Mother:
Your brother went to the war
and never returned.

I never forget –
Help me! Help me, Mother,
he cried,
if I go to the war now,
I fear I'd never come back
alive.

He knew his destiny.

A box of ashes came home.
And the world around me
      was
shattered.

One month after his death
the day of liberation came.
Just one month after . . .

Daughter:
In another war
you lost your daughter.
My sister.

Born a girl
in the year of the horse
she was the daughter
with a wild temper.

She sang in a voice
sharp as a knife,
danced in the night
like the flame of a torch.

Her ambition grew
like the grapes on the vine.
But then she was
in disgrace
for being a woman.

Another war broke.

And she flitted
from one illusion
to another.

One rainy day
she ironed her dress
with pretense
and
drank the water
of sweet death.

A virgin –
dead.
At twenty one.

She was buried
in the wilderness.

In the wilderness
where the virgin soul was
      destined
to linger
eternally.

Mother wailed.

The pain and anguish
nailed hard
on her bosom
and rusted
in all the years of her life.

Now

in apathy –

Mother:
I prayed God,
I prayed Buddha.

to take away my life
instead of my children.

God and Buddha
they left me
long ago
when the war broke.

But nothing matters.
Nothing –

Daughter:
It matters, Mother.
It matters that you are
my Mother.

Through you
I had a vision
of life
different from yours.

Through you
I learned the wisdom
to seek
for freedom.

You paved the way

for my journey
into the world
unknown.

Through you
I gained the courage
to survive.

It matters
that I am your daughter.

Mirror to mirror
through myself
I see you.
You see me.

Are you not happy that I
    came
to see you?

Show me a smile
however faint.
Open your heart
just one more time.

Mother:
Tears, my tears . . .
Strange . . . you bring my
    tears back.
Am I alive?

Daughter:
You are, Mother,
eternally . . .

Susan Neulander Faulkner to her mother Elsa Liebes Miner, 1979

Susan and her mother and sister fled Nazi Germany in 1938, when Susan was 17. Her father was put to death in Auschwitz in 1942. Her mother started her own business in the United States and worked until partial blindness forced her to retire at the age of 68.

Susan had wanted to be a doctor, but she had to leave school at 15 and go to work as a secretary to help support her family. At 21 she married, and several years later she and her husband adopted two children; the marriage subsequently deteriorated and they were divorced. Susan started college at the age of 38, and fourteen years later earned her PhD in English. For several years she enjoyed teaching in college. She is now retired and lives in New

York, where she writes, participates in groups, attends concerts, films and plays, and spends time with her friends.

She writes:

'My mother, possessive and domineering, with an instinct for the jugular, was a darkly beautiful woman, with a queenly walk, gorgeous legs, magnetic charm and strong sex appeal, all of which she used to advantage; she was also a highly successful businesswoman and talented artist. Her love for me was always qualified by my imperfections, and I soon came to fear her rages – she slapped me hard numerous times for trivial offenses, even after I was grown. I feared even more her withdrawing her love from me for some reason; at times she would look through me with an icy glance and refuse to talk to me for days.

'In her last years my mother, wanting to bind me to her once more, did so by giving me money over protracted periods. I accepted gratefully, since my husband had died penniless shortly after our divorce, and I had to help my daughter, who was ill for several years. I also knew that these gifts were my mother's way of repaying me for those early years of sacrifice. Tragically, she never learned that love cannot be forced or bought, and that only by giving it freely and in full measure can one receive love in abundance.'

1979

Dear Mother,

A week ago you died, and at last I am free – and quite alone. Free from that presence hovering perpetually in the wings I could never stop looking to for the warmth and affection, the unreserved approval, that I knew only too well would never be there. And yet, while you were alive, I kept hoping in my innermost being that – some day, some time – you would become that mythical 'mother' that I had yearned for since childhood. I never recall your eyes looking at me with affection and pride, although others told me many times that you loved me and were proud of me, and indeed in your later years you did many loving and caring things for me. Yet that yearning for the never-to-be fulfillment of a lifetime dream never left me but remained obstinately throughout my life to haunt my hours of happiness with family, with friends, with lovers, even with my children. 'More,' 'I want more,' 'I need more,' this was the unspoken urge within me. Now that your death has finally foreclosed the possibility that my persistent hope might be fulfilled after all, I can free myself of my obsession and see you for what you were: a woman who enjoyed and endured much, who fought hard, loved a few people, and who labored greatly and successfully. If you could not love me in the way I would have wanted you to, that was not so much a failing on your part as the outgrowth of your own desperate desire to have your father love you – not just to admire and respect you, which he did, but to LOVE you. This unfulfilled want colored all your relationships, especially with your daughters; you would so much have wanted me, the elder one, to be a boy, to replace the void left by the death of your only beloved brother, killed in the First World War. None of us could ever satisfy your longing, just as all the love I've had in my entire life could never make up to me for your love I felt I had been denied.

Now I am alone – my body feels hollow inside, just as – I imagine – a woman must feel after giving birth. For in a strange way, you were like a physical entity within me, a part of me that belonged to my body, that filled a void within me, and that I was always aware of. Yesterday, when Tracy Austin won the US Open Women's Singles championship, my first impulse was to pick up the phone and call you: 'What did you think of the match?' And then it came to me like a gentle pull within me that you were no longer at the other end of the phone, that the circle had narrowed irrevocably, and that the one quintessential person in my world was gone. Last week, after the funeral, I sat at home in the darkness, listening to the 'Messiah' for hours and crying like a child who 'was despised, rejected,' left all alone in the dark. But out of that communion with the abandoned child within me, when I felt empty, hollowed-out, finally came a new sense of wholeness, a sense of myself as an independent adult, no longer cared for by that non-existent, magical 'mother' that I had wished for all my life, but now left to make my own way, however haltingly and alone.

Your shadowy dominance has been removed from my life, a dominance in latter years based more on my remembrance of what you once were than on present-day reality, and now I can no longer count on either your faint praise or your persistent need to control my life in some measure. Now I can finally look at my life, one filled with achievements and tragedies of my own, with love, with friendships, with an irrepressible zest for living, and say to myself what you somehow could never say to me wholeheartedly: 'Well done.' And now I can look back at you, my mother, and say, truthfully, 'I admired your achievements, Mother; I loved you imperfectly as your love for me was imperfect. And what finally remains in my memory of you are the many years we lived through – together in some amazingly close-linked fashion, like two lifeboats keeping each other afloat – the experiences we shared, and the feeling, in spite of everything, that you were there for me when it counted, in your own marvellously egocentric, domineering, matriarchal way – and for all that I thank you.'

Marion Cohen and her mother, 1977

Marion Cohen is a mathematician, poet, teacher and mother of three children, Marielle, Arin and Bret. (Another daughter, Kerin, died two days after birth.) Marion grew up in a Jewish family in New Jersey; her father worked as a high-school history teacher and her mother as a teacher in an elementary school. Coming from a family of atheist intellectuals, Marion faced an unusual set of criticisms when, at the age of 21, she married Jeff, a practising Jew: Marion could never be 'liberated' enough to suit her mother.

The incident which provoked this letter was a telephone call in which Marion's mother said she could not come to help out when Marion and Jeff were ill simultaneously, because she had a bar mitzvah to attend in two weeks. She suggested instead that Jeff 'call a cleaning woman' or that Marion should come home with her. But when Marion continued to feel ill, she consented to come and help out for one day. However, the offer was made in such a way that Marion said she would feel uncomfortable having her around. Later that day, Marion wrote to her mother:

5 June 1977

Dear Mother,

. . . I look upon yesterday's phone conversation as the first time I've ever 'stood up to' you. Oh, I know I had temper tantrums as a child, and I know I wasn't the perfect teenager, but for various reasons – most of them connected with guilt and fear, but also because of your heart condition – I have refrained from speaking the truth, and have just gone along with a lot of things – like your recent supposedly casual comments about how Bob does the dishes, or about how So-and-So had a big wedding and isn't that terrible? . . . or telling me all about what's wrong with my friends, and everybody else that isn't you or Daddy or our immediate family, but mostly everybody else connected with Jeff . . . I have refrained from dealing with these things as they come up, and I'm sick and tired of it. Even though each 'incident' only bothers me for a short while, it's still unfair.

. . . Once you told me that one of these days I'm going to have to decide how I feel about you and Daddy. Well, Ma – I already *know* how I feel; I just haven't told you. In short, I feel pressured, nervous and incapable of ever possibly pleasing you – even more incapable of Jeff's ever possibly pleasing you. I feel judged – and judged guilty. And I feel as though you and Daddy and Sis have a little 'club', a little clique, going (the purpose of which is vague but has something to do with art, music, Freud and politics), a club which I don't belong to, don't want to belong to, but feel that I should belong to. Also a club that I pretend, in your presence, to belong to, and this pretense makes me feel nervous. I feel that you have a Family Tradition going, a tradition which is infinitely more destructive than either Catholic or Orthodox Jewish tradition. (I may be exaggerating here!) . . .

Anyway, what I've been trying to say is that I view my 'phone call to you as the first time I ever 'stood up' to you, the first time I ever said 'Oh, *Mother!*' (It's not that I haven't *been* independent of you; I *always* have been – I just never *declared* independence. I guess that must be because I wasn't *entirely* independent.) ANYWAY, I've finally stood up to you – and I feel guilty as hell! It was soooo hard for me to do what I did, knowing as I was doing it that I was displeasing you, 'upsetting' you. It was very hard. I *feel* so anxious to please you.

. . . But mostly it's hard for me because of guilt – and fear. I suppose everybody has the little-girl fear of Something Terrible Happening And It All Being My Fault. And I suppose everyone hesitates to rock the boat, for fear they are Entirely Wrong After All. That's my main fear – that all along I've been wrong. That, if I confront you, then you'll counter-confront with some startling piece of information about Jeff, such as that he's in charge of distribution of Nestlé's infant formula to underdeveloped countries! That's the ultimate, of course. (I seem to have a very Kafka-esque mind.) The next-ultimate is that you'll *prove* me wrong – in the same way you 'proved' to me 15 years or so ago that pre-marital sex wasn't such a hot idea. (It seemed so logical, the way you put it; only an hour later, alone in my room, I realized the flaws.) . . . I'm afraid of you. And when you get into your 'bad moods' (which, from my point of view, are unpredictable), this fear runs rampant.

Away from you, however, I am almost completely sane. I feel even saner since this latest happening. It all seems clearer, somehow. You are (among other things) simply a person who has disappointed me . . . Then *you* try to pull a guilt trip on *me* by saying I'm 'discarding' you. If I *did* discard you, in self-defense, you could hardly blame me – but I'm not. I was simply too proud to have you come, when it was so obvious to me that you didn't want to. I was also, as I said, afraid.

But the main thing is: I can't understand what's the big deal about Jeff. You never gave him a chance. He was a 19-year-old kid when I first fell in love with him; what did you want from him? (Yeah, I know Daddy read *Kapital* when he was 20, but Gauguin started *his* work at age 40-something.) . . . my friends – young, old, radicals, lesbian separatists, artists, etc. – all like and respect him and think we have a great marriage. I really fail to understand why *your* standards are so high.

Just because he doesn't have the 'lingo', or the personality, or the same beliefs Daddy has doesn't mean he doesn't have 'integrity'. And if you say you can't respect Jeff because of his politics, then go right ahead and stop respecting me. *My* politics aren't the same as Daddy's, either. And while you're at it, stop respecting Florence, and Molly, and Beverly, and all your other friends. I guess what I'm trying to say is: Do you resent having a son-in-law? Did you want me to marry? Like in my poem, 'What are the plans for me?' And it is obvious to me that – *à la* the next line – I am *not* 'fulfilling that plan'.

It's hard for me to prove to you (and, as a mathematician, and as a person full of guilt feelings, I *need* to prove things – I imagine the whole issue appearing before a jury) just *how* you never gave Jeff a chance. It began so long ago, and you've always been so subtle about it. Most of the time I never knew when you would 'attack'. But it was right from the beginning that you let me know Jeff wasn't in your plans for me. One evening, shortly after I told you we were in love, we were doing the dishes together and you suddenly started telling me I should consider whether Jeff was the one for me, as (a) he was kosher, and (b) he wasn't musical. So right away I knew how you felt. How could I *not* tense up? How could I not continue to be tense with you throughout the years? I suppose things might have been better if I had actually explained to you at length *why* I had fallen in love with Jeff, what it was we found together; I suppose – thinking back – what *you* needed then was reassurance, reassurance from me. But fear kept me from being this adult about the whole thing. (Remember, I was only 17.) Fear that, if I confronted you, you might win. Or 'prove' to me . . . that I was wrong and Jeff really *wasn't* the one for me. Intense and new as my love for him was then, I was still afraid to face you concerning it. If I had been stronger, I would have.

. . . I don't know what happens next. *I* didn't mention 'discarding'; you did. But one thing you have to know: If I have to discard you, I will. As I said, you don't have to be friends with Jeff. He doesn't have to – and he doesn't – come along every time I visit you. (So don't pull the maneuver of calling me 'unliberated', or anything equivalent.) If you're sick, I can come take care of you and leave the kids with Jeff. But if *I'm* sick, you can't take me home with you. If you want to help, you have to come to me. My immediate family is Jeff and Elle and Arin. You don't take better care of me than Jeff. It's just that right now Jeff is sick, too. Otherwise he would do everything, as he did when I had bronchitis and when I was recuperating from the D and C. You act as if I need a mother to care for me because Jeff isn't doing his job. I don't believe I'm imagining this (or 'misinterpreting', as you always say).

Gee, when I started this letter, I felt 'guilty as hell'. Now I find I don't even feel guilty as purgatory! As you say, I guess I'm the type to 'bounce back' very quickly. In that respect I'm very strong. Too bad I'm so hesitant taking the action in the first place. 34 years old and I've finally gotten the nerve to say 'Oh, *Mother!*'

I think of all the good things. The duets. Your interest in my endeavors. The childhood happinesses. The things you've said that really made an impression and affected my life. Like about marrying 'someone who breaks through your loneliness'. Or how one shouldn't feel guilty or embarrassed about things *other* people did. And other things which I can't remember right now. And your emphasis on 'values'. Although it still makes me feel pressured (I do have what I call a 'radical' hang-up, which is due to you and Daddy, I'm sure, but which is my responsibility to deal with), it also, I'm sure, has helped shape my life. Indeed, you did lots of things right, and I'm sure you had a lot to do with 'what I am today' (which is something I'm quite pleased with!). I think of the good things. All that baby-sitting when Elle was an infant. (It came just when we needed it.) Some nice things you bought us. Your pleasure at my wedding. (Wish you hadn't spoiled the pre-wedding period for me, though.) Your sending me to Arts High. I think of the good things. There were good things. There *are* good things. Our recent deepening friendship. (But with my still not confronting you on the matters of this letter.) There *are* good things.

But there are *always* good things. As Anne Frank said, 'there is some good in everybody', and while she seemed to think this a positive idea, I find it annoying: The 'some good' confuses the issue. Politically, it is detrimental. What I really mean is: Just because there are good things doesn't mean I'm not allowed to confront you – and confront you strongly – with the bad.

As I say, I am fearful of what you will confront me back with. Will it be the ultimate? ('Well, okay, I'll tell you. I didn't want to, but now I see I have to. Jeff is a Nestlé's distributor.) Or will you use one of the classic maneuvers, used unconsciously by parents everywhere? ('I want you to know how much you've upset me.' 'I could tell you a few things – but I won't.' 'After all I've done for you . . .' 'If you could remember some of the things you did when you were little . . .' 'I see you've given up all your (meaning 'our') principles.' 'I see that husband of yours is poisoning your mind.' 'But, in spite of it all, I want you to know that you're very important to us, that we still love you.') What will you say? What evidence will you come up with that I am totally unaware of?

I'm sorry, but I can't end with, 'But I love you anyway.' That's just not my style – as a writer, and as a person. I can only end with – just this –

Marion

A week or so after this first letter, there was a visit and a tense, terse conversation in which Marion's mother mentioned how 'hurt' she was. Marion wrote again:

7 July 1977

Dear Ma,

Just a quickie this time . . . I find it hard to level with you in person. You always put on that bad-mood expression, or at least so it seems to me. At any rate, it plays on the guilt feelings I already feel, and it renders me incapable of saying what I would normally say. It sort-of paralyzes me.

The main thing I want to say is that you got the wrong impression (or *I gave* you the wrong impression) from the ending of my last letter.

I *didn't* mean that I don't love you – I *do* love you – I just meant exactly what I said, that, considering the mood I was in, I couldn't bring myself to end the letter on a 'love-note'. It would, at least for me, play down everything else I said in the letter, and, as I said there, it would seem too cliché-ish. So I'm sorry if you got the wrong idea.

One other thing: Maybe it's expecting too much of you, but I think it's childish of you to just keep repeating how 'hurt' my letter made you:

1) *I'm* hurt, too. I've been hurt for a long time. But I didn't even mention it (before this), because that's understood. Of *course* we're both hurt. Frank-ness always starts with hurt feelings. To quote an old cliché, the truth hurts.

2) I *knew* you would be hurt (and I knew you would not hide the hurt), and *that's* why I've waited so long. Perhaps I shouldn't have. But I really believe you would have been just as hurt had I spoken up 16 years ago.

3) Being hurt doesn't make you right. (Here's one of my political sayings: Suffering doesn't make you a radical. Hitler was in prison, and in any revolution, the oppressor, as well as the oppressed, suffers greatly.)

4) Ask yourself honestly – aren't you sub-consciously – *very* sub-consciously – as *everyone* does – as we *all* do – as *I* do – using your 'being hurt' as a weapon, or at least a defense mechanism? I mean, it *does* play on my guilt feelings (and my guilt feelings are not unique).

5) I disagree with you that the way I 'hurt' you is much more serious than the way most children 'hurt' their parents at one time or another. Most parents probably really *have* been 'discarded' (as you say) by their children at some point. All *you've* gotten is a belated 'Oh, Mother!' and an honest lengthy account of my feelings.

6) Speaking of my feelings, you seem to be shy-ing away from the question: Are they justified? Are they at least *partially* justified? After all, I'm not a malicious person. And I'm not a poorly adjusted person. If I feel a certain way, there must be a reason.

No matter how hurt you are, and no matter how much you wallow in that hurt (I know that hurts, too), it won't erase the above question.

7) Maybe you *need* time to wallow in the hurt. But, if you're an adult, you won't take forever. I'm *not* a bad little girl; I'm 34 years old, mother of 3, mathematician, political writer, etc. Whole audiences have taken me seriously. If you're adult, you'll eventually be able to see *me* as adult, too. When you're ready, we can discuss as adults – with the underlying, and compassionate, assumption that we're *both* 'hurt'. ('Adult' isn't really the word I mean to use; I use it for want of a better word.)

One other thing: I *do* realize that the intensity of my guilty-little-girl feelings may be a defect in *my* personality. *Maybe*. I somehow doubt it, but maybe. Anyway, I'm dealing with it. Right? I'm not letting the *feelings* get in my way. (I've already discounted any idea that *feeling* guilty mean you *are* guilty. I once read that innocent people on trial usually feel guilty at some point or points. And Kafka has certainly had an effect on me along those lines. Plus my own writing.) BUT I'm willing to admit that I *might* have *exaggerated* (but not *imagined*) your anti-Jeff slurs because of my excess of daughter-guilt feelings. I'm willing to admit that. To some extent at least, I may be simply blaming you ('blame' for want of a better word) for being my mother.

In fact, as I confront you more and more, I find myself able to be more objective along these lines, and more objective in general. So *that's* good . . .

Love,
Marion

July 1977

Dear Marion

Now that I'm actually sitting down to write to you, I don't know what to say. If I question some of your statements, it might sound as if I were challenging you. If I ask for clarification, it would sound as if I were getting bogged down on petty details. If I talk about feeling, it might seem that I'm hurt. If I deny what you ascribed to me, it puts you on a guilt trip. If I stand on my principles or quote from my heroines or heroes, it might sound pompous or self-righteous.

Nonetheless, I do have to say a few things. I wasn't 'hurt' (although I may have said that to you). My immediate feeling was humiliation, a powerful wave of humiliation that almost knocked me over. A few days later, this changed to anger. But all the time, I was thinking. I read your letter, sentence by sentence, and made copious comments in the margins. I racked my lousy memory to recall some of the things you wrote about. One bitter day, I listened to a Mozart quintet. Tears dropped into my lap, one after another, and I wrote a note to you and put it in my will.

Well, time passed. I erased the comments and tore up the note. We talked a little and saw each other. I know that I love and care for you, perhaps as Johann says at the end of *Scenes from a Marriage*, '– in my inadequate way', and I think you love and care for me, too. So what more is there to say?

Love,
Mom

Joannie Fritz and her mother Gloria, 1980–82

Joannie Fritz, a writer and actor living in New York, grew up in Los Angeles, San Francisco and New York. A graduate of New York University, she has written and produced three full-length plays: *You Told Me That the Carousel Was Crystal, Frames* and *Inside*. She co-authored, with David Steven Rappaport, a children's musical, *Frognapped*, and was co-founder, with Larry Pellegrini, of Kidwerks, a children's theatre collective in New York. She has been a collaborator and performer of street and experimental theatre with MOMO, a New York theatre collective, as well as appearing as a solo performer in New York, California, Nevada, and in Europe.

Her mother, Gloria Hieger, also has two sons, Carl and Bobby, A classical musician, Gloria previewed at Times Hall as a pianist when she was 20, and subsequently worked with the Pittsburgh Symphony and the Baker Symphony in Pennsylvania, and the Pasadena and San Gabriel Symphonies in California. She has coached vocalists and served as accompanist for Joannie and Carl. Gloria is now retired after twenty-five years of working for the County of Los Angeles, where she handled eligibility for food stamps. She is continuing her part-time work as accompanist and coach for the Los Angeles Cultural Arts Center and as a private teacher. She plans to return full-time to music, and perhaps to return to university to further her education.

Joannie wrote this letter during a trying time in her life and in her relationship with her mother. She then decided not to send it:

8 May 1980

Dear Mom?

How are you?

Got your letter?

I am suffering, that's how I am. You write sentimental thoughts, sweet, 'wish you were here'. I was once sweet but my hands are bruised from repeated slaps. I am getting wrinkles and I am no longer sweet . . .

I am struggling, Momma, much like I suppose you struggled at a similar age . . .

My old friend G.B., the crazy old marxist somewhat-known writer and my first mentor, told me during my last visit to California, 'Well, Joannie, you made it past thirty and you didn't cop out.' Truthfully, I'm more concerned with thirty-one, rapidly approaching on my left shoulder.

Thirty-one is a good age to give up. You left Pittsburgh for Los Angeles about that time and shortly thereafter you gave up your musical aspirations. You had responsibilities: two small children, a new life. Somewhat begrudgingly you put your personal pursuits on hold.

At thirty, I am also in transition. My 'family', the artist's cooperative comprised of one roommate and one roommate/lover, is getting a divorce. My 'children' say they are leaving, yet they ask for my help and emotional support. Much as I've asked of you in the past. But I got my hands slapped too many times. So I've stopped asking.

You write that your youngest son, Bobby, has reached eighteen. Your long awaited rite of passage – the children have reached adulthood. All three of your children – 'Very Wanted', 'Wanted and Paid for in Pain' and 'Oops!' – has grown up and started; is unable to start; and is more than ready to start (respectively) lives of their own. And at long last, you can resume yours.

Cliché and cloying, the message of aging womanhood, the *balabusta*,* the ascent from *hetaira*† to matriarch; your subsequent desexualization (or more aptly the relinquishment of your never-understood and greatly feared sexuality) – it is this you pass on to me as matrilineal folklore, from mother to only daughter. Ironic that you pass this sad legacy on to the only daughter whom you've viewed as corrupter of your husband and sons, this only daughter with whom you've carried on a lifetime love/hate affair. As sure as fathers pass on the title and the kingdom, you transmit the message of motherhood – to your sterile, bisexual, divorced, bohemian daughter. You give it with the same sense of futility that I receive it. I can only half-listen. It's almost embarrassing to read your words. Although you have my sympathies, you really do, for that plight that we as women jointly face, I can only wonder *why* you want to tell me these things. They are as incomprehensible to me as my lifestyle is to you.

It would be of more help to me if we could frankly discuss the current situation with my roommate/lover Deckla, but I know it would be impossible to get past word one without arousing your ire or offending your sensibilities. And if only we could have this hypothetical conversation about the aforesaid intensely painful relationship, I think you'd find it interesting to note how closely my relationship with Deckla parallels ours. The two of you have in turn been Hydra, Medusa, Medea and Venus to me. I have hated and scorned the both of you; at the same time desperate for your support, acceptance and love. And I have often been less than kind to both of you, I am ashamed to say. It's also uncanny how much I've learned about *all* my relationships, past and present, by having this liaison with Deckla, this unit which you have patently condemned.

But then again, you've found every loyalty of mine outside our nuclear family condemnable, regarded them as direct threats to my feelings about you. My friends were turncoats who exploited me. No one was as faithful as my family, everyone would betray me. No one was ever good enough, and yet I was 'trash'. My husband was a 'hick'.

---

*Yiddish: 'matriarchal head of household'.
†Greek: strictly, 'courtesan'.

My lover Blue was a 'bum'. And as for Deckla – well, for the sake of peace we agreed to not discuss her at all.

. . . I am dying a slow death of kow-towing to what I think are the demands and needs of others, lest I be rejected for my unnamed crime. Yet I am, after all, above reproach: the good mother. Indeed, I am Mother Courage, archetypal survivor and inept protector of my children in the face of insurmountable odds, am I not? I try to be kind – and I end up being misunderstood. I try to be zen about the whole thing — and am condemned for my selfishness and ambivalence. I try to stay calm and handle things less explosively than you would – but my clumsy handling is as ineffective as screamed epithets and flying bookcases.

For that reason, lest I become a clone of you, I have been 'kind and giving' to my ex-husband (and resented it). I have supported my ex-lovers in their subsequent, and sometimes concurrent affairs, made love for old time's sake (and swallowed my bile with a shudder). They all say I love unconditionally. 'Joannie always understands.' Yep, I'm just one hell of a girl – just like the one that married dear old Dad.

Except I lack your honesty about my resentment. No one wants to listen to me unless I scream, and I don't know if I want to be heard that badly. The other night I looked in the mirror and I thought, 'You know, the only difference between you and your mother –' (You self-righteous smart-ass self-flagellating bitch) – 'is that she has the honesty to scream when she's in pain. You, on the other hand –' (stoic idiot hypocrite that you are) '– turn it in on yourself.'

At that moment, I understood you in a way I never had before . . .

love,
Joannie

March 1982

Dear Mom,

After two years I am sending you the [above] enclosed letter which until now I didn't have the courage (or vindictiveness) to send . . . So much has happened since I wrote that fiery missive in 1980. We've both grown up. It's hard to send you this letter now, because it no longer accurately reflects my sentiments about you, about me, about women, about life in general. There is much yet to be angry about, but my anger has moved out of the realm of protracted rebellion. I'm angry about more far-reaching things now, like war and poverty and hunger, tangible things to which one can address oneself effectively if one has handled one's own *mishegas*.*

The anger between us has been expressed by prolonged periods of verbal violence and mutual abuse, and long periods of silence, but

---

*Yiddish: 'craziness or insanity'.

finally we have attained a most incredible and civilized peace. Perhaps that's why I never sent that letter to you. The letter was really for me. Moreover, it was the beginning of a long healing process . . .

Now I tremble in apprehension at the reaction you may have upon reading it. I was wise not to send it two years ago because had I done so, we may never have transcended our difficulties. But I *do* want it to be published, Momma, for many reasons, one of which is I think it might be of value to other women; after all, all women are daughters, whether or not they ever become mothers. Further, the catalytic effect the writing of this letter has had on our relationship (unbeknownst to you until now) bears witness to the power of purgation, however painful. I feel it's only ethical of me to share it with you prior to publication . . .

There is no longer time or energy to be angry about my failings or my childishness or my lack of 'success'. Some might call *that* giving up. In the past I have judged you harshly for your choices, Mom; yet I haven't changed so much that I would seek marriage or aspire toward suburbabliss; I've come to terms with my life. I'm not interested in slapping anyone's hands any more, least of all yours.

Gloria, two months ago, I'd gotten to the point of giving up, I'd lived my fuckin' life like the fuckin' rebel I've always been, angry sand-paperish wench. We are sweet women, you and I, covered by bandages and thorns; brave, carrying on in our miniature *la gloire*. We are small in stature, big in scope, influence, power. We fear our own manipulative ability; we fear rejection; we fear we won't be noticed. And sometimes we're not. I will empty myself now, Gloria, as I emptied myself to you when I reached those California shores on my last visit home. I was so empty by that time, and you were there, wanting to fill me, your firstborn only daughter – whatever she was/has-been/will be – you loved and nurtured me in my infantile regression until I was once again strong enough to go on. When I was younger I upbraided you for not giving me your tit when I was an infant. Now, at long last, you have suckled me when I have most needed it. On mother's milk, I am reborn.

love, Joannie

28 July 1982

Dear Joannie,

. . . I've been thinking of answering your letter for days now . . . Both letters touched me very deeply. You can express yourself so beautifully – you are truly gifted. Not many people understand you – but I'm beginning to know my daughter and I love you more than ever. You are at a beautiful age now, make the most of it . . .

Take care and keep in touch,
I love you infinitely,
Mom

Ann Scott and her mother Joan, 1971–75

Ann Scott is a writer, recently co-author (with Ruth First) of a biography of
Olive Schreiner. She is completing a PhD on psychoanalytic theories of religion, and is working on a book about the psychoanalyst Karen Horney. She
also teaches classes on psychoanalytic thought for the Extra-Mural Studies
Department in the University of London.

Joan was active in the women's liberation movement and worked for many
years for the Family Planning Association. She died of cancer in 1976.

Ann has written the following memoir and commentary on the letters she
exchanged with Joan in the last five years of Joan's life:

'Simone de Beauvoir has recounted how forcefully she was struck by the first
line of *L'Asphyxie*, Violette Leduc's memoir of her childhood – "My mother
never gave me her hand." Leduc was then an unknown writer, had submitted
her manuscript for publication, and de Beauvoir was asked to read it. I came
across a description of the incident four years after my mother's death, just
when I was beginning to sort through her letters to me for this anthology; it
rang out in my mind straight away as an echo of my experience and an organising principle for my thoughts. Yes, I'd always found my mother so distant,
cool, fatigued; and I had never relinquished my need for her to have been
different; and for this book I would write something that showed it thus. So it
came as quite a shock, when I went systematically through the correspondence, to discover its buoyancy, to see her now as someone who had
rebuilt a lifestyle for herself after her marriage ended; had remained lonely,
but never fully given in to the depressions to which she was prone; indeed
faced mortal illness with courage and even wry humour.

'None of this detracts from the sensation of being emotionally deprived as a
child, but it does imply questions about the passage of time and the balance
between one's own fantasy and somebody else's reality. My mother *was*
somewhat withdrawn (family memories back that up) but she wasn't as all-
denying as my Leduc-ish image of her would have it. She had found motherhood largely unrewarding, certainly not something she was cut out for (she
would often say she should have been a university don instead) – but my
internal sense of her as being out to destroy my vitality far outweighed anything that could have taken place between us. And by the time my sister and I
were going through university, living away from home, and so on, she was
able to put the immediate responsibilities of parenting behind her and think
about the state of her own life. This later period is the context for the group of
letters that I quote from here.

'The letters that survive date virtually without exception from the first half
of the 1970s, when Joan was in her late fifties and living alone and I, then in
my early twenties, was an undergraduate in Cambridge and after that a journalist on *Spare Rib*. My parents had separated in 1971, after nearly thirty
years of marriage, and Joan now had a demanding administrative job with
the Family Planning Association (FPA). In her own words she felt a need to

"act fast" – she was keen to make a fresh start and was only too aware that old age would be upon her within a matter of years – and she soon got involved in a local consciousness-raising group affiliated to the Women's Liberation Workshop, then the main co-ordinating body for London groups. Later on she volunteered for one of the administrative positions within the Women's National Co-ordinating Committee (WNCC), a larger outfit.

'The Women's Movement now assumed a primary significance in Joan's life. A lifelong humanist and pacifist, she rued the day she had settled for domesticity in the face of an equally strongly-felt pressure to conform. The early writings of the movement spoke to her previous condition as a house-wife and she became a fervent collector of pamphlets, conference papers and books. When it came to organisation, on the other hand, she may have felt out of her depth, perhaps also somewhat out of sympathy. Although she'd lived the greater part of her adult life as a wife and mother she had a long history of volunteer work, in the Campaign for Nuclear Disarmament, the Women's International League for Peace and Freedom, the Campaign for the Restoration of Democracy in Greece, and the birth control work of the FPA. She had kept a book called *The ABC of Chairmanship* by her bed at home and the informality of the early women's groups would have been difficult for her to negotiate. I would have said that she suffered from the lack of older women in the movement at that time if I didn't also remember her becoming rather prickly at my suggestion that she link up with one of the first such groups being formed; she valued young women's acceptance of her and saw no need for anything else. Similarly, she never identified herself with one strand of feminism rather than another, and we rarely discussed movement issues as such. Joan was someone with unshakeable convictions which she would defend against all comers, and for her "the movement" was primarily a source of ongoing personal inspiration and solidarity with other women. She never, to my knowledge, engaged actively with its main theoretical debates – virtually never passed judgement on tactics or strategy adopted – and chose instead to advocate unity and collective action above all else.

'Because we were both active in feminism, we could take a lot for granted about each other's perceptions of the world. But the very closeness of our basic ideas meant that a lot was left unsaid, and a certain amount is still unclear. I don't know, for instance, whether Joan had read Simone de Beauvoir before the feminism of the Sixties surfaced: that is, I don't know whether her sense of herself as a feminist was recent or long-standing, dating from youth, albeit unexpressed; or whether it sprang to life in her fifties us a means of making sense of her own subjugation and the degree to which she had acquiesced in it. As you will see, de Beauvoir crops up on and off throughout the letters, from Joan's reading of *A Very Easy Death* to a period of intensive correspondence between us in the summer of 1971 on themes of personal autonomy, independence and growth. De Beauvoir's relationship with Jean-Paul Sartre stood for aspirations that both of us shared but never verbalised directly: for dignity, frankness, self-determination, and the like.

What's odd is simply the fact that we never spoke face-to-face about it all.

'Our relationship when we were together was by no means high-flown. People often imagine that sharing a perspective on the position of women – indeed seeing one another at workshops and knowing the same people – somehow erases the usual mother–daughter tensions. We bickered, I would withdraw, Joan probably *did* try to live through me too much, and I could certainly be cruel and withholding. On the other hand, the letters show that our contact could also be intimate, but that the intimacy was spasmodic and precarious. We seem to have been able to open up more to each other in writing than in person: the emotion in the letters was not necessarily followed up when we met. And in my letters to her I also detect a yearning for something more reassuring in our relationship than I felt I got, but which I drew back from demanding; on her side she would make great efforts to create a proper space between us as two adults. I'm still not clear how much the correspondence, blessed with its lack of inhibition, constituted the "innocent" dimension of our relationship; or how much the difficulties in our face-to-face interaction suffused it.

'Most of Joan's letters to me in Cambridge were short, rapidly hand-written affairs, factual, lively, letting me in on her doings and those of her friends and colleagues; her thoughts about the women's group and the political activities she was involved in. But one letter stands out from this period as quite exceptional. In October 1971, a year before she developed breast cancer and when she'd been living on her own for about six months, she wrote me a long, typewritten letter beginning, "I have nothing of any interest to report, but I feel out of touch with you and don't like it. It seems a long time since we last talked at all." She asks how I am – "how is your health/room/stereo/morale/work?" – and then describes a busy life: anxiety about an imminent promotion at work, concern about her storage heaters, double glazing, the state of her social life, and so on. I think this was written on a Saturday night; on the following morning, at 8 a.m. (for she was in the habit of putting a time to things), she added a coda, which strikes me now and struck me at the time as being written in a whirlwind of emotion':

October 1971

. . . What has really done it is reading de Beauvoir's *Une Mort Tres Douce**** – but in English – the translation I bought in Skegness. (Shall I ever go back there? Almost certainly never, and who cares – but it was a seminal place, for me anyway.)† One is overwhelmed with sorrow

---

*'*A Very Easy Death* is Simone de Beauvoir's short, hour-by-hour account of her mother's death. She describes in detail her own and her sister Poupette's reactions.'

†' "Skegness" is a reference to the place where one of the first national Women's Liberation Conferences was held. The movement was then embroiled in an organizational and strategic fight with Maoist women, and this was one of the rare occasions when Joan took a stand on an internal issue. She got involved in the WNCC's administrative work in its attempt to forestall a Maoist takeover.'

for Simone's mother, and at the same time one enters utterly into Simone's conflict of feeling, so lucidly expressed, between suffering and the detachment that the living must feel for the dying. And for oneself, as Poupette said – one must come to it oneself, 'otherwise it wouldn't be fair'. And an added pang for me, as perhaps you can imagine – twenty years on, will it be you and your sister and me? It was very similar for Jocelyn and Ruth [*her sisters-in-law*] in their mother's death: *very* similar. I wouldn't like to ask Jocelyn if she's read it – perhaps she has. I know that my mother-in-law asked at one point, 'Oh, why don't I die?', and that in one of her easier moments she went through all our names . . . thinking of each and I suppose saying good-bye in her mind. So, having read it last night and this morning, in two great gulps, I want to concentrate on the main impression it has made on me – that when one is in one's terminal illness it is too late to talk about one's feelings, past and actual – one is simply too tired to bother, and an indifference settles on one – one is sunk fathoms deep in self-absorption – it takes a long time to 'come to the surface of one's eyes', as Simone describes her mother doing, and *see* the people around, who once were all-important to one. So I want to tell you now, for you to remember then (in case I don't get another moment like this in the next twenty years) that I love you devotedly, no matter how bitchy you are sometimes; that I think you are getting to be a bigger and better person as you grow older; that I admire you for your struggles to mature and liberate yourself; that I respect your intellect; that I am proud to have had a hand in your upbringing; and that I hope we shall be friends as long as I live. It's strange that I have this attachment to you, since we are such different characters.

'I remember very clearly receiving this letter. I had been in London with a boyfriend for the weekend, and can still see myself collecting my mail on returning to college, recognizing my mother's handwriting, going up to my room with my boyfriend, and sitting down on the floor and reading it; the first couple of pages a fairly familiar account of my mother's life. I was glad that she seemed so confident; there was a strange liveliness, even a gaiety, in the chaotic typing: something like a speedy enthusiasm for life. As for the last page – I can't remember whether it reduced me to tears, but it did induce a state of intense exaltation, a feeling that at last, after having experienced my mother as cold for so many years, she seemed to be giving so much.

'Perhaps the physical break with her past, the establishment of her own home – albeit a small one in an indifferent, modern block of flats – brought up the desire for a completely new way of life, freer, less inhibited? It was immensely important to Joan that she had been able to get out of her marriage and the achievement gave her self-confidence a great boost. In this letter it seems also to have given her the capacity to think backwards and forwards in time – from her mother-in-law's death some twenty years previously to a question mark about her own 'twenty years on': it gives the letter the feel of a wide open space, one that she was now free to survey. But it's also typical of our relationship that the letter should stand apart so: I don't recall how it was between us when we next met; to my shame I can't remember writing back straight away, even if only to say her letter had come and I was taking it in. I'm not saying this didn't happen; only that any experience of feedback from me is buried. The paradox, of course, is that I was so affected by it all.

'Letters from the previous years trace the growth of Joan's feelings of independence. At the end of 1970, when she was beginning to look for a place of her own to live in, she wrote me the following letter, showing that she remained closely involved in the detail of my life. She asked whether I'd heard that the *Black Dwarf*, a newspaper that I'd worked on before I went to university, had now folded; she jostled with me in an unusually relaxed way over using commercial vs. natural medicines (she has a mild tonsillitis and is "suppressing it sternly with *Contac* (commercial)"). Most tellingly of all she ended with "Much love, Mummy/Joan", an acknowledgement that our relationship was in transition':

I took a day off work today for flat-hunting, and have actually put a deposit on a mansion flat in the totally unfashionable area of Anson Road N7. It has three rooms, k & b, some good points and various bad – but it has possibilities, it is a reasonable price, and above all it's *available*. I got badly disheartened toiling around from one desirable area to another and finding that there was simply nothing to see or that what there was was either horrid or beyond my means. Whether it will actually come to anything I don't know – it takes some three months to finalise these matters, the agent said. And who knows what will happen in that time? But there it is, anyway. You could have a room?

'Six months later she'd moved house (not to the flat mentioned above, by the way), and had begun to work out her lifestyle as a woman alone. A brisk, cheerful letter of May '71 evokes this early period well. The numbered political comments were not non-stop, actually, but interspersed with news about the state of the church bell opposite her flat and the fact that her window cleaner had turned out to be a member of the National Front. (When she speaks about being accepted on equal terms she is referring to her age and inevitable lack of experience in the local libertarian subculture.)':

2) I have joined the Holloway women's lib group, and must away in a minute to my second meeting. Very small group and very pleasant girls, except one case – hardened survivor of the Committee of 100 who is a nuisance. They have apparently accepted me, on equal terms I mean, and I hope this will last. It's a new group and we're all groping,

which makes things easier. We are going to discuss the current issue of *Shrew* this evening. It's a good one, on the family – have you seen it? . . .

7) I have seen *The Battle of Algiers* and absolutely agree with you. The women's planting of the bombs among children and young people I thought quite unjustifiable, particularly in view of the leader's forthright statement that 'you don't win wars with outrages – or revolutions.' But apart from that I thought it was a splendid film.*

'A few months later I was in quite bad shape – in the throes of a difficult relationship with a man and having attacks of physical panic':

10 August 1971

Darling A,

I hope you have had my card, though it didn't get posted till I got back . . . I have thought of you very often since last Thursday. The visit made me feel better myself, but I can't help wondering if it had any effect on you. I am especially anxious to know whether you have started your psychotherapy – and also whether you have had a period. Please answer! As for what you said about a change of scene – that it didn't really make much difference to one's troubles – basically I know that's true, but I must say my weekend in Dorset did me good, and I think it might help you to get away from Cambridge, even if only briefly. I repeat what I said about your using this flat over the Bank Holiday weekend, if I'm in Scotland.

. . . As I enjoyed Dorset so much, I am thinking of driving down there for a week. Would you like to come? It's incredibly lovely, remote and restful there! I daresay Janet Martin would put us both up. Alternatively, you and Ed could stay on in the flat, if you'd like that. Only I need to know your feelings, because if you don't care to come to Dorset I might ask Suzette [*a colleague at work*] or someone to go.

. . . Now, Anno, let me hear from you with the answers to all my questions. I am picturing you [in your room]. I left Paul Swezy's book after all, didn't I? Never mind, I'll get it another time. Kisses and a big hug from me.

Mummy x

'Then later the same month it was my mother's turn to be low; she came to Cambridge and was apparently "very grateful" for my help. In this letter she links us together, feeling that perhaps a painful era is coming to an end for

---

*'I'm rather surprised at myself here. At the time I was close to a Trotskyist group and can't imagine how I could have allowed myself to express anxiety or revulsion at physical violence in the name of revolution.' (A.S.)

both of us. Unfortunately I can't remember why she was so gloomy just then, and whether it really was prompted only by anxiety at work':

22 August 1971

Dearest A —

I am back home, feeling very much the better for my short trip, which took me away (physically) from my gloom and has improved my morale considerably. The more I think of my state this week the more I feel I was right to go to the doctor – in fact I went just in time, even though I haven't fetched the prescription. Can't think why I didn't ask for it when buying Contac this afternoon – must be because unconsciously I now don't want to take Mogadon! But the experience of true depression has been a revelation, and has given me a yardstick against which to check future symptoms.

The assurance that I am to change my job, putting an end to several weeks of uncertainty, disappointment, anxiety, etc., didn't seem to penetrate, somehow, until today. I think I have been through a difficult time.

I enjoyed our afternoon, and look back with pleasure to meeting Kitty [Ann's landlady] and being her guest: and Shulamith Firestone's book [The Dialectic of Sex] will always remind me of this visit. I read steadily all the way to Liverpool Street, and I see with pleasure and sadness that indeed the American movement is infinitely ahead of ours in theory . . . there is valuable ammunition in the book for use against the politicos.*

It's nine o'clock, and I am thinking of you and hoping you're re-united with Ed and having a happy evening at May's. Let me know what you decide to do, if you go away. I'll give you a ring before the weekend, in case you're there; and again on September 1, when I'll be passing through London. Perhaps I'll find you here!

It was a weight off my mind to see you more cheerful, and I hope that perhaps the worst is over for both of us.

'Our lives settled down and we continued writing regularly. From this period I've selected a letter which illustrates Joan at her most outgoing, some eight months before her cancer developed. I've omitted details about holiday dates, trees coming into leaf, and so on. Here she really is in the swing of an independent life: although it apparently contained no romantic attachment or expression of sexuality, it was filled with political and cultural activity, and she was respected and admired by many people. She was in expansive mood, obviously pleased that I was happier now. It was a relatively placid time for me and I'd written to her enthusiastically about my work and friends in Cambridge':

---

*'The Dialectic of Sex was the "book of the year" for feminists; and the "politicos" would be the Maoist women against whom the WNCC were campaigning.'

Darling A –

Have returned home to find your letter, which I was so glad to get . . . I was amazed and delighted to read that you have no problems at all – can I believe this?! It's absolutely years since you said anything of the kind. Have things taken a turn at last? Anyway, it's the best possible news. And that Ed is happy. Long may this continue.

. . . I have done an astonishingly self-indulgent thing – put my name down for a trip to Italy with a party of strangers – but I would be going to see Florence and Pisa etc. again, not for togetherness – and I hope they would be a civilized crowd, and that I would be able to talk to some of them.

But the main reason I started to write to you now is to let you know my commitments for this coming weekend, when you suggested we might meet, which I'd very much like to do. I'm going to Irene and Stefan for lunch on Sunday, and to Kenwood for a George Eliot programme that evening. But I hope you will be free at some other time. I feel better than when I sent you my despairing post-card: but we haven't talked for a long time.

xx Mummy

'Her letters could also be sharp, and she would often make acerbic, though not ill-natured, comments in the margins. Then there was a casual, friendly tone – at one level we were like sisters in the feminist sense – in her P.S. on one occasion: 'Do you want me to put your name down for that December 11 meeting on Victorian attitudes to women?'' (I must have been an inadequate correspondent, for she had to ask me about this one again.) And one aspect of our relationship that marked it out as perhaps unusual for women of her generation was its apparent openness about sexuality and bodily functions, sometimes expressed in practical terms, at others obliquely and humorously. Early in 1972, for instance, I sent her a postcard of a Hogarth painting in the Fitzwilliam Museum in Cambridge, Part One of which is entitled *Before*, Part Two *After*. I sent her *Before* (a delicate young maiden, her hand raised in shy refusal of the advances of her suitor, who appears to have his flies open) with the quiet comment: "Dear Joan – I think this looks like an advert for the FPA." "I didn't know that Hogarth," Joan wrote back the same week, "and it *would* do for the FPA." Indeed, three years later, by which time I was back in London, Joan must have been in Cambridge on work and sent me *After* (the two are now slumped against a tree, clothes awry and cheeks bright red): "Do you remember sending me Part 1 of this? Have just seen them side by side in the Fitzwilliam. What a poignant pair!" Notes and letters were full of gestures like these; "Any response to letter?", tacked sideways onto a card she sent one summer, was a reference to a love letter I'd sent to someone I was rather forlornly chasing at the time. Still, I was often frustrated by the emotional reticence that she displayed when I was with her.

'By contrast with my mother's letters, which in retrospect seem to have both dignity and self-possession, my own letters as an undergraduate are almost unreadable: brittle, and full of clever witticisms. Even so, the first letter which I have is one in which I do come out and acknowledge guilt at having perhaps spoiled her Easter holiday, the first in her new flat. Here I express anxiety about the difficulty of adjusting to a changing parent–daughter relationship. As in all the letters of mine that I'm quoting from here I find myself held in by the rather fey monotone I cultivated at the time . . . the issues, of course, were real enough.'

May 1971

. . . I don't know what went wrong, I don't think it had anything to do with being used to living with young people, but more with the way in which it's very difficult (at least I find it difficult) to relate to a parent once you're past the parent–daughter stage if it also involves living together, like this holiday, and I know that I didn't make much effort to really communicate with you. I hope I didn't really ruin things.

'I found my letters among her papers after her death and saw that she had underlined some of the passages in them (including the last sentence of the letter above), a lifelong habit with letters and newspapers.

'Many of my letters were sent to "Dear Joan", though some were to "Dear Mummy". One to Mummy, for example, described how I'd been overworking for exams and had been doing eight hours a day for three weeks. A few months later the old ambiguity asserted itself and I wrote to "Dear Joan/Mummy". Now I told her about my new diaphragm and how liberating it felt not to be tied to the pill any more. At the end of the letter I tried to come clean, in a less self-conscious way than usual, about what I took to be her difficulties in being alone and being independent; again, I sense an evanescent closeness, which comes only a few months before her letter to me about de Beauvoir's *A Very Easy Death*':

Dear Joan/Mummy,

I'm glad you were cheered up by coming up here. I was very depressed after you left, I think mainly because the current structure of the family doesn't really accommodate parents being upset like it does children being upset . . . I hope you're not having too difficult a time becoming indifferent to [*Ann's father*]; all I can say is that now you've got a room of your own, and maybe that helps a bit. I think you must try to be less polite. I don't mean that in a straight verbal sense – I don't mean actually to be rude to people, but say the things that upset you, even if it means ringing me (or anyone else) up at 1 in the morning. It was OK for me after you'd left, because I could cycle to the University and just be with other people who had hang-ups of their own . . . But now that you're living on your own, I think it's more difficult to put hang-ups in perspective. You've got to find a sort of balance between independence and aloneness. I find that very difficult and what I'm trying to work out now in my relationship with Ed . . . is whether I can do it myself. I'm determined not to be possessive, so that sometimes I find myself physically, muscularly tense . . . But I don't want to get involved in a repeat performance of the relationship with Matthew which went on far too long.

Have I said all this before? Some of it I think I have. I'm very worried that I'm not independent. But that's another story altogether, and I think I've talked enough about myself for the moment.

'In another letter at around that time I went over some of the same ground, for this new relationship I was in was taxing all my emotional resources. I was concerned to establish the relationship as one in which I could tolerate separations "not in a martyred but in a constructive, S. de Beauvoir way". I think that "S. de Beauvoir" here meant the ability to retain a sense of one's life and projects independently of a lover's presence: I describe having tried to re-read Elizabeth Smart's *By Grand Central Station I Sat Down And Wept* for the first time since the age of sixteen and "the amazing thing was that it seemed so puerile – all the frantic tears of betrayal seem out of place – I think if the girl in the story had some self and integrity she wouldn't be so hurt. So maybe I'm learning a bit."

'A few months later I see my own urge to communicate with her at work again. I try to describe "how I want to exist as a person", and Joan responds in her own way with her underlinings, presumably marking the comments of mine that she most wanted to remember and consider. I let her know that I seem to be getting into a pattern of pre-menstrual sensitivity, and then depression when I ovulate. I ask her advice on a contraceptive detail; she replies to this at length. Now I'm not sure quite what this amounts to; as an FPA worker she lacked all prudishness about the technicalities of sex, but our emotional contact was never so straightforward. I suspect too this was the time when I discovered that Eleanor Marx and Olive Schreiner,* friends in the 1880s, talked about their feelings about menstruation and I was so touched by the thought that I tried to put it into practice with my mother. With hindsight I can see how I'd got a number of categories confused: mother/daughter; sisters in the biological sense; sisters in a friendship, comradely, or feminist sense. At the time I think I wanted to be my mother's sister and for her to be mine.

'Because my mother developed breast cancer when I was a student and we were separated geographically, there are regular letters from that period, late '72 and early '73; there are far fewer letters for the year leading up to her death

*See pp. 134–9.

in 1976, when both of us were in London. But letters or no letters, and although much of the complexity of my relationship with her has only become clear as a result of my psychoanalysis, it was obvious at the time that our relationship changed dramatically once she developed secondary cancer in her bones. For when a mother becomes fatally ill her daughter must be able to mother: in our case the transition from my being a rather resisting, ostentatious undergraduate to a more capable caretaker who could sustain a supportive relationship with Joan did begin in 1972 when Joan had a mastectomy.

'She wrote from the hospital a week or so after her operation':

Darling Anno,

I must share with you a little piece of *good* news for a change – not the prognosis, I haven't had that yet – but my admired Sister Simmonds has just come and told me that I am doing so well that I may go for a walk *outside the hospital* – 'go and have tea at Heal's,' said she! It's beautiful sunny weather here, which probably prompted the thought. But I can't really imagine having the energy to walk that far . . .

Now, darling A, another and important reason for my writing is to thank you for your beautiful letter,* which I shall think of and keep till the day I die – however soon or late that may be. And the way you took my news, when I told you in your room at Girton [*that she had a lump – I burst into tears*], is another of my really treasured memories. It's much easier to write these things than to say them (I've got tears in my eyes now as it is), but I must let you know what a wonderful support you have been to me in the last couple of weeks, when I have needed help in a unique way. Sister Simmonds has told [my surgeon] that I want and can stand the truth, so we have some prospect of knowing it, and acting accordingly.

'The prognosis was fairly good and within a month we were discussing plans for Christmas, with Joan commenting poignantly: "I'll be able to look after you (I hope)." I sense also how important it was for her to feel she could still sometimes be my adviser, and for me to feel I could go on confiding in her; it was reassuring for both of us that some familiar patterns could be maintained. Indeed within a couple of months she was back at work having adjusted pretty rapidly to her changed self-image and the physical discomfort of a mastectomy. She writes to me at Girton in January 1973 that she's immersed in life again; she still gets tired after a full day's work but is confident that this will pass. Then she describes her imminent divorce proceedings, the problems in getting a new car, a film or two that she's seen. She'd

---

*'This letter is too private to include here.'

also gone back to the weekly Workers Educational Association class on women's history that she'd been attending until her operation, and she decides to go to their summer school on 'Women and their Struggle'. It was a buoyant period, an Indian summer for her. Her letters, now signed "Joan", were a mix of news, work for the FPA, and her pleasure at "returning to the dinner party scene". Some months before my finals, she sent me an airy, spacious note: "I feel like coming for another lunch one Sunday", full of the excitement of having to all intents and purposes made a really good recovery; she'd been visiting friends in Scotland who'd been converting their old barn, and she'd pulled "hundreds of nails" out with her own hands and a hammer.

'On the verge of her collapse with bone cancer two years later there was a very different state of affairs. Things in the family were at a very low ebb. Nevertheless she had it in her to ponder my "lesbian triangle" (her own term) with non-judgemental curiosity, and she still had recourse to her basic feminism in describing, quite fiercely, a friend whom she had recently stayed with as "a vivid example of women's oppression": the woman kept putting her creative work last and tended to her family's needs unceasingly. This is a reminder for me of our shared language; despite personal suffering she had not become completely turned in on herself nor had she forgotten how to perceive in a political light. I certainly don't want to idealise the past; the summer of '75 was probably one of the worst in all our lives, but Joan had unsuspected reserves of strength. After a protracted spell in hospital (she now had less than a year to live) she went to Dorset in October to convalesce and sent me an exceptionally calm and warm letter which ends, "Have your usual deep- · going week!"

'The letters to me end at this point. I wasn't writing to her now; we were both in London; most of the time she was in hospital and I usually visited her every day. After her death I read the letters that she received from friends during these stays in hospital, and they showed me how much of her experience she had been unable to share with me; not because she hadn't wanted to, necessarily, but because by definition I couldn't supply all that she needed now – I was at the beginning of my adult life and I was not mortally ill. The letters which she exchanged with a younger friend, herself receiving hospital treatment for thrombosis at the time of Joan's death, have a quality of private, instinctive solidarity that shows how much Joan had valued discretion about pain. And I think the thing which I've come most to appreciate about her is that she never sacrificed her intellect by allowing physical debility to narrow her interest in books and newspapers and the problems of her friends. Nor did she give in to sentimentality about fear or loneliness.

'Six months before her death, for instance, she composed a reply to a letter about breast cancer that had appeared in *Spare Rib*. I still don't know whether she ever sent it in; I have only the rough draft. I want to include part of it because I think it shows Joan at her best, even though it's not a letter to me:'

You're quite right about facing one's own death alone (unless one's religious, when presumably one just looks ahead to a painless eternity). Like you I haven't the physical or psychic energy to initiate anything, and yet I couldn't just ignore your letter. Our difficulty is going to be that all women (men too) in our position, realising that they are probably in their terminal illness, even though they have no idea how long they've got or what the rest of life is going to be like, are preoccupied with their own situation plus the wear and tear of the daily activities that they're trying to carry on. I can hardly bear it myself, and we have to keep in mind that this is the human predicament, not just a feminine or an ill person's one – sooner or later we have to admit to ourselves that we are *all* mortal, and our own mortality is catching up with us now.

'However the word "feminine" might irritate me now, Joan's notion of the human predicament is a dignified and powerful one. It was thoroughly in keeping with her outlook on life for as long as I can remember it, that even when severely ill she should be writing a letter to a periodical, and on a rationalist theme. (Of course, luck was involved too: whereas some cancers – or their treatment – are more devastating at an earlier stage, Joan was able to write and read more or less comfortably until 24 hours before her death.) But in trying to understand why I so much needed her to stay mentally alert – and valued the fact that she was able to do so – I realised something quite basic about her, my attitudes to women, and, by extension, to the women's movement.

'I was reminded of how I've often wondered, in a probably foolish way that doesn't have much to do with my conscious awareness of women's oppression, why there needs to be feminism. Recently I read a book on infancy which began to unlock my confusion on it – the author pointed out how roles and values learned within the family exert a much stronger influence on a child's development than those outside the home. Many of the women in my family had careers as well as children. Joan, although she lived largely as a housewife, had been to Oxford, brought me and my sister up to have ambition for our lives, pursue intellectual studies, appreciate the arts, and campaign against prejudice, and I have never understood how anyone could think women are inherently men's inferiors. The taken-for-grantedness of all of that is very deep in me. I am not talking here about unconscious experience or conflict, of course, which would complicate the issues and open up contradictory pulls and impulses; but about my sense of what should be available to women culturally, politically and economically as their birthright. For in that I think Joan stood us in very good stead. I never learned conventional "femininity" at her hands – and so never had to unlearn it either. Yes, I had to do battle with her emotionally, but I never had to reject her in order to make something of my life.'

Morena and her mother Celia, 1977–78

Morena was born in 1953 to a young couple of mixed race in Seattle, Washington. Her mother, Celia, is white, and had run away from her own mother when she was 16, after being raped by her stepfather. She dropped out of school and was working as a secretary when she met and married Morena's father, a local black musician. They were divorced, largely because of his drinking problem, shortly after the birth of their second child, Toni; Morena was then 3. Celia, left with two young daughters to support, often took in lodgers to make ends meet; some of these lodgers also served as baby-sitters and, at the age of 7, Morena was sexually molested by one of them. A few years later, another man who was living in the house woke her in the middle of the night, standing naked over her bed. She was terrified of him, but even more afraid to tell her mother, who needed the money the lodgers brought in.

Celia married a local high-school teacher when Morena was 11. When Morena discovered her stepfather secretly watching her in the bath, she complained to her mother. Celia told her it was her own fault. Morena later wrote:

'I didn't want to believe it was really happening. I was no older than twelve but her marriage was new and fragile. This was the man she loved. Part of me asked what had happened to her love for me? In later years, when I got into trouble for writing in my journal that I hated him, no one ever questioned how he happened to be reading my diary in the first place or why I felt the way I did. I envied other children their happy existence. I envy now my friends and the wonderful relationships they have with their mothers.'

Coming from a working-class background and having little education herself, Celia worked hard to send her daughters to a private school and to impress upon them the importance of going to college. They always lived in an inter-racial neighbourhood and, after a few upsetting experiences in the predominantly white private school, Morena and Toni were sent to an integrated school. Celia loved the out of doors and considered moving to the country, but she didn't want to isolate her daughters from black people. Morena says:

'I love and respect her for that and I'm grateful to her for her foresight. I must say I have contempt for white parents who choose to have mixed children only to raise them with no sense of racial identity. Robbing them of their colored identity breeds nothing but self-hatred. The same self-hate I would feel if I did not relate to my blackness at all while the rest of the world related to it in a negative way. I carry an equal amount of pride in my Scandinavian half as I do in my African half. It's simply that black is my primary identification.

'When I was young, I sometimes used my half-whiteness as a privilege. I thought if people knew I was half white they would like me better. Mostly, white people were indifferent to me except when they would want to know what nationality I was. Something exotic, like Hawaiian or Indonesian? I used to feel complimented. As my awareness grew I came to realize that they were saying, in effect, that black is not exotic. They were trying very hard to make me something other than what I was. After all, I couldn't be black and beautiful too. I came to defend my blackness as well as finding great pride in it. I began answering simply that I was black – and watching their faces fall.

'Mama is very idealistic. She sees the world through the eyes of a humanist; she felt it was one of the kindest things she had to teach me. For her, a white woman, it was easier to carry this attitude through life. Humanism is a luxury I, being black, cannot always afford. While I think my idealism has been a survival technique, I believe it was a mistake not to arm me with the tools to fight the racism I was bound to come up against. As a result, I grew up think-ing there was no such thing as prejudice, and I personalized every rebuff I encountered.'

By the time Morena reached her teens, Celia's drinking had progressed along with her husband's. She had had a drink problem before she remarried, but now there were terrible fights and Morena spent an increasing amount of time taking care of her mother when she drank. The marriage broke up several times and Celia was lonely whether they were together or apart. Morena recalls:

'I prayed and prayed they'd stop fighting. I banged and banged my head on the floor, screaming for them to stop. I thought if they realized I wanted them to stop enough to hurt myself, they would. The whole house was screaming: they at each other, me at them, my sister at me to please shut up.

'My stepfather was a child and my mother became a martyr immersed in pain and self-pity. All I knew was that I had to take care of her, that I didn't want to see her hurting, that I hated anyone who caused her pain (including myself), that I wanted to prove to her she wasn't a failure, but I didn't know how. I promised to build her a house in the country. It gave us both hope. I loved it when I made her smile. My job was caretaker and I grew familiar with her stages of drinking. Getting her to bed before she reached the emotional depths wasn't easy but when I succeeded I felt infinitely relieved. I felt neces-sary and our mutual dependence on one another grew. However, it often felt impossible to measure up to what I thought she wanted of me.

'It's difficult for me to view mama objectively, separating my needs as a child from who she was as an individual, her conditioning as a woman, and the circumstances of single parenthood. I have thought many times that the men in her life meant more to her than her children. I must be wrong, but I have felt it. It is still very hard to make sense of my experiences of child molestation. As a child who was being mistreated and molested by baby-sitters, including women, without the knowledge and support of my mother (or anyone else), I had no sense of power. I still find myself trying to make sense of irrational minds in figuring out, "why me?" I know it's futile.'

Morena became pregnant six times between the ages of 13 and 22. She says:

'I needed approval. I had no idea I had a right to "no" especially if it was going to make them angry or hurt. Somewhere in my head sex meant caring. At fourteen I gave it to a man forty years my senior who later offered me money. That's when I learned that the combination of sex and money meant even greater caring. My long-term relationships were often with these men and not so much with boys my own age. I learned to play well the role of innocent child, yet never fucking for less than $20. Money itself wasn't the issue since I held steady jobs.

'To my way of thinking, I've had many emotional bottoms in my lifetime. How could my mother not have known about the drugs and pregnancies? How could she, living with me every day, miss what everyone else saw? The morning sickness, marijuana smell, alcohol giddiness or LSD insanity? I haven't completely resolved my resentments on this question, although rationally I know we see what we can afford to see and she was often involved in her own drinking and other dramas. At least some part of me must know that it was nothing to do with lack of love.'

Her mother knew about the first pregnancy, which ended in a miscarriage necessitating major surgery. She kept the next two pregnancies secret and had illegal backstreet abortions which landed her in hospital with complications. When pregnant again at 17, she had wanted to keep the child and she tried to keep the pregnancy secret for as long as possible. When, at a very late stage, her parents discovered it, they took her to Oregon to have a legal saline abortion. She later had another abortion and another miscarriage. She writes about her forced saline abortion:

'I hated them for a time, especially mama. Isn't it sad how we give our mothers the brunt of the blame? And I never let her forget it, making sure she felt as bad as I did. When I finally began to understand her side and forgave her we cried in each other's arms.

'I had been labelled a whore long before I knew what a busted cherry was, so at this point I felt I had nothing to prove in terms of chastity. Mama must have worried about me like crazy. We had awful fights and called each other tramp. It was so sad because all the while there was deep love between us, but sometimes it demonstrated itself in really perverted ways. When she says she's been a failure as a mother, what is she saying about the way I've turned out?'

Morena started working in regular part-time jobs at the age of 15. She drank and used drugs, but gave up speed and then downers after a nearly successful suicide attempt and brief incarceration in a mental institution. She fell in love with her best friend, Sharon, when she was 15, but continued to form her sexual relationships with men until her mid-twenties.

At the age of 18, Morena moved in with a boy she'd been going out with, although she had sworn never to live with a man. She didn't love him but she wanted independence from her mother. He was an alcoholic and the relationship was distressing throughout the three years they stayed together. Finally Morena rebelled: 'It took me a complete loss of all human dignity in a violent and dehumanizing situation to re-evaluate what I thought I was worth and what I wanted my life to be.'

She began to have sexual relationships with women and to make a commitment to being with women. Wanting to prove that she wasn't just reacting to her former boyfriend's cruelty, she became the lover of a very gentle man and, at the same time, of a loving and patient woman. At the age of 22 she left both her lovers to go to Trinidad. She became involved with Gene, a hotel worker who was very good to her; they corresponded after she left Trinidad and he offered her a one-way ticket to come back to him. She returned and made two important discoveries: feminism and Gene's addiction to alcohol. She left him and returned home to watch her father die of cancer of the pancreas. 'But,' she says, 'I know it by another name, alcoholism.' Her stepfather died soon after and her mother was operated on for cancer. Morena writes about the contradictory emotions she felt during that period:

'I felt that mama definitely wanted me to be with men and that she wanted me to be with Gene. That trip to Trinidad was living out a faraway dream of her own. I empathize with that but a marriage with him would have been impossible. Aside from my lesbianism, he was a drunk! A beautiful drunk, if there is such a thing. Today all the patterns are much clearer than they were then, but at the time I did not understand the complexities of alcoholism.

'Sad to say, my lesbianism didn't alter my attachment to drunks or to Bacardi rum. Debbie, my first lover, is now a recovering alcoholic but during our three years as a couple we drank together constantly. Finally with my own alcoholic denial and my co-alcoholism in full bloom I accused her of excessive drinking and demanded that she stop. She had a dry spell or two but didn't attempt sobriety until long after I left Seattle.'

In 1977, Morena moved to California, wanting to break away from the confines of her family and her small lesbian community. She says:

'The lesbians there were particularly dogmatic in their downward mobility. I remember wearing slacks to an event once and some of the women, all white, remarked disapprovingly how 'dressed up' I was. The pressure got so great that when my corduroys tore beyond repair I rolled up the pant leg, afraid to wear a new pair. That's when I knew I needed to be around my own culture. Poor people don't need to prove they're poor. Proud people would do anything to keep from looking like a scrounge. It's only the rich in their guilt and denial who can really afford to be downwardly mobile.

'I'd met my first black lesbian while she was on tour speaking about feminism. Having had no contact with black lesbians up until this time, I was in awe of her. Margaret isn't a woman who wastes time where matters of the heart are concerned and I was infatuated. Within a few months I'd made the trek from Seattle to live with Margaret and her ten-year-old daughter Kathy in San Francisco.

'What followed was a time when my mother's and my relationship suffered immensely. There is no way to know what went on with her. I know I felt tremendous guilt. I was haunted by memories of her saying, 'I always wanted two daughters and you were my firstborn. You're just like me, honey. You're all I have now.' I had abandoned her and my promise to build her a house in the country. It didn't help that most of my letters went unanswered by her. Guilt meshed with anger. With insight and love Margaret coaxed me into therapy.'

The letters which follow were written during those early months in California. Morena included several entries from her journal with the letters to her mother:

2 June 1977

Mommy Mommy Mommy

First of all I want to say I love you, more, I'm sure, than you'll ever know. Up until lately it's been more tense between us than ever in my life as far as I can remember. So much has gone unspoken. I am defensive. I see things differently than you – I defend my views, myself. And you, you bore me, raised me, protected me – you feel guilty about what I have grown into. At Uncle Alvin's memorial service I felt a stranger to you and you felt it too, I saw it in your face. I wanted to talk, I know and could not. A letter, a letter, give me some paper, I will splatter ink over a page, for now it's the only way. Trying to think of you simply as another human being rather than mommy (and what mommy represents to me) is so hard but it's necessary in order to record true and complete feelings instead of witholding for fear of repercussions.

Since I've been in California I've been able to uncover layers and layers of emotions I have around daughter and motherhood. Before I share with you my deepest thoughts and emotions, both confusing and clear, I want you to know *I need* you. I need for you to bare yourself to *me* instead of everyone but me when it concerns us. I need to bare myself to you. Mommy, we need each other. Because we've always been so connected it is an extremely painful adjustment now that I have developed my own lifestyle that happens to differ from your interpretation of happiness. But we need each other.

Journal – 18 April 1977
'I don't feel right when people tell me I've got to live my own life and be happy. I still feel guilty when I can pass a few days in happiness. Then it comes as a rush: her image, her world and I feel guilty. Guilty and sad.'

9 May 1977 – notes after the Black Women's Support group. *
'The room flowed with tides of pain, guilt and love and anger. As women, mothers and daughters, told their story I realized the umbilical cord is never cut.

'. . . that mom takes up half of me and if she were to die I too would, literally, *die*. The fear and fantasy of her death has haunted me so that there is no means of escape left. I can recall her every story of guilt, of struggle, of sacrifice, of suffering throughout her life. It's always been the three of us, 2 girl children and one mother alone. She white, us black. All of us finding refuge from a cold world in family womanlove. I have grown up feeling responsible for all her hurt yet I know I am wrong. She has projected her own feeling into her child. It is so hard to try to stand apart from that to claim and build my wholeness.

'– I bet she thought my lesbianism was a phase but even without directly confronting her it's more than obvious my life revolves around women, not just mommy, and though she's never admitted it I feel certain that realization is hitting her very hard.'

May 19 – on coming home for Uncle Alvin's funeral – and you.
'– She gives birth and half the world tells her it is wrong to have black children. She clings to us, we to her, with love and protection, we are all she has. And for the majority of our lives we are all she has had, the most secure, surest point of her life. Now, whenever we move from her breast into our own lives, she feels totally alone and we are suddenly "having the time of our lives" and "we don't love her". While I think I may know most of where it all starts – her grandmother's, her mother's, her own guilt,† and now ours (or mine) – I don't know the answers. She feels guilty, an unworthy mother, so we grow up feeling we have to continuously prove our love and worth to her even if it means denying our own right to life.

'It tears me apart to see her drinking – I can handle her when she's drunk, keeping her humored or avoiding her without antagonizing her, but this does not help empty her rivers of resentment, anger, defeat and loneliness. She is tired; she gives up sometimes. Must I take that burden and responsibility? Can I do that, and live my own life? That I don't know yet and until I do, will feel such guilt and consternation.'

Mommy, my lesbianism should certainly not be a source of guilt for you, but a reason for thankfulness. How do I convince you? Will time convince you of what I cannot? Mommy, I've been pregnant *six* times!

---

*'This was a lesbian rap group, but I didn't say so to Mom because the issue of sexuality was so volatile between us.'
†Celia was raped by her stepfather when she was 16.

Do you really think nature was trying to say, 'Have a baby'? I think more like, 'Stay away, it's not natural.' You yourself have gone through two disastrous alcoholic marriages yet it seems you'd rather see me with Gene, an alcoholic, because 'he seems so sweet'. The two of you have never met and you're talking about a lifetime. A lifetime of what you had with Daddy and B. [*Celia's second husband*]. Since acting on my lesbianism, I have developed more as a woman, a human, reclaimed more lost hopes, and realized more dreams than ever before. Can't you see it? All those years they told you it wasn't good or right – so that even you who has wanted women had to deny yourself. So now, in spite of the obvious, you'd rather see me lay and live with a man. NO! . . .

A play! Can you believe it? The last thing in the whole world I ever thought I'd do. Never! Never! NEVER! Paint, poetry, writing, these things I can do in hiding, but a play? ME? Public? It makes me wonder how much we have within that we never discover. I think about you, your art, your beauty, your brilliance. But you wanted children and we were your priority. Do you really think we were worth it? . . .

I see little girls all over the place following their natural inclination to love women. Then around 10, 11, 12, etc., peer-group pressure and the trouble with boys begins. Some of us escape after 10, 20, 30 years and return to ourselves, some know from the beginning where they belong . . .

Many paragraphs in my journal speak of you – apart from what I've shared here – of your life, your fears, your love and how it affects me. I think of how I'd like to see you – on a farm of course, and of what a good marriage would have meant to you.

I know that even though this letter says a lot, it also leaves a lot to be desired. I have no guesses as to how this will hit you but I want you to know it took a lot of faltering and forceful determination and need to send this letter. What to expect in return? Hell, I don't mind saying I'm scared silly, but if we are friends then honesty is essential as is facing up to a lot of hidden junk. If you think I'm way off base, say so. We need that exchange. I love you very much and I love myself too. I don't want us to lose one another yet I need you to recognize and accept what I have been. If you cannot, well . . .

Love,
Morena

Five months later, Morena had not received a reply to any of her letters:

13 November 1977

Dear Mama,

Again, the first move, but I've been concerned how you're doing. There are conflicting emotions running through my veins, a lot of angry, hurt, resentful feelings towards you. I think what you're doing is really unfair. Over a month ago I began a letter to you: 'I feel humiliated so this is most likely my last attempt at communication with you until I get some response.' Any response is better than feeling totally ignored. It's as if we are nothing! Remembering your excuses and reasons for not writing while I re-read some of the letters you wrote to me in Trinidad, three long letters and three telegrams in a period of only three months! In the seven months I've been here now, not one letter. I received the binder you sent as a birthday present (which was very thoughtful indeed) but as I said in my thank-you note, still a poor substitute. You have allowed me to expose myself and make myself totally vulnerable to you *more than once*, still no response except 'still don't have time to write'!! I find it hard to believe!

I feel like you've manipulated people a lot, including me. I don't mean to be sarcastic or vicious, not here. Female manipulation can be called survival but nevertheless you *must* have known that not facing up to my last letters would hurt when I was trying to bridge a widening gap between us. And you criticize *me* for insensitivity.

I think you're afraid of my honesty. I also think you're jealous of me. You can talk *about* me to other people, but you can't talk *with* me. Not even in a letter. I'm going to keep trying not to care, but that isn't even an option right now, because it would mean pretending I don't need you or love you. So instead I feel angry and ripped off. I *hate* going on assumptions!! It would be nice just to know how you're doing, what's going on in *your* life at least, if nothing else. My job is doing well, as is the rest of my life right now. I feel very fortunate and forever growing . . .

You might be interested to know that another woman and myself will be the cover subject of Worklife Magazine, put out by the U.S. Department of Labor in Washington D.C. Ellen and I were contacted by the magazine through Women in Apprenticeship – an advocate group in San Francisco that assists women who are in, or would like to enter, blue collar trades. As to what month we'll show up I've no idea but I'll let you know. It's really exciting to imagine the encouragement that cover will provide to other women.

Time to close. Anything else would be further risk. It's your turn now. One last time, *please* write. I mean *write*!

With love,
Morena

Two months later she had still had no reply. She remembers: 'I was in my room, filling in my journal when all of a sudden I wrote':

Finally I can say to myself, I hate you! but even now I cannot cry aloud. You fooled me all of these years. I would rip you apart if I could. A silent scream. You would fog if you were glass. I'm trying to understand you.

All my life, you invaded every pore, every crevice, each part of me and I want no more of you! I can't be cleansed of you because I have felt desires to caress you. I can't be cleansed because you bore me out of your need for love. I can't be cleansed because for 24 years you've strung me along as you would a man. I still want you to love me and I hate you for it. I thought we were close because you said we were, but you used me to call yourself a slut. I would die rather than reproduce what you have, in the end, produced. We run with the same stride. I hope I tire more easily than you.

Please please, mommy, touch my face, feel the tears you bore. FEEL THEM, stop hiding behind your own. I've had dreams of you being my mother, my lover, but we're strangers to each other. Touch but don't look. No, no, especially not inwards.

After seven months of silence, her mother replied:

9 January 1978

Dear Morena,

Just got down here on my night job and there's a note from my boss telling me there's nothing to do tonight, I have to be at school at 6:30 for my class and I know when I get home at 10:00 I'll be lucky if my eyes are still open, so decided I'd better try to scribble a few lines to you now . . .

I just can't figure out what do you mean by the statement: 'You have such out-of-the-way ideas of what's going on with me! I realize I expected too much'? Morena, I have *no* idea of what's going on with you. I don't know why you're so cold towards me. If you're angry with me, I don't know why. I certainly don't know what you mean when you say you realize you expected too much. I'm now wondering, does that mean you expected more from me as a mother? Have I been even more a failure in your eyes than even I'm conscious of? I can't figure out what's going on, what I've done – or is it something else? Morena, I'm in the dark. You seem so angry with me, and I guess – your family as a whole. I can't figure out why you flew off the handle at me and told me you never wanted me to call you again. The way you've been acting towards me ever since you left here has been a complete mystery to me.

That first letter you wrote hurt me deeply. I cried and cried for a long time afterward every time I let myself think about it. I'm going to have to answer it I guess, but it seems so useless, because I can't think of anything to say I haven't said to you with all my heart before, and if you didn't hear me then, why I should think you'd hear me now when you've become so distant, when you seem to have forgotten everything that I *am*. I thought we knew each other so well, and were so close. It's an awful blow to me to find out that evidently we're not at all. I've bared myself to you more than any other mother I know and it seems you haven't seen me at all, that it was all for nothing.

You said that you felt a stranger to me at Uncle Alvin's service and that I felt it too, that you could see it in my face. Morena, you may have *thought* you saw it, but *you did not!* I didn't feel any distance between us, not even from you. Maybe that was unperceptive of me, but I was too full of grief and shock over the loss of someone I had been very close to and who I had loved dearly for a few years longer than you have been alive. Alvin and I had been two outsiders in our family, and we were very dear and close friends for many years. I thought you understood what I was feeling.

Honey, I've got to go to my night class now. I'm going to mail this as soon as I can get to the Post Office for stamps, then write some more as soon as possible.

My love always,
Mama

Four years later, Morena explains some of the recent changes in her life and how they relate to this exchange of letters:

'A year after this letter I met Naomi, the woman of my dreams. As was the pattern, I moved from one lover to the next, one addict to the next. Luckily I had done some growing up by now or at least growing tired of being on the run. This, besides being in love for the first time in my adult life, provided me with a firm foundation to survive the next two-and-a-half years. It was sheer tenacity and my new commitment to be willing to struggle through anything, no matter how difficult, that kept me going. Naomi and I were trysted, or married, in Los Angeles by our local black lesbian witch.* It was beautiful. I wondered about inviting mama but she now had a job as a merchant marine and she was in Alaska at the time so I was relieved of the dilemma. My sister was my attendant. Naomi's mother was angered at receiving an invitation. After all, we didn't have to "flaunt" the most important day of our lives in her face. I thought about my mama. It would have been such a special thing to have her there. I wondered if she'd ever accept my lifestyle just on the basis of my happiness with it. My choices don't jive with her hopes for me, but I get greater rewards from being a non-traditional worker and a lesbian – a liberated woman. Obviously we have completely different ideas about what the "good life" is. Somehow I got the message, despite the lipservice she gave to the contrary, that my major directions in life weren't okay for her. I have had to battle between being true to myself and accommodating (or manipulating) others; I know the answer now.

'My sister went back to Seattle with stories of the happiness and growth

---

*'To me a witch is really all women; it names the natural state of woman.'

she'd seen in me as well as testimonials to Naomi's beauty and fine spirit. I'm grateful for that because mama sent back her blessings. It was a miracle to me. A great joy. For the first time in years she seemed interested in how I was, open to hearing about my life, at least in relationship to the mate I'd chosen. I am reminded of the anger and bitterness I'd felt through the years in thinking she didn't care. Now I realize that we have been operating by two different sets of standards. And that we each have a right to our own process of growth. Mama did what she had to do and she did the best she could. Who are we to sit in judgement of one another? It has nothing to do with her not loving me, only to do with not knowing me or understanding this life of mine. For her silence was the remedy. For me silence breeds insanity.

'In 1981 there was an overhaul in Naomi's life and my own. An overhaul that saved our relationship and our lives, bringing us physical and emotional sobriety. I'd had enough of her addiction to alcohol and marijuana. By focusing on outside circumstances, by pointing the finger everywhere but inward I was conveniently able to overlook my own patterns. I was an expert at analyzing everyone else's problems, but I'm the one whose every major relationship has been with an addict, primarily alcoholics. Why?! They are the mirrors to my own soul. It is no coincidence that my self-esteem was low and that I chose to be with people who were incapable of giving me the emotional support I craved. I measured my value by their successes and failures and by how much I suffered. I was a great martyr, having learned that the more one suffers the more worthy or superior one is. There was no glory in happiness.

'I couldn't articulate any of this at the time. Finally all I knew was that I was tired and I was suicidal. My life had become totally unmanageable. Of course, it was all Naomi's fault! If she'd stop drinking, life would be perfect. Our therapist suggested I go to AlAnon, an anonymous organization for the friends and families of alcoholics. It was in AlAnon I learned that I was not only obsessed with Naomi's behavior but that I too was addicted – to the alcoholic. I decided that to insure my own emotional sobriety I could no longer live with an active alcoholic. It was impossible to force change on someone else but I could make some changes with myself . . . This was the only action that could ensure sanity.

'By this time I had also come to grips with my own alcoholism and had begun attending lesbian A.A. meetings. Finally the puzzle of my life was beginning to come together in a way that made sense. If it was really love I wanted, I first had to believe myself deserving of it. I am perfectly capable of giving to myself anything which I think I need as well as seeking out relationships that are healthy. Once I made the conscious choice to seek happiness, I started learning how to stop undermining my chances.

'The greatest act of love I'd ever performed was to leave Naomi. To stop nagging and return her the dignity to find her own way. All the best intentions in the world didn't negate the harm I was doing us both. When she fell it was without me and when she rose it was also without me. I stood not over her, but at a distance in case she *asked* for help. That our love for each other and for ourselves was great enough to survive this when families are separating every day, is a miracle I am still in awe of. The greatest gift we have allowed ourselves is to die in a real way and be born all over again. We are children in this new world of sobriety. The worst day now is better than the best day then. Only now do I have the chance to live and die as an adult.

'Emotional sobriety can be much trickier than physical sobriety. Until very recently I often found myself thinking along the lines, "Well now that I've saved Naomi I'll go save my mama." Thankfully I've absorbed enough of the twelve steps of AlAnon and Alcoholics Anonymous to cut that shit, but quick! In fact, I can see that mama's and my relationship has made subtle progression, although we still go through periods of arguing and not speaking to each other. At least I am learning a new way of relating to her. The old way has eaten away at me long enough. I reached a pinnacle of obsession with negativity. When the bitterness, the anger and the guilt all but cut off my oxygen flow, I found myself willing to seek alternatives. Joy now provides the same motivation that sorrow once did.

'It was probably inevitable, considering my family history, that I would acquire considerable strength as well as become a great alcoholic and co-alcoholic, addict to both people and substances.

'It is plain to see how those dynamics have been played out on both sides of the family down through the years. But the understanding that active alcoholism makes maturity impossible has helped me get back the love I have for mama. In separating the disease from the innocence and wisdom of the woman it becomes easier to let go of blaming her.

'For a long while I didn't know what to feel. Disrespect got confused with anger, cynicism with hurt. I tried to separate myself from her. I just couldn't bear that she wasn't what I needed as a child, nor who I wanted her to be now. I expected my mother to be perfect. Instead what I got was a mortal, full of human frailties and all my life I've held it against us both. Whose standard was it that defined what a mother and daughter should be to each other when every relationship is unique unto itself? Who was it that passed down the image of mother as madonna and Virgin Mary? Why is it that all the responsibility for perfection lies on mothers and other women?

'It is a cruel trip to lay on any child. My mother is a courageous woman to have split from an unhappy situation when she was only sixteen years old and to venture out on her own. To support herself in any way she could rather than go back. To marry the man she loved in spite of society pressures. If you know what it's like in a racist world now, can you imagine what it must have been like for her in the 40s and 50s? Then she had the babies she wanted, raising us by herself, ignoring what certain people said or the way they looked at us. She never once hid from the choices she made. I've learned my alcoholic behavior from her, but I've also learned courage and strength and survival. Oh I'm not saying I don't miss the long talks we never really had or the eye-to-eye honesty I craved. I'm not saying I don't still have resentments sometimes or that I always understand what's going on, but compassion has entered the picture at last, for both of us. Compassion that allows tolerance and an even greater capability for being honest. It is just that now I am accepting both the sides she gave me, unlike ever before. For years I fought against any notion that we were alike. My own tunnel vision, my own self-hatred prevented me from translating anything positive into our similarities. Non-acceptance of my likeness to my mother is no less than non-acceptance of myself. Since facing that very real fact I've felt my love for her return and my own life expand.

'The choices are there and each one of us chooses. Mama continues to drink because she wants to. I don't have to grapple with the extremes of all or nothing anymore, such as, "Either she stops her alcoholic behavior or she cannot be in my life." I could do that with others but not with mama. The truth is I don't want to let go of her. There is a connection to her unlike that to any other human being. She is my mother, a fact I no longer want to deny. It feels that I am learning what love is, apart from my personal desires, separate from my own neuroses. And I realize that if I change others around me change. Mama is a pretty incredible woman. She may stop drinking or change in other ways I've dreamed about. She may go to A.A. and then again she may never be so moved. It's really none of my business, a circumstance over which I have no control anyway. Her choices and her responsibilities are not mine: this is a far cry from how I felt in May, 1977.

'I've been a lesbian for seven years now, a feminist for six, a carpenter for five, an advocate of women entering skilled trades for four, trysted for three and a practicing witch for two. Naomi and I are moving in exciting directions. She is eleven years older than me and neither of us have been in a relationship that's lasted this long or felt this stable. We're part of a "working class women and self-esteem group" where I have been able to examine, among other things, the unconscious limitations I've set upon myself. We'd eventually like to buy a home, which would give me a chance to resolve my guilt about possessing more materially than mama does. Someday I'd like to return to live in Seattle, to my native land, so to speak. But I don't yet trust that I'd be able to maintain any kind of serenity without distance between mama and me. Today no matter how much I dream of running into her arms, I know how easily I could get pulled back into unhealthy patterns.

'The letters and journal entries that are included here helped facilitate all the changes in a subtle yet profound way. I had to feel the loss, the abandonment and the contempt. I had to hate her before I could really learn to appreciate our bond. As I let go of my hurt, replacing it with empathy, it becomes less necessary for her to reciprocate.

'I thought I had reached this point back in 1978 when I responded to the letter my mother had finally written after months of my pleading. It has taken me four years to realize that my reply was just the beginning of my journey:'

1 February 1978

Dear Mama,

I only know one way to begin this letter and that is to dive right into it. As I write I'll try not to preface certain thoughts with apologies as I so often do in my speech. I'll try to stay very clear in my message. Also, hoping to eliminate as much defensiveness and conflict as possible, I want to say that I am *not* finding fault with you. I am the product of particular circumstances and realities. There is a great need to *examine* the why's and how's, to recognize them and to move on in a healthy manner.

Many times over many years and spanning all of your moods you've expressed guilt and fear that you were little short of a failure as a mother. (Don't you see how that, if true, would reflect on me? I certainly don't consider myself a failure.) I see you as a strong woman who gave what she had and the best she had learned. There were circumstances beyond your control, there were mistakes and there was a lot of work. What I'm trying to do now is to examine how all of this affected me as a growing child to developing woman. In the process I hope to re-evaluate myself and redefine my relationship with you.

I'm free now to love the woman of my choice but you were the first woman. It was you I looked to for nurturance and love. I imagine that you felt that pressure many times. I imagine you sometimes felt incapable and fearful, guilty and terrified of ever making a mistake. I cannot rid you of your guilt, I cannot save you from your life. I realize that now. That's something you've got to do yourself. You are a strong and capable woman. It is both that strength and the guilt you've passed on to me.

I've never doubted that you love me. The hand I have in disciplining Kathy (the 11-year-old who lives here) reminds me so much of your own, this only strengthens my lesson that we raise 'our' children in much of the same way we ourselves were raised.

When I was a child, you were the most beautiful woman in the world to me, the smartest and the most sensitive. I always felt so proud of you, so terribly proud and protective. As a child, though, I missed you a lot. You had other responsibilities and needs and a life of your own. I was *among* your priorities. It killed me to see you unhappy. Always in the back of my mind I took responsibility for your suffering. After all, weren't you working to support me? Aside from your own loneliness, didn't you feel it necessary to marry so that I would have a father, therefore a 'real' home?

I got in trouble because I wrote in my diary that I hated my stepfather. Why didn't you ever try to *talk* to me, to find out *why* I felt the way I did or at least to let me know you were there for me? When I was 11 or 12 and I told you how he peeked at me through the vent while I bathed, you said I 'asked' for it. My rational mind can tell me at 24 why you acted this way, but as a child I didn't understand. Nor did I understand why you never confronted your brother about his attempt to rape me. It's that type of anger and hurt you have received these past months. It is not my intention to blame you but to make you realize what it is I've been experiencing and where it's taking me. So I idolized you, yet you weren't always there for me. You had your own needs, your own insecurities and attachments that had nothing directly to do with me yet affected me in a very profound way.

When you cried in frustration, feeling as though you'd never get out, I promised, 'Mommy, I'll build you a house in the country.' It was the promise of a child who felt responsible for your situation, and therefore I felt I had to get you out of it. I'm just now beginning to see how unrealistic that is. You made your 'choices' before I could possibly have any influence, and if I ever build you a home in the country, it will not be out of obligation but out of love.

In your most recent letter to me you said you have *no idea* of what's going on with me. That stung because as I go over the 8 pages I sent you in June I wonder why you still have NO idea.

When I moved to California I experienced a great deal of guilt and pain because we had never been separated in such a way. I felt the guilt and pain was undeserved. Confusion and conflict consumed me until I felt no longer in control. I began therapy and what a blessing it came to be.

When I wrote to you during the summer and fall, I not only needed a response but *expected* one. That was my mistake. When I received nothing it brought many nightmares and a great sense of rejection.

Haven't you ever resented your ties to me? Not even for a moment?

What part of yourself did your own mother give to you when you were growing up? Why did you run from her at sixteen? It was not your fault that you could not always give for no-one ever really gave to you. Still, we both suffered. *Why* was I afraid to tell you about Bobby, the boarder who you left to babysit? I waited for you to come home after my screaming forced him to leave, but once you, my security, arrived I couldn't tell you why I was afraid to return to bed. I still don't know the answer. I wonder sometimes, what parts of my childhood I've hidden from myself.

Is it so hard to understand why I would be defensive of my lifestyle? It's never been too popular with any of the family. How many times did I scream at you when I overheard while you talked about me to your friends? I couldn't understand why you wouldn't tell *me* those things, why you were afraid of me. I resented you because I never felt I could or wanted to live up to your dreams, to your idea of success and happiness. There were many times I truly *believed* you would have *preferred* someone else for a daughter.

I am not angry with you, nor am I angry with *any member* of the family. My anger stems from the first time I was molested as a child and only now, sixteen years later, is it being released. I wanted you to understand and respond with immediate honesty and warmth. That is what I meant when I said my expectations were too high. I wasn't being fair. I believe all of what I'm saying to be valid, but recognizing it must have hit you pretty hard. It certainly did me. It scares me to realize I'm only beginning to scratch the surface, but it feels good to be more honest.

I no longer feel unworthy or guilty. I know I have not deserted you. When we meet it will be on my terms because finally I've begun to come to terms with myself, who I am and why I am. I don't love you because you are my *biological* mother. I love you for who you are, the energy you've put into me and because I believe you love me. I see now with much clarity many of your shortcomings (along with your strength) but in working through their effects on me, and realizing I have much more control over who I am than I thought, I can more easily understand and feel compassion towards you. We are all products of our environment. I want us to be friends, though I believe mutual anger, resentments, misgivings and rewards to be eternal. We will move at our own pace, grow at our own speed and let go as we can.

I think what I feel best about is that I don't have my hopes up as I did before for you to respond to me in an equal way. Of course I would love it if you did. I don't feel as vulnerable, nor do I feel it necessary to hide my vulnerability. The most important thing to me at this point is to express to you how I am feeling. What you do with that is your own choice. The pressure is off!

I am both appreciative and grateful for your last letter. I do hope another follows. I'm especially appreciative for your explanation of what you were going through at Uncle Alvin's funeral. I admit I could have been wrong in what I said. What I was feeling could have indeed shadowed my perception of what you were experiencing. I'm glad you let me in.

This letter seems terribly incomplete. It has only touched surfaces, at least, for me. I have a lot of work ahead. I imagine you will feel many emotions from what I've written so far, including defenses, disagreements, agreement, guilt, some satisfaction –

I hope somewhere you begin to understand.

Take a good look at me. I'm a survivor. I have fears and guilts and faults. I've learned well my lesson not to trust, not to give overmuch. In that process I've learned to rely on my own inner resources and develop my strengths. In relationships I'd like to act on impulse more than I do, but too often I'm purposeful and calculating. I lack discipline, preventing me from realizing my fullest potential. I am sensitive and terribly afraid. I'm introspective, gifted and fairly articulate.

Strong, capable and stubborn. I have courage, determination, and a strong drive to live and know life. I try to be honest with myself. There is conflict and contradiction but also the desire to make new discoveries, to continue growing. I'll never be stagnant. I'm your daughter. You gave me both sides.

With much love,
Morena

Permissions

1951. Used by permission of Sir Ralph Verney and Constable and Co.

Extract from 'Cassandra' by Florence Nightingale, first published in *The Cause* by Ray Strachey, Virago, 1978. Reprinted by permission of Virago.

from the Alcott Family Collection (7706), Barrett Library. Used by permission of the University of Virginia.

from *Your Dear Letter: Private Correspondence of Queen Victoria and the Crown Princess of Prussia, 1865–1871*, ed. by Roger Fulford, Evans Brothers Ltd, 1971. By gracious permission of Her Majesty the Queen.

from *Calamity Jane's letters to her Daughter*, shameless hussy press, 1976. © Stella A. Foote. Used by permission of shameless hussy press and The Women's Press.

from a private collection of Eastman family letters. © Yvette Eastman. Used by permission of Yvette Eastman.

Hellen Keller's letters quoted by permission of the American Foundation for the Blind, New York.

from 'Why Men Need Woman Suffrage' by Helen Keller, *Helen Keller: Her Socialist Years*, International Publishers, 1967. Used by permission of International Publishers.

from *Testament of Youth* and *Testament of Experience* by Vera Brittain, first published by Gollancz, 1933 and 1957. Used by permission of Paul Berry and Geoffrey Handley-Taylor.

from *Lady Into Woman* by Vera Brittain, Andrew Dakers Ltd, 1953. Used by permission of Paul Berry and Geoffrey Handley-Taylor.

from *Selected Letters of Winifred Holtby and Vera Britain 1920–1935*, A. Brown & Co., 1960. Used by permission of Paul Berry and Geoffrey Handley-Taylor.

from *Soaring Wings* by George Palmer Putnam. Used by permission of George C. Harrap & Co. Ltd.

from *Hannah Senesh: Her Life and Diary*, trans. by Marta Cohn, 1971. Used by permission of Vallentine, Mitchell and Co., Ltd.

from *Dying We Live*, ed. by Helmut Gollwitzer, Kathe Kuhn and Reinhold Schneider, The Harvill Press Ltd, 1956. Used by permission of Random House.

from *Our Mothers' Daughters* by Judith Arcana, shameless hussy press, 1979. Used by permission of shameless hussy press and The Women's Press.

from *Going Too Far: The Personal Chronicles of a Feminist*, © 1977 Robin Morgan. Reprinted by permission of Random House and Robin Morgan.

from *GynEcology* by Mary Daly, Beacon Press, 1978. Used by permission of Beacon Press and The Women's Press.

from *Of Woman Born* by Adrienne Rich, W. W. Norton & Co. Inc., © 1976 Adrienne Rich. Used by permission of W. W. Norton & Co. Inc. and Virago.

from *My Mother/My Self* by Nancy Friday, Delacorte Press, 1977. Used by permission of Nancy Friday.

References

Part One

I called her after the heroine . . . 'Professions for Women' by Virginia Woolf, in *Women and Writing*, ed. by Michele Barrett, p. 58

Very little is known about women . . . 'Women and Fiction' by Virginia Woolf, in *Women and Writing, ibid.*, p. 44

While I was writing this review . . . *ibid.*, pp. 58–59

Chapter 1

Until I was 28 . . . 'The Art of Poetry: Anne Sexton' in *Anne Sexton: The Artist and Her critics*, ed. by J.D. McClatchy, p. 3

Write down your feelings . . . 'Anne Sexton: Somehow to Endure', *ibid.*, p. 245

With Sylvia Plath . . . *Sylvia Plath and Anne Sexton: A Reference Guide* by Caeron Northouse and Thomas P. Walsh, p. 119

Always life with Anne . . . *Anne Sexton: A Self Portrait in Letters*, ed. by Linda Gray Sexton and Lois Ames, p. 23

Anne's death was not unexpected . . . *ibid.*, p. 423

Chapter 2

Why does the incest victim . . . 'Father-Daughter Incest' by Judith Herman and Lisa Hirschman, p. 739

Part Two

There was a bird's egg once . . . *Woman and Labour* by Olive Schreiner, p. 222

Chapter 3

We should place . . . *Marie Curie* by Eve Curie, p. 372

Women must convert . . . *Women and Madness* by Phyllis Chesler, p. 298

The issue of women's entrance . . . *Sexual Politics* by Kate Millett, p. 85

Women naturally took the heavy . . . *Woman and Labour* by Olive Schreiner, p. 155

I would endure some inconvenience . . . *Seven Adventurous Women* by Winifred Holmes, p. 30

a very singular person . . . *Some Famous Women of Wit and Beauty* by John Fyvie, p. 120

women are at their best . . . *The Times* editorial, quoted in 'Frederika Bremer Centenary' by Marta Tamm-Gotlund, *International Women's News*, April 1966, p. 35

The first letter I wrote . . . *My Life* by George Sand, p. 225

My business in life . . . 'The Rights and Wrongs of Women: Mary Wollstonecraft, Harriet Martineau, Simone de Beauvoir' by Margaret Walters, in *The Rights and Wrongs of Women*, ed. Juliet Mitchell and Ann Oakley, p. 330

I felt more determined than ever . . . *Pioneer Work* by Elizabeth Blackwell, p. 23

She was the first person . . . *Lucy Stone: Pioneer Woman Suffragist* by Alice Stone Blackwell, p. 94

My present life . . . *Florence Nightingale* by Cecil Woodham-Smith, p. 86

There were furiously resentful . . . *ibid.*, p. 92

Why have women . . . 'Cassandra' in *The Cause* by Ray Strachey, pp. 396–404 *passim*

It would be useless . . . Woodham-Smith, *op. cit.*, p. 116

Her appointment caused a sensation . . . *ibid.*, p. 141

The Government has asked . . . *Florence Nightingale* by Margaret Goldsmith, p. 137

to give expression . . . Woodham-Smith, *op. cit.*, p. 236

I wish we had her in the War Office . . . *ibid.*, p. 265

I have an intellectual nature . . . *ibid*, p. 77

as a consummate confidence-trickster . . . *Times Literary Supplement*, 28 May 1982

The REAL fathers and mothers . . . Woodham-Smith, *op. cit.*, p. 307

You say women . . . *ibid.*, p. 384

that women should have the suffrage . . . *ibid.*, p. 487

I cannot remember a time . . . *ibid.*, p. 549

Work is, and always has been . . . *Louisa May* by Martha Saxton, p. 319

'Happy Women' was the title . . . *Louisa May Alcott: Her Life, Letters and Journals*, ed. Ednah D. Cheney, p. 197

Girls write . . . *ibid.*, p. 201

the most vital . . . Saxton, *op. cit.*, p. 366

A woman has a right . . . *ibid.*, p. 339

I think I shall soon . . . Cheney, *op. cit.*, p. 300

work slowly for fear . . . *ibid.*, p. 269

Too much work . . . *ibid.*, p. 199

failure is impossible . . . *Susan B. Anthony* by Katherine Anthony, p. 498

Now, Minnie, you know very well . . . *Life and Letters of Mary Putnam Jacobi*, ed. Ruth Putnam, p. 67

Do I not . . . *ibid.*, p. 81

cried much . . . *Queen Victoria* by Lytton Strachey, p. 27

was extremely crushed . . . *Victoria and her Daughters* by Nina Epton, p. 12

they did me such immense harm . . . *Life of Olive Schreiner* by Samuel Cronwright-Schreiner, p. 250

unnatural and unmotherly . . . *Olive Schreiner* by Ruth First and Ann Scott, p. 47

of my whole life . . . First and Scott, *ibid.*, p. 181

tried to understand . . . *ibid.*, p. 23

The great love . . . unpublished writing about Crystal by Max Eastman

When Susan B. Anthony . . . from 'The Hero As Parent' in *Heroes I Have Known* by Max Eastman, pp. 2–3

Life was never dull . . . 'Crystal: Mother Worship' in *The Nation*, 16 March 1927

We children . . . ibid.

She fought injustice . . . *Love & Revolution* by Max Eastman, p. 504

Crystal made . . . Frances Perkins, excerpt from letter to Max Eastman, 30 July 1928

I don't give a damn . . . *Helen and Teacher* by Joseph P. Lash, p. 426

Women insist on their inalienable rights . . . *Helen Keller: Her Socialist Years*, ed. Philip Foner, p. 67

I feel almost . . . *Lella Secor: A Life in Letters*, ed. Barbara Moench Florence, p. 88

What mattered about a book . . . *Testament of Experience* by Vera Brittain, p. 80

I ended the First World War . . . *ibid.*, quoted in the introduction to the Virago edition by Paul Berry, pp. 8–9

The word 'career' . . . *ibid.*, p. 37

Now, inspired by . . . *ibid.*, p. 80

Even the humiliations . . . *Humiliation with Honour* by Vera Brittain, p. 80

From the end of the First World War . . . *Testament of Experience*, pp. 472–4

Unlike my mother . . . Interview with Shirley Williams by Angela Phillips, *Spare Rib*, Issue 112, Nov. 1981, p. 26

resent[ing] all inequality . . . *ibid.*, p. 26

In my view . . . private letter, 1981

She belonged to the elect . . . obituary of Winifred Holtby by Rebecca West, *Daily Telegraph*, 30 September 1935

her months in South Africa . . . *Testament of Friendship* by Vera Brittain, p. 160

There are some things . . . *Soaring Wings* by George Palmer Putnam, p. 78

With these activities . . . *Last Flight* by Amelia Earhart, p. 12

In the papers she left . . . Putnam, *op. cit.*, p. 60

no child if mine . . . *Letters Home* by Sylvia Plath, ed. Aurelia Schober Plath, p. 5

In December, she closed . . . *ibid.*, p. 48

Her physical energies . . . *ibid.*, p. 500

Commonly accepted channels . . . *Prisons and Prisoners* by Constance Lytton, p. 37

This is where my life's ambition . . . *Hannah Senesh: Her Life and Diary*, trans. Marta Cohn, p. 81

How long will this go on? . . . *ibid.*, p. 125

Where did this girl . . . *ibid.*, p. 194

Part Three

We must live as if our dreams . . . *Our Mothers' Daughters* by Judith Arcana, p. 215

Chapter 5

They said we were anti-motherhood . . . *Going Too Far* by Robin Morgan, p. 7 and p. 52

Many of my friends . . . 'Awaiting Quintana: A Journal of Adoption' by Nan Bauer Maglin

I hope Alice Walker's description . . . *ibid.*

Chapter 6

sisterhood, like female friendship . . . *GynEcology* by Mary Daly, p. 369

The most important thing one woman can do . . . *Of Woman Born* by Adrienne Rich, p. 246

Chapter 7

I no longer have fantasies . . . Rich, *op. cit.*, p. 224

My mother never gave me her hand . . . quoted in Simone de Beauvoir's foreword to *La Bâtarde* by Violette Leduc, p. 5

Bibliography

GENERAL

Abbott, Sydney and Love, Barbara, *Sappho Was a Right-On Woman: A Liberated View of Lesbianism*, Stein and Day, 1972; reprinted 1977.

Alvarez, A., *The Savage God: A Study of Suicide*, Random House, 1972; Penguin, 1974.

Arcana, Judith, *Our Mothers' Daughters*, shameless hussy press, 1979; The Women's Press, 1981.

Ariès, Philippe, *Centuries of Childhood: A Social History of Family Life*, Jonathan Cape, 1962; Penguin, 1973; Peregrine, 1979.

Beauvoir, Simone de, *A Very Easy Death*, trans. by Patrick O'Brien, Deutsch, 1976; Penguin, 1977.
  The Second Sex, trans. and ed. by H.M. Parshley, Jonathan Cape, 1953; Knopf, 1953; Penguin, 1972; Vintage, 1974.

Belotti, Elena Gianini, *Little Girls*, intro. by Margaret Drabble, Writers and Readers Cooperative, 1975.

Bernard, Jessie, *The Future of Motherhood*, Dial Press, 1974; Penguin, 1974; reprinted as *The Future of Parenthood: The New Role of Mothers*, Calder & Boyars, 1975.

Boston Women's Health Book Collective, *Our Bodies, Ourselves*, Simon and Schuster, 1973; revised 1975; U.K. edition by Phillips, Angela and Rakusen, Jill, Allen Lane, 1978; Penguin, 1978.

Brittain, Vera, *Lady Into Woman: A History of Women from Victoria to Elizabeth II*, Andrew Dakers Ltd, 1953.

Brown, Rita Mae, *Rubyfruit Jungle*, Daughters Inc., 1973; Corgi, 1978.

Brownmiller, Susan, *Against Our Will: Men, Women and Rape*, Simon and Schuster, 1975; Secker and Warburg, 1975; Bantam, 1976; Penguin, 1977.

Butler, Sandra, *Conspiracy of Silence*, New Glide Publications, 1978; Bantam, 1979.

Cate, Curtis, *George Sand*, Avon Books, 1975; Hamish Hamilton 1975.

Chicago, Judy, *The Dinner Party: A Symbol of Our Heritage*, Anchor Press/Doubleday, 1979.

Chesler, Phyllis, *About Men*, Simon and Schuster 1978; The Women's Press, 1978.
   Women and Madness, Doubleday, 1972; Avon, 1973; Allen Lane, 1974.

Chodorow, Nancy, *The Reproduction of Mothering: Psychoanalysis and the Sociology of Gender*, University of California Press, 1978.

Connor, Eva B., ed., *Letters to Children*, Macmillan, 1938.

Corrective Collective, *Never Done: Three Centuries of Women's Work in Canada*, Canadian Women's Educational Press, 1974.

Daly, Mary, *GynEcology: The Metaethics of Radical Feminism*, Beacon Press, 1978; The Women's Press, 1979.

Davidson, Cathy N. and Broner, E.M., eds, *The Lost Tradition: Mothers and Daughters in Literature*, Frederick Ungar, 1980.

Dinnerstein, Dorothy, *The Mermaid and the Minotaur: Sexual Arrangements and Human Malaise*, Harper and Row, 1976; Colophon Books, 1977; in the U.K. under the title, *The Rocking of the Cradle: And the Ruling of the World*, Souvenir Press, 1978.

Dworkin, Andrea, *Woman Hating*, E.P. Dutton, 1974.

Dowrick, Stephanie and Grundberg, Sibyl, eds, *Why Children*, The Women's Press, 1980; Harcourt, Brace, Jovanovich, 1981.

Eichenbaum, Luise and Orbach, Susie, *Outside In, Inside Out: Women's Psychology A Feminist Psychoanalytic Approach*, Penguin Books, 1982.

Eisenstein, Zillah R., ed., *Capitalist Patriarchy and the Case for Socialist Feminism*, Monthly Review Press, 1979.

Elbogen, Paul, *Dearest Mother: Letters of Famour Sons to their Mothers*, L.B. Fisher, 1942.

Esterson, A.L. and Laing, R.D., *Sanity, Madness and the Family*, Pelican Books, 1970

Ettore, E.M., *Lesbians, Women and Society*, Routledge and Kegan Paul, 1980.

Faderman, Lillian, *Surpassing the Love of Men: Romantic Friendship and Love Between Women from the Renaissance to the Present*, Morrow, 1981; Junction Books, 1981.

Fallaci, Oriana, *Letter to a Child Never Born*, trans. by John Shepley, Simon and Schuster, 1976; Arlington Books, 1976.

Flax, Jane, 'The Conflict Between Nurturance and Autonomy in Mother-Daughter Relationships and Within Feminism', *Feminist Studies*, Vol. 4, no. 2, June 1978.

Feminist Studies: 'Toward a Feminist Theory of Motherhood', Vol. 4, no. 2, June 1978.

Friday, Nancy, *My Mother/My Self: The Daughter's Search for Identity*, Delacorte Press, 1977; Dell Books, 1977; Sheldon Press, 1979; Fontana, 1979.

Hammer, Signe, *Mothers and Daughters/Daughters and Mothers*, Quadrangle, 1975; Hutchinson, 1976.

Henderson, Kathy and Armstrong, Frankie and Kerr, Sandra, eds, *My Song Is My Own: 100 Women's Songs*, Pluto Press, 1979.

Herman, Judith and Hirschman, Lisa, 'Father-Daughter Incest', *Signs: Journal of Women in Culture and Society*, Vol., 2, no. 4, 1977.

Jackins, Harvey, *The Benign Reality*, Rational Island Publishers, 1981.

Laing, R.D., *The Politics of the Family and Other Essays*, Pantheon Books, 1969;

Lapidus, Jackie, *Ready to Survive*, Hanging Loose, 1975.
  Starting Over, Out and Out Books, 1978.

Lazarre, Jane, *The Mother Knot*, Dell Publishing Co. 1976.

Leduc, Violette, *La Bâtarde*, trans. by Derek Coltman, Peter Owen, 1965; Dell Publishing Co., 1966.

Liddington, Jill and Norris, Jill, *One Hand Tied Behind Us: The Rise of the Women's Suffrage Movement*, Virago, 1978.

Lifshin, Lyn, ed., *Ariadne's Thread: A Collection of Contemporary Women's Journals*, Harper and Row, 1982.

Llewellyn Davis, Margaret, *Maternity: Letters from Working Women*, collected by the Women's Cooperative Guild, new intro. by Gloden Davis, Virago, 1978.

Mause, Lloyd de, *The History of Childhood*, Psychohistory Press, 1974; Souvenir Press, 1976.

Mazow, Julia, ed., *The Woman Who Lost Her Names: Selected Writings by American Jewish Women*, Harper and Row, 1980.

Miller, Kathy, 'It's Great to be Female', *Re-evaluation Sisters*, no. 5, Rational Island Publishers, 1979.

Millett, Kate, *Sexual Politics*, Doubleday, 1970; Rupert Hart Davis Ltd, Granada Publishers, 1971; Virago, 1977.

Mitchell, Juliet, *Psychoanalysis and Feminism*, Pantheon, 1974; Vintage Books, 1975; Allen Lane, 1974; Penguin, 1975.

Mitchell, Juliet and Oakley, Ann, eds, *The Rights and Wrongs of Women*, Penguin, 1976.

Moers, Ellen, *Literary Women*, Doubleday, 1976; Anchor, 1977; W.H. Allen, 1977; The Women's Press, 1978.

Moffat, Mary Jane and Painter, Charlotte, eds, *Revelations: Diaries of Women*, Random House, New York, 1974; Vintage Books, 1975.

Morgan, Robin, *Going Too Far: The Personal Chronicle of a Feminist*, Random House, 1977; Vintage Books, 1978.
    ed., *Sisterhood is Powerful*, Random House, 1970.

Nightingale, Florence, *Cassandra and Notes on Nursing*, forthcoming from Virago, 1984.

Olsen, Tillie, *Silences*, Delacorte Press/Seymour Lawrence, 1978; Virago, 1980.
    Tell Me a Riddle, Lippincott, 1961; Faber, 1964; Virago, 1980.
    Yonnondio: From the Thirties, Delacorte Press, 1974; Faber, 1975; Virago, 1980.

Phillips, Melanie, *The Divided House: Women at Westminster*, Sidgewick and Jackson, 1980.

Plath, Sylvia, *The Bell Jar*, William Heinemann, 1963; Faber, 1966; Harper & Row, 1971.

Rasmussen, Linda and Rasmussen, Lorna and Savage, Candace and Wheeler, Anne, eds, *A Harvest Yet to Reap: A History of Prairie Women*, The Canadian Women's Educational Press, 1976.

Rich, Adrienne, *Of Woman Born: Motherhood as Experience and Institution*, W.W. Norton and Co., Inc., 1976; Virago, 1977.
    On Lies, Secrets and Silence: Selected Prose 1946–1978, W.W. Norton and Co., 1979; Virago, 1980.

Rowbotham, Sheila, *Hidden from History: 300 Years of Women's Oppression and the Fight Against It*, Pluto Press, 1973.

Rush, Florence, 'The Freudian Cover-Up: The Sexual Abuse of Children', *Chrysalis*, no. 1, 1977.

Sartre, Jean Paul, *Search for a Method*, trans. by Hazel E. Barnes, Alfred A. Knopf, 1963.

Schreiner, Olive, *Woman and Labour*, preface by Jane Graves, Virago, 1978.
Trooper Peter Halket of Mashonaland, intro. by Marion Friedmann, Adriaan Donker, 1974.

van Doren, Dorothy, *The Lost Art*, Coward-McCann, 1929.

van Doren, Charles, *Letters to Mother: An Anthology*, Channel Press, 1959.

Wheeler, G.C., *Letters to Mother*, Allen and Unwin, 1933.

Woolf, Virginia, *A Room of One's Own*, Hogarth Press, 1929; Harcourt, Brace and World, 1957; Penguin, 1963; Triad, 1977.
Women and Writing, ed. with intro. by Michele Barrett. The Women's Press, 1979.

BIOGRAPHY
Alcott, Louisa, *Louisa May Alcott: Her Life, Letters and Journals*, ed. by Ednah D. Cheney, Little Brown and Company, 1899.

Anthony, Katherine, *Susan B. Anthony: Her Personal History and Her Era*, Doubleday, 1954.

Bernard, Jessie, *Self-Portrait of a Family*, Beacon Press, 1978.

Blackwell, Elizabeth, *Pioneer Work in Opening the Medical Profession to Women: Autobiographical Sketches*, Longmans, Green and Co., 1895; with new intro. by Mary Roth Walsh, Schocken, 1977.

Bremer, Frederika, *Life, Letters and Posthumous Works of Frederika Bremer*, trans. by F. Milow, Hurd and Houghton, 1868.

Brittain, Vera, *Humiliation with Honour*, Andrew Dakers Ltd, 1942.
Testament of Experience: An Autobiographical Story of the Years 1925–1950, Gollancz, 1957; intro. by Paul Berry, Virago, 1979; Fontana, 1980.
Testament of Friendship, Macmillan, 1940; afterword by Rosalind Delmar, Virago, 1980; Fontana, 1981.
Testament of Youth, Gollancz, 1933; preface by Shirley Williams, Gollancz, 1978; Virago, 1978; Fontana 1979.

Brittain, Vera and Handley-Taylor, Geoffrey, eds, *Selected Letters of Winifred Holtby and Vera Brittain 1920–1935*, A. Brown and Sons, 1960.

Cronwright Schreiner, S.C., *The Life of Olive Schreiner*, T. Fisher Unwin Ltd., 1924.

Curie, Eve, *Madame Curie*, trans. by Vincent Sheen, Pocket Books, 1946.

Dinesen, Isak, *Letters from Africa*, ed. by Frans Lasson, trans. by Anne Born, University of Chicago Press, 1981; Weidenfeld and Nicolson, 1981.

Earhart, Amelia, *Last Flight*, arranged by George P. Putnam, Harcourt, Brace and Co., 1937.

Eastman, Crystal, *Crystal Eastman on Women and Revolution*, ed. by Blanche Wiesen Cook, Oxford University Press, 1978.

Epton, Nina, *Victoria and Her Daughters*, Weidenfeld and Nicolson, 1971.

First, Ruth and Scott, Ann, *Olive Schreiner*, Andre Deutsch, 1980; Schocken, 1980.

Friedmann, Marion, *Olive Schreiner: A Study in Latent Meanings*, Witwatersrand University Press, 1955.

Fyvie, John, *Some Famous Women of Wit and Beauty*, Archibald Constable and Co., 1905.

Goldsmith, Margaret, *Florence Nightingale: The Woman and the Legend*, Hodder and Stoughton, 1937.

Harper Ida Husted, *The Life and Works of Susan B. Anthony*, Vols 1–3, Bowen-Merril Co., Ltd, 1898.

Holmes, Winifred, *Seven Adventurous Women*, G. Bell and Son, 1953.

Jacobi, Mary Putnam, *Life and Letters of Mary Putnam Jacobi*, ed. by Ruth Putnam, P. Putnam's Sons, 1925.

James, Edward T., ed., *Notable American Women*, The Belknap Press of Harvard University Press, 1971.

Keller, Helen, *Helen Keller: Her Socialist Years*, ed. with intro. by Philip S. Foner, International Publishers, 1967.

Lash, Philip P., *Helen and Teacher*, Allen Lane, 1980.

Lytton, Constance, *Prisons and Prisoners: Some Personal Experiences*, William Heinemann, 1914.

Maglin, Nan Bauer, 'Awaiting Quintana: A Journal of Adoption', *Frontiers*, Vol. III, no. 2, 1978.

Martineau, Harriet, *Harriet Martineau's Autobiography*, Smith, Elder and Co., 1877; Virago, 1983.

McClatchy, J.D., ed., *Anne Sexton: The Artist and Her Critics*, Indiana University Press, 1979.

Northouse, Cameron and Walsh, Thomas, *Sylvia Plath and Anne Sexton: A Reference Guide*, G.K. Hall & Co., 1974.

Perry, Gillian, *Paula Modersohn Becker: Her Life and Work*, The Women's Press, 1979; Harper & Row, 1979.

Plath, Sylvia, *Letters Home*, ed. by Aurelia S. Plath, Harper and Row, 1975; Faber, 1978.

Putnam, George Palmer, *Soaring Wings*, Harrap, 1940.

Sand, George, *My Life*, ed and trans. by Dan Hofstadter, Victor Gollancz Ltd, 1979.

Saxton, Martha, *Louisa May: A Modern Biography of Louisa May Alcott*, Houghton Mifflin Co., 1977.

Secor, Lella, *Lella Secor: A Diary in Letters 1915–1922*, ed. by Barbara Moench Florence, Burt Franklin and Co., 1978.

Senesh, Hannah, *Hannah Senesh: Her Life and Diary*, trans. by Marta Cohn, Vallentine, Mitchell and Co., Ltd, 1971.

Showalter, Elaine, 'Florence Nightingale's Feminist Complaint: Women, Religion, and "Suggestions of Thought",' *Signs: Journal of Women in Culture and Society*, Vol. 6, no. 3, 1981.

Stone Blackwell, Alice, *Lucy Stone: Pioneer Woman Suffragist*, Alice Stone Blackwell Committee, 1930

Stowe, C.E. *Life of Harriet Beecher Stowe: Her Letters and Journals*, Sampson, Low, Marston, Searle and Rivington, 1889.

Stowe, Harriet Elizabeth (Beecher), *Life and Letters of Harriet Beecher Stowe*, ed. by Annie Fields, Sampson, Low, Marston, Searle and Rivington, 1897.

Strachey, Lytton, *Eminent Victorians*, Chatto and Windus, 1918; Putnam, 1918; Penguin, 1971.
    Queen Victoria, Chatto and Windus, 1921; Harcourt Brace Jovanovich, 1921; Penguin, 1971.

Victoria, Queen of England, *Your Dear Letter: Private Correspondence of Queen Victoria and the Crown Princess of Prussia 1865–1871*, ed. by Roger Fulford, Evans Brothers Ltd, 1971.

Webb, R.K., *Harriet Martineau: A Radical Vision*, Heinemann, 1960.

Woodham-Smith, Cecil, *Florence Nightingale 1820–1910*, Constable and Co., 1950; McGraw Hill 1951; Fontana, 1977.
    Queen Victoria: Her Life and Times, Hamish Hamilton, 1972.

Index